SILCHESTER
THE ROMAN TOWN OF
CALLEVA

SILCHESTER
THE ROMAN TOWN OF
CALLEVA

GEORGE C. BOON
F.S.A.

with a folding plan of the town showing
details traced from aerial photographs,
40 photographs and 42 drawings

DAVID & CHARLES
NEWTON ABBOT LONDON
NORTH POMFRET (VT) VANCOUVER

ISBN 0 7153 6339 5

First published as *Roman Silchester* in 1957
by Max Parrish & Co Ltd
This completely revised and expanded edition
published by David & Charles in 1974

Set in 11 on 13 pt Granjon and printed in Great
Britain by John Sherratt and Son Ltd Altrincham
for David & Charles (Holdings) Limited South Devon
House Newton Abbot Devon

Published in the United States of America by David &
Charles Inc North Pomfret Vermont 05053 USA

Published in Canada by Douglas David & Charles
Limited 3645 McKechnie Drive West Vancouver BC

IN MEMORY OF

GERALD, 7th DUKE OF WELLINGTON
FRANCIS NEEDHAM
and
WILLIAM SAMUEL EVANS
Rector of Silchester

Silchester is a place that a lover of antiquity will visit with great delight.

WILLIAM STUKELEY

Contents

Illustrations

PLATES

8

FIGURES

Foreword

The basis of this book is my *Roman Silchester* (1957), the work of a young man in haste. Time has done a little, if only a little, to correct his imperfect knowledge of Roman affairs.

The excavations of Silchester were largely carried on at a time when there was little realisation of the possibility of extracting a chronological framework from operations designed principally to reveal a plan. But this primitive aspect of the work ensured rapid coverage of the large area within the walls, and Calleva remains to this day the most widely-explored of all the Romano-British towns and of all towns of its kind in the Roman Empire. The questions which may legitimately be asked, in consequence, are those of a general nature, above all as to what the plan tells of the success or failure of the earliest phase of true urbanisation in our country. The most important new matters to be found in these pages are a study of the original street-plan cadastre and an examination of the agricultural basis of the economy. In returning, however, to Joyce's *Journal,* to the *Archaeologia* reports (which are scarcely more than printed versions of the annual lectures to the Society of Antiquaries on the results of excavations), and to the great collection of antiquities deposited since 1891 at Reading Museum by successive Dukes of Wellington, it has fallen to my lot to re-interpret certain discoveries and to fill out the picture previously presented in many ways, for example as regards the plan of the most important building in the town, the basilica; and in respect of the church, it has at last appeared possible to demonstrate the Christian identification.

As regards the history of Calleva, I could but cobble and mend some of the tattered threads, by reference to the huge and still growing body of comparative evidence, mostly of recent acquisition. Fortunately, the site is not the emptied sepulchre of Victorian and Edwardian archaeology that it is commonly reputed to be. Selective re-examination of buildings cleared only in part, or to floor-level, holds promise, and it is now established by aerial survey that there are many which the accidents of trenching passed by. These are the precious growing-points of a fuller Callevan chronology.

Considerations of textual length have compelled me to abandon the survey of the tribal area, which I had hoped to attempt on the model of Edith Wightman's *Roman Trier and the Treveri*. The chapter in *Roman Silchester* dealing with the course of the roads near the town is also omitted, for I have done no fieldwork on their lines since 1956. On the other hand, the book is wide-ranging in its search for helpful comparisons, for not the least achievement of Roman provincial archaeology is its revelation of the astonishing ubiquity of an identical material culture which, diversified as it may be by regional peculiarities serving only to emphasize the underlying unity, existed throughout the immense area where men sought to become Romans.

The story here unfolded is in parts complex and in others not fully satisfactory, because archaeological evidence is rarely instantly accessible or indeed to be taken at its face-value. The qualifications with which many explanations are offered of course reflect this uncertainty, and inevitably extend to many important matters of daily life where the record is imperfect, not only at Silchester but everywhere else. The critical apparatus in the notes and references is therefore rather extensive, for plain, unsupported asseverations are an imposition upon the credulity of the reader, especially the general reader whose interests the writer of a book of this kind should above all bear in mind, by providing at least some means whereby statements can be checked and the evidence indicated for independent assessment.

Immense strides have been made in Roman archaeology since 1957 and my debt to other scholars, living and dead, is fully apparent and is, I hope, fully acknowledged in the notes. These remarks may fitly end with a quotation from Stukeley's preface to the *Itinerarium Curiosum* (1724): 'above all I avoided prejudice . . . and if my sentiments . . . happen not to coincide with what has been wrote before me; 'twas not that I differ from them, but things did not so appear to me'.

There remains a grateful duty to acknowledge the complete assistance afforded by the Director of Reading Museum, Mr T. L. Gwatkin, and Mrs J. Greenaway, Archaeological Assistant. I have also to thank the Council of the Society of Antiquaries for permission to reproduce drawings from the Fox Collection and from *Archaeologia*. These and similar acknowledgements appear in the underlines. The other plates are from negatives, sometimes prints, in the possession of Reading Museum. The drawings of objects and the plans are in many cases preserved from the first edition, being in the one case by Mr T. L. Gwatkin and in the other by Miss S. Y. Townend: they are supplemented by myself. The main plan is the fruit of much anxious consultation between myself and my colleague at the National Museum of Wales, Mr Colin Williams. Mr John Hopkins, Librarian of the Society of Antiquaries, has been as always a most helpful friend. My wife has nobly supported me in the very long hours, extending over several years, of private study and writing at home, where the entire work was prepared. To her, and to the three friends named in the memorial dedication, I owe more than need be explained here in words.

Penarth, February 1973   GEORGE C. BOON

PART ONE

HISTORICAL

I

Silchester: A Mirror of British Archaeology

*Hrim on lime**

SILCHESTER is a scattered village 13 km. south-west of Reading, just over the Hampshire border which kinks curiously northwards to bring the area of the Saxon manor within the county. CALLEVA ATREBATUM occupies a spur of quaternary gravel overlooking the wide, gentle valley of the Loddon to the east; it commands views open enough today, but was once so enshrouded in forest as to give rise to a name which meant 'the woodland place of the Atrebates'.[1] The use of the tribal name indicates a capital of a Romano-British self-governing community or *civitas;* but the Atrebates had migrated to Britain from northern Gaul long before Roman times, and by the early years of our era had already established a capital at Silchester. In this book, the Roman town chiefly concerns us. Its existence is proclaimed by the stout nonagonal ring of its walls, solid and impressive even in advanced decay; by an outer earthwork compared by Aubrey, in 1667, to that with 'an externall graff . . . as now in Oxford at New-parks'; and by the perennial emergence of its regular street-plan in the ripening corn—'a straung thing' to Leland in 1540, but correctly interpreted by the local folk, as Camden records in 1586 (pl. 7).[2] The differences in soil-moisture which largely account for this phenomenon are capable of the most delicate delineation, not only of streets, but of the outlines of buildings warm and watertight 1,600 years ago and more (pl. 8). Today, no foundations are exposed, and the parish church of St. Mary the Virgin, together with the Manor Farm, are the only buildings within the 40 ha. of the walled town.

The manor of Silchester was bought in 1828 by the Parliamentary Trustees as an addition to the estate of Stratfield Saye bestowed by the nation upon

---

* 'There is hoar-frost on the mortar'—from 'The Ruin', an eighth-century West Saxon poem in the *Exeter Book,* dealing probably with Bath.

the victor of Waterloo. The great Duke of Wellington appears to have had scant patience with antiquaries; and is said to have told one who raised the subject of Silchester that 'he had better go to Rome, where he might find much finer remains'. There had already been a phase of fieldwork and excavation, as we shall see; but the fame of Silchester stems from the time of the second and third Dukes, who respectively initiated excavations in 1864, and acceded in 1890 to the desire of the Society of Antiquaries to excavate the walled town completely.[3] The work is reported in *Archaeologia,* but by present standards the accounts are primitive. Excavation is an art which has developed only since the twenties, and here we have what nineteenth-century minds thought worthy of record in what nineteenth-century eyes perceived. Excavations in 1938-9 and 1954-61 have supplied some elements of a skeletal chronology, but have been very small in extent, and the reader cannot expect to find the same finesse of chronological detail which arises from excavations in Romano-British towns today. It might be said that the work of the Revd J. G. Joyce and of the Society of Antiquaries has itself become an archaeological feature, to be treated as such in Silchester studies.

This said, it is salutary to remind ourselves of the contribution of Silchester to our knowledge of the earliest urbanisation in Britain—a contribution which, as Sir Mortimer Wheeler said, 'gave at once, and with a rough accuracy, the general impression of a Romano-British town such as fifty years of subsequent and often more careful work have failed to equal . . .; who among . . . later and wiser excavators has not constantly referred . . . with profit to the crude primitive assemblage of Silchester?' Nothing had been learnt previously of the chief building, the forum-basilica, which such towns contained; little of the density of buildings within insulae very much larger than those of Mediterranean towns; scarcely more of the characteristics of the individual dwellings. At Silchester, too, were initiated some of the technological examinations of material which are today an inseparable part of any excavation of consequence. The task of this book is to present the Silchester 'assemblage', perhaps less crude, after all, than may be supposed; and in so doing to bring a little nearer realisation the aim—the blind aim—of 1890 'to reveal the whole life and history, as seen in its remains, of a Romano-British city'.[4]

DERIVATION OF THE NAME

'The Ruin', of which a phrase is cited at the beginning of this chapter, already enshrines the belief that towns such as Calleva were the work of giants: some would have said of the Devil, and at Silchester we have the

Devil's Highway, which is the Roman road to the east, and Grim's Bank, an earthwork on Padworth Common. Silchester, too, had its giant: Hearne, cantankerous and accurate, explains his name, Onion, as a misreading of that of Constantine upon coins—Onion's pennies, as they were called. Onion, who dwelt in a cavity of the wall (the spot is represented by a fallen section on the south side), hurled the Imp Stone, which is probably the stump of a Roman milliary, to its present position at the west end of Silchester Common, 700 m. south of the actual line of the Roman road to the west. In 1280, the stone was called *hyneston* (*hyrneston?*) and marked a corner of the bounds of Pamber Forest. Another legend, first recorded by Stukeley, is that the town was 'taken by sparrows', and this may perhaps merely be mystificatory, depending on a play of words (Old English *spearwe*, sparrow; *spere*, spear).[5]

The name Calleva has been applied to Silchester only since the eighteenth century. Horsley demonstrated the identification in his posthumous *Britannia Romana* of 1732; but we know from Hearne that Edmund Halley had been ready to do as much in 1718. It is curious that Stukeley, who knew his *Antonine Itinerary* as well as anyone—and therefore that Calleva was mentioned four times in it—and knew moreover that 'many were the *roman* roads that met' at Silchester, should have clung to the prevalent belief that

1. Inscription to Hercules Saegontius, forum, 1744. Scale, about 1/6

this was the *Vindomis* of a single route, twice transcribed: but the identification had Camden's magisterial authority. Like Humphrey Lhuyd, whose seminal influence upon the *Britannia* still remains incompletely acknowledged, Camden held that Calleva was at Wallingford; or, as he put it, Gallena was at Guallenford. A further hindrance, inherited by Camden from Henry of Huntingdon (1139), was that Silchester had been the *Caer Segont* (*recte* Kair Segeint and really Caernarvon-Segontium) of the list of twenty-eight cities of Britain found in a manuscript of Nennius' ninth-century *Historia Brittonum*. It followed that Silchester was the city of the Segontiaci mentioned by Caesar, and in consequence could not be a town of the Atrebates. In 1744 this opinion was reinforced by the discovery of an inscription purporting to mention 'the god Hercules of the Segontiaci' (fig. 1). We know now that what is common to these names is the Celtic *sego*—'strong', applicable to river, tribe, or god. Such difficulties would not have arisen if the modern name had kept any semblance of the old: but it is Silcestre in *Domesday Book,* the earliest mention, and Geoffrey of Monmouth knew it only by its modern name, despite its appearance as back-cloth to one or two episodes in his myth-history. Medieval C-forms, related by etymological gymnastics to Calleva, have little value; and it is generally accepted that the modern name is derived, at some removes, from the Saxon *sealh +* *ceaster,* 'sallow-tree chester', the tree being common there still. While the nomenclating Briton saw the 'wood', the Saxon saw the 'trees', doubtless because, in the intervening years, Romano-British agriculture had largely cleared the wood from around the town.[6]

An inscription containing the word CALLEVA was eventually exhumed in 1907 (pl. 11, p. 172); but, to find it, the scholar had had to leave his study and accept Sir Richard Colt Hoare's advice: 'be a spade and shovel antiquary, a real working one, or none at all!' Let us now follow in these footsteps.[7]

JOHN STAIR (1708–82)

It is a highly remarkable fact that a Hampshire villager should have been among the first ever to attempt detailed archaeological fieldwork in Britain. Little is known of his life. As a lad, John Stair's imagination was probably fired by Rector Betham,* who had amassed a large collection of antiquities

---

* Robert Betham, Rector of Silchester 1698–1719, rebuilt the rectory (now a private house in grounds on the south side of the lane from the Calleva Museum to the site) and according to Hearne (from whom the following details are taken) had a library reputed to be worth £800. He was tutor to the thirteen-year-old orphan James, Viscount Ikerrin, grandson of the Earl of Blessington, Lord of the Manor. In 1712, Betham took the boy with him to London, where the 'sad, vain' Dawson, minister

from the site. By 1733, he was in the service of Rector Paris *de quo, nisi opera loquantur, siletur;*** after whose death in 1743 he moved to Aldermaston and became a cobbler, and then the inn-keeper; before 1770, he was parish clerk. His Silchester activities are described in letters from John Collet of Newbury to John Ward of Gresham College, London, one of the most prominent antiquaries of the time.[8] Stair's first claim to notice arose from his discovery of the inscription in 1744; it then transpired that he had been working on a plan of the town for some years:

Newbury Jan. 5: 1744/5

S^r

According to your desire I now send you the Plan of the Ancient City of Silchester, as drawn by Mr John Stair of Aldermaston. . . .

The method he took to discover where the Streets formerly ran, was by observing just before Harvest, for several years, the places where the Corn was stunted. . . . Then upon digging here, he found a great deal of Rubbish &ca, & the plain Ruins & foundations of Houses on each side of the Streets. Whereas in the middle of the Squares there is no such Rubbish, nor any appearance of the ruins of foundations of houses, & moreover the Corn flourishes there very well.

By digging in these places Mr Stair found the inside of the Market place to have been above 90 Yards in length from North to South and above 50 Yards in breadth. . . .

As to the Plan I now send you, Mr Stair has not drawn it out exactly by rule, so that 'tis only a rough Draught. . . . He measur'd the Wall on the outside, going as near to it as he possibly could, for the Bushes which grow about it.

He has also measur'd 2 sides of 2 of the Squares & noted them down in the plan.

And he further says, that the two principal Streets that lead to the 4 Gates of the City were about 8 Yards broad, whereas the other Streets were but 6 yards in breadth as near as he could discover.

I had almost forgot to mention one very remarkable Circumstance Mr Stair assur'd me; That in digging below the foundations of some of the Houses, he discover'd the remains of some other foundations made of Flint stones cemented

---

of Windsor and Betham's brother-in-law, was confined for debt in the Fleet Prison. James was murdered by footpads as he walked in the vicinity, and his body was thrown into the Fleet Ditch. By a strange coincidence, Betham himself suffered a like fate seven years later: in 1721, a highwayman confessed to this crime, but James's murderer was never found. There is a handsome tablet to the young Viscount on the north side of the chancel of Silchester church; the epitaph ends with a hexameter line from Martial (*Epigrams*, VI, 29): *Immodicis brevis est aetas, et rara senectus* 'For the surpassing, life's course is short, and old age rare.' Betham was buried to the east of the north porch of the church.

** 'Concerning whom there is silence, unless his works speak'—a reference to his replacement of the bells, which had been lost during the Rebellion. The phrase is on his epitaph, next to Ikerrin's.

together with Mortar. This Mortar was quite decay'd, & he could easily crumble it with his Fingers, whereas the Mortar of the upper Foundations was of quite a different Texture & as hard as the Stones themselves, & below the upper Foundations some loose pieces of Mortar coarsely painted of several dull colours, as Green, Yellow, Red & White . . . without any figures or agreeable variety. . . . These things inclin'd him to imagine that probably here might have been anciently an old British Town, & that the Romans rebuilt this City upon the remains & foundations of it. . . .

I am S^r your most oblig'd humble
Servant,

John Collet

Ward was puzzled by the octagonal outline of the walls on the 1741 plan submitted: Stukeley had made a parallelogram of it, as had Aubrey, though neither had walked the full perimeter; and unknown to all, an estate-plan of 1653, now at Stratfield Saye, showed the outline correctly. So, later in that year of the Forty-Five, Ward went to Aldermaston, stayed with Stair, recruited a professional surveyor, and saw to the measurement of a new plan on the spot. The finished drawing (pl. 1) reached him in the following May, but Stair's name had unhappily been left off, and was furthermore not included in the published version in the *Philosophical Transactions* of 1748, though Ward acknowledged his part in tracing the street-lines 'to a considerable exactitude'. Stair continued his Silchester work, and Taylor's great county map of 1759 shows fragmentary buildings west of the forum. Stair's collection, viewed by Gough in 1768, passed to his son (also John, 1745–1820) and then out of sight, though he himself had long since sold the inscription and the bronze pedestal-frame found nearby (p. 111). His rarest coin, the gold Allectus (fig. 10) found by the ploughboy in 1746, is beyond doubt a specimen now in the British Museum.

THE REVD J. G. JOYCE (1819–78)

Between Stair's time and the beginning of continuous excavation in 1864, only two events require notice. In 1833 occurred the random opening of a 'villa'—the baths of the inn, p. 141; and in 1850, the most valuable mapping of the site, with hachured relief added to the parish tithe-map taken as the original, by Henry Maclauchlan (1792–1882), not long before he undertook his famous survey of Hadrian's Wall for the Duke of Northumberland.[9] We have copied that map, with modernisation of the earthwork-detail, for the inset of the main folding plan in this book.

James Gerald Joyce, Rector of Stratfield Saye from 1855, was the second Duke of Wellington's choice as excavator (pl. 3). The son of a merchant of Clonmel, Co. Tipperary, he went up to Magdalen Hall, Oxford, at the rather late age of 24, graduating in 1846 and taking Holy Orders. In the words of his obituary in the *Proceedings* of the Society of Antiquaries, to which he was elected in 1867:

> As an artist and an archaeologist, Mr. Joyce exhibited powers of a high order. No one can be surprised that in early life he was urged to make Art his profession who examines that remarkable folio on the Fairford Windows [Fairford church, Glos.] published under the sanction of the Science and Art Department in 1872, and dedicated to his wife, 'The Honourable Ellen Joyce, the sharer of this and every other labour of the author' . . . the extreme delicacy and beauty of the illustrations, and the great amount of learning and culture crowded into the letterpress, give to the work a character of a very high excellence. . . . everyone will be struck with the shrewdness and sagacity with which Mr. Joyce felt his way at the threshold of the . . . excavation of Silchester . . . he examined wisely and warily every trace which could put him on the road to . . . discovery, entering in his 'Journal of the Excavation' every fact and measurement . . . noting with skill and discrimination every surface laid bare, every object exhumed, every coin discovered, and, in short, enabling the reader . . . to follow every step. . . .

Joyce's achievements, with four labourers, were the opening of the north, south, east and amphitheatre gates; the forum-basilica; the temple in Insula VII, and several houses, notably the I.1 and XXIII.1.* Not all are published in his three (two posthumous) papers in *Archaeologia* XL and XLVI; but by great good fortune, Reading Museum was able to acquire the two volumes of his *Journal* and a large sketchbook in 1934. The *Journal* is profusely illustrated with pen and watercolour drawings of building-details, plans, objects, and—a great rarity for the time—some sections. A copy of the *Journal* was made for the Duke by Joyce's successor, and contains trifling Additions from 1878 to 1884: these volumes are at Stratfield Saye.[10]

In Joyce we see a man ahead of his time. He was, I believe, the first to realise, however dimly and hesitantly, the cardinal archaeological principle of dating structures by means of associated objects. Addressing the Society of Antiquaries in 1867, he proposed:

> . . . to take one liberty only . . . and that is to treat each stage of [I.1] as if it might be regarded to be of the date of the coins found in it. I am aware that strictly speaking such a deduction is incapable of proof, because the coins may have been in circulation a long time . . . but in absence of any other guide

---

* His Blocks II and III. In this book, the 1890–1909 nomenclature is used. Thus I.1 means Insula I, House 1; and the addition of a B, e.g. VI.B1, designates a building styled a 'block' in 1890–1909. Improvements in knowledge of the street-plan have led me to divide some of the insulae, e.g. XVIIIA, XVIIIB, but the original numbering of houses and blocks has not been altered.

whatever I venture to suppose that a coin may be deemed sufficient index of a date, to be accepted where it is impossible that any other information can ever be accessible. . . .

Nothing then was known of the dating of any kind of Roman pottery: Roach Smith's paper of 1849, the first scholarly treatment of *terra sigillata,* has no word on dating; and at the very end of the century, G. E. Fox's notes on the pottery found at Silchester show how little it meant chronologically even then. The advances in knowledge were to come largely too late for Silchester. Here, however, is Joyce demonstrating his theory:

> . . . in clearing the western ambulatory . . . traces of the most ancient floor were met with; to arrive at them, we had already dug to below the footing of a later wall. . . . Fifteen inches perpendicular of gravel below the lowest course . . . lay the level bed of concrete upon which the ancient floor had been laid. . . . Lying here . . . was a coin of the Emperor Commodus. We may not be wrong, therefore, in attributing the alteration, in the process of which this coin must have been dropped here by a workman, to the date 180 or 190 of the Christian era; certainly it could not be earlier, or no coin of Commodus could be there. . . .

His judgement could not always be so felicitous; and from the middle of 1876 the long-sustained *Journal* entries cease under the distraction of ill-health. The latest record links his work with early soil-science. Darwin was then assembling materials for that most beguiling of scientific books, *The Earthworm* (1881); and his sons Francis and Horace came to Silchester in November, to conduct studies on the subsidence of floors, the penetration of walls by earthworms, and the texture of the superficial mould. Darwin's monograph contains some woodcuts from Joyce's section-drawings.

The Darwins stayed at the Rectory, and we learn from Joyce's parochial diary, of which a volume survives at Stratfield Saye church, that Dr [Horace] Darwin addressed the temperance society formed in the parish some months earlier. Great though Joyce's devotion to his Silchester work was, and long the hours consumed in recording it, we are thus reminded that he was a busy parish priest in the Wilberforcian style of 'good churchmanship', having been ordained under the new Cuddesden régime in 1847 after a brief diaconate in the slums of St. Michael's, Coventry, and a short spell at Wing (Bucks.). In 1850 he went to the living of Burford (Oxon.) and there began to exercise his archaeological gifts for the first time, on the Fairford windows. Bishop Sumner made him rural dean at Stratfield Saye, and he came to be regarded as 'the confidential friend' of more than one occupant of the Winchester see, Wilberforce among them from 1869. As rural dean, he helped to establish diocesan conferences, and together with his wife founded the North Hampshire Choral Union in the year before his Silchester work began. And there were, besides, the multifarious duties of which the parochial diary is full. Those were days of great rural indigence, and here are recorded all the minutiae of the blanket fund, the coal allowances, the night-school for the illiterate, and so forth; sick visits with gifts, death-bed readings, and the like. Until 1877, when ill-health forced the move, he had appointed no curate, for he was very far from rich; and in the last months his brother clergy often took his services. He died aged 59 on 28 June 1878, from the effects of a cold which had turned to bronchitis. It may be thought that the dedication of *Fairford Windows* gracefully acknowledges the part played by Ellen Joyce in all these parochial labours of a remarkable man.

THE SILCHESTER EXCAVATION FUND, 1890–1909

The languishing excavations were stopped on the death of the second Duke in 1884; but thoughts were turning already towards their renewal on a much greater scale. The prime mover was F. G. Hilton Price, a banker and a prominent antiquary, who had caused an accurate survey to be made of the baths of the inn, revealed since Joyce's death. By 1889, complete excavation was being mooted:

4, Grosvenor Gardens, S.W.
June 25th 1889

General Pitt Rivers presents his compliments to the Duke of Wellington and writes to say that he called this morning in his capacity of Gov^t. Inspector of Ancient Monuments to inquire his views and wishes as to the excavation of Silchester.

The Antiquaries are very anxious that it should be thoroughly dug out and afterwards covered in again, after plans and a model had been made of it. Being a Monument of great National interest it appears desirable that it should be done, but General Rivers did not wish to take part in any agitation for the accomplishment of such a purpose without first ascertaining the Duke's wishes on the subject.

No doubt if the place were thoroughly explored after proper compensation to the tenant, it would be best, in this climate, to cover it over again, as it could not be put under cover without great expense. The matter would thus be concluded and there would be no further desire to meddle with the land. . . .

His Grace
The Duke of Wellington

Pitt Rivers later conveyed a memorandum to the Duke which set out the proposals, whereby the work would be managed by the Society of Antiquaries. In approving the scheme, the Duke offered a site for a museum, a contribution to its cost, and assistance towards roofing over any remains thought worthy of being kept open. The ground thus prepared, George E. Fox (1833–1908), artist-architect and student of Roman Britain, and W. H. St. J. Hope (1854–1919), medievalist and the senior official of the society, laid a memoir before the meeting of 27 February 1890. This stated that

> The complete excavation of a site of 100 acres is of course a stupendous work, and the large size of the area as seen from the walls is enough to dishearten a good many people. If however we give way to such feelings, Silchester will never be excavated at all, and even if it will take more than one man's lifetime to do it thoroughly, that is no reason why the work begun by Mr Joyce should not systematically be resumed and carried out unflinchingly year after year.

Work began under the direction of Fox and Hope on 23 June. To the former are due numerous highly-finished coloured drawings of mosaics (pl. 4 shows him at work) and minutely accurate studies of architectural and other details. These he later presented to the society and some are published here for the first time: many appear in the *Archaeologia* reports. To Hope we owe the excellent plans of buildings, most notably that of the public baths in which he distinguished six periods of work (cf. fig. 15). Others helped in the supervision of the excavations; but Mill Stephenson (1857–1937) made the third member of the usual triumvirate. He was a leading authority on monumental brasses, and a numismatist; essentially of a practical turn of mind and little interested in the speculative side of archaeology, he was invaluable at Silchester, and acted as foreman during some of the six-month seasons: he had a ready sympathy with the men and an understanding of their country ways which inspired affection in return—so much from his obituary, and as much from the late Mr Fred Smith of Silchester, in his declining years custodian of the Calleva Museum (opened as the village's contribution to the Festival of Britain and as a memorial to Lt-Col J. B. P. Karslake), who had been one of the twenty or so employed. Fox, Hope and Stephenson are shown in pl. 5, together with Haverfield (1860–1919), greatest of all Romano-British scholars, and Gowland (1842–1922), whose long sojourn in Meiji Japan brought an insight into primitive metallurgy which he applied at Silchester and elsewhere.

The Silchester Excavation Fund (cf. fig. 2) was supported by public subscription as well as by the Society of Antiquaries. Wages accounted for between £250 and £500 a year, the only other sizeable expense being rent for the ground occupied, which was usually in the region of £40. The labour-force was drawn from villages up to 8 km. distant; the men walked to their work, which began at 6 a.m., and for which they received half-a-crown

2. Design of brown-paper bag for finds, 1892. Scale about 1/2

a day, plus a few extras in payment of the dirty work entailed in clearing out pits and wells, or for special finds: coins, a halfpenny; inscriptions, three-pence a letter; a sovereign for the two finders of a hoard of silver coins in 1894. Some of the labourers acted as guides for the visitors who flocked to the site on Sundays, coming by trap from Mortimer or Bramley station: they probably supplemented their wages quite considerably in this manner, and no doubt a good many 'trifles' then passed into private hands, including—one may suspect—the gold piece of Carausius shown in fig. 10.

The area was dug by insulae wherever possible, and their erratic sequence on the plan attests the degree to which the farmer's interests supervened. The procedure was to lay out parallel diagonal trenches; any structure found was isolated and cleared to floor-level. Finally, a workman went round the trenches with an iron bar, to test for soft spots concealing the mouths of pits and wells not already discovered. The completeness of the resultant plan is a matter with which we must deal later (p. 49): but it is at least evident that this mode of working is likely to have left much undisturbed, and was not well-devised to deal with any but substantial structures and especially not with those of timber, references to which are usually, not always, as matters of inference.[11]

'The result of the excavations', the Society of Antiquaries was told, 'will be to reveal to the world the whole life and history, as seen in its remains, of a Romano-British city. . . . All walls and buildings must be carefully measured up, and to ensure accuracy be plotted and drawn on the spot to a uniform scale, with sections and models where necessary. All objects found must be properly labelled and registered, and the exact spot where found fully recorded.' Coloured as these intentions were by the practice of General Pitt Rivers, and probably insisted upon by that Olympian figure, they represented an ideal which experience was to shatter. The plans are good, and each year's results were copied on to Henry Hodge's cartographical *tour de force,* the seven-fold enlargement of the Ordnance Survey 1:2500 plan, still kept at Burlington House. Some good ruin-models were made, now mostly at the Calleva Museum. Vessels from many pits and wells were marked, and a good many other objects of importance are more or less closely provenanced. But for the vast majority of finds there is no such record, and the day-to-day notebooks have not survived as they have in the case of the contemporary excavations of Caerwent.

It is the easiest thing in the world to attack the standard of the excavations at Silchester, but it is done with hindsight. When those promises were made, there was no conception of the mountainous quantities of finds to be expected from a town-site, and the persistent ignorance of the dating-value of material hindered the development of stratigraphical technique. Funds were never to run to the employment of assistants, Pitt Rivers' acknowledged keystone of his own labours in Cranbourne Chase; but even so, the General was no better placed to carry through the interpretation of his sites by the evidence so painfully recorded: that was left to another, and the significance of his system was therefore masked. Finally, did not Haverfield himself roundly deny the existence at Silchester of 'successive' deposits, scorning Joyce's claims? In such an intellectual fog, we must be wary of discerning meanings in the 1890 statement which its authors could not possibly have intended.[12]

As already mentioned, the scientific examination of metallurgical and organic remains was established at Silchester as a routine, for the first time in Britain. Joyce had obtained geological determinations from Murchison; now Gowland studied the residue of silver-refining, and other fundamental work was done. The list of economic plants in Godwin's *History of the British Flora* (1956) contains fifteen Roman introductions, and eleven are supplied by Silchester from the work of A. H. Lyell in picking over samples of mud from the bottoms of pits and wells, and of Clement Reid in identifying the seeds thus recovered. The total, of all species, numbered over 160. Such work, of course, was not new: Otto Heer had brought out an extensive list from the Swiss Lake-Dwellings in 1866, and the earliest botanical determination from an English site appears to be the *Buxus sempervirens* from one of the Bartlow Hills tumuli (1840). Lyell's also was the work which enabled C. O. Waterhouse, god-child of Darwin, to list over seventy species of insects, etc., including—interestingly enough if not very significantly—the 'furniture' beetle, *Anobium*. The list was never published *in extenso*. By contrast, the treatment of mammalian remains is summary, and disappointing by other standards of the day set by Pitt Rivers, Bulleid and Gray at Glastonbury, and Ewart at Newstead; though the bird and fish indentifications are important.[13]

The effect of the excavations, supplemented as they were by those of Caerwent, was profound. Scarcely a book, from Haverfield's *Ancient Town Planning* (1913) to Garcia y Bellido's *Urbanistica de las grandes ciudades del mundo antiguo* (1966) fails to reproduce the plan; scarcely a book on Roman Britain fails to do the same and to enter with greater or lesser detail into the discoveries. An uncritical apogee was reached in 1924 with James Thomson's *A Great Free City: the Book of Silchester,* 'two large volumes [which] while they contain some useful photographs and information, are far too discursive to do justice to so great a subject'.[14] The truth is that the *gloire* was fast fading. The early gains of stratigraphical excavation elsewhere were beginning to hint that much had been overlooked: indeed, as early as 1908 there was a pathetic comment by Mill Stephenson at an Antiquaries' meeting: '. . . attempts had often been made to take advantage of stratification at Silchester, but always without success', while Haverfield looked to the excavation of the cemeteries, vainly planned for 1909, to provide the chronological background so largely missing.[15]

As an appendix to the Antiquaries' excavations, the work of J. B. P. Karslake (1868-1942), albeit on the smallest scale, requires mention. It was in the garden of his house at Silchester* that he had found the head of Sarapis (pl. 18, p. 166) which probably served as his introduction to the triumvirate in 1899. Towards the end of the campaigns, he interested himself

---

* Acre House, now demolished and replaced, stood at the north-east corner of Silchester Common. It was originally a Victorian farmhouse. Many visitors to Silchester will remember it as a prominent landmark by reason of the third storey 'on stilts' devised by Karslake himself, after an architect had pronounced the foundations of the building insufficient to support another storey unaided. The writer remembers with pleasure the many kindnesses extended to him in this house by the late Mrs Leonora Karslake and Miss Kate Karslake.

in the outer earthwork, recording burials in its bank, and later tracing the path which it took on the east of the town. His also was the discovery of the Roman and later tilery at Little London, where many of the bricks and tiles of Calleva must have been made (p. 277). John Karslake was a type-specimen of that stalwart race, the English amateur archaeologist, whose influence has always been so potent; who but such a one, for example, would have sought out all instances of the name 'Little London'—of which there are not a few—to demonstrate its frequent association with potteries or tileworks?[16]

MODERN EXCAVATIONS

More recent work will illuminate our discussion of particular points as we come to them, and needs but listing here. Mrs M. Aylwin Cotton's excavation of the defences (initiated by the then Office of Works, now the Department of the Environment, in advance of the consolidation of the northern stretches of the town-wall) brought important chronological results in 1938-9, extended as it was to the outer earthwork. My own excavations of 1954-8, on behalf of Reading Museum and the Silchester Excavation Committee, were mainly concerned with the recently-discovered inner earthwork and the question of the pre-Roman occupation. In 1961, the Committee re-examined the Roman church near the forum, the work being directed by the late Sir Ian Richmond and myself: the account of the building in Chapter 14 below is provisional and personal.

We may look forward to the gradual preservation of the remaining sectors of the wall, since difficulties in the way of its becoming a Guardianship Monument of the Department of the Environment were solved by the generosity of the Wellington Estate and of the only other private owner, Mr A. P. D. Smyth of Rye House. It is to be hoped that there will again be excavation on the large scale desirable to settle its chronology and remaining details before the masons commence: so far only a small beginning has been made, and meanwhile the structure continues to moulder at a growing rate.[17]

In December 1972, the site of Calleva was sold with other lands at Silchester after 144 years in the possession of the Wellington family. 'Now a person of a moderate fortune may buy a whole *roman* city, which once half a kingdom could not do: and a gentleman may be lord of the soyl where formerly princes and emperors commanded.' So Stukeley closed his account of his visit, and we fitly end this section.

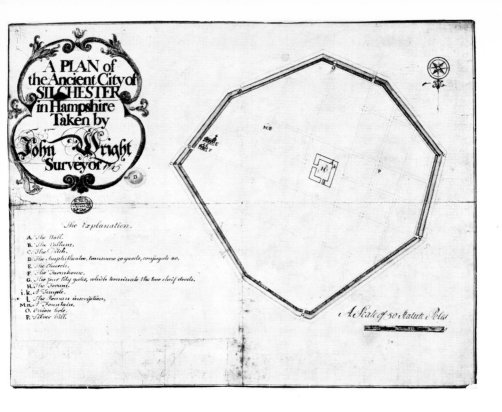

1 Plan of Silchester by John Wright, 1745, showing the streets laid down by
John Stair
2 The amphitheatre, 1724

The Side view of the Amphitheater at Silchester. May 8. 1724.

3   The Revd J. G. Joyce, about 1860
4   G. E. Fox drawing the mosaics in the gallery of XIV.2, 1895. Note the inserted fireplace
in the room shown in the foreground
5   Directors of the Silchester Excavation Fund, 1900, in XXIII.1. L.-R. Mill Stephenson,
F. Haverfield, Wm Gowland, G. E. Fox, and W. H. St. J. Hope. Note the hypocaust in the
foreground

THE SILCHESTER COLLECTION

Strathfield Saye House
Mortimer R.S.O.
Berks.

Feb. 27. 91.

The Duke of Wellington presents his compliments to Dr Stevens, he has an idea that it might be a beneficial thing for the neighbourhood & the Town of Reading, if he offered the articles lately discovered at Silchester, to the Museum at Reading as a loan Collection, there being at present no suitable place to exhibit them on the spot, & as it is desirable that they should be able to be seen in the neighbourhood of their discovery. If Dr Stevens would kindly communicate to the Duke of Wellington his views on the subject, the particulars of the loan could easily be settled hereafter.

Such was the letter received by Joseph Stevens, founder and honorary curator of Reading Museum. At a subsequent interview, the Duke explained that he was a life-holder, and could not make a gift of the material; but since his successor would be in the same position and unlikely to build a museum on the site, the loan could be looked upon as a virtual permanency. And so it has remained to this day. It was to include all that had been, and would be discovered; and indeed, apart from Joyce's 'great prize', the bronze eagle from the basilica (pl. 34c), the *Genius familiaris* (pl. 34e) and a few other things remaining at Stratfield Saye, all that excavation has yielded in modern times is in public care.[18] It may be said with some justice that Reading Museum has well sustained the burden which the presence of a collection of international renown imposed. Ancillary material includes the surviving photographic negatives taken by a local firm in 1890–1909, and also a few dating back to Joyce's time (pl. 25): they were the gift of Charles Keyser, the ecclesiologist. The catalogue of the collection was begun in 1951.

35

Early Settlement and the Establishment of the Town

Broad fingers of plateau-gravel, about 90 m. above sea-level, are a prominent feature of the Hampshire-Berkshire borderland; and it was on the tip of such a spur that Calleva was founded. In the natural state, this terrain supports light woodland or scrub, very easily cleared by fire as the autumnal blackened wastes of neighbouring heaths all too plainly show. Though the humus is scanty where agriculture is not now practised, signs of medieval cultivation on Silchester Common prove that a living could be wrung from it, and there is abundant water at the junction of the gravel with the underlying London Clay. The contrast between this vegetation and that of the lower-lying ground must have been very striking at one time, as we can still half-glimpse by looking from the edge of the Common across the attenuated remnant of Pamber Forest, with its thickets, lanky trees and sparse marshy clearings, towards the chalk Downs above Basingstoke, probably as bare then as now.

Round barrows on Mortimer Heath and a few stray relics of Neolithic and Bronze Age date from Silchester suggest that the plateau was colonised in early times, and in the Silchester collection itself a coloured glass bead of a kind identical with a pair from a princess's grave at Reinheim, and a small iron cheek-piece with bronze rosettes from a helmet of Montefortino affinity (fig. 3) suggest that barrows of the Early Iron Age, about the fourth century B.C., may have been levelled within the walled area; a La Tène I bronze brooch may not be much later.[1] Towards the end of the second century B.C. came the first waves of Belgic invaders from north Gaulish homelands, and coin-finds suggest that the future site of Calleva may not have been unknown to some of these folk. Two of the coins, rather later in date (c 40 B.C.), are especially interesting because they are issues of the Atrebates, a tribe from the neighbourhood of Arras which was to establish a kingdom in what is now Sussex, Hampshire, Berkshire, and parts of Surrey and Wiltshire. Their king at this time was Commius, once the friend of Caesar and his emissary to these shores in 55 B.C., but later the implacable enemy

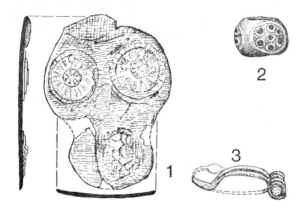

3. Early Iron Age remains. 1, iron helmet cheek-piece with bronze rosettes. 2, glass bead (turquoise, brown eyes, blue spots, outlined in white). 3, la Tène I bronze brooch.
Scales, 1,3: 1/2; 2: 1/1

of the Romans, who escaped from Gaul some time after the revolt of Vercingetorix, probably about 50 B.C. One of these two coins (fig. 4,1) was found near a sub-rectangular enclosure of about 1.6 ha., known as the Frith (Pond Farm, fig. 5), on the north edge of the Silchester spur; the other, a contemporary plated counterfeit, came from the walled area, close to which, on the south-west, there was probably another enclosure of similar type: part was later embodied in the 'salient' of the outer earthwork in Rampier copse.[2] There may also have been occupation-sites on Mortimer Common, for dykes running across the neck of a spur in that region (fig. 5G) seem best regarded as being of early Belgic date. But when circumstances favoured the creation of a larger settlement, or *oppidum,* the Silchester spur was chosen because it was the most southerly, and therefore one to be secured against seizure by hostile forces who might then overrun the rest of the plateau. The choice, of course, was that of a very primitive community, who thought more of safety in remoteness than of the potential arising from a position on a trading-route such as the Thames; at the same time it must be realised that for decades on either side of the birth of Christ the Thames ran as frontier between the Atrebates and the hostile Catuvellauni to the north, and Reading, however favourably situated for Thames and Kennet trade, would have been far too exposed a position to be developed until that frontier had ceased to be of consequence.[3] The main strength of the Atrebates, moreover, seems always to have resided in the south of their area, in Sussex.

37

CALLEVA UNDER THE ATREBATES

Commius had come to Britain vowing never to set eyes on another Roman; but he was not averse to Romanised ways, and his was the first indigenous coinage in this island to display a legend in Roman lettering. In the years after about 35 B.C., COMMIOS gold staters (fig. 4,2 from Reading) penetrated thinly throughout the area described above, and since five of the dozen or so known come from Basingstoke, Basingstoke-Odiham, Guildford and Reading (which produced two), political conditions were evidently appropriate for the establishment of Calleva. For proof of its existence, however, we have to await the brief reign of Eppillus (about A.D. 5–10), one of the three rulers described as 'Son of Commius' on their coins. Eppillus seems to have dispossessed his elder brother Tincommius (cf. fig. 4,3, from Emmer Green, on the Oxfordshire side of Reading) by A.D. 7, and was in turn dispossessed by the last brother, Verica, identifiable with the 'certain Berikos', suppliant at the court of Claudius in A.D. 43. Tincommius' later coins, from about 15 B.C.,

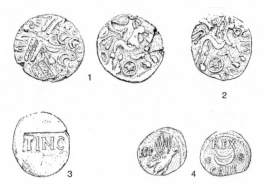

4. Atrebatic coins. 1, gold stater, Pond Farm woods, c. 50–35 B.C. (J. S. Eyton coll.). 2, gold stater of Commius, Reading, c. 35–20 B.C., reverse only. 3, gold stater of Tincommius, Emmer Green, c. 15 B.C.-A.D. 5, obverse only. 4, silver quarter-stater of Eppillus, King at Calleva, c. A.D. 5–10 (British Museum)

are of a Romanised design, and hint at the presence of technicians from the continent: it has been suggested that there was a kind of 'treaty-relationship' between Rome and the Atrebates, as if Rome here played her age-old game of *divide et impera:* it would not do for the Catuvellauni, nominally defeated by Caesar, to become too powerful. Be this as it may, Eppillus was the first in all the long annals of coinage in Britain to employ the title REX; yet his exceedingly rare gold and silver coins (fig. 4,4) have an even greater significance for us, because they name Calleva (CALLEV, CALLE). There was no

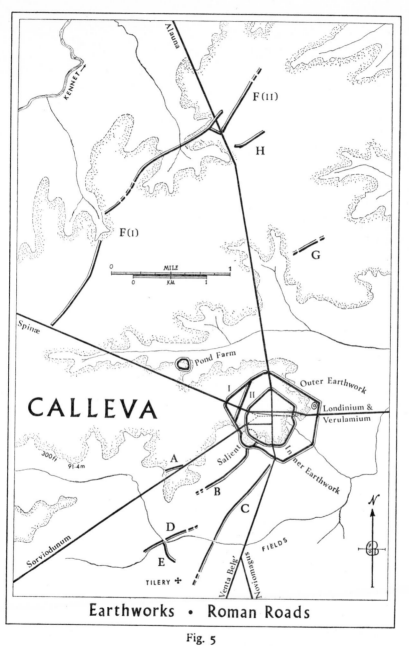

Earthworks · Roman Roads

Fig. 5

other Calleva; and since British coins were issued at capitals, no doubt in the close entourage of the king, these show that the Silchester *oppidum* had come into being by the early years of our era.[4]

So much, as it were, *in vacuo*. No structural feature at Silchester has yet been assigned on any certain grounds to the earliest *oppidum*. It is possible, however, that the Flex Ditch and the more westerly of the two trailing lines of dyke south of the walled town are to be understood in this context. The first (fig. 5A) cuts off a small side-spur south of Silchester Common, to bar direct access to the plateau by this convenient route; the second (fig. 5B) faced south-east in the direction of the southern Atrebatic capital near Chichester, and probably stretched across open or cleared ground as an obstacle to chariotry approaching by a track which fell into disuse only when the Roman road from Noviomagus to Calleva was constructed in the late first century A.D. (p. 45). It will be noticed that neither earthwork has very much relevance to a settlement on the walled site, and the Eppillan centre may have lain elsewhere; it is known, however, that Belgic *oppida* were sometimes very dispersed.[5]

If the Eppillan *oppidum* was scattered we are very fortunate indeed to possess some material from the excavations of the walled area which reflects occupation in the earliest decades of the first century A.D. The most important is the glossy red Italic sigillata (Arretine ware) of which about forty vessels are represented. This was the *de luxe* table-ware of the Augusto-Tiberian period; later, south and central Gaulish imitations began to supplant it, and even found their way into Britain. Arretine of the type considered here ceased to be manufactured before the Roman invasion of A.D. 43, though vessels were treasured and many survived in use at that time. Most of the Silchester Arretine vessels were plain cups and dishes, some bearing potter's stamps mainly of the great Arezzo firm of *Ateius* (about 5 B.C.—A.D. 20, cf. fig. 6,2). Three others are interesting because they are not paralleled in the much larger list from Camulodunum, founded about A.D. 10: they are those of *Sextus Annius, Mena slave of Avillius*, and *Jucundus,* the last on a bowl of provincial manufacture, but very early in shape (fig. 6,1). Scraps of moulded bowls also appear. Some Tiberian Gallic stamps are also drawn (fig. 6,3).[6] Whether some fragments of Mediterranean amphorae are also pre-Roman is uncertain: they may well be.[7] A piece of polychrome glass inlay and a piece of cased blue vessel-glass with opaque twisted white threads are pre-Roman, beyond much doubt.[8] Another kind of pottery illustrated is Gallo-Belgic black or red ware, often with potter's stamps. Some, as also some of the fine light-coloured butt-shaped beakers and other table wares, entered Silchester before the Roman period.[9] As for local pottery, the dozen

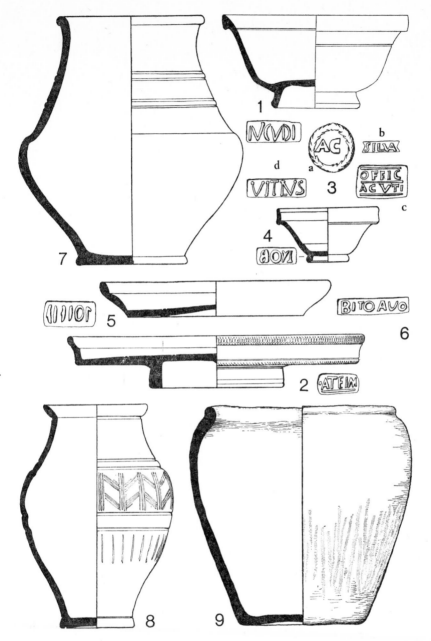

6. Early pottery. 1. provincial Italic cup, Augustan, with stamp of Jucundus. 2, Arretine plate, Tiberian, with stamp 'by the hand of Ateius'. 3, stamps on Tiberian Gaulish wares: (a) on cup, Acutus of Montans and la Graufesenque; (b) on cup, Silvanus of la Graufesenque; (c) on cup. 'Acutus' workshop', see above; (d) Vit(u)lus of Lezoux, on decorated bowl (form 29). 4, black Gallo-Belgic cup, with stamp of Boutus. 5, plate, similar ware, illiterate stamp. 6, stamp BITO(s) AVO(t) 'Bitos made this', on another black plate. 7, typical wheel-made Belgic jar, grey ware. 8, typical small butt-shaped beaker, orange ware, import. 9, typical jar in coarse flint-gritted brownish-grey local 'Silchester' ware. Scales, stamps 1/1; rest, 1/3, but no. 1, 3/8

vessels in the ritual deposit found in the area of Insula XII (p. 164) are pre-Roman and possibly as early as Eppillus.[10] The continental imports suggest that a small series of Gaulish base-metal coins is to be linked with pre-Roman trade.[11]

CALLEVA UNDER CATUVELLAUNIAN OCCUPATION

Verica's reign was one of disaster for the Atrebates. The Silchester region was lost: if we accept the general belief that the occurrence of British coins in any number within a particular area denotes political control by the issuing authority, we have to admit that about A.D 25 the whole northern part of the realm was lost to the Catuvellauni led by Epaticcus, brother of the famous Cunobelin.[12] A small silver-plated counterfeit from Calleva closely resembles a coin of this ruler, but the name EPATI has gone, and it may just conceivably have been a coin of Caratacus, identical apart from the name CARA.[13]

Under the Catuvellauni, Calleva remained a place of some importance and was probably the capital of Epaticcus and Caratacus (from about A.D. 40). A suggestive clue is provided by fragments of pitted clay moulds (fig. 40,2) in which flans for a base silver coinage were cast:[14] they are very similar to moulds from Camulodunum, Verulamium and elsewhere, but as far as is known, the Atrebatic rulers preferred to strike tiny silver minims and did not issue the billon attested by analysis. It is to the Catuvellaunian period, too, that the only definite trace of pre-Roman domestic occupation so far discovered at Calleva is to be assigned. In 1957–8, excavations below the bank of the inner earthwork south of the walled town (p. 44) revealed traces of a hut and an adjacent deep rubbish-pit. A great deal of pottery was collected, none Roman, almost every piece of native manufacture; and among it were several bases from pedestal-urns. These are a diagnostically Catuvellaunian type and are rare south of the middle Thames.[15] The hut lies within the line of the more easterly of the two dykes on the south of the walled town (fig. 5c), and it is possible to envisage that dyke as a defence against a Verican counter-offensive from the south-east. The flight of that unhappy ruler to Claudius, however, shows that the Catuvellauni eventually swept over his kingdom entirely, and there is pedestal-urn material from Selsey to indicate as much.[16]

TIBERIUS CLAUDIUS COGIDUBNUS, KING-LEGATE

The disruption of the power-balance in Britain gave the Romans a *casus belli* which the emperor Claudius, avid for military fame, seized. Four legions and supporting troops landed in 43 at Richborough in Kent and probably also in the vicinity of Chichester. The Catuvellauni were quickly defeated; Caratacus fled to the Silures of south Wales, and continued to lead war-bands against the petty tribal states of the periphery of the nascent province.[17] It is not explicitly stated that the Atrebatic kingdom was restored, though this is implicit in the action taken to vanquish the proud Catuvellauni, and also in the fact that a kingdom is known to have existed in southern Britain after 43. But we do not hear more of the elderly Verica; the ruler known to history is Cogidubnus, whose relationship to the Commian dynasty is obscure.

Only two sources refer to Cogidubnus. In the *Agricola*, Tacitus remarks that 'certain tribal communities' (*civitates*) were 'given' to him, and that he remained very faithful up to the time of his own recollection.[18] The reference occurs in a sequence of events and can thus be dated to about A.D. 50–1. Whether Cogidubnus was newly-appointed then, or whether he had been King since 43, we do not know. The second source is an inscription from Chichester, which may be of Claudian or Neronian date: it records the erection of a temple of Neptune and Minerva *ex auctoritate Ti(berii) Claud(ii) Cogidubni R(egis), Legati Aug(usti) in Britannia*,[19] and shows that Cogidubnus was a Roman citizen (presumably by the grant of the emperor Claudius, whose names he bore). The legatine title is extraordinary, and scholars have long speculated upon its meaning. The only colourable parallel concerns Herod the Great, who was awarded the honorary standing of procurator in the province of Syria.[20] Since Tacitus does not mention Cogidubnus' legature, we may be sure that it, too, was purely honorary; and from the further continuation of the passage in the *Agricola* '. . . that [the Roman people] might employ even kings as instruments of servitude' it seems clear that the additional *civitates,* if indeed they were additional, were ruled by Cogidubnus as king and not in any sense as legate. The governors of Britain were indeed legates, but not all legates were governors of Britain, or of any territorial province, and 'Emperor's delegate' is a better rendering of their title.

The kingdom of Cogidubnus is believed to have lain in the south around Chichester, because the inscription was found there, and because the *Antonine Itinerary* refers to the town as *Regno*. It has been doubted, however, that this word has any true relationship to the Latin *regnum*, 'kingdom',[21] and the inscription by itself does not locate the kingdom or its capital any more closely, for example, than the foundation-stone of the National Museum of Wales locates the kingdom and capital of George V. All that can be said is that it would be strange to discover that an area later designated as the *civitas Atrebatum,* centring upon Silchester, lay outside the *regnum Cogidubni.*

The date of Cogidubnus' death can only be guessed, and the unusual assignment of two distinguished juridical legates to Britain in the period 81–6 has been connected with the dismemberment of the kingdom and the creation in its place of the three cantons of Atrebates, Belgae and 'Regini'. In 81, however, Agricola had already been governor for three years. If Cogidubnus had died during this time, it seems unlikely that Tacitus would have phrased his reference to him as in fact he did. Most probably, he died before 78; and if the tile from the public baths of Silchester bearing Nero's name, i.e. of 54–68, is of local origin (p. 278, fig. 7, 1) he may have died long before, for the tilery is likely to have been established upon royal domain of some kind acquired by the Roman state by conquest or by testamentary deposition.[22]

CALLEVA AND KING COGIDUBNUS

The Revd John Skinner committed to his diary of February 1821, the speculative suggestion that Cogidubnus was associated with Calleva.[23] Of late years, evidence has come to light which strongly points in that direction, for the first great defensive enclosure, the inner earthwork, is of an entirely native style, but it is adapted in a very striking manner to the course of the main Roman road from London westwards to the campaigning areas of the south Wales borderland.

The inner earthwork encompassed about 32.5 ha. and was of simple but massive type, being laid out in a series of straightish lengths with re-entrants on the south, east and west (folding plan). Its ditch was 13.5 m. wide (wider on the south, where it was cut in sand) and 3.5 m. deep, with a flat bottom 3.5 m. across; the bank was of similar width, and its height was increased by material scraped up to its rear; a small bank on the counterscarp lip of the ditch brought the minimum overall relief to 7 m. The profile is very reminiscent of a type of late pre-Roman fortification in Belgic Gaul—the 'Fécamp' type—of which several other examples have been found, as modifications of older defences, in southern England, most recently at Danebury, near Stockbridge (Hants.). There the overall dimensions are not far different, but the ditch has a much wider flat bottom—closer, in fact, to the French prototypes—than at Silchester, where attention had to be paid to the angle of rest of the subsoil.

As already mentioned, the bank overlies the 'Catuvellaunian' hut discovered in 1957–8 (p. 42), and the defence as a whole must consequently belong to a period after A.D. 25. To go into details for a moment, the bank was found to have slumped deeply into the filling of the pit adjacent to the hut, and active settlement furthermore continued even after the levelling of the bank to its present negligible contour. It may be concluded that if the bank had stood for long, its weight would have compressed the filling of the pit to such a degree that no consolidation would have continued when most of that weight had been removed. Levelling is known to have taken place within a year or two of A.D. 50, and it follows that the construction of the earthwork cannot well have occurred until the eve of the Roman invasion or even later. But since the east and west entrances correspond to the line of the Roman strategic road, and are not otherwise explainable, it is the second of the alternatives that must be chosen. In other words, this great earthwork was erected by British allies of the Romans, who enjoyed considerable power and complete trust. We might almost hazard the guess that Cogidubnus' legatine authority recognised his military contribution as an ally of Rome and was equivalent to that of a legionary commander.

The entrance on the south is interesting in a different way, for the Roman road to Winchester (Venta Belgarum) is not aligned from it, but from a point somewhat to the south-east. Most probably it corresponded to the line of a trackway to Chichester taking a somewhat different course from the later Roman road, which branches off the Winchester road about 1.5 km. south of the town. Here, then, is another demonstration of the relatively early date of the inner earthwork, when a link to Chichester was required, but before the construction of the properly engineered roads to Chichester and Winchester.

The behaviour of the Portway, the Roman road to Sorviodunum and eventually to Exeter (Isca Dumnoniorum), is also very interesting. This road assumed great importance in 47 as a link between London and the southern extremity of the frontier-zone then established on the base-line of the Fosse Way (Exeter to Lincoln). At Calleva, however, the road very clearly passes directly over the inner earthwork, which was obsolete, evidently, at the time of its construction. Earlier, no doubt, the Portway was unmetalled and diverged from the west entrance of the inner earthwork not very far to the north. We can very probably deduce from the construction of the metalled line across the site of the earthwork that the creation of the new frontier-zone had rendered this great enclosure obsolete; and indeed the excavations of 1955 showed very clearly that the infilling of the ditch was begun about A.D 50. By Flavian times, when the regular street-grid of Calleva was laid out, a good deal of the circuit had no doubt been obliterated;

but owing to the gradual sinkage of the filling the process was not completed until the latest years of the second century.[24]

A much larger defensive circuit of 95 ha., the outer earthwork, seems to have been erected in its place almost immediately, for the only pottery found underneath the bank is Claudio-Neronian. The new work was of much slighter elevation, and had a V-shaped ditch 5.5 m. wide and 1.8 m. deep. Except on the west, where there was a considerable extension, it ran at a fairly even distance around the kernel of the town (folder). The new line was interrupted for the passage of the Roman road to the west, and presumably for all the other roads: on the south, the entrance will have lain on the line of the trackway to Chichester, thus well to the south-east of the entrance in the inner earthwork, and will have governed the alignment-point for the road leading to Winchester and Chichester. This primary outer earthwork may also be envisaged as belonging to the regal phase.

Subsequently, the earthwork was reduced to about 86 ha. by cutting off the westerly projection. The height of the rampart was greatly increased by the addition of material scraped up from the interior, and in Rampier copse —named from the great bank—these hollows can still be traced. The total elevation here, embracing as it did part of the early farmstead enclosure (p. 37), was in excess of 7.5 m.; and on the north-west too the secondary outer earthwork still stands to an impressive height: Wall-lane passes through it near Rye House. The final phase of work involved the construction of a low flint revetment on the outer side of the bank, and some of the materials can still be seen among the roots of the great hollies crowding the bank in Rampier copse; the ditch was also re-cut at the same time. It is surmised that the secondary outer earthwork dates from Boudica's rebellion in A.D. 60–1;[25] the revetment and ditch-cutting are almost certainly later, dating probably to the period when the street-plan was laid out in Flavian times.

THE EARLY TOWN

What was the character of the settlement developing within these successive barriers? We may certainly look for public buildings constructed to Roman design and in Romanised technique, for the Chichester inscription shows that the *Regnum* of Cogidubnus in no way lagged behind the rest of the province in such particulars. As already mentioned, the public baths of Insula XXXIIIA produced a tile bearing the stamp of an imperial manufactory of the time of Nero (54–68), and this discovery has generally been accepted as affording some indication of the early date of the baths, despite the curious fact that only one stamped tile was found. That the baths were early, however, is certain from the fact that the portico was demolished when the street was laid outside on the regular grid-alignment (pl. 20, p. 93).[26] If we turn to the folding plan, we see that the reason for this procedure lay in the fact that the building is at an angle of 9° to the streets.

A glance at the plan shows that a great many buildings—as many as a third of the total—are not built in accordance with the streets, and must in very many cases be of earlier origin. The most significant of them have been 'adapted' to the streets by the addition of a porch (XXIII.2) or an extension of some sort (XVIIIA.3); sometimes merely the projecting front was rebuilt, as at the baths, or in several of the houses (e.g. IX.3). Some years ago, Lady Fox proposed an 'old town plan' arranged on an axis approximating to that of the baths, but in accepting divergences as varied as 2° to 16° from the line of the streets implied that the original layout was haphazard.[27] The subsequent discovery of the inner earthwork has thrown new light on this matter. Nearly all the unaligned buildings are within its circuit, and those which are not can in many cases be explained by reference to some local peculiarity such as the sloping ground in the south-east of the town, or the run of the later Roman defences. Furthermore, the axis of the baths corresponds to a direct line across the inner earthwork enclosure from the east to the west entrance. Some thirty buildings conform to the same deflection from the streets, and five of them are 'adapted': they unquestionably point to a rectangular partition of the ground based on the line of the actual route from east to west. Such a town-plan, of course, can never have reached the stage of having metalled streets between the plots: otherwise, there would have been no reason to change the alignment later. Nor should too much be made of this early attempt at town-planning: not too much was in fact made of it, as we see from the varying alignment of properties in Insulae I or XXIII: compare, for example, XXIIA.2 and XXIII.2.[28]

This chapter may be closed with reference to some articles of Roman military equipment. The inner and primary outer earthworks were presumably manned, if required, by the native troops for whom they had been designed: that such troops existed, in early days, is attested by Tacitus.[29] The presence of Roman military equipment, though often and rightly taken, in southern Britain, to point to the existence of a Roman fort, can hardly be so interpreted here;[30] and in any case the most notable deposit, the brass hinges, lace-hooks and rosettes from a legionary segmented cuirass (fig. 8.1), found in a pit of Insula XXIII, is of Flavian date rather than earlier. A tinned bronze mess-can (fig. 35,1) from the same pit bears the stamp CIPI AVG, i.e. of a member of the bronze-founding firm of the Cipii of Capua, who seem to have had a sizeable army contract.[31] No doubt some of the military gear, not all legionary (and by no means all of first-century date, as we shall see) could well have been lost by troops passing through the town. But the contents of the pit may hint at a settled stay, and very possibly a detachment of legionaries was sent to Calleva as a police-force during the period of transition which must have followed upon the death of Cogidubnus. Some fragments of leather sheeting from the panels of leather ridge-tents (*papiliones*, 'butterflies') used by the Roman army were found in the silt of the inner earthwork ditch, at a spot where it was open as late as about A.D. 100: possibly the detachment envisaged lived *sub pellibus*.[32]

3

The Success of Urbanisation

Calleva has the most complete plan of any peregrine town in the Roman Empire, though it is chronologically undifferentiated; the street-grid and the inner ring of defences, however, afford a means of distinguishing early from later developments and of gauging the success of urbanisation. But just because the plan is fuller than any other comparable plan, a basic problem must not be forgotten: how complete is the pattern of buildings?

The extensive cover of aerial photographs, in particular those taken recently by the National Monuments Record under the supervision of Mr John Hampton, provides an excellent check on the accuracy of the excavated town-plan. The photographs immediately reveal a much more complex 'history' in the soil of Calleva than that plan suggests: all the difference, in fact, between a full tonal gradation and a line-block, and more besides, for unrecorded buildings also appear. Some corrections can also be made to lines of streets, and some extramural streets can be inserted. Turning to pl. 8, which shows parts of Insulae XIIA, XXVI, IX and I north of the modern track across the site, it becomes quickly apparent that the number of undiscovered buildings, and buildings incompletely opened, is impressive (see the folding plan).

	EXCAVATED PLAN			AERIAL PHOTOGRAPHS		
	Unaligned	*Aligned*	*Total*	Unaligned	Aligned	Total
Rectangular Insulae						
XIIA	–	2[=1]	1	2*	5	7
XXVI	3	4	7	5*	9	14
IX	2	1	3	2	6	8
Square Insulae						
XXIII	4	1	5	5	4	9
I	1	2	3	1	2	3
Total	10	10[=9]	19	15	26	41

(* *timber*—dark lines in gravel spreads)

The known total of buildings in this wonderfully distinct region is thus more than doubled. If repeated on a similar scale throughout the town, such additions would dramatically change the familiar plan. So far, however, we do not possess a complete aerial cover of the same fidelity, and caution is necessary before this deduction is accepted. In the first place, since we are dealing with insulae bounded by a street-system which regularised a largely haphazard existing development, the houses which are neither aligned with the streets nor adapted to them must be left out of account. The square insulae thus continue to be dominated by the pair of large houses which each contains, and these houses continue to be surrounded by much open ground. The additions occur predominantly in the rectangular insulae and mostly take the form of smallish buildings. It seems conceivable that the large insulae were created expressly for large establishments, and the small insulae for those of lesser account. It is furthermore possible to use the apparent contradictions of this suggestion in its support, for, to take Insula XIV, the two large dwellings which are found on the plan clearly developed from much smaller originals.

Secondly, the density of building in IX or XXVI, as now revealed, is still very similar to that long planned for XVII or XVIIIA. In other words, what the aerial photographs show, and permit us summarily to correct, is the varying efficiency of exploration in different parts of the town. Of course allowance must be made for deficiencies not at present controllable by a near-perfect aerial cover: in III and V, for instance, we might expect a greater density of buildings.

Thirdly, the centripetal pattern of development conveyed by the 1908 plan is very strongly confirmed by the line taken for the inner Roman defences. These truncate the peripheral insulae in such a way as to suggest that all extant buildings were to be encompassed: XXIV.1 and 2, for example, are included at the cost of a 400 m. run of ditch, bank and eventual wall otherwise unnecessary; and there must be something important within the north-east corner to account for the projection of the defences at that point. XXIV.1 and 2 are large houses, but we see that exactly the same attention was paid to the smaller properties in the western insulae. We may conclude that nothing on the same scale as the development here, or as closely grouped, can have existed to the west or north in parts cut off when the inner defences were established.

On the spacing of buildings within the insulae in general we shall have more to say in Chapter 7, when we come to deal with the original metation of the streets. For the present, it is enough to note that even in those insulae which contained more buildings than were actually excavated, there still

6 North-west sector of the town wall, showing the structure sagging into the filling of the ditch of the inner earthwork

7 Aerial view of Silchester from the west, showing the streets, and traces of the inner earthwork and (fore-ground, left) the primary outer earthwork

8 Aerial view of parts of western insulae, showing detail which includes buildings omitted in the 1908 town-plan

9 Aerial view of the extramural region west of the walled town, showing field-boundaries, etc

remains much open ground, proportionately as much around each building as there is around the large houses elsewhere. The photographs do not, and cannot, show everything that existed at any time; nor is what they show necessarily clear without excavation. A Calleva of huts, for example, has largely escaped detection.[1] Nevertheless, the plan as we now have it shows fairly clearly what existed in the second to fourth centuries,[2] as well as a fair proportion of structures dating basically from the first century. In short, there are about 150 known buildings aligned with the streets, or adapted to them, and about half that number are unaligned and unadapted.

THE PATTERN OF URBANISATION

A regular street-plan was a mark of civilisation, and some small towns never acquired it;[3] but because—in our view—Calleva was not constituted as a regular local-government capital until after the death of King Cogidubnus, its streets were not laid out until the Flavian period, say about A.D. 80, and the metalling of peripheral lines was still proceeding under Hadrian, say about 130.[4] The length of time taken to complete the grid is understandable, since the streets were not destined to be flanked by continuous rows of buildings, and there could have been little sense of urgency. Indeed, we may be tempted to imagine that Calleva could have managed perfectly well without its grid. The streets, however, were taken as far as the reduced outer earthwork, on the west side at least; and originally, therefore, hopes were high that an area of some 86 ha. might be built up. This is about three-quarters the area of Roman London and about the same as Verulamium; among towns of lesser status, it is second only to Corinium (Cirencester). However, when the inner defences were erected in late Antonine times, all buildings of consequence were contained, as we have seen, within less than half the original area (40 ha.).[5]

The very spacious planning of the insulae and the isolated settings of many of the houses offer a clue as to the reason why the development of the town did not exceed that limit. The yards and minor structures found near many of the houses (p. 255) reflect the agriculture which remained the essential basis of life; the contrast with the much more crowded shops and small premises along the main east-west street is very striking. Even so, desirable though a main-street position evidently was, there is no really continuous frontage, and the shops are not numerous in relation to the ordinary houses. We may remember that the site of Calleva was chosen in response to the requirements of a small, primitive agricultural community, and that it only later became, for political and military reasons, an *oppidum* of consequence. Trade, like

S.—D

the Roman roads, came to Calleva because it existed, and was a good distributive outlet; not because it lay on a natural trade-route or because the townsfolk were able in any important way to develop a local commerce. The manufacturing industries were all small in scale and designed for the local needs of the town itself and the surrounding countryside only. The early tanning-industry (probably continued in later centuries, though the evidence is far from clear) is the chief detectable exception: but as a product of animal husbandry it must point to the agricultural surpluses which can alone account for the comfortable standard of life maintained in many of the houses, which will have depended partly on direct farming, and partly on the contributions of tenants, in all probability.

It was on a basically agricultural community, therefore, that the urban civilisation of Rome was veneered. Yet the result was not a garden city: as Haverfield observed, 'I will not call it a "garden city", for a garden city represents an attempt to add some features of the country to a town. Silchester . . . represents the exact opposite. It is an attempt to insert urban features into a countryside.'[6] These features were, in particular, the grid of streets, the shops, the baths, and the forum-basilica or market-place and administrative centre. They were interspersed with other buildings, including a few temples which in no way differ from the rural pattern, and houses and home farms. But although paddocks, barns and byres might be situated conveniently near the dwellings, the fields were at a distance (Chapter 19). The chief restrictive factor lies here. The practical limits of arable farming from a single centre are illustrated by the modest extent of the built-up area of Calleva.

So much for the general picture. As we examine the plan in greater detail, we perceive that indications of continuous development along the new lines of street are very meagre. An urban mentality could not be conjured up *pari passu* with the imposition of the grid and the spread of Romanised building-methods. There are perhaps three blocks adjacent to the central insula containing the forum-basilica which might be classed as typically urban, consisting as they do of a number of conjoined chambers which are likely to have been in the same ownership and to have been let to individual shop-keepers. These blocks are found at the south-east corner of Insula III (four rooms with a colonnade in front)[7] and midway along the southern margin of Insula I (five rooms with a yard at the back);[8] but the third is far more interesting, and takes us back to a date before the street-plan was imposed. Let us look into it.

The forum-basilica lies at an angle of about 2° to the street-grid, and there are about three dozen other buildings which conform to this alignment.

In some cases the deflection may be wholly fortuitous: but at least six have been adapted to the grid,[9] and for that matter so has the forum, the main east entrance of which was brought 1.5 m. south of the axial line in order to make it correspond to the division between Insulae V and VI.[10] Slight as the deflection is, therefore, it seems to merit study; and just as the alignment of the baths could be said to be related to the direct path across the site from the east to the west entrance of the inner earthwork (p. 47), so the alignment of the forum can colourably be said to answer that of the Roman road approaching Calleva from the east. If continued straight across the site, without need for an adjustment just north of the present parish church, as recent aerial photographs now show, this road would meet prolongations of the west and south-west highways in a simple Y-fork near the south-east corner of the future Insula XIII.[11] Such a correspondence can hardly be accidental, but must on the contrary have been planned. That the plan was not executed is perhaps to be attributed to the existence of the sacred enclosure and temples (Insula XXX) which such a road must unavoidably have cut in two. Be this as it may, it seems likely that the forum-basilica was aligned in accordance with a proposal to extend the Roman road directly across the site; and that a *grand boulevard* fully 12 m. wide was planned on the line of that road, so that it would sweep up to the main entrance of the forum like the *via praetoria* of a legionary fortress to the main entrance of the *principia*. On the corner of the projected boulevard a block of ten lock-up shops was built (VI.B1, fig. 29, 1), exactly answering, in its alignment and colonnaded façade, the external portico of the great building opposite.[12] But, as the *temenos* of Insula XXX remained inviolate, the boulevard never took shape as planned, and the Roman road was connected to the street-plan of Flavian times by a dog-leg bend. The street opposite the forum became one of the least important in the entire town, leading nowhere. Buildings encroached upon it and eventually upon the block of shops. Thus this early Callevan venture—civic venture, in all probability—into urban planning and into real-estate cannot have been much of a success.

In sum, the degree of urbanisation in matters of planning was lowly, and by modern standards the term is barely admissible. Yet it is not by modern standards, nor yet by those of the Roman Mediterranean, that we should judge. Mindful of the great fact that Calleva and the other towns of Roman Britain were the very first ever to be created in this island, among peoples to whom the urban concept was almost wholly novel, it is the evidence of success within practical limits that should be sought out, not the evidence of failure. If an ambitious scheme was a failure, it does not follow that the entire experiment in urban living was also a failure. Calleva, on the contrary, maintained an urban vitality within lesser limits. The streets, for example, were kept in good order, always clean, and their central rainwater gutter is a late feature (p. 89). The baths, the chief place of social venue, were constantly altered; the forum-basilica, unlike that of Wroxeter which lay in ruins after a fire about the end of the third century, was rebuilt after destruction perhaps at that very time (p. 71); and towards the end of the fourth century, the little cathedral church—for such it may have been—arose in the shadow of this great neighbour.

Of the nineteen principal towns of Roman Britain, only five besides Calleva have not remained important urban centres. Except in the case of Isurium (Aldborough) a good deal is known of their general plans: but only at Caerwent does the area enclosed correspond at all narrowly to what was built up (18 ha.).[13] At Caerwent, indeed, special circumstances existed, for in some degree it served as the township of the neighbouring legionary fortress of Caerleon, where the civil settlement seems never to have developed very far. At the one attested *municipium,* Verulamium (80 ha.), and at Wroxeter (83 ha.) there are large insulae and widely-spaced buildings:[14] but although neither of these towns passed through the chrysalid regal phase of Calleva, they show no more real sign of civic planning in accordance with the street-lines, and Caistor St. Edmund does not do so. The four *coloniae* are overbuilt, but were no larger than peregrine towns; on the other hand, a few significant details emerge from their sites. Lincoln, for example, possessed an excellent aqueduct for which the water had to be considerably raised artificially, and a corresponding system of deep main drainage—in Britain a mark of the more 'Roman' as opposed to the more 'British' side of urbanisation.[15] Again, it is at Camulodunum that we find other evidence of buildings which seem to exemplify a landlord-tenant relationship.[16] London, then as now, was by far the largest town (about 133 ha.): understandably, little is known of the density of Roman building there. In a wider context, it is often said that British towns compare ill with those of Gaul. While they certainly appear small by the standards of Nîmes or Arles, Augustan *coloniae* of 200 ha. or more,[17] they are similar in size to many other Gallic towns, such as Sens (Augustodunum of the Senones). The real question, however, is not crudely one of size, but one of the relative density and character of buildings. The enquirer abroad is as frequently defeated by modern overbuilding as in Britain, but it must appear from the fragmentary continental plans known, e.g. of Vaison, Augst, Xanten, Aquincum or Cambodunum,[18] that a much denser standard of building applied than was the case in Britain. There is also far more evidence on the continent of great wealth lavished on public buildings and fine monuments.

THE STATUS OF CALLEVA

The civil zone of Britain contained, under the general direction and control of the imperial governor and the independent financial administration of the procurator, various kinds of self-governing communities (*civitates*). This was the usual Roman arrangement. Four of these communities were *coloniae,* perhaps more: in three known cases they were first-century plantations of retired legionaries outside former legionary bases (Camulodunum, Gloucester, Lincoln), and in the fourth, outside an active legionary base (York). Another type of chartered community was the *municipium,* of which Verulamium, on the authority of Tacitus, was an early example. So far as we know, the other communities were native or, as the Romans called them, *civitates peregrinae,* and for the most part were formed from existing tribal divisions. They had Romanised administrations modelled on the chartered pattern, but they did not enjoy the Roman citizenship or the Latin franchise appropriate to Verulamium. Their citizens possessed merely their tribal citizenship, which carried collateral rights and obligations, but was not of great account in a world dominated by *cives Romani.* As time went on, however, their magistrates would have acquired Roman citizenship, and their members who had served in the Roman auxiliary forces would have brought it back on retirement, leading thus to a noticeable spread of the *civitas Romana* within the peregrine territories, especially because (until about 140) the official grant to soldiers extended to existing children. Thus by the end of the second century, there would have been appreciable numbers of Roman citizens at Calleva; and though the surviving epigraphic record of their presence is very small, it may be observed that three out of the five stones which retain some portion of a name relate to Roman citizens, three of them members of the family of the Tammonii. In 212, the Roman franchise was extended to provincials generally under the terms of the famous edict of Caracalla known as the *Constitutio Antoniniana.*[19]

The question of the status in law of the chief towns of the peregrine communities has been much discussed in recent years.[20] The coupling of the tribal name to the place-name, as in the case of Calleva Atrebatum, Venta Silurum and eight more, does at least enable us to identify the principal administrative centres. Beyond this point there is uncertainty. Was such a town not merely the administrative centre of its *civitas* but its actual core, as was certainly so in the case of the chartered communities? Or were the peregrine communities of the first century so very large and backward that this is altogether too sophisticated a notion? In that case, the town would have had a separate existence as but one (albeit the largest and most important) settlement upon the soil of the *civitas*. In Britain we have one inscription, from Brough-upon-Humber, which may show that this was so. It specifically refers to the *vicus Pet(uariensis* or *-uariensium)*, i.e. the recognised settlement, if we may so call it, of Petuaria or the folk of Petuaria. It may also refer to the *civitas Parisiorum* in which Petuaria lay, but this is far from certain. It would be difficult, nevertheless, to point to another settlement which could be regarded as a likely *civitas*-capital in this region. An inscription from Sens, which mentions a man who was a magistrate both of the *civitas Senonum* and of the *vicani* of Agedincum, is the most important piece of evidence to have a bearing on the matter, and again it enables us to suggest that *civitas*-capitals did rank as *vici*. Inscriptions from Wroxeter and Caerwent, relating in the one case to the dedication of the forum by the *civitas Cornoviorum* and in the other to the erection of a statue by the *respublica civitatis Silurum,* make no mention of the town or the town-authority; but since neither of these actions need have concerned it, these inscriptions cannot be adduced in evidence against its existence.[21]

If, in addition to sheltering the administration of the *civitas,* Calleva possessed an urban administration of its own, we may perhaps ask of our very extensive town-plan where its offices were situated. If we may assume that the forum-basilica was the seat of the *civitas*-government, they can hardly have been there. Possibly the rectangular building with an apsidal end (*schola,* p. 158) at the south-east corner of Insula XXI might be regarded as a candidate.

Three Purbeck marble inscriptions from statue-bases, found in the Insula XXXV temple (p. 154), have sometimes been adduced in favour of the suggestion that Calleva had acquired chartered rank by the early third century. They refer to a *collegium peregrinorum consistentium Callevae* (cf. pl. 11);[22] and if there was need for such an 'association of foreigners resident at Silchester', it is argued, that Callevans themselves could no longer be classed as *peregrini*. The argument is neat, but depends on the assumption that the inscriptions are earlier than 212, when Roman citizenship was awarded generally. Fatal to it, therefore, is the continuing mention of *peregrini* in inscriptions of certainly later date, notably one of 232 from a small place in the Vosges.[23] In these cases, the *peregrini* must have been just as much Roman citizens as the inhabitants, and the distinction must lie between non-possessors and possessors of the local citizenship which, far from being extinguished by the edict of Caracalla, seems to have been fostered by it.

The inscriptions are therefore irrelevant to the question of the later status of Calleva, which remains entirely open. There is the shadow of a possibility, however, that such a change is implicit in the addition of the great late-Antonine statue of the Tutela (p. 119) to the central shrine of the basilica. This statue, of which a few scraps survive (pl. 10), is one of two works of art by an accomplished continental sculptor working in a British medium, Portland stone: the other, of very similar style, is a head of Sarapis (p. 166, pl. 18) which can certainly be no earlier. The existence of an Antonine Tutela, or personification of the community, begs the question of what may or may not have preceded it, and why an earlier statue, if it existed, should have been changed. However, argument along these lines is far too vague for comfort.[24]

THE ADMINISTRATION

We know very little directly of the government of peregrine communities in Britain, and can but presume that such shreds of evidence as exist indicate constitutions modelled on those of the chartered towns, as was the case in Gaul.[25] The Caerwent pedestal (p. 58) tells us that there was an *ordo* (council) which governed by decree: so too at Noviomagus (Chichester) in the Cogidubnian period, where we have a colourable reference to a *s(enatus) c(onsultum)*— interestingly enough the term used to describe the decisions of the Roman Senate, but in this case those of a local body.[26] We do not know, however, how many councillors *(decuriones)* there were: not even that there was a standard number: and we do not know at what level the necessary property-qualification was fixed.[27] It is clear from the plan of Silchester or the plan of Caerwent that not all the *decuriones* lived in town, and indeed we should not expect this in the case of large *civitates*. We may, however, hazard the guess that the property-qualification was modest, for it is clear that the largest houses of the second to fourth centuries either grew out of much smaller houses (e.g. XIV.1, fig. 29.8) as wealth increased, or else were built on the sites of smaller dwellings (e.g. I.1).

The normal colonial constitution provided for a number of annually-elected pairs of magistrates. The chief of these were the *duoviri juredicundo*, who were charged with the administration of justice. In peregrine circumstances, before 212, they would have applied customary tribal law; and all capital, important civil, and cases involving a Roman citizen, were sent up to the imperial governor's court. A fragmentary inscription from Corinium (Cirencester) appears to refer to a *duovir:* otherwise, British evidence relates to the *coloniae,* as at Glevum (Gloucester), where the products of the municipal tilery bore their initals as a means of dating akin to that used in

59

the empire at large, where the consuls' names were so employed. The model constitution also provided a pair of *duoviri aediles,* who attended to public works, and a pair of *quaestores,* whose responsibility lay with finance. We know of an aedile at *vicus*-level and of a *'questorius'* at *civitas*-level, in Roman Britain.[28]

In the first and second centuries, these magistracies were coveted as honours. There was no emolument; and those elected from the *ordo* to fill them were expected to commemorate their term of office by shows and public works. The aedile of the *vicus Petuariensium* already mentioned, for instance, donated a stage for the theatre. The stately Rhenish Corinthian columns of Silchester basilica (pl. 17) might well have marked the munificence of an early *duovir,* and alterations at the baths might have been carried out at the expense of an aedile. Under the later empire, however, members of the *ordo* risked a personal surcharge for any deficiency in the taxes rendered to the imperial government, and the erstwhile honour of the civic posts became a burden. There is on the whole much less sign of wealth in the late houses of Silchester than in those of earlier date: the mosaics are of an inferior standard, and in the largest house of all (XIV.1) the older floors remained in use, patched here and there. It looks as if, in a time when taxes were certainly much heavier than previously, the somewhat narrow basis of the Callevan economy was unable to meet demands without some retrenchment, but perhaps a greater proportion of the rich members of the community no longer dwelt in the town, preferring their country estates at a distance. We need certainly not imagine that the condition of the ruling class was irremediably depressed as a result of fiscal measures.[29]

The financial affairs of the *civitas* embraced the raising of both imperial— as just hinted—and local revenue. Peregrines paid a tax on real-estate *(tributum soli)* and a poll-tax *(tributum capitis).* In addition, there was a tax assessed upon the community as a whole, the *annona,* or requisition of grain and other supplies. At first this seems to have been raised as required, the produce being paid for at a nominal rate.[30] Later, it became a regular exaction. Among other taxes may be mentioned the *aurum coronarium,* payable on the elevation of a new emperor, and the 5% inheritance-duty *(vicesima hereditatum)* to which Roman citizens were liable—it was even suggested that the main reason for the edict of 212 lay in the enhanced revenue from this tax arising from the universal extension of the citizenship. Other burdens included the upkeep of the imperial highways within the community's area, and the maintenance of the imperial posting-service *(cursus publicus)* which used them. The latter commitment would have been heavy at Calleva, for the town was at an important road-junction. In the first to third centuries there must have been much official traffic on the western highway to Caerleon, seat of the Second Augustan Legion, and in the fourth century on the same road to Cirencester, created capital of the province of Britannia Prima by Diocletian. A large inn or *praetorium* was provided in Insula VIII for official and other travellers (p. 138).

As regards local revenue, the most important elements were rent for public lands and tax levied on private lands; there may have been something in the way of customs-duties at the frontiers of the *civitas,* but there is no evidence that this was so. On a smaller scale, leases and town-dues would have supported the *vicus*-administration.

POPULATION

There can be very little doubt that the Callevans were, in general, young. A Roman actuarial computation puts the life-expectancy of persons aged up to 20 years as only 30: the figure is close to that for late Stuart England.[31] Infant-mortality, not included, would have been severe—20–25%.[32] The sinking of wells in areas honeycombed with refuse-pits and cess-pits, where numerous pupae of flies tell their tale,[33] cannot have promoted good public health, and medical ignorance vastly multiplied the illnesses considered inoperable or incurable today. Trade and movement through the town, especially of troops from far afield, may have introduced diseases, and only the wide spacing of houses acted as a safeguard. The cemeteries, however, are virtually unexplored and we have no biometrical data from Silchester at all. The average ages attained by civilians in Britain, on the basis of 220 epitaphs, were 34.6 for men, and 27.8 for women, worn out by drudgery and childbirth. The recent study of skeletons from a cemetery of Roman York led to the pithy observation that 'our middle age was their elderly'.[34]

Added to the high natural rate of child-mortality, there is the question of infanticide, though we do not know to what degree the numerous baby-burials exhumed throughout Britain are due to this.[35] 'Several skull-bones of very young babies' were nevertheless recovered from a drain at the public baths; and although 'it would be highly speculative to account for their presence', there is little alternative to supposing that a person could be found at the baths to dispose of unwanted babies.[36]

Estimates of the population of Calleva have ranged from 1000 to 7500, and obviously no reliable means of computation exists. *Peccavi et ego:* in *Roman Silchester,* I proposed 4000 on the basis of a notional total of 200 houses occupied at any one time, and an estimate of 8 to 12 in family, based on the number of bedrooms discernible in the plans of the large houses

(p. 194), leading to a household maximum of 20 souls when slaves and dependents were included. But the number of occupied houses is not likely to have exceeded about 150, and the first-century total was less, perhaps only half on the showing of the known unaligned buildings. Even if the figure of 20 did apply to the large houses, moreover, it cannot have applied to the smaller, sometimes quite small, dwellings which make up nine-tenths of the total.

We have no idea how large the family actually was; but as the population was mostly young, it is more likely to have embraced two, rather than three, generations; and infant-mortality will have kept the numbers of children down. An average figure of six in family may well be too high; but taking it, doubling it to allow for servants in 15 large houses, and adding two to it to allow for servants in the 135 small houses, we reach a second to fourth century total in the region of 1200. It is cold comfort to add that all population figures before the first national census (1801) are also approximate. However, for a period which in many ways might be thought demographically similar to the Romano-British, we might take the later seventeenth century when the hearth-tax lists were compiled. It is on the basis of these lists that estimates of the local populations of the period are generally made and it is customary to multiply the crude numbers of dwellings indicated in the rolls by something between four and five to give an estimate of a particular population. On this basis, the population of Silchester in the second to fourth centuries would be only 600 to 750, and the first-century population perhaps only 300 to 375. These figures seem very low; is there a means of control? Obviously, nothing definitely of service: but the public baths (fig. 15) are designed to the scale of those provided for an auxiliary regiment of 1000 men, e.g. at Castell Collen fort in Radnorshire;[37] and on the first-century dating of the primary baths, this would mean that if the figure for the population, based on the analogy of the hearth-tax computation, is anything like correct, then an allowance for growth not of 100%, but of 200%, was envisaged when the building was laid out. This itself seems unlikely: yet we already know that the town-plan itself was to be created on a far grander scale than was ever matched in actual development.

LITERACY AND LANGUAGE

As in other towns, evidence of literacy is profuse. Without reckoning the stone inscriptions—about a score—there are over fifty personal names scratched to denote ownership on pots, etc.; fourteen remarks scrawled on tiles laid out to dry before firing; and sundry other graffiti. About 150 bone,

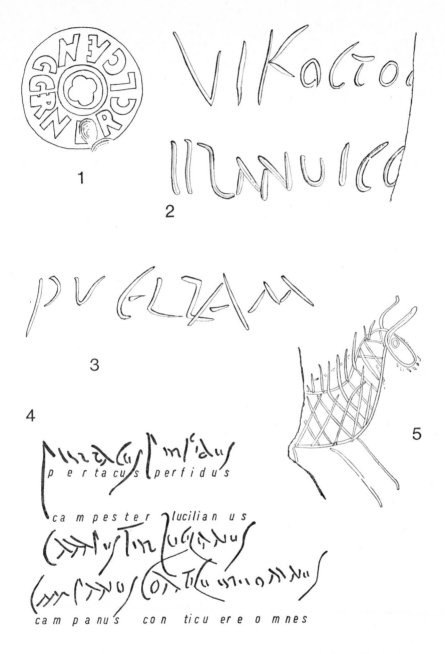

7. Tile-stamp and graffiti on tiles. 1, Neronian tile-stamp from the public baths, A.D. 54–68. 2, 'Sixth day before the Kalends of October [Sept. 26], by the hand of Icc--'. 3, '. . . girl . . .'. 4' 'Pertacus *perfidus* [untrustworthy], Campester, Lucilianus, Campanus, all fell silent'. 5, shaggy-coated ox. Scale 1/2

bronze, or iron stili (fig. 34,11) together with part of a fir writing-tablet,[38] indicate the widespread use of waxed tablets for accounts, memoranda and correspondence, as do little bronze seal-boxes, often gaily enamelled, which were used to protect the soft wax impressions of signets. Pen writing, doubt-less on tablets more often than on imported papyrus, is attested by metal or pottery inkwells (cf. fig. 21,10).[39] What is particularly interesting is the humble level of society which this evidence in general embraces: if a tile-maker, for example, could not only write his name and total up his production, and perhaps date it according to the Roman system, but also scribble a remark about a girl, it can certainly be concluded that literacy was prevalent (fig. 7,2–3).[40]

Some of the graffiti display practised hands, none more so than the example which ends with a tag from Virgil's *Aeneid* (Book II, line 1: *conticuere omnes [intentique ora tenebant]* 'all fell silent [and held their gaze intent], fig. 7,4). This was probably a writing-lesson which was meant to be copied.[41] The unmanageable shape of the specimen, an unbaked flue-tile (or *tubulus,* as another Silchester graffito names it)[42] subsequently returned to stock, fired, and sold, suggests that the lesson was given at the tilery, in order that workmen should have the necessary skill to keep their tallies and mark each batch appropriately. The circumstances which may have led learners beyond this stage are quite obscure.

How far do these graffiti reflect the regular use of Latin speech among the tile-makers and, by implication, among the artisans, traders and retailers of Calleva, the clerks of the administration, the stewards of the various estates and their proprietors who used the writing-instruments listed above? Latin was the only language written and read, and therefore heard, if only because silent reading was a rare accomplishment.[43] Furthermore, it was necessary to use Latin words for which an equivalent did not exist in Celtic, *tubulus* for a start. Among the Latin loan-words which emerge eventually in Welsh, however, there are some which are decidedly odd: they include names of parts of the body, for instance, and even for 'fish'. The displacement of perfectly good Celtic words of this kind is remarkable, and can but illustrate the dominance of the intrusive tongue: 'men sought to become Romans'. A place such as Silchester saw a good deal of through-traffic, civil and military; and foreigners settled there, as our inscriptions prove. It was a centre not only for the dissemination of Roman manufactures, but of the entire mode of life which went with them; and Latin must consequently have been in very wide use indeed.[44]

4

Change in the Third and Fourth Centuries

THE TOWN WALL

As we have seen, when the time came for the defences to be renewed, only about half the original area was enclosed. By 1909, it had been realised that the new inner defences had consisted first only of a bank and ditch, and that the wall was a subsequent addition. Discoveries made in that year also showed that the system as a whole could not be earlier than the middle of the second century; and in 1938 Mrs Cotton's work suggested that the bank had been erected about 160–70 and that the wall was erected about 190–210.[1]

The amount of ground which can be opened in search of datable relics usefully associated with the building of defences is never very large in relation to an entire circuit—here 2.4 km—and it is always difficult to know how far any particular finds can be relied upon to indicate a close date. But at least it can be said that the bank-wall sequence is repeated at numerous other towns, and that in none of these cases is there any evidence for the construction of the bank later than *c.* 200. Antonine banks, however, are an insular phenomenon: few Gallic towns received defences until the later third century.[2] Accordingly, the explanation of these banks must also be insular. Choice falls most readily upon events at the close of the second century, when the governor Albinus stripped the island of troops for his war of 196–7 against Septimius Severus, rival for the throne. The frontier districts of the west and north would then have been left without the garrisons which kept the natives in check; and men's thoughts must have turned to the possibility of an outbreak of violence unseen since the days of Boudica 130 years before.

This explanation seems sound enough to apply to many cases; but at Cirencester the elaborate stone-built east gate was a primary element in the system, earlier—if only marginally—than the adjoining earthen rampart. Since timber gates of the simplest pattern could alone be provided at a time of crisis, the Cirencester evidence must tend to suggest that not all the second-century earthwork defences are a product of the Albinian episode.[3] The scale of the Cirencester stone gateway allows us to suppose that this town at least, and probably others, had embarked on long-term schemes designed to be carried out as funds and labour were available. The Augustan architect Vitruvius gives defences a high priority in his account of town-planning and buildings. Prudent authorities, moreover, had only to seek permission to built fortifications or to modify what was already in existence; and unrest in Antonine Wales and the north may have provided the impetus.[4]

The completion of the defences by a wall involved the community in a very heavy commitment of resources. It is calculated that over 45,000 loads of bonding-stone and 105,000 loads of flint went into Silchester wall (p. 101). There is no hint that the provincial government helped in any way, and we can only suppose that the work of construction was spread over a fair term of years, so that the annual commitment—above all of labour normally devoted to agricultural production—could be brought within reasonable bounds. The town-wall is not well-dated: a denarius of 193 was found in 1909 deep behind, and close to, the back of it—i.e. in the filling between it and the original bank, which had been cut back—and offers a minimal date. The remarkably neat workmanship of the rear face (pl. 14) suggests that the wall was probably designed to be free-standing, however, so we cannot be sure even of this. By the late third century the mound had been built up. It is possible that the wall itself should be placed in this period rather than before.[5]

THE GARRISON

Nothing certain is known of the provision for manning the defences of a Romano-British town at any period. The considerable regional autonomy enjoyed by each *civitas* imposed, however, duties of public security and law-enforcement which called for the creation of a modest *gendarmerie;*[6] but a few military objects of the third–fourth centuries suggest that government troops may have been stationed at Silchester and other towns. The most important is a roundel from a belt (fig. 8,3) bearing the motto, completed on other elements not here found, but of standard type: OPTIME MAXIME CON*(serva)*/NUMERUM OMNIUM MILITANTIUM—'[Jupiter] Best [and] Greatest, protect [us] a troop of fighting-men all'. A closely similar roundel occurred at the northern fort of High Rochester, where the third-century garrison included a *Numerus* (i.e. an irregular unit); and parts of a

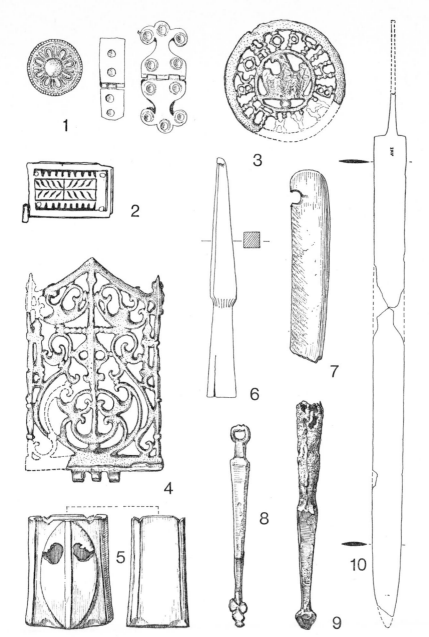

8. Military objects. 1, brass rosette and hinges from a segmental cuirass, first century
A.D. (Pit 10, Insula XXIII). 2, tinned bronze belt-plate, first century. 3, roundel from
belt, third century. 4, tinned bronze or base silver belt-plate, third century. 5, bone
scabbard-chape, third century. 6, iron head from ballista-bolt. 7, bone tip from a bow,
third century? 8, sword-scabbard loop, bronze, third century. 9, iron spear-butt. 10,
iron sword with stamped numeral, fourth century (1890 'hoard' of ironwork, Insula
I). Scales, 1/2, no. 10 about 1/5

numerum omnium plaque and of two heart-shaped *militantium* terminals were turned up at Aldborough, the Romanised capital of the Brigantes.[7] There may be some likelihood that *numeri* were stationed in towns, either as their garrison, or to protect imperial installations there.

Other military remains are shown in fig. 8. The handsome openwork belt-plate of tinned bronze or base silver, its centrepiece in the form of an ornamental spear-head of the kind carried by the adjutants (*beneficiarii*) of high officials, is of about the same date.[8] The signet-ring stone, of apple-green plasma, shown in fig. 24,2, carries the same emblem.[9] The only article directly associated with the defences, however, is a bone splint from the tip of a composite (horn and sinew) bow, found at the west gate. Such bows were manufactured at the legionary fortress of Caerleon, and of course elsewhere, in the third century, as were bone scabbard-chapes.[10] A military bronze spur of continental pattern is a recent stray find (fig. 21,1).[11] Weapons from Silchester are few: there are a number of spear-heads and arrowheads of doubtful relevance, an iron *ballista*-bolt (illustrated) and a caltrop or anti-personnel spike. A sword from the large deposit of ironwork buried towards the end of the fourth century in Insula I (p. 268) bears a stamped numeral, probably XVI wrongly arranged, and may have been made in one of the government arms-factories of Gaul.[12]

In the fourth century, there were certain modifications to the defences. Gateways were blocked or narrowed, and a wide outer ditch was dug to hinder an enemy's approach to the wall: this may have been done in connection with a plan to equip the enceinte with projecting towers as at Caerwent, but if so no tower seems actually to have been built. Indeed the Caerwent series, a feeble reflection of the towers to be seen at Cardiff fort not far away, is itself incomplete. Such towers would have been manned by archers, and would have offered a means of providing enfilading fire if an enemy approached too close to the wall: they are far too small to have served in any regular way as emplacements for *ballistae,* or arrow-shooting catapults, as archaeologists have sometimes supposed.[13]

Silchester is one of the towns and other sites which have produced buckles and tags from the straps fastening the broad military belt affected in the late and increasingly German imperial army. A theory, widely held and with much to recommend it, sees in these strays a trace of Germanic mercenary garrisons stationed, under the authority of the chief civil governor of late Roman Britain, the *vicarius,* in towns and the countryside for the protection and defence of the population. Some of the specimens of buckles found in Britain, e.g. at Winchester, dating to the middle of the fourth century, are of continental manufacture. Others are British imitations, like

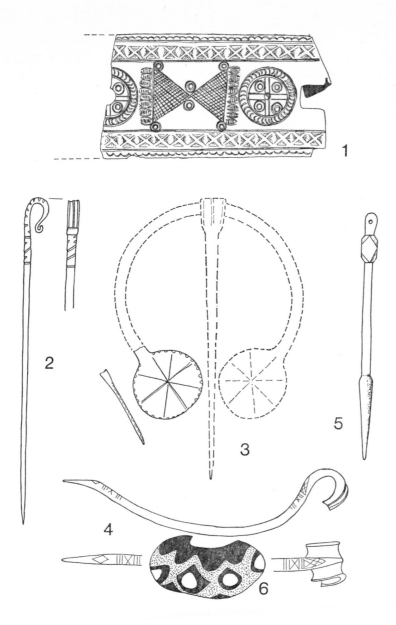

9. Late objects, 1–5 in bronze. 1, buckle-plate, military. 2, Celtic brooch-pin. 3, terminal, Celtic penannular brooch. 4, pin, large Celtic penannular brooch. 5, Saxon linked pin. 6, glass eye-bead (black, with white spots outlined in opaque red). Scales, 1 : 2/1; rest 1/1

the worn example found in a grave of a Germanic? woman at Dorchester-upon-Thames. The Silchester material is all British (buckle-plate, fig. 9,1): its earliest piece, from the forum, is exactly matched by a buckle from Lydney temple, dating to the later fourth century; its latest resemble others in an early Saxon grave at Reading, about 450, and in a woman's grave at the early Saxon cemetery at Blewburton Hill near Newbury. Provincial Roman women did not favour belted dresses, and it can be supposed that Germanic women obtained these buckles from their menfolk. A few beads in the collection—black glass inlaid with zigzags of opaque white, red, yellow or turquoise; rock-crystal with short-axis perforation; lenticular amethystine quartz; and discoid amber—are of Migration Period type (fig. 9,6) and could also have belonged to Germanic wives.[14] Until graves can be excavated, however, it is best merely to register this as a possibility.

CALLEVA IN THE LATE THIRD AND FOURTH CENTURIES

We may now retrace our steps a little. Were the walls ever manned against a foe, other perhaps than some late roving band? No mention of the town can be found in any of the works of ancient historians; and Haverfield called it 'a typical country town, where life was easy and commonplace. . . Such a town can have no history, and Silchester has none'.[15] But if nothing of consequence occurred there sufficient to rouse the distant Clio, that Muse cannot be said to have been particularly wide-awake in the third or fourth century. It is not entirely fanciful to suppose that Silchester was caught up in a late third-century crisis.

The story of Carausius, once Admiral of the Fleet of Britain, usurping emperor in the island from 286 until his death in 293 at the hands of his finance-minister Allectus, who ruled until 296, need not be repeated.[16] Gold coins of both have been found at Silchester (fig. 10).[17]

10. Gold pieces (*aurei*) of the British usurpers Carausius and Allectus, A.D. 286–93 and 293–6. Scale, 1/1

The recapture of Britain was planned as a pincer-movement. Constantius I was to land in Kent and make for London, while his general Asclepiodotus was to neutralise the naval-base in the Solent, and march to join his master. In the outcome, the brunt of the campaign seems to have fallen upon Asclepiodotus, and a decisive battle was fought in terrain characterised by hills and level ground, a description which could well apply to the Silchester region—all the more so because of its nodal position in the road-system along which both the separatist and central government's forces must have marched. Joyce cherished the romantic notion that the bronze eagle (pl. 34c) which he discovered in the basilica was 'once the imperial standard of a Roman legion . . . some aquilifer of the revolted troops shut up here as a last stand, despairing of its safety and of his own life, and whilst the whole western side of the basilica was beleaguered, rather than surrender his trust tore away the bird from . . . its staff, wrenched off its wings . . . and hid it in the wooden ceiling of the *aerarium* . . . and so the eagle [remained] until the final fires, kindled by barbarian hands long after the Romans had ceased to dwell here . . . buried the Roman bird in that venerable grave from which he has happily been rescued'.[18] Alas! neither the stratification, carefully recorded as showing the eagle below the upper of two layers of burnt material, nor the mark not only of damage, but also of repair (p. 119), allows such a picture; and what can be said of the eagle can likewise be said of the great Antonine statue of the Tutela (pl. 10, p. 119): both bear signs of wanton damage repaired and re-inflicted; and since the basilica showed signs of destruction by fire on two occasions, it would be perverse not to associate the repairs of these objects with the restoration after the first fire.

That event is undated: if Joyce had any numismatic warrant for placing it at the end of the third century, he would probably have recorded it in the *Journal*, if nowhere else. But there are also repairs to the south tower of the east gate (p. 102), and the conception of a 'last stand' may not be altogether wide of the mark, even though the devoted standard-bearer need not figure in it. It is at least fairly certain that the destruction of the Tutela statue, and its repair, cannot well have lain earlier than the third century, and from the strategic point of view Calleva could well have suffered in 296.

In the past few years, our view of third and fourth century urban history in Britain has been greatly modified, largely because of excavations at Verulamium. It seems that the city visited by S. Germanus in 429 can have borne scant resemblance to the mouldering ruin pictured in earlier research.[19] So, too, elsewhere, and doubtless at Silchester, though in justification of this statement we can at present rely only on our gleanings from the published accounts, the *Journal*, and the collection at Reading.

In any assessment of town-life, there could be no more vital evidence than that provided by the baths, the most popular and levelling of all the public institutions of the Empire. Bath-houses everywhere show evidence of constant alteration, and that of Insula XXXIIIA is no exception. Hope recognised six structural 'periods', one dated to the fourth century by a coin of *c.* 317–26 sealed below a floor:[20] as late as *c.* 320, therefore, large-scale renovations were taking place at the baths, and no doubt elsewhere. Coins relating to the latest frequentation of buildings, however, will not be structurally sealed and may not be sealed at all. From the forum there are numerous coins of the Theodosian dynasty (from 383 onwards), terminating with Arcadius *c.* 395–402. The latest certain coin from the inn, Insula VIII, is of Valens (364–78), and one of the Insula XXX temples yielded another.[21] The temples in Insulae VII and XXXV were probably destroyed before the end of the Roman period, perhaps when official Christianity reached the town.

It was the hope of 1892, when the church near the forum (Chapter 14) was discovered, that Calleva would prove to contain others. This hope arose from the very small size of the building, 13 by 9 m. overall, and from the knowledge that Timgad, for example, possessed several churches. But the analogy was fallacious; and in due course it became clear that Calleva possessed no other church identifiable as such by plan alone. Small and unpretentious though the Insula IV building was, it is ranged next to the seat of civil power in the centre of the town, and in front are the remains of a baptistery, recognised by the late Sir Ian Richmond. Since, in the early church, baptism was a rite administered only by bishops,[22] and since this building (unlike those attached to churches in some of the late forts of the Rhineland) appears in a *civitas*-capital, it seems possible to regard the building as the cathedral of an Atrebatic diocese. There is no record of such a diocese; but the Gallic church was divided into territorial dioceses centred upon the *civitas*-capitals, in a system which seems to have sprung into being directly upon the promulgation of Constantine's celebrated edict of 313. The style of the British bishops attending the Council of Arles in the very next year contains in each case the expression . . . *de civitate* . . . and shows that some of the British sees (in that case those of the capitals of three of the four small provinces into which the island had been divided by Diocletian *c.* 300) were founded equally early, and on the same model.[23] There are difficulties in assigning the Silchester church to such an early date: the plan, basilical with vestigial transept, is a miniature of one of the great Constantinian basilicas of Rome itself; and it seems unlikely that such a plan could penetrate to Britain before the last years of the fourth century. Unfortunately, coins from the black filling of hollows in the nave-floor, discovered in 1961, are totally irrelevant to the question of when the building was erected.[24]

Turning lastly, in this brief survey, to the houses, several show developments at dates reasonably placed in the fourth century, and so coincide with what has been discovered in other towns: XXVII.1 is an example, and XIV.2 with its richly-floored gallery (pl. 32), destined to be covered by a subsequent floor of which a few patches of cement bedding remained, is another. In general there is little sign of late opulence in domestic design and appointments, such as elaborate and finely-worked mosaics: the gallery of XIV.2 had only small panels set within large expanses of coarsely-patterned red and buff tessellation. Rich mosaics are indeed for the most part features of the grand villas of the late Romano-British countryside, and their occurrence at Corinium, capital of the Diocletianic province of Britannia Prima, is evidently a special case, easily understood. In XXVII.1 there is at least one mosaic of the fourth century, with a bust of one of the Seasons (pl. 31), and in XXXIV.1 we find a large but rather coarse mosaic in the style of the 'Corinium' school of artists.[25] In XIV.1, XXIII.2 and also XXVII.1, floors considered to be of the second century were retained, and survived, crudely patched with rough tesserae or with bricks, as long as the houses remained in occupation. Joyce's detailed plan of XXIII.1 gives a revealing insight into the state of the floors of many Silchester houses about the close of the Roman period, as does a published photograph of XXIV.2.[26] No coin-lists survive for the period 1890–1908; but taking Joyce's lists as a reasonable sample, it is worth note that in I.1 there is evidence of occupation as late as Honorius, while in XXXIV.1, which he partly opened, the latest was of Arcadius. Similar instances are likely to have abounded.[27]

The latest coin from Silchester, recorded by Thomas Hearne, who was an excellent numismatist, was of 'y^t Constantine that was proclaimed Emperor here by the British Army in the year 407'.[28] To admit the historical context would be to turn our wheel full circle to Chapter 1: it is a possibility considered in medieval times, and one of which the truth can never be averred. The Theodosian coins from Silchester number about 700,[29] half the totals for the later Constantinian and for the Valentinianic periods (337–64, 364–83). Verulamium presents an almost identical pattern, and life there, as we now know, continued well into the fifth century.[30] Apart from coins, we can recognise only a few objects which are indisputably imports of the late fourth or early fifth centuries: a little glass, and among the pottery most clearly a piece of Argonne sigillata bearing a rouletted design assigned by recent research to c. 395–420; and most interesting of all, a north African lamp (pl. 33f) in red-surfaced pottery, bearing a figure of a horse: it is of about the same date.[31]

5

The End: A Problem

In 410, the Emperor Honorius wrote to the 'cities in Britain' that they were to take measures for their own defence[1] against the barbarian invaders descending upon the island; Gaul was equally vexed. A last usurper, Constantine, had led the remains of the army to the continent, and the Britons expelled his governors in an endeavour to convince the central authorities that they wished to return to allegiance. Few scholars would maintain, however, that imperial troops ever entered into Britain again.

The first great figure of the fifth century, the 'proud tyrant' Vortigern, has gone down into history as author of the blunder of calling in 'Saxon' aid against the Picts, somewhere about 430. In due course, Hengist and Horsa rebelled; but the historical judgement, originating with the British cleric Gildas who wrote about a century later, is unjust because Germanic elements had long been allowed, even encouraged, to settle near towns and country estates in return for an undertaking to protect them: we have noted the possibility of Germanic soldier-settlers at Calleva (p. 68), and that is but one town of a number. However, rebel they did: once the immediate troubles of 410 had been overcome, life in Britain under the government of the *civitates* seems to have continued much as before, though the imperial tax-burden was no more. Of the exactions levied for the army, we can only guess: the rise to supreme power of one of its generals was inevitable. The rebellion of Germanic settlers opened the island to invasion, and in 446–54 a last, vain appeal to the Roman commander in Gaul, Aëtius, was made. Thereafter the Britons had to rely upon their own prowess entirely, and by the great victory of about 500 at Badon Hill they halted the onward progress of the Saxons for very many years. At that date, British territories seem still to have survived east, as well as west, of the area of primary Saxon settlement in the upper Thames valley, and may not have become totally submerged until the 570's. South of the Thames, the campaigns of Cynric and Ceawlin must finally have destroyed whatever may have remained of Romano-

74

British civilisation between 552 and 568. A self-supporting, perhaps increasingly self-reliant community at Calleva, behind strong walls sufficient to baulk primitive Saxon warriors may conceivably have survived towards this period.[2]

Little effort is needed to visualise the town of 410, which must in essentials have resembled that of 310 fairly closely. Thereafter, the archaeological perspective swiftly darkens: coins, for example, no longer arrived in any number, and the use of money seems to have passed away by 430 at the outside.[3] Thus the last coins and recognisable imports at Calleva are merely à cheval between the fourth and fifth centuries. Perhaps organised life was extinguished very soon after 410: since its foundation as a royal oppidum in Belgic times, Calleva had been the seat of administration, and it was this alone which had elevated it above the level and condition of a backwoods agricultural settlement. Slow devolution for 150 years, or swift extinction: these are the alternatives to be considered.

SOME CELTIC FRAGMENTS

In the Silchester collection there are four objects which have a western or northern Celtic affinity: three pins (one, perhaps two, from a type of penannular brooch), and a terminal from a penannular brooch.[4] Advanced dates have been claimed for all four. The first is a well-made pin of yellow bronze or brass (fig. 16, 1): the little silver ring which passes through the lug suggests that it was one of a linked pair of dress-pins. Its affinities are primarily Scottish. Examples are known both with and without the red enamel which decorates this specimen, some having more elaborately-cut heads in which a zoömorphic element is reasonably discernible: they are probably later than the simple type in question. Though this pin has been regarded as late or sub-Roman, it is best matched by one from a Flavian level at Newstead; and another—a very large bronze cloak-pin of not dissimilar design—was found in barracks at Caerleon, and might well have been an Antonine legionary's souvenir of service in north Britain.[5]

The other material appears in fig. 9. The pin with a tubular head belonged to a penannular brooch about 6 cm. in diameter, with terminals no doubt modelled as stylised duck's heads, as on the handsome Caerwent example. The distribution of the type is northern and western, and it was to give rise, in time, to the fantastically ornate Irish penannular series. A few outliers in the south include specimens from Oldbury (Wilts.) and Abingdon (Berks.). Again, very late dates have been claimed for brooches of this sort.

Bits of two, used as a detached pin as here, and as a bracelet, have been found in pagan Saxon graves, but so has much other obsolete Romano-British material. Better for a late dating, if only the circumstances of discovery were clear, are two complete brooches from a Frisian homestead-mound, thought to have been deposited towards 500. On the other hand, early dates can also be claimed, earliest of all an example from Scotland said to have been found with a bronze skillet and a buckle of Antonine pattern. At Holyhead, too, there was another, associated with part of a strongly-ribbed penannular hoop very like one from a wall of the Kingsweston villa, near Bristol, dated around 270-300. The Silchester pin, therefore, is no type-fossil of the fifth century.[6]

The pin with shepherd's crook head is a rare type. There are approximate parallels, mainly in iron and mainly Irish, but one in a Mendip cave where the latest Roman object was a Theodosian coin. The terminal much resembles that of a late Roman bronze razor from Silchester (fig. 16,6), and the spiral filed on the shank is a device found on the tubular-headed brooch-pin mentioned above. The present pin may also come from a brooch or loose-ring-headed pin.[7]

It would be interesting to know whether the flat discoid terminal concluding the little series was found with the pin just discussed. That it is properly described as coming from a penannular brooch is clear from the parallels. The most striking of these is a brooch from Co. Galway in the National Museum of Ireland, though the terminals are only half the size, and the decoration is ring-and-dot for inlay and not a simple incised pattern. The Irish brooch may date around 600; nearer to the Silchester terminal is the linear ornament of a small penannular from Linney Burrows (Pemb.), probably sub-Roman.[8]

There are about thirty penannulars of ordinary Romano-British type in the Silchester collection (fig. 19, 10), some late; it is thus evident that the Celtic specimens discussed can do no more, at the most, than indicate the survival of life at Calleva after 410, and they do not necessarily indicate even this. If they were supported by other material, e.g. by the eastern Mediterranean pottery found predominantly on western sites, but also in London,[9] we should be better placed to estimate the intensity of the occupation; but so far not one scrap has been found. Furthermore, the Celtic material is numerically overshadowed by the purely Saxon (cf. fig. 9, 5);[10] and that is still small enough in quantity to be classed as the casual losses of peasants tilling the ground among the ruins, the forerunners of the little community recorded in Domesday Book, or of chance travellers along the Roman roads.[11]

THE OGHAM STONE

One famous relic, intrinsic proof of the presence of Irish elements at Calleva about the year 500, remains to be considered. The Ogham stone was found two-thirds of the way down a Roman well sunk through the corridor of an early house, IX.1.[12] It is a stubby baluster pillar of friable yellowish sandstone from north Berkshire. When it was washed, 'there appeared on one side a curious series of markings not unlike the characters of an Ogham inscription,' and as soon as a photograph (pl. 12) had been taken, the stone was sent off to London, where it was examined by Sir John Rhys, the leading Celtic scholar of the day.

Ogham writing was probably devised in fourth-century Ireland. Its characters consist of strokes in relation to a vertical axis, usually the arris of a massive block, here an incised line, because a lathe-turned pillar was the readiest sort of large stone available at Calleva. The characters have been traced to a grouping of the letters of the Latin alphabet by late Roman grammarians. Thus B L V S N are denoted by one, two, three, four and five strokes at right-angles to the axis and on the right; H D T C Q by one to five strokes similarly, on the left; M G Ng Z R by one to five strokes, normally oblique, across the axis, and the vowels A O U E 1 by one to five short strokes or notches on the axis. Our text is thus transliterated:

EBICATOS/[MA]QI MUCO[I (. . . .)]

'(The tombstone) of Ebicatus, son of the kin of [. . .]'. This is an unexceptional text in Irish Celtic, though the name is probably a mis-spelling of *Ivacat*[*t*]*us*. The last word, completing the genealogy, is missing together with the capital of the column, for the upper end of the stone has been severely battered. Cases are known where a zealous Christian hand has defaced a pagan genealogy: even if it could not be read, the pattern of the strokes forming *maqi mucoi* would have been familiar.[13] Under Christian influence, most of the Oghams in Britain have an accompanying Latin text.

Two things give the Silchester Ogham its unique interest: it is by far the most easterly known,[14] and its presence at Calleva appears to contrast with the evidence of Germanic occupation at Dorchester-upon-Thames and Winchester.[15] The relevance of the second point must depend on the date of the inscription. Oghams belong to the fifth, sixth, and earlier seventh centuries, apart from an artificial 'scholastic' later group. Otherwise they are not easy to date. Rhys suggested that the perpendicular, rather than oblique, form of the M was 'a mark of antiquity'; Sir Ifor Williams proposed a date of *c.* 450, and Professor K. H. Jackson's most recent estimate is 'not much earlier than *c.* 500, on linguistic and epigraphic grounds'.[16] Who was Ebicatus? For O. G. S. Crawford, he was 'a belated pilgrim caught in the incipient turmoils of the Dark Ages' while traversing the long, overland route from Ireland to Rome.[17] This may be so, though a Christian pilgrim might more probably have been accorded a monument couched in Latin characters. Of one thing, however, we can be justly certain; that by 500 little if anything can have remained of the Romanised local authority which had for centuries maintained the wholesome legality of extramural burial. It seems to follow that pagan Irishmen at Calleva around that date, whether or not any of the trinkets discussed above belonged to them, can hardly have been mercenaries in Callevan service, and the apparent contrast between Silchester and Dorchester or Winchester cannot take on a political significance. If we prefer Sir Ifor William's earlier date of *c.* 450, we merely set an earlier end to the organised life of the town.

GRIM'S BANK, PADWORTH

Three km. north-west of Calleva, there is a substantial earthwork known as Grim's Bank (fig. 5F), first seriously studied by B. H. St. J. O'Neil. In another article, he described cross-ridge dykes on Crookham and Greenham Commons 9 to 16 km. west of the town, and in a third sketched a picture of the Silchester region in the fifth and sixth centuries, when these earthworks, he thought, defined British territory against Saxon encroachment. The town itself, he suggested, was 'the abode of a civilised society during much, if not all, of the fifth century'.[18] Further, J. N. L. Myres had observed that there is plentiful evidence of fifth-century Saxon settlements along the south bank of the Thames below Oxford, their cemeteries frequently coinciding with what had been small riverside communities in Romano-British times:[19] Reading, where there is an early cemetery, for example attests Roman occupation at least down to *c.* 400.[20] Some of these Saxon communities, who have left traces in the early place-names of the region, ending in -*ing* ('-*ingas*', 'folk of . . .') such as Sonning, Reading, Pangbourne (*Pægeingaburnan*, 'stream of Pæge's folk'), Goring, Wasing, and possibly Pinge within 6 or 8 km. of Calleva,[21] were originally perhaps composed of soldier-settlers planted among these villages. The Thames, in other words, was re-assuming its earlier rôle of frontier, as once between the Atrebates and the Catuvellauni. On the south of Calleva, there seems to have been little Saxon settlement of early date until the environs of Winchester are reached; but the names Basing and Worting suggest that archaeological evidence is incomplete, and that the Loddon, like other tributaries of the Thames, offered a line of penetration.[22] Myres concludes that until severe Saxon attacks began, *c.* 450, 'some sub-Roman power centred in the [Silchester] area was in a position to hold hostile barbarians at arm's length, and perhaps to employ friendly ones to defend its northern frontiers in the Thames Valley'.[23]

O'Neil's studies appeared three years before C. F. C. Hawkes's detailed assessment of Pitt Rivers's excavations on Cranbourne Chase.[24] Hawkes showed conclusively that linear earthworks were erected in late Roman times as well as at other periods. Bokerly Dyke, excavated by Pitt Rivers, was constructed *c.* 325–50 as an estate-boundary, and was extended across the Old Sarum-Dorchester road (it is about 50 km. from Dorchester), possibly to impede the approach of marauders in 367–8; and it was again refurbished in the late fourth or early fifth century. The only evidence for the date of any of the Silchester dykes under consideration consists of shards of two Roman pots from near the base of Bury's Bank, Greenham Common. They are of disparate date: one is of first-second century manufacture, and the other is of *c.* 300 or somewhat later.[25] Leaving on one side the problem of how they came to reach their find-spot, it is sufficient to point out that Bury's Bank need not be later than Bokerly Dyke, Phase I, and that it may have had a similar purpose, viz. in delimiting the town-lands.

Grim's Bank, Padworth runs from one Roman road to another, and is thus entirely different in concept from the trailing Belgic lines south of Calleva, which we studied in Chapter 2. It is well-preserved in parts, and can be seen in and near the east end of the Aldermaston Atomic Research Station enclosure; the original relief was some 3 m., but in its course of some 3.8 km. the dyke is interrupted midway where, perhaps, there was dense scrub. The behaviour of the dyke in relation to the Roman roads differs very strikingly at either end: on the south-west, it begins abruptly, but not nearer than 73 m. to the highway to the west; on the north-east, however, the earthwork is carried across the line of the road to Dorchester-upon-Thames and some 60 m. beyond, while a short distance to the south, an earlier cross-ridge dyke (Grim's Bank II), traversed by the road very close to its western end, was apparently brought into use once more, and a short branch extends to it from the rear of Grim's Bank itself (fig. 5).

The extension of the dyke across the Roman road has become clear only since aerial survey established the course of the road further north, in the Kennet valley.[26] We now know that between Calleva and the river there is only one re-alignment point, to the rear of the dyke 3 km. from the town, at Pond Slade, where one of the numerous steep little valleys cutting into the edge of the gravel plateau is avoided. The elaboration of the works around the Dorchester road shows that danger was apprehended from that direction, rather than from the west. There were early Germanic settlers at Dorchester, from *c.* 400, and by 450 Saxon settlements were springing up in the Thames valley. In the next half-century, Saxon elements penetrated westward, and their great cemetery at East Shefford, not very far from the Cirencester branch of the western highway, was then commenced.[27] It follows that if Grim's Bank was erected in the period of equilibrium which supervened upon Badon, the road westwards from Silchester would have been covered in the same way as the Dorchester road. It seems that Grim's Bank cannot be as late as *c.* 500, and in all probability is not later than *c.* 450, if indeed it is so late.

The most immediate comparison of the blocking of the Dorchester road lies with Bokerly, Phase II; but there is a difference. Here, traffic to Calleva was still permissible, even if it had to make its way around the end of Grim's Bank and was thereupon faced by the works to the rear before it could regain the cambered road. Such a scheme of control is likely to reflect a period when traffic and intercourse between communities was still vital, and the erection of the dyke, which was no light task, is most probably to be referred either to 367–8 or to 410.

THE END OF CALLEVA

G. R. Elton has observed that 'historical study is not the study of the past but the study of present traces of the past'.[28] No doubt he would find some difficulty in accepting the picture sketched in the preceding pages as 'history', even though it is the only sort towards which the archaeologist can fumble his way. The wise reader will make up his own mind as to the probable course of events which left Calleva, in their outcome, the scene of peaceful medieval agriculture, its buildings forgotten. The strength of archaeological enquiries lies in the different field to which the rest of this book is devoted.

Left to themselves, historians in the past were largely content to take the testimony of Gildas, and that of the Anglo-Saxon Chronicle, to the effect that the towns of Roman Britain perished in fire and slaughter:

> . . . the fire of righteous vengeance . . . blazed from sea to sea. . . . All the settlements were brought low with the frequent shocks of battering-rams; the inhabitants, along with bishops of the church, were thrown together mown down to the ground, both priests and people, while swords gleamed on every side; and . . . there were seen in the middle of the streets, the bottom stones of towers with lofty doors cast down, and of high walls, sacred altars, fragments of bodies covered with clots . . . of red blood, in confusion as in a kind of horrible wine-press. There was no sepulture of any kind save the ruins of houses. . . .

—and some escaped to the hills, were killed or made slaves, and so on; for this is Gildas at his most impassioned, writing of the period which followed the rebellion of the Saxons invited by the 'proud tyrant'.[29] As for the laconic Chronicle, under 491 we find 'Ælle and Cissa beset Andredes-ceaster [Pevensey, a Saxon Shore fort] and slew all who dwelt therein, nor was one Briton left'.

Traces of fire and slaughter are very difficult to evaluate; and the Silchester excavations played a part in the formulation of the archaeological view that towns gradually decayed and were abandoned. The seminal article was Haverfield's in 1904: Silchester produced no signs of general conflagration and no skeletons of murdered persons.[30] Haverfield drew a parallel with the last years of the Danubian province of Noricum Ripense, where towns were abandoned and where the population was eventually transplanted to Italy. Frere has painted in more of the same picture: 'We have the Germanic garrisons, not much use, given to panic and not loved by the populace. We have the ineffectiveness of barbarian attempts to capture a walled town unless everyone was at mass. We have the lack of determination on the part of the provincials to defend themselves: we have the sack of some towns, the famine at others, and the evacuation of still others. We have the appearance of unofficial leaders . . . who replace the official. . . . But . . . we have the continued existence of Romanised life of a sort'.[31]

Which of these varied fates was the lot of the Callevans? We have seen that the site is in general shallow, and much disturbed by cultivation. If floors were often wrecked by the plough, then well-defined burnt levels will also have been torn up, since they too were superficial and were never to be protected, as were the signs of the Boudican fire of London, by later structures and deposits. I myself well remember the 1940 fire-storm in Bristol, the air filled for days with ash, like black snowflakes; and I later exca-vated in the ruins. There was surprisingly little left after ten years' exposure to the elements, the accumulation of blown dust and the growth of weeds, to mark this disaster in any clear or obvious way, or even to make it plain how the buildings had been destroyed: of course most of the rubble had by then been cleared away, as indeed the rubble of Silchester has largely been cleared away, though by a far slower process. Only the buried burnt levels at the basilica are an exception.

Haverfield stated that no skeletons had been found at Silchester. This was untrue and became more so. Caution is needed in assessing what was found; but the skeleton of a man, revealed by the excavators of 1833 in the cold plunge-bath of the inn baths, may tell us something of the end of Calleva. In a leaden pipe 'upwards of 200 Roman brass coins' were discovered,[32] but are nowhere described: since the building served its ordinary purpose until the late fourth century (p. 72) they cannot well have been of earlier date. In any case, the skeleton must be of a time when civilised standards had so decayed that an unburied corpse was tolerable—that, or else there was no one to see to burial. If, as seems likely, the skeleton and the hoard are to be associated, c. 430 is the latest date which can be applied. Human remains were found elsewhere: in a pit of Insula XXI, thought by the excavators to be of the Roman period;[33] a skeleton was found in VI.1, and part of the body of a child had been thrown down a well in the same insula[34]. Two or three skulls from the forum, and the greater part of a skeleton 'subsequent to the deeper portion of the bed of ruin' marking the destruction of the basilica in the latest fourth or fifth century—if the Theodosian coins from the site are any guide—may tell a similar tale of violence,[35] as also fragments of another skull from the west gate.[36] But the bed of ash in the basilica and Stair's reported references to burning in the forum are the only signs recorded, as far as I know, of a final destruction by fire.[37] There are far too few skeletons to indicate wholesale massacre of an inhabited town, and none is reported as bearing sword-cuts. There are also far too few to suggest the incidence of the plague which Gildas also mentions.[38] The evidence we have seems best explained as the result of casual lawlessness at a time when duly-constituted authority had disappeared. That this time may not have been very much advanced in the fifth century, is suggested by a neglected source to which Morris has drawn attention, for it seems to describe such conditions in the Britain of about 411.[39] It is submitted that 'the present traces of the past' do not entitle us to suppose that recognisable town-life persisted at Silchester beyond c. 450, and that for all we know to the contrary, may by then have been extinguished, leaving the site as cold-harbourage to wandering Irishmen, and a home to a few peasants whose descendants were merged unnoticeably into the substratum of Ceawlin's Wessex. To some such final period as this must belong the last signs of occupancy so far noted, the dirt and ashes of a squatter's shelter in the ruins of that ultimate imperial monument, the church of Insula IV.

PART TWO

ARCHITECTURAL

6

Water Supply and Drainage

WATER SUPPLY: WELLS

The early inhabitants were able to obtain water in plenty, merely by digging at the edges of the superficial gravel.[1] These springs draw upon charged sandy clays beneath: thus there is always water at Silchester wherever the gravel cap has been pierced. Wells remained the chief source of supply when the Romano-British town came into existence. The situation precluded an extensive system of piped water supplied by leat or aqueduct. No doubt there were times when the wells ran low or dry through prolonged drought, and the few streams captured for specific purposes shrank; no doubt also, the water normally filtered and purified by the gravel bed became contaminated by seepage from pits: such, however, was the common lot until recent times. Several wells occurred in each insula, some clearly belonging to particular premises, others serving paddocks or dwellings swept away in the course of time. The wells were of regular construction, and were usually carried to a depth of about twice that of the gravel, on an average 6 m.[2] Often the gravel was firm enough to stand alone, so that the shafts were dug at minimal width: but in Insula XXIII, a well had collapsed almost at the point of completion, the workmen having escaped only to leave their ladder below.[3] Another well produced a perfect antler pick, an interesting if by no means unique instance of such a primitive tool in a Roman context.[4]

The much more unstable nature of the sand below the gravel, however, generally made a lining imperative, at that depth at least. A stout oak curb was inserted as soon as the danger-point was reached; then sometimes a flint lining was built course by course downwards, as the ground was excavated below. Finally, the curb lay at the bottom, and on it a square frame of riven oak boards, roughly jointed at the corners and sometimes braced by short struts was constructed, generally 1 m. square and high; but a height of over 4 m. of boarding was reported. Another type of lining

85

employed old wine-barrels (pl. 40, p. 263): their dimensions, roughly 1 by 2 m., made them very suitable for the purpose, and fifteen instances occur. Only rarely were complete flint or brick linings discovered, for the essential was speed and simplicity of work in the dark, cold, cramped and rapidly-flooding space.[5] The only mention of a well-head structure is a stone surround with a 42 cm. piercing; doubtless, more careful work would have revealed post-holes for windlasses, pulley-housings, or roofs.[6]

Water was hauled up in a great variety of containers, ranging from small stave-built buckets in fir or oak, with iron bands and handles, to a pewter bucket and a handsome bronze amphora with one handle missing, which had been pressed into service (fig. 35, 3). One of the pots used had retained a length of plaited bark rope around the neck.[7]

THE FORCE-PUMP

The oak pump-stock found in an early deposit below XIV.1 in 1895 remains the only British specimen of a type supposed to have been invented by the Alexandrian scientist Ctesibius in the second-century B.C. The finest examples are in cast bronze, and are quite small, such as the Bolsena pumps in the British Museum and that from the Sotiel-Coronada mine in Spain, in the Museo Arqueológico Nacional at Madrid: it is fitted with a squirt on a universal head, and was evidently a fire-fighting appliance. Several wooden stocks have been found on the continent.[8]

As fig. 11 shows, the stock has decayed to reveal the central reservoir, which must have been covered by a plate of wood or lead. On either side, there are complete vertical piercings for the cylinders, which were found in place but were removed to prevent the splitting of the wood upon drying: they are 55 cm. long and 7.5 cm. in diameter. The flanges at the top fitted over the stock and were there secured with nails; and as they are not pierced to correspond with the passages leading to the reservoir, we see how much wood has been lost at the top. Like all Roman lead-piping, the cylinders have a joint, in this case lapped and soldered—one of the first-recognised proofs of the use of soft-solder in Britain. Gowland showed that the lead contained just over 1% of tin, probably added designedly to improve the durability of the metal in wear.[9]

The pistons, which are missing, were worked reciprocally by a hand-lever pivoted between them and above. Thus, when the left piston was raised, suction caused the flap-valve at the bottom of the reservoir on that side to close, and water entered the cylinder. At the same time, the right piston was depressed, forcing the valve at the end to close, and the inner valve to open under the pressure of the water lodged in the cylinder from the previous stroke; and on entering the reservoir, this water displaced the previous contents up the rising-pipe. A stroke of 25 cm., 20 times per minute, would have delivered about 22 l. at 50% efficiency.[10] A small lead weight from one of the terminal valves was found.

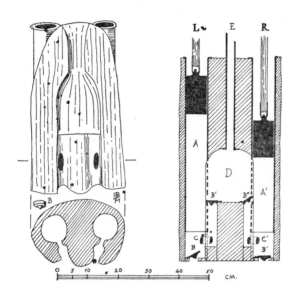

11. Stock of wooden force-pump with leaden cylinders; and restored section

The appliance required a rigid housing. Possibly a board pierced with holes, found at the botom of a well in Insula VI,[11] would have been a suitable support: but I doubt whether the pump could have been very effectively worked at the bottom of a well, owing to the play in the long coupling-rods to the handle. If used at the top, long pipes would have been necessary to reach water-level, and priming would have been necessary. The most satisfactory use of the pump would have been in raising water from a tank at ground-level to an overhead cistern supplying a bath-house or domestic purposes. A case in point is the reservoir of the baths of the inn, fed by an underground spring. The brick-lined chamber has a floor level with that of the hypocaust-basement adjacent, and water could have been drawn off directly for the cold bath at the far end of the building; but a pump would probably have been necessary to fill the supply-tanks of the hot-water boilers of the *caldaria* (cf. p. 128).[12]

CHANNELLED AND PIPED SUPPLY

A stream runs near the site of the public baths, and a watercourse passed under the portico to flush the latrine, but there is no sign of a reservoir on the plan of the building. There must accordingly have been a gravity-supply from the higher ground to the west. A line of piles, with associated vertical and horizontal members ('camp shedding') runs along the northern margin of the insula, and there are traces of a branch on the west side of the building. Probably these timbers mark the course of a trough which carried water from some source in the Insula VI or XXXV area, for they appeared to continue beyond the north-west corner of Insula XXXIIIA.[13] Curiously enough, an unusually large and well-made oak trough was traced running southwards from a well in Insula VI, and it may have discharged very near the line of timbers. The well was of unusual construction, with a deep wooden framework slotted into corner posts; the trough began about 0.5 m. from the mouth of the well, as if there had been a pump at the top of the well: it cannot have been merely an 'overflow' as the report suggests. The eastern extension of VI.2 truncated the trough, and therefore the arrangement suggested cannot have obtained for more than a limited period.[14] Unfortunately, this is all that can be said about the water supply of the baths. In the building itself, all was too ruined to reveal anything of the system of distribution which must have existed.

The last subject in this section is the wooden pipe-line which ran along the southern margins of Insulae XV and XVI and so into III, where it appeared to serve an early building, possibly a small bath-house, sealed by a spread of gravel.[15] The pipes themselves did not survive, but the iron collars used to join them remained, and showed that they had been about 2 m. long. The collars are 11.5 cm. in diameter and 4 cm. wide, and have a central stop-ridge: in use, a circular seating was made with a ring-punch in the ends of the pipes to be joined, the collar inserted into one, and the second pipe gently knocked home. Since the wood was maintained in a swollen condition by the water conveyed, the joint was reasonably water-tight, for no high-pressure system was involved. At the time of discovery, there was no known British parallel to this 215 m. run of wooden pipe-line, but many similar mains have been found since. Judging by Caerwent evidence, the bore—laboriously drilled by augurs of increasing size—is unlikely to have exceeded 5 cm.[16]

The pipe-line passed deeply below the inner defences and must be of earlier date. A rough mass of flintwork found in the ditch immediately outside may perhaps have been the foundation of a water-tower destroyed when the ditch was cut: it would have been necessary to raise the supply at some point, because the stream which was presumably tapped, about 150 m. further to the west, is at a somewhat low level, and there are considerable variations in the level of the pipes within the town. It may also be noted that the pipe-line was discovered entirely by accident, when the sides of a later rubbish-pit were being cleared down, and had been sealed in part by a gravel spread upon which a later building was constructed. There may well be other pipe-lines of this kind at Silchester; but as the streams are not numerous, they will not have been many.

DRAINAGE AND WASTE DISPOSAL

Our towns are enormous by ancient standards, and questions of public health demand highly effective means of evacuating sewage and waste waters, and of eliminating mountainous quantities of refuse. The elaborate drainage-systems of today depend upon almost unlimited supplies of running water provided, augmented by the run-off from streets surfaced with impermeable materials. Conditions were far different at Calleva, where the supply of running water was very limited, and the storm-water drainage of the streets was rudimentary. There does not seem to have been any regular provision of side-drains: at least, I have never found any; and it was not until some date in the third century that the final remetalling of the streets incorporated a central, flint-lined gutter, prominent upon aerial photographs (pl. 8).[17] Another striking difference between Roman and modern practice was the omission of gutters along the tiled eaves of buildings, which projected so that the water was shed well away from the foot of the walls. This was so even at the forum, where the eaves' drainage was absorbed by the deep gravel metalling of the courtyard, and seeped through to a large box-drain under the main east entrance, and so passed into a central gutter in the street.[18] Where buildings were set close together, the question of *stillicidium*, or eaves' drainage, was a fruitful source of litigation, as may be imagined:[19] though at Silchester, except here and there along the main east-west street, there could hardly have been any difficulty.

Special arrangements were necessary for the two largest users of water, the public baths and the baths of the inn. In both cases, the problem was increased by the erection of the inner defences, which in some measure blocked the natural drainage to the south-east.[20] The latrine of the baths was flushed by the overflow, probably, of the channel which brought water to the building, and was discharged into a timber-lined cesspool which would have required periodic cleaning.[21] The stream near the baths used to rise within Insula XXXIV, but otherwise seems to have existed in Roman times much as now: presumably the baths-drainage joined it, and was carried through the wall, when that was built, in a culvert, of which traces were found.[22] The drainage of the various basins was not followed up, but in Period V (p. 129), when the cold bath was on the west or uphill side, the water was discharged on to a brick apron, and apparently allowed to find its own way round to the south-east; there is an arched culvert below the floor of the furnace-room at the south end of the building.[23] Probably the large body of water in the cold bath was but rarely changed. In the baths of the inn, there was a considerable slope to the sewer between the cold bath, etc. and the latrine; and Fox thought that the periodic release of water from the *piscina* served to flush it. Outside, the effluent was conducted into the ditch of the inner defences by timber-built drains leading through the south-east gate (p. 105). A well-preserved section of timberwork, 2.74 m. long, consisted of a baulk 79 cm. wide and 23 cm. thick, with a longitudinal channel 33 cm. wide cut in it, and a covering plank,[24] found out of place, was probably a duct rather than a drain.

A room near the porter's lodge of XIV.2, fitted with a small tile-drain into the street, recalls the centurion's privy in the Myrtle Cottage barracks at Caerleon,[25] but it is difficult to point to any other drainage of this kind.[26] No house had a flushed latrine to compare with one or two examples at Caerwent, probably inns, or with arrangements at Wroxeter, where surplus water from the town-leat ran into the street-gutters and flushed domestic privies. Indeed, throughout the cities of the Empire, a flushed latrine was seldom found in a domestic setting.[27] The chamber-pot was in universal use, and its contents went into rubbish-holes; or, composted with kitchen-refuse, were stored in manure-pits, to be spread on the fields: a scatter of small bones, shells, shards etc. around many Roman sites shows this to have been the ordinary practice, well-attested by Columella, and continued until recent times: the early nineteenth-century improvers of working-class housing not infrequently made a point of the value of collecting sewage for this purpose.[28] A manure-pit below XXXV.1 proved to contain much solid matter, in which the seeds of some 40 plants, including apple, blackberry, cherry, fig, large plum, poppy (as a condiment) and sloe were identified.[29]

Lastly, two great middens of industrial waste may be mentioned; both are very early. One partly underlay the forum and spread over some 750 sq. m. of ground to the east: it was composed purely of oyster-shells (p. 291).[30] The other, below the block of shops contemporary with the forum at the north-west corner of Insula VI, covered some 230 sq. m. and was composed almost wholly of the lower jaws of oxen (p. 290).[31]

7

In the Steps of the Roman Street-Surveyor

Doubtless the greater part of the street-plan of Calleva had been laid out at one time; certainly the main north-south street, for which a Flavian dating has been obtained (p. 53), must have been among the first to be metalled, even though minor lines on the periphery were not made up until the second century, and others never. Now that various additions and corrections, both intramural and extramural, can be made to the grid on the basis of aerial photographs (see the folding plan at the back of this book), the governing principles of such a regular layout should be discoverable; the large square insulae, for example, which form a vertical row in the centre and appear to have been especially devised for large properties (p. 50), share top and bottom borders with rectangular insulae to left and right, which have evidently been laid out at two-thirds the width of the others. Clearly, however, there are peculiarities which must in general stem from the prior existence of important buildings—notably the forum-basilica, the public baths, the sacred area on the east (Insula XXX) and probably the amphitheatre—which had to be respected.

Yet in tracing the steps of the Roman surveyor we find his work doubly veiled. In the first place, he was concerned with setting out *lines:* but these are represented only by the subsequent *streets,* on which buildings or even plots of land have here and there encroached. In the second place, the modern plans upon which any examination of his work has to be founded are, like all plans, approximate, and our first concern must be to test their reliability. A word, however, about the streets themselves: as Stair had noted in the middle of the eighteenth century, they vary in width from less than 6 m. to 7.6 m. in the case of the two main thoroughfares. They were made of rammed gravel, often with a natural clayey matrix which helped to consolidate the surface, sometimes intensely hard. There is a marked camber at the sides; the top is flattish, or shouldered by light wheeled traffic, rarely rutted or pot-holed. The thickness varied according to the ground beneath: on solid ground, perhaps only 30 cm.; deeper over soft ground or disturbed areas. Usually there are signs of one to four remakings, the last of these containing the central rainwater gutter (p. 89).[1]

THE ACCURACY OF THE STREET-PLAN

As already mentioned, the general plan of Calleva is based upon a seven-times enlargement of the Ordnance Survey 1:2500 plan. The vast extent of paper provided ample space on which to set out buildings individually reproduced to scale, but the main lines cannot possibly be more accurate than the Government survey, except where excavation suggested corrections of detail. The published plans of 1887, 1891, 1898, and 1908 form a typical sequence of copies based on copies. According to the printed scale on each, the overall north-south measurement of the town, from outer face of wall to outer face, is respectively 741, 756, 762, and 765 m.,[2] while the Ordnance Survey, within its accuracy-limit of 2.4 m., suggests 750 m. Although in itself a reasonably consistent and indeed irreplaceable record, therefore, it is clear that the 1908 plan cannot safely be used for detailed scaled measurements.

The insulae were individually planned on the spot to a scale of 1:96, and many fair copies still exist at the Society of Antiquaries. They were published at the scale of 1:2500 × 7. In many cases, included dimensions prove that they are highly accurate; but in others, discrepancies can be found.[3] Furthermore, there are other instances where measurements specified in the text of the reports turn out to be wrong, through hasty proof-reading or otherwise. In sum, a careful collation of all available evidence of measurements is necessary before significant dimensions can be accepted.

THE WORK OF THE SURVEYOR

Not the least interesting feature of the grid is its alignment, only 4° west of true north. The ancient surveyors preferred a northerly setting whenever the terrain permitted; other instances among Romano-British towns include Caerwent and London. The architect Vitruvius stresses the value of excluding wind from the streets;[4] and since in Britain the prevailing wind is south-westerly, we need seek no further explanation. Vitruvius and the surveyor Hyginus describe the mode of determining the meridian, viz. by marking the points where the shadow of a gnomon at the centre of a drawn circle strikes the circumference at a particular interval before and after noon, and then bisecting the arc.[5]

The instrument used in the survey of Calleva was no doubt a *groma,* which consisted, to judge from the sole known specimen found at Pompeii,[6] of an accurately-made bronze cross about 1 m. from end to end, pivoted horizontally on a bracket at the top of a stout pole. A plumb-line *(nervia)* depended from the tip of each arm, and another from the pivotal point, so that the instrument could be set up over a precise spot. The surveyor stood back from the *groma,* and by sighting through each pair of *nerviae* in turn, was enabled to lay out the first two main lines-of-sight *(rigores)*—the *cardo maximus* running north and south on the meridian already determined, and the *decumanus maximus* running east and west. These lines were marked out by ranging-poles *(perpendiculi),* and measurements along them with a graduated cord swiftly gave the points of intersection *(tetrantes)* of the desired lesser *cardines* and *decumani.* The *groma* was moved to each of these, and the whole area was gradually squared off.[7] The last stage was to lay off the widths of the streets from these lines, and to mark the corners of the resultant insulae by posts. Traces of these are reported from God-manchester (Hunts.).[8] There is proof at Silchester that the middle of the streets represents the survey-line. The portico of the public baths projected across the southern edge of the street; and IX.3 did likewise on the north of the main east-west street. It is obvious that both buildings would have impeded the respective lines-of-sight if these had not been central to the track of the future streets.

The *groma* was simple, sturdy, and reliable in patient hands, but its lines took some time to come to rest and were easily agitated by the wind, as was remarked by Hero of Alexandria in his attempt to promote the *dioptra,* a kind of primitive theodolite of his own invention. Gromatical surveys consequently often display inaccuracies, which are accentuated by sloping ground. Except on the south-east and, to a lesser extent, the south-west, Calleva can be regarded as a flat site, and the inaccuracies which can be found may be accepted as falling within the limits of reasonable tolerance. Thus the *cardo* street on the west of X-XIX departs by about 4 m. in 400, or 1%, from perfect parallelism, and the *decumanus* on the south of XV-XXXIV by about 3 m. in 600, or 0.5%. It is interesting to note that the error is much greater on the east side of the town, where the valley containing the public baths was traversed. On the assumption that the street on the west of XXX is part of the original layout, the departure from parallelism with the *cardines* to the west is no less than 18 m. in 360, or 5%. No reliable indications of the ancient module of the plan are likely to be found in that sector.

On a military analogy, the primary station of the *groma* would have been in front of the main entrance to the forum; but the alignment of that building, and the fact that it was already under construction when the street-plan was to be laid out (p. 55), show that this cannot have been so in our case. The *cardo maximus,* of course, is represented by the main north-south street immediately west of the forum-basilica; this line permitted a direct junction with the Roman road on the north of the town and, in the other direction, was carried through the original south entrance of the inner earthwork almost centrally. Where, then, was the *decumanus maximus?* Was it, as might naturally be supposed, on the line of the main east-west street, see-ing that this offered a direct junction with the Roman road to the west, via the west entrance of the inner earthwork? Perhaps; yet the curious position of this street some distance north of the forum-basilica is anomalous, for a line directly passing the building—like the *cardo maximus*—would still have made an acceptable junction with the western highway and on the east would still have cleared the corner of the *temenos* of XXX. Probably the real key to the problem is the amphitheatre, to the rear of which a *decumanus* street (i.e. that on the north of X-XXXVIA, see folder) extends. Since the size of the insulae must have been decided in advance, the *locus gromae* could therefore well have been at the centre of the future cross-roads north-west of Insula I; while the distance between this point and the forum could well have led to the slight deviation of the street-grid from the alignment of the latter (p. 54).

It would be satisfactory to state that the amphitheatre was in fact of earlier date than the street-grid; but, alas, it has not been excavated. The legionary amphitheatres of Caerleon and Chester are of course Flavian; but a more apposite case is that of Corinium, originally timber-built in the first century.[9] The Neolithic 'henge' monument of Maumbury Rings, Dorchester (Dorset), may well also have been transformed into an amphitheatre by that period,[10] and an amphitheatre in the pre-street phase at Silchester is thus not unlikely.

Let us now consider the insulae in more detail. As remarked above, the rectangles were laid out at two-thirds the width of the squares, and we thus have two principal insula-types answering respectively to the proportions of 3 × 3 and 3 × 2 'units' (i.e. thirds). The 'unit' may accordingly be expected to apply widely to the plan of Calleva, and this is so: we have to do with an authentic and verifiable measurement. The clearest example lies in the strip of Insula IV south of the forum-basilica. Here there are three divisions, (a) from the street on the west to a wall beside the lane which runs up to the forum but is not centred upon the south side-entrance; (b) from this wall across the lane to another wall on the west of the church; and (c) from that wall to the street on the east. Naturally, all lanes within an insula, being subsequent to the layout of the grid, have to be reckoned inclusively, and on the accurate insula-plan[11] these divisions (a-c) measure respectively 37.19, 39.93 and 41.15 m.; but if the back wall of the basilica is allowed to govern the width of parcel (a), the figure rises in that case to 38.41 m. Probably the variation of less than 1.5 m. from the notional 'unit' of 39.83 m. is not of great practical importance, owing to the possibility of inaccuracy arising from the placing of boundaries at much later dates. The length of the first space (a), from the corner of the basilica to the street on the south, is equal to a 'unit' almost precisely, and it is also precisely here that such a measurement would show, because of the slight obliquity of the forum-basilica. Further, the corresponding space on the north of the basilica is almost exactly half a 'unit' in height, exclusive of the street which flanks the building. The divisions of the strip on the north do not conform to our notion very well, but another space on the east of the forum, containing a small house, is one 'unit' in height and three-quarters of a unit in width.

Insula IV is full of odd plots of ground, because it had to contain the forum-basilica. The north-south measurement of the entire plot, however, does not come to the four 'units' which a casual glance suggests, unless a 4% error can be accepted. That we may be right in accepting an error of this magnitude is indicated by similar errors in the other insulae of the same vertical range. Only Insula I seems to be a nearly perfect square of three 'units' (117.34 × 118.26 m.); the height of XXIII, as corrected by aerial survey, is 113.39 m., and VII, 115.82 m. The length of IV, moreover, was probably governed by a desire to run a street past the entrance of the public baths in XXXIIIA although, as things worked out, the survey-line was too close to the portico at one point, and it became necessary to rebuild the façade (p. 129).

A few other examples of 'unit'-division may be given. On the east of VII, the lateral lane beside the *temenos* occurs at a reasonably correct interval from the northern margin of the insula; on the north side of VIII, the inn is placed at about the requisite distance of a 'unit' from the northern border, and half a 'unit' separates VIII.1–2 from the north-west corner. On the south side of XI, a lane leaves the main east-west street half a unit from the eastern boundary. The reader may be interested to try other situations upon the folding plan, by means of proportional dividers, and to check the results with the original *Archaeologia* reports and plans.

In terms of 'square units' or likely fractions there is also much to discover. Taking Insula I, we see that the two big houses in the northern corners fit quite well into a 'square unit', though they doubtless had much more land than this, as must be the case of XXIII.2, an oblique house of early origin. The row of shops and other small premises along the southern margin of I looks very much as if the individual plots ran back for the depth of half a 'unit', though the widths vary somewhat.[12] Similar buildings in adjoining westerly insulae answer to the same depth, though the limit is overbuilt here and there. In X and the eastern half of XI, there are signs of a regular vertical division of the corresponding strip into half- and quarter-'units'. These and other indications suggest that the square and rectangular insulae were basically partitioned into nine and six 'square units' respectively, there being also provision for multiple holdings and fractional division. This theory helps to explain the otherwise merely capricious siting of many of the buildings of Calleva.

THE TRANSLATION OF THE 'UNIT'

The only previous attempt to relate the insulation of Calleva to measurement in terms of Roman feet (*pedes monetales,* so called from the Temple of Juno Moneta in Rome where the standard, equivalent to 0.296 m., was laid up) is that of Haverfield, who saw the possible use of a dimension of 240 *pedes* in the small insulae east and west of the forum.[13] The vertical measurement of the northerly row containing II and V is close to this; but the widths do not correspond, and neither does the height of the more southerly row containing III and VI. We return below to the question of these insulae; it may be added that a unit of 240 or even 120 *pedes* is nowhere else discernible on the plan, unless actual measurements are rounded off in a highly arbitrary fashion which involves the assumption that the Roman survey was 14 or 15% in error: the largest detected error is 5%, and we have no right to assume errors three times as great. Furthermore, it is impossible to detect a dimension of 240 or 120 *pedes* (or any likely multiple or fraction thereof) in what is known of the insulation of British towns, except as rarely as here at Silchester.[14] The most perfect of all Roman planned towns, Timgad, does not show such dimensions,[15] and two insulae at Augst which have been very carefully studied recently with a view to elucidating their subdivisions measure 210 by 172 *pedes* in one case, and 200 by 160 in the other.[16]

Taking Insula I as the most perfect square, we find it measures in round figures 395 by 400 *pedes;* and that IX, a typical rectangle adjoining, is 280 *pedes* wide. Collating this with our Insula IV findings, it would appear that our 'unit' measured between 130 and 140 *pedes.* Unless the latter figure happens to be particularly faithful, therefore, there does not seem to be a clear sign of a dimension easily divisible into the halves and quarters which the plan itself displays.

It must be pointed out that calculations in terms of a Roman *pes* of 0.296 m. are bound to be approximate, because that figure is in itself an approximation, the standard having gone. Even so, it is known from a comparison of foot-rules and other ascertainable measurements that the *pes* varied from place to place, because in each locality it would have been merely a copy, at *n*th hand no doubt, of the standard. Thus a folding rule from Caerleon (which, being a legionary site, might be expected to produce something close to the official standard) measures 0.2945 m., and a half-rule from Silchester (fig. 41, 19, p. 293) yields a foot of 0.291 m.[17] It would be nonsensical to apply that measure to the insulation, for there is nothing to connect the rule with the surveyor, and there is no reason to suppose that all rules in use at Calleva were of identical length: certainly, the weights are not identical (p. 292).

What, then, of the 'unit'? It so happens that the surveyor Hyginus warns his reader to make diligent enquiry as to the measure used everywhere outside Italy.[18] The implication is that the *pes monetalis* was not in universal use, and two exceptions are noted, one in Egypt and the other in the Tongres region of northern Gaul. Here the *pes Drusianus* was current, and was equivalent to a *pes monetalis et sescuncia*, 1 ft. 1½ in. Roman measure, or 0.322 m.[19] Given the north Gaulish origin of the British Atrebates, one may wonder whether the problems before us might not better work out in terms of the Tongres foot. Coincidentally or not, the module of the survey answers almost perfectly in terms of 120 *p.D.* (39.83 m. divided by 120 = 0.3319). So much for Insula IV; the dimensions of I and the width of IX work out with a less breathtaking exactitude, viz. 354 by 357, and 253 *p.D.*, but still within the known 5% margin of error. Now it may be observed that the unit of 240 Roman feet mentioned by Haverfield is equivalent to one side of a rectangle 120 *pedes* wide, having the area of one *jugerum* (about 0.4 ha.) and containing two *actus quadrati* of 120 by 120 *pedes*. A square Silchester 'unit', accordingly, might be an *actus quadratus* of Tungrian measure; and thus the square and rectangular insulae will have contained respectively nine and six *actus* of this kind.

FURTHER DETAILS OF THE STREET-PLAN

The squares and rectangles which we have just discussed are the most important categories, but there are others which remain to be examined. The wide rectangular insulae on the east of the vertical standard range through XXI–XXXV seem to reflect the necessity of avoiding the north-east corner of the public baths in XXXIIIA; the clearest indication of the width of the row comes from XXVII, where the eastern boundary-street comes strongly through in crop-mark year by year, but for some reason appears to have been difficult to define during the excavations.[20] This width is 101.19 m. or about 305 p.D., and was perhaps intended to measure 2½ 'units' (300 p.D.), suggestive of a notional area of 7½ Tungrian *actus*. In Insula XXXVIA to the east again, the original width may have been two 'units', the walled enclosure containing B1 and the street on its west side accounting for one. But in this part of the plan the insulation is very imperfect.

The double range of small insulae east and west of the forum coincide in height with Insula IV, four 'units' in height. The street which divides each pair had therefore to be taken out of this area, either from each component equally, or (as was decided) from one only, that on the north. In this way, it was possible to run the dividing street between V and VI more or less opposite the centre of the east front of the forum, though not exactly, hence the alteration, on which we have already commented, to the entrance (p. 55).

Lastly, the height of the lateral range through Insula VIII, as far as it was metalled, corresponds within about 3 p.D. to the figure of three 'units', but only on the evidence of the insula-plan.[21]

UNALIGNED LANES

These very large insulae must often have been crossed by lanes and footpaths, and some of those which were metalled show on aerial photographs. Several appear to follow the grid-alignment as in VII or XI, but others are oblique. Among them may be relics of the haphazard pre-street development, as in the case, perhaps, of the oblique lane in XXIIB; among them too are accommo-dation-tracks as in VIII, leading to the court of the baths and to the public entrance. One or two other lanes are marked in the extramural area, but interest centres more particularly on the region west of the outer earthwork, where tracks leading to cultivated ground have been observed (pl. 9, and folder), and in one case to a secondary entrance in the original line of the earthwork, excavated in 1956.[22] On the east, further lanes of a similar kind have been seen, as far as 500 m. from the east gate; but unfortunately the conditions of soil-moisture in this part of the ground render the pattern indistinct.

In conclusion, it is worth remarking that the more one studies the regular Callevan street-plan, and the more one comprehends the difficulties which faced the ancient surveyor, the greater becomes one's respect for the logical and versatile manner in which he imposed his scheme over an area so widely encumbered with obstacles. Who was he? One thing seems certain: the Roman foot was not used, and he is not likely, therefore, to have been an army *mensor*.

8

The Town Wall: An Expensive Undertaking

The town wall stands 4.5 m. high near the south gate, not much above the bank inside. There would have been a walk on top of that bank; traces occurred at Caerwent, probably, and York certainly.[1] Supporting troops and munitions could be gathered there without impeding the parapet-walk above. The Silchester wall was in all likelihood about 6 m. high, plus a parapet of say 1.8 m. The wall is nearly 3 m. thick at the base, and stands on a slight flint foundation covered externally by a plinth, which is chamfered near the gateways. On the south-east, and where it crosses the line of the inner earthwork on the north-west (pl. 6), the wall is supported on piles.[2] An internal scarcement about 2.5 m. above the base reduces the upper thickness of the wall to about 2.3 m., but at intervals of some 60 m., and near each of the nine corners, the basal thickness is carried up to form shallow buttress-like projections about 3.7 m. long. These might be thought to mark turrets, but the floor-area would be so small that the suggestion must be abandoned; much more probably, the projections marked access-stairs and crossing-places.[3] A *ballista* could be mounted upon them at a pinch, if need arose.

The external corners are not rounded, except on the north-east and south-west, where the angle is unusually sharp. Little remains, however, of the external facing. The inner face was finished with equal care (pl. 14), and it may have been intended to remove the earlier bank entirely. The structure is of roughly-coursed flint, set in a strong concrete of gravel, sand and lime; the facing-stones are hammer-dressed. The most striking feature is the series of levelling-courses, which are composed, not of brick as at Verulamium and elsewhere, but very largely of Jurassic limestone brought from a distance of 70 or 80 km.[4] and otherwise of local ironstone; brick was used only in the facings of gateways and in their arches. This bold use of stone is very curious. We are led to infer that the local brickworks were incapable of turning out the immense quantities required; but this in turn brings further questions to mind. Was the industry incapable of expansion because the potential labour-force had been taken to dig the flints, the gravel and the sand, and to burn the lime? And if there was an imperial tilery in the time of Nero at Little London,[5] did it no longer operate? Or, seeing that the limestone quarries were within the borders of another *civitas,* that of the the Belgae to whom Ptolemy attributes Bath,[6] did those quarries lie on imperial property, and if so was there any accommodation made to assist the Atrebates in the matter of the defences of Calleva? Or were there private pockets to be lined? Such questions as these, natural and important, vex the archaeologist, who is never likely to be able to answer them formally, and must be content, as so often, to report a bare fact or a primary deduction. Firstly, if it is not a fact, then it is such a deduction, that the construction of the wall must have been spread over a fair term of years (p. 66): the pressure on manpower, therefore, can hardly have been so acute as to prevent the expansion of the brickworks. Secondly, imperial or not, the Little London works were in production in the period 80–150/200 because the site has yielded a fragment of roller-patterned flue-tile, a waster now in Basingstoke Museum, made at that period (cf. p. 278). Evidence regarding the quarries is more elusive. Just south of Bath, there is a building which was clearly the administrative headquarters *(principia)* of an imperial domain, managed by a freedman, who rebuilt the headquarters *c.* 212–17.[7] We do not know how large the estate was, or in what its principal interests lay: but quarries are likely to have been included.

The wall of Calleva was constructed in horizontal stages of about 1 m. or less, consisting of four or five courses of flint, sometimes fewer, capped by one, two or rarely three layers of bonding-stone, replaced here and there by sections of fragments laid herringbone-wise, as if every piece had to be used with economy. Little is known of the working-lengths allotted to different gangs. The parapet, to judge by one of its semicylindrical coping-stones,[8] was about 75 cm. thick. It will have had merlons and embrasures of about equal dimensions, appropriate to what we must assume was a small garrison, and thus quite different from the wide embrasures seen on Trajan's Column or in the Castra Praetoria at Rome,[9] in any case much earlier: the tendency in Roman fortification was to reduce the width of the embrasures as time went on.

The construction of the wall involved a heavy commitment of all kinds of resources, as mentioned before (p. 66). Taking an average cross-section as 16.45 sq. m. and the length as 2,430 m., the volume is nearly 40,000 cu. m., not counting gateways. In terms of a wagon-load of 500 kg.,[10] the number of loads of bonding-stone would have been around 45,000 and the number of loads of flint around 105,000, to say nothing of the 10,000 cu. m. of concrete which, as the visitor immediately sees, was somewhat liberally used.[11]

GATEWAYS

There are eight gates. The east and west are a pair of similar plan, with double carriageways and flanking towers; the north and south gates also form a pair, but have only single carriageways. The others (south-west, amphitheatre, and south-east gates, together with an unfinished, blocked gate on the north-east) are simple passages. All no doubt corresponded to gates constructed, or for which allowance was made, in the primary or 'bank' period of the inner defences. The east gate may well belong to that period, all the more probably because it is the 'London' gate: the curtain-wall, when eventually constructed, was block-bonded to it.[12] On the south, a trace of an original wider gate survives just to the west of the extant structure, which was built separately from the wall, though presumably as part of the same scheme.[13] Only on the west, in fact, does the gate appear to be perfectly contemporary with the curtain.

The west, south and north gates are fairly deeply recessed, a feature of Greek origin found in the British Iron Age, and in Roman forts from the Flavian to the Hadrianic period, less frequently later: notably in timber at Oakwood, Scotland, where there were twin passageways and flanking towers, and in stone at Haltwhistle Burn, Northumberland, where the passages were single. Carausian Portchester, Hants., is perhaps the latest known.[14] The creation of a forecourt ensured that attackers would be subjected to destructive fire from the inturn of the walls on either side. From the Antonine period onwards, however, military architects particularly favoured projecting towers.[15] Caerwent is an interesting case: the original defences, probably Hadrianic or Antonine, had inturned entrances on the east and west; but when the wall was built, the corresponding gateways were of the partly-projecting type, and were built over the filling of the earlier ditch.[16]

It is strange that there should not have been a deeply-inturned entrance on the east, at Silchester, since only a very small projection of the wall on either side would have produced it: at present there is no satisfactory explanation of the matter. The west gate (pl. 13),[17] rather more than 16 by 7 m. overall, was better preserved than the east gate, similar but a little larger.[18] The plan is very simple, and there are no side-passages for pedestrians such as we find at Verulamium, Cirencester and elsewhere, though it is worthy of note that the main road from London westwards via Silchester left by a

Roman Newgate without pedestrian passages.[19] The rectangular towers had two small rooms at ground-level: the walls, about 1 m. thick, were evidently of some considerable height, probably one storey above the first-floor, which would have corresponded to the level of the parapet-walk (6 m.). The second storey probably had a flat roof with battlements, serving as an elevated fighting-platform.[20] The passageways are almost 4 m. wide, and are recessed nearly that distance from the face of the towers. The plan clearly shows the stout wall between them, and the projections front and back which carried the brick-turned arches—a voussoir was found. The superstructure would have taken the form of a crenellated platform at parapet-walk level. The construction throughout was excellent: the flint core of the walling was faced with stone, there were stone quoins and simply-moulded ironstone imposts, and brick was used in bonding-courses and in the jambs of the tower doorways. All the work was rendered in pink cement—lime-mortar containing ground brick for added strength and resistance to damp—and the walls of the tower rooms were painted in red and white stripes. The thresholds were of timber, and a piercing of the wall between the passageways, just behind the front arch-pier, allowed sufficient play for periodic removal and replacement. A similar arrangement occurred, well-preserved, at the north gate, and it could there be seen that the threshold-beam was of 25 cm. scantling. The doors were nearly 12 cm. thick, and as usual were pivoted: a piece of iron strap and a cylindrical pivot-shoe furnish these details. None of the gates produced a stone pivot-socket, so the corresponding bearings must have been let into the threshold and lintel-beams. From the outside, the west gate may have looked as in fig. 12.

The north and south gates,[21] built separately from the curtain-wall, had passageways a little over 3.5 m. wide. The side-walls are again 1 m. thick, and were no doubt carried up to the same height as the towers at the east and west gates; but the overlap of curtain and tower is so small that it is questionable whether there was direct access to the first floor from the parapet-walk, except possibly at the north gate, unless some sort of timber staging was provided. The same difficulty applies to the east gate.

The other, minor, gates somewhat resemble the north and south gates of Caerwent, but those were built to a squarish plan, projecting inwards well behind the line of the wall, and were probably surmounted by towers.[22] That cannot have been the case here, and the parapet-walk must have been carried uninterruptedly above the archways. The south-west and amphitheatre gates were about 3.5 m. wide.[23] The former was fairly well-preserved (pl. 14), and it is clear that the portal was recessed about 1 m. from the face of the wall; the whole of the vaulted passage was cement-rendered. The outer arch

PLAN

12. Plan of west gate, with imaginative restoration

was carried on slightly-projecting piers, the surviving northern plinth being badly scarred by wheeled traffic. The inner arch was flush with the wall, and the bank behind was gently sloped down to the roadway, in order to avoid the need for a revetment of the kind found at the south-east gate. It is curious that the main road to Sorviodunum and the south-west left by such an insignificant gate, but more so that there was a gate here at all, for the main west gate, from which that road could easily have diverged, is only 150 m. to the north. Among the articles turned up in the gateway were another piece of strap and a pivot-shoe; of seven impost-stones, all of different patterns, only one could have belonged to the gate, in Fox's estimation. The rest came from the blocking-wall mentioned below.

The unfinished postern, 215 m. north-west of the amphitheatre gate, does not correspond to a street of the regular grid.[24] In this, and in its width of only 1.4 m., it resembles the south-east gate. The decision to have a gateway at this point at all seems to have been secondary, for the plinth of the wall is carried across the opening, and at the other gates it is omitted. Quoins were laid to the height of the internal scarcement of the curtain-wall, but then the gap was filled with masonry, and the upper part of the wall carried over the site.

The south-east gate (pl. 15) is a somewhat problematical structure.[25] Initially, it was clearly designed as a narrow postern, in this case with a projecting inner archway, of which some brickwork and the basal stone blocks remained: the work is similar to that of the west gate. Below the floor of the passage ran the box-drain carrying the waste waters of the baths of the nearby inn (p. 90). At some later date, the arch-piers were extended, and enclosed vertical, cement-lined shafts for timbers of 30 cm. scantling, joined at the base by a sill, and presumably by a lintel overhead. The secondary character of this work was not appreciated, though it is clear on the photographs, and the whole was identified as a sluice-gate. 'From this framework', wrote Hope, 'hung the sluice-gate [working] in grooved uprights, for which vertical rebates are cut out . . .'. At the same time as the additions mentioned were made, the approach to the gate, originally timber-revetted, was lined with retaining-walls, and the area between was cemented. But the 'sluice-gate' lies only in a very small declivity, not at the foot of the decided valley in this part of the site: the stream which still runs there was conveyed through the wall in a simple culvert (p. 90) and took with it the waste waters of the public baths, very much greater in quantity than those of the baths of the inn. We may well wonder whence was to come the enormous volume of water which would have justified the erection of such a large sluice-gate. The vertical shafts are the key, and possibly held uprights for some sort of tower or staging on the wall above; I cannot see the 'rebates' on the photographs, and unfortunately no detailed plan of the gateway appears to exist. In may be added that some sort of provision for the escape of water through the wall might be expected on the south-east side of the circuit, where there is another small valley from which a stream issues: a modern land-drain pierces the wall here.

THE DITCH AND THE CROSSINGS

There are two ditches in front of the wall, an inner ditch cut originally for the bank, 7 m. wide and 2 m. deep, and a later, outer ditch of about double these dimensions but of saucer-shaped profile. It is assumed that the inner ditch was superseded when the wall was built; but the reason for cutting back the rampart was to find room for the wall to stand, as we see in various other cases. The inner ditch remained largely open or was filled with loose material; a solid clay filling is known at one spot, and between the south-west and west gates a narrow metalled track seems to have been laid on the filling.[26] A second ditch at a fair distance from the wall is a feature of fourth-century town-defences, as at Caerwent: undoubtedly here also. The spoil was thrown into the inner ditch or spread along the outer lip of the new ditch as a low glacis.[27] A vague indication of the date at which these modifications to the ditch-system were carried out is provided by coins from a rude hut erected on the glacis: they were mostly worn-out rubbish, the latest being of c. 364–83.[28] A fair interval of time must have elapsed between the completion of the glacis and the date at which the authorities would have permitted such a hut to stand in this position.

It is probable that the inner ditch was originally spanned by bridges opposite each of the gates. The clearest evidence comes from the north gate, where a solid gravel abutment, containing an emplacement for a large sole-beam, was revealed on the inner lip of the ditch, and two large flint-packed postholes, 9.7 m. apart, on the outer lip.[29] But there were also signs that the bridge was later replaced by a causeway across both ditches, and such may have been the case on the south and also on the west: of the east gate we cannot speak, for the excavators had to content themselves with permission to open the guard-chambers and passageways, and no exploration of the ditch beyond took place. Surface relief suggests that there were bridges at the south-west and amphitheatre gates: possibly the gates were not used in the fourth century.

MODIFICATIONS TO THE GATES

As the final subject of this chapter we may record certain blockings and narrowings of the gates. On an earlier page, mention was made of the addition of projecting towers to the walls of many Romano-British towns, though not at Silchester, as far as is known,[30] though the cutting of the new outer ditch may well denote an intention to provide them, which for one reason or another was never carried out. At some sites, where towers were provided, the gateways were also modified in imitation of the latest pattern of military architecture, the forts of the 'Saxon Shore', built around the end of the third century. In these, the entrances are both fewer and narrower than in earlier forts, and it is not surprising to find that the gateways of some of the latter were modified to correspond, for example at Greatchesters on Hadrian's Wall. At Caerwent, though we cannot speak of the main east and west gates, the south gate was completely blocked, and the north gate reduced to a low sallyport.[31]

At Silchester, the south carriageway of the west gate was walled up, the blocking contained part of a Corinthian capital from the basilica—probably one which had been damaged in the first fire (p. 71)—a section of double column, and a coping-stone from the wall itself. At the north and south gates, columnar material was also found and suggests that there were block-ings; so does the inscription found in 1732 on the bank adjacent to the north gate, probably placed there when the entrance was reopened for agricultural purposes in the middle ages. The south-west gate was also reduced at some period, but at a date after the roadway had been raised by over 1 m. in thickness, to only 2 m. in width: the blocking-wall is of good workmanship, as it also is at the south-east gate, though composed there merely of lumps of concrete laid between courses of brick. Two large stones reported by Joyce as lying in the amphitheatre gate may also tell of a blocking. Nothing is known of a blocking at the east gate, but the remains were so reduced that little, if anything, would have survived.[32]

The garrison of Calleva was discussed earlier, on page 66.

9

The Forum-Basilica

The forum-basilica measures about 84.5 m. from north to south and 95.5 m. from east to west (fig. 13).[1] As we have seen (p. 94) the foundations were laid before the street-grid was imposed *c.* 85; the vicinity was cleared of huts, the great mound of shells to the east was levelled, and the whole area surfaced with clean gravel. Traces of an early precinct of shops and a *grand boulevard* on the east have also been mentioned. It is not possible at present to date the building more precisely: Joyce found a piece of plain samian deep beneath the east wall; and that piece is Flavian; he also recorded coins of emperors running down to Domitian (81–96) in the mortar of one of the apses of the great hall, some heavily encrusted with mortar, but adds 'or lying close by the walls' or deep in 'the débris on the floor'. All things considered, the building must belong to the late first century, and this is the period to which corresponding buildings at Winchester and Chichester, in the other *civitas*-capitals formed in the former kingdom of Cogidubnus, appear to belong.[2] The great building to be described in this chapter would have taken a considerable time to complete. Clearly construction had not advanced very far when the street-grid was laid, because it was still possible to modify the position of the main east entrance (p. 55). The Corinthian columns of the basilica are of a Rhenish style known at Bath, Caerwent, and other British sites also, and considered to belong to the early second century.[3]

An external portico ran around the entire building, broken only on the east where the entrance was marked by a double archway 6.7 m. wide: the engaged Tuscan column found at the south gate appears to have belonged to it. Inside, the court, 44 by 36.5 m., was lined on three sides by a portico, from which shops and offices opened. Side-entrances divided these ranges from the basilica, which closed the fourth side of the court. The great hall of the basilica, some 82 by 17.5 m., terminated in apsidal (later rectangular) recesses, probably juridicial *tribunalia* for the *duoviri* (p. 59); along the

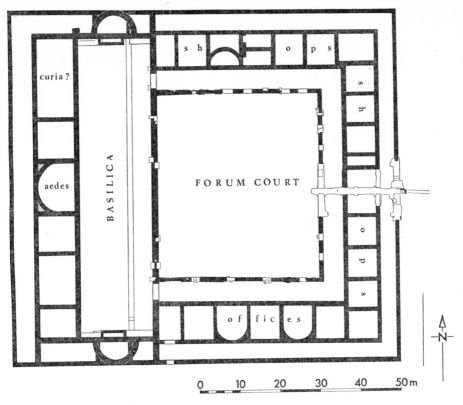

13. Plan of the forum-basilica

west side was a suite of large chambers, that in the centre, again apsidal, being probably the civic temple, and that at the north end, of double size, being probably the council-chamber.

The plan is like that of the headquarters of a legionary fortress, fully evolved by the time of Nero. Here we see the same court and ranges of rooms, the same basilica, *tribunalia,* and office-range on either side of a central *aedes.*[4] Most Romano-British fora are of this pattern, and the connection has therefore been held to be both direct and simple. In a province lacking any indigenous architectural tradition worth the name, the services of military architects may well have been made available to local authorities desirous of following the governor Agricola's 'private encouragement' to erect precisely this, among other types of buildings: indeed may have been included in the help given *publice,* i.e. from state resources, for them to do so.[5]

The origin of the basic design has been traced to late Republican and early imperial public architecture in northern Italy,[6] and it is therefore possible that the Silchester building may not, after all, be a simple adaptation of a military type. But the military parallel is compelling, extending as it does to the exclusion of a third element—the *capitolium*—which, in continental fora and probably at Camulodunum if not at Lincoln, stands in its own court beyond the forum square.[7] It may be added, for what the observation is worth, that the Silchester forum-basilica seems to have been laid out according to the official Roman foot rather than the provincial variety which was used in the setting-out of the street-grid (p. 97).[8]

Joyce saw in the Silchester forum-basilica 'in effect the very plan itself upon which was constructed the world-famed Forum of Trajan with the Basilica Ulpia by its side'. Scholars have recognised the same influence at Augst and Alesia.[9] Are all such basilicas, with apsidal terminations and central apse—features which do not occur in the military parallels—scaled-down replicas of the noble concept of Apollodorus? The Ulpian basilica was begun in 98; and if the theory is true, we are in a difficulty over our date of shortly before 85 for the Silchester building. However, there is little warrant for the Trajanic dating of Augst or Alesia; and the modest civil basilica of Kempten reveals the apsidal design as early as the time of Claudius. Indeed, the great terminal hemicycles of the Ulpian basilica can be found in the Augusto-Tiberian *Caesareum* at Cyrene or, for that matter, in the practically identical design of the mid-Flavian basilica of Corinium,[10] though in both these cases at one end only.

THE FORUM

The three ranges of rooms around the gravelled piazza vary from 9 to 10 m. in depth; the widest is on the south, where there is a suite of five well-proportioned chambers alternately square and apsidal.[11] As Joyce suggested, these were probably public offices, the two apsidal rooms being intended for the *aediles* (p. 60). The paucity of finds in these rooms lends some support to this belief. The other ranges consisted mainly of shops, of which those at the north-east and south-east corners opened on to the outer portico only. In the centre of the east side, there was a vestibule between the inner and outer faces of the archway; and the narrow apartment next to it may have contained steps to the terrace or upper storey which must have existed to balance the lofty height of the adjoining basilica. On the north side, one of the rooms has been laterally partitioned, and next to it an apse has been built to face the court. Close to this spot, Stair found the inscription to Hercules *Saegontius* (fig. 1), a brick pedestal, to the cladding of which the inscription may have belonged, and a heavy moulded bronze frame probably also from the pedestal.[12] Presumably, therefore, a statue stood in this recess.

Joyce made specific suggestions as to the uses to which some of the other chambers were put. Three north of the 'staircase-well' on the east side would have been butchers' shops, on the grounds that all but one of the steelyard hooks found came from them; and the last but one on the south of the same range was 'the favourite luncheon bar of the forum', where 'the favourite food was oysters'. In this case, his view of the stratification was confused, for, as the 1892 re-examination established, the shells belonged to an altogether earlier midden (p. 291). On the other hand, a great pot had been walled into a corner of the chamber, and may indeed have held shellfish or other comestibles: it is a feature reminiscent of many a *popina* at Pompeii or Ostia.[13] Another shop, in the north range, was identified as a manufacturing jeweller's, since a small bar of silver was found there, partly used. At this juncture, we may mention the stone moulds for pewter dishes found in the débris of the forum by Fox (p. 274). The laterally-divided room in the same range was, according to Joyce, a banker's: here were found not only an unusually large number of coins ranging from Claudius II (268-9) to Valens (364-78), but also 'recesses' in the west wall, into which strong-boxes could have been built. *Nummularii* would have had their place, for it is far from certain that the copper coins and the gold or silver were freely interchangeable as in modern systems, even under the early Empire; while in the fourth century we read of 'buying' gold pieces for settling taxes levied in gold.[14] However, the coins mentioned are probably only a scattered hoard, and the recesses may merely be a trace of a different period of building. Nevertheless, Joyce's suggestions conjure up a lively, if generalised, picture of the forum in its heyday. The steelyard hooks, for example, remind us of the well-known relief at Dresden of an open-fronted butcher's shop, the husband cutting up chops, the wife doing the accounts, seated in a high-backed chair; joints hang on a frame at the rear; and in front, a big steelyard has been swung out of the way.[15] There are numerous genre scenes of this kind among the ancient reliefs and terracottas (see further, p. 188). The largely open, metalled ground around the outside of the building suggests that cattle-markets may have been held there, the dealers doing their business in the shade of the outer portico.

The picture of the building, however, is vague, for we have scarcely touched upon its elevation. Parts lay so close to the old surface of the ground that the plough has long since torn up almost every vestige of the superstructure, and even most of the floors, of red brick tessellation, have gone. Fox is the only scholar to have studied the problem, and his arguments and conclusions are still valid.[16] It may be assumed that all three ranges were of the same height, and that the southern range, the widest, governed that height. Here the apsidal rooms would have had vaulted ceilings terminating in half-domes, probably of hollow tiles as in the case of the somewhat later vault in XXXIV.1 (p. 197); these vaults would have been covered externally with tiled roofs. The lathe-turned Tuscan columns of the inner porticoes stood about 4.6 m. high,[17] and at about 4.4 m. centres; allowing for the architrave and minimal walling above, the level of the window-sills in the gable-ends of the vaulted rooms—the only means of external lighting—cannot have been less than 8 m. above the floor, supposing there to have been a pentice roof at only 20° slope above the portico. But the rooms would thus have been disproportionately high, and Fox therefore envisaged a terrace-roof above the portico, bringing the level of the windows to a more reasonable 6 m. or so. Since the vaults were 3.5 m. in radius, the ridge of their tiled cover would have been about 12.8 m. above the ground, in this case; and such a height allowed ample headroom in a storey above the shops in the other ranges, for storage or living-accommodation. A relief in the Uffizi portrays something like this, though without the terrace: we see cloth being shown to customers in the open front of a shop, where columns support an upper floor, the rectangular shuttered windows of which are seen below tiled eaves.[18]

THE BASILICA

This part of the building everywhere presented to Joyce 'the comminuted smash of a great fabric'. Enough was left, however, to provide evidence of reconstruction after the first disastrous fire (p. 71) which left, for example, signs of charred ceiling-beams at 60 to 90 cm. intervals across the room at the south-west corner. The alteration of the *tribunalia* from an apsed to a rectangular plan, involving the raising of their floors 74 cm. above the level of the hall and the facing of their fronts with grey-green Purbeck marble, dates from the reconstruction.

The great hall appears somewhat narrow in comparison with various others,[19] but there is a reason for this. The most prevalent design for a basilica incorporated a nave and two aisles divided by colonnades supporting a clerestory like that of a great church, its lineal descendant. Lighting, and the difficulty of spanning a considerable width in one, were thereby respectively contrived and obviated. In our case, there would otherwise have been a requirement for beams some 19 m. in length; and although such were to be had—the *aula palatina* at Trier required beams some 27 m. long— they must have been rare and expensive; and the natural British structural timber, oak, would probably have been available only in shorter lengths.[20]

This picture of an ideal basilica is upset by the curious fact that the excavations brought to light only one of the massive stereobates on which colonnades were erected. Both Joyce and Fox carefully sought the other. Joyce lamely concluded that 'any architect will at once see . . . that such a wall must originally have existed . . . in accordance with the strict conditions of symmetrical arrangement always observed in the works of the ancients', and Fox could find no more than 'a fragment of wall' a little south of the centre, and a 'ragged projection' from the lateral foundation next to the southern apse. To anyone who has had the experience of excavating a Roman basilica, as has twice fallen to my lot at Caerleon, Fox's results are a highly unconvincing demonstration of the substructures of a great colonnade. The fragment of walling found near the centre was too slight to mark on any plan; and there is no certainty that the ragged stump at the south end was part of an otherwise robbed stereobate; the filling of the trench would in any case have stood out in strong contrast to the natural gravel. We have to conclude, therefore, that there was never more than a single colonnade in Silchester basilica, and that the dotted lines marked on Fox's plan which indicate the course of a western and an 'original' eastern stereobate must be expunged. The single-aisled basilica has a respectable Hellenistic ancestry at Magnesia or Priene; the great hall of the *tabularium* in Rome is of this kind, as are the market-basilica of Pompeii and basilicas at Zuglio and Vidy-Lausanne; somewhat later, the basilica of Caistor St. Edmund follows the same model; and if the basilicas of the permanent legionary fortresses are all double-aisled, single aisles appear in timber-built structures at Haltern and Inchtuthil, while the same pattern is followed in stone at Chesters or House-steads auxiliary forts, and many others.[21]

What, then, of the symmetry? The truth is that neither Joyce nor Fox was in a position to appreciate the essentially two-fold character of basilical design. Their thoughts were limited to one type only, the long-axis type where attention was concentrated upon the far end of a long perspective, as in the Basilica Aemilia at Rome or in the Corinium basilica already cited. There is however a second type, the short-axis type where interest centred upon a feature on that axis, opposite a main entrance. Instances include above all the Basilica Ulpia, with Trajan's Column as the focal point; in the legionary headquarters, with their double colonnades, it is the *aedes* or temple of the standards, and it is the *aedes* at Silchester. The wide areas to left and right, in such buildings, were available for other purposes: the architecture, whether or not reduced to a single colonnade, remains perfectly symmetrical to either side. It can be seen from the plan that the single stereobate encroaches a little on the east side of the terminal apses. In the double-aisled basilica at Augst (Period I), a similar feature was calculated to lend a spacious air to the apses by concealing their point of junction with the end-walls.[22] At Silchester, the effect would have been very unbalanced if not counteracted in some way; and that this was done seems clear from the existence of lateral foundations which would have carried engaged columns of the same height and order as those of the colonnade; one of them would have projected to cover the western return of the apse at either end of the hall.

The great Bath stone columns had shafts about 86 cm. in diameter at the base, and on the assumption that they were 20 modules, 10 diameters, in overall height, we reach a figure of 8.6 m., about five-eighths of the height of the columns in the porch of the Pantheon at Rome. Only the merest fragments survived: among them, however, were some fluted drums, which may have framed the central *aedes*.[23] The capitals, one of which is shown restored in pl. 17, measured 96 cm. in height and 110 cm. across the volutes. Allowing for an architrave proportionate to the height of the columns, and for an entablature, as well also for the vault above the *aedes* (5.8 m. radius) springing from the level of the architrave, the basilica could not have stood less than 18 m. in height to the eaves, and the ridge of the roof must have approached 22 m. above ground-level. Joyce found pieces of window-glass and also star-shaped iron corner-pieces from window-grilles, but whether all these came from the clerestory remains doubtful.

The present account differs from Fox's in another important particular. He represents the forum-front of the basilica as extremely plain; and indeed his plan shows none of the masses of stone which appear so carefully marked along the great east wall on Joyce's, and of which measurements are given in the *Journal*. Presumably, they had all disappeared by Fox's time. They compare with the masses noted by him along the forum peristyle, and must likewise indicate columns, or perhaps piers. Among smaller columns attested were some about 56 to 60 cm. in diameter, and others only 38 cm.; the former may have come from the bases marked by the masses of stone. One of these is in line with the north side of the *aedes,* and there were probably five intercolumniations of about 3 m. on either side of the main entrance. The faced walling mentioned by Fox cannot have extended further than the forum-porticoes on either side, and in each case was pierced by a doorway into the basilica. Not a few basilicas were open along their length in this way: Augst (Period II) is a good example, and Krischen in his reconstruction-drawing shows doors with windows above as infillings, and these may well have existed in the case of Silchester. Caerwent is another British example, if we may judge from the worn state of the steps running the full length of the forum-front.[24] The design is common in military headquarters.

The rooms on the west of the hall, apart from the *aedes,* are five in number: three to the south, and two to the north, including there the large chamber (19 by 9 m.) which probably served as the *curia.* Others must have been a *tabularium,* or record-office, an *aerarium* or treasury, and other offices. They probably had wide entrances from the main hall, and their ceilings—for which there is evidence already quoted—would have been at the level of the entablature of the colonnade. Their lighting presents no difficulty, for all except the *aedes* could have had external windows; the *aedes* would have been adequately lit from the clerestory above the single colonnade.

The floor of the *aedes* was raised 78 cm. above that of the main hall, and was gained by three steps running the full width of the opening: it was here that fragments of the statue of the Tutela occurred and, when taken with the military parallel to the use of the central chamber in the range, leave little doubt of the correctness of our identification. Fox states that the floors of the apsidal *tribunalia* were raised very nearly as much; but a careful reading of his text and an examination of the plan make it plain that he was referring to the later rectangular recesses.

The floor of the main hall was apparently of plain cement: Joyce makes the point that there was no sign of tesserae having been embedded in it. Funds perhaps originally ran only to white tessellation (hard-chalk) in the three apses. Later floors were of the ubiquitous red tessellation, eventually patched with bricks here and there. Great use was made of Purbeck marble wall-facings in both periods: some remained in position on the front of the southern rectangular tribunal when first opened, and a large slab from IX.2, still highly polished, with cramp-holes in the edges, must have come from the basilica. Otherwise, fragments attest panelled decoration outlined by simple mouldings of the same material, and divided by narrow strips of sawn hard-chalk, some with mitred corners.[25] The *aedes* possessed a white Italian marble dado, and presumably the green and white Pyrenean marble found in Insula I-II came from this room also.[26] The plaster above the dado was painted in large areas of plain salmon-red, pale blue and green; the prevalent, rather sombre grey-green coloration of the main hall was substantially relieved by the massive creamy line of the columns, left so far as we know unpainted; so that the total effect was very striking, supplemented and heightened as it was by a considerable body of colour applied to the upper parts of the walls. Fragments of painted plaster from the northern apse display the favourite combination of light-red and ochre-yellow, together

14. Imaginative reconstruction of the east or forum front of the basilica

with white, and with traces of green and yellow draperies.[27] A reconstruction
of the building is offered in fig. 14.

FURNITURE, INSCRIPTIONS AND STATUARY

Two side-tables with monolithic tops, one in Purbeck marble and the other
in Bath stone, both decorated in the 'chip-carved' manner along the leading
edge, may be mentioned first of all.[28] Tables of this kind are well-known,
especially in the third- and fourth-century villas of the west-country; they
were probably *monopodia*.[29] In general, however, furniture was probably
sparse. In the offices there would have been what was necessary for the
transaction of business, the safe-keeping of monies, and the preservation of
records: a few good tables, seats for officials, chests, and racks for the
storage of documents would no doubt cover most possibilities;[30] and there
would have been charcoal braziers in the offices during the winter, for no
other form of heating was installed.

About a dozen inscriptions were turned up in and around the forum-
basilica. None is complete; most are represented by single scraps of thin
Purbeck sheets. We are thus deprived, at very least, of the names of the
chief persons of the town, of the offices which they held, and no doubt much
else. The most important, from the sheer size of its lettering (28 cm. high,
painted in red as the custom was), must have extended over a long frieze of
closely-butted panels. Not so much as a complete letter remains. An inscription in relief is indicated by part of a bronze A about 15 cm. tall. Otherwise, the most interesting epigraphic relic is a stone which named the
civitas Atrebatum, found in the presumed *curia*.[31]

Four important statues are also represented. The Portland stone statue

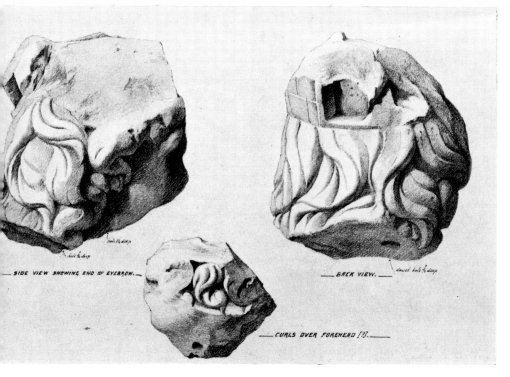

SIDE VIEW SHOWING END OF EYEBROW.

BACK VIEW.

CURLS OVER FOREHEAD (?)

10   Fragments of the head of the Tutela, Portland stone
11   Purbeck marble inscription from the temple in Insula XXXV, naming the town
   [CALLEVAE] and a *collegium peregrinorum*, or 'strangers' association'
12   The Ogham stone, from a well in Insula IX, as found

13 (above left)
The west gate, showing foundations of the southern tower, enclosing guard-rooms

14 (below left)
The south-west gate, showing the partial blocking (left of the ranging-pole) and the neat interior face of the town-wall

15 (above right)
The south-east gate, showing brick piers and blocking

16 (below right)
Walling at the public baths, Insula XXXIIIA, carried on alder piles

of the Tutela, previously mentioned, is stylistically linked with the Sarapis head (p. 166) also in this material, and is Antonine or Severan. All we have, apart from one or two lumps of damaged draperies, are two pieces from the head (pl. 10) showing the mural crown which characterises such personifications. Fox carefully marks the dowel-holes in the fractured surfaces, showing where repairs were executed after the first destruction of the basilica. It is impossible to tell whether this was a standing or a seated figure: in either case, the superhuman scale made it a dominant work of art, and it is one of the few known to have been fabricated in Britain out of native stone by a first-rate continental sculptor.[32] Another statue, this time in yellowish sandstone but again of superhuman scale, is represented by a fragment of a sandalled foot. It presumably came from an imperial statue.[33]

Another imperial statue, likewise of superhuman size, but in bronze, also stood in the basilica. The only piece certainly belonging to it is a lappet (*pteryx*) from the heavy kilt of the ceremonial armour worn by emperors and generals, best represented by the Prima Porta statue of Augustus. The fragment (pl. 34g) has been bent upwards and fractured from the parent mass, which would have been composed, as far as possible, of prefabricated elements brazed together. Very few cuirassed bronze statues have been reported from Britain: parts of a *pteryx* and cloak (*paludamentum*) were found in the headquarters-building at the legionary fortress of Caerleon, and part of another *pteryx* in the headquarters at Segontium fort. The present statue may have been as much as a century older than the Tutela, for long *pteryges* of the type in evidence tended to disappear in favour of a shorter and less cumbersome variety in the course of the second century.[34]

Joyce's 'great prize' from the basilica, the bronze eagle now at Stratfield Saye, has been left to the last. Described by Professor Jocelyn Toynbee as 'by far the most superbly naturalistic rendering of any bird or beast as yet yielded by Roman Britain', the eagle—a hollow casting 23 cm. from beak to tail, 15 cm. high and weighing 1.6 kg.—was found, in circumstances already described (p. 71), in the most southerly of the offices. The modelling of the body is excellent (pl. 34c) and was achieved by casting, without *ciselure*. The attitude is as poised for flight, the head being raised and turned to the right. The wings are missing, but the modelling beneath them is so good that they must certainly have been extended and raised. The legs are separately made and inserted, somewhat crude, and almost certainly part of the repairs executed after the first destruction of the basilica. The back has been greatly modified to form a seating for a second pair of wings; the impression of their feathering on a small ridge of brazing-metal shows that the workmanship was rough. A torn and raised edge at one corner of the slot is connected with the ultimate Roman fate of the eagle, which, like the cuirassed statue mentioned above, was smashed to pieces for the sake of its metal, no doubt in latest or sub-Roman times.

As we have seen, Joyce drew parallels from Trajan's Column, which he had studied in the course of a visit to Rome, to suggest that this had been a legionary eagle. However, the presence of such a standard at Silchester can never have been more than momentary, and the history of repair and subsequent damage leads to the conclusion that the bronze, like the Tutela which experienced the same vicissitudes, was a permanent ornament of the basilica. It was probably part of a larger composition, accompanying a statue of an emperor, or of Jupiter, or possibly was surmounted by a small bust of Jupiter or the like.[35] Joyce also says that it was gilded, but it seems probable that he mistook a gleam of the metal underlying the thin grey-green patina for gilding.

A strip of decorated bronze, bearing acanthus-foliage partly covered in silver-foil (pl. 34f) may close this chapter. Fox thought it may have come from an official throne, but parallels are not close, and it is more likely that it formed part of the framing of a statue-pedestal.[36]

10

The Public Baths

After following the original layout, it will be sufficient for our purposes to indicate the most important changes which took place in this great building of Insula XXXIIIA.[1] The rooms were arranged in a row, the usual design, and as likely as not the hand of a military architect is to be detected in the plan (fig. 15).[2] From first to last, the accommodation comprised the following: (1) an entrance porch (*porticus*); (2) a latrine (*latrina*); (3) an exercise-yard (*palaestra*); (4) an undressing-room (*apodyterium*), as the Romans called it; (5) a cold room with plunge-bath and provision for a shower (*frigidarium*); (6) a warm room, serving mainly as an antechamber to those leading off (*tepidarium*); (7) a hot room containing a hot bath and a laver of cool water (*caldarium*); and (8) a hot dry room, the so-called 'Spartan' bath (*laconicum* or *sudatorium*). Various other rooms were also provided, some probably as massage-rooms (*unctoria*). The original building measured some 43.5 m. from north to south and 23 m. from east to west.

Cleansing the body by means of perspiration is a very ancient practice and is found throughout Europe and beyond. In Roman times, the process depended firstly on the inducement of perspiration by exercise; and the dirt and sweat, oil too if applied at this stage, were removed with a hollow-bladed strigil in the hot room. Several strigils have been found at Silchester (fig. 16, 10), as well as fragments of the small oil-bottles (fig. 36, 9) which often made a set with a pair of these implements, and a fragment of a bronze dipper. A dip in the cold bath, or a shower, to close the pores of the skin, was the next and often the final stage. The wraps and towels used would have been of fine wool or linen, and not the Turkish cotton towelling in use today. Soap was not used.[3]

There is a small possibility that the baths were divided in Periods III-V, so that men and women could use them at the same time: otherwise, following the usual practice, women would have bathed in the mornings—i.e. before the rooms had reached their highest temperature—and men in the

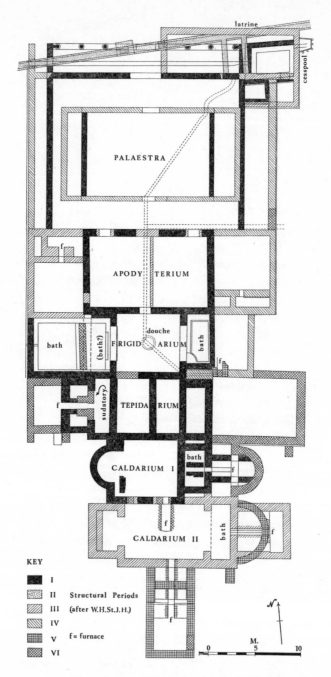

KEY

- ■ I
- ▨ II — Structural Periods
- ▨ III — (after W.H.St.J.H.)
- ▨ IV
- ▦ V — f = furnace
- ▦ VI

latrine

cesspool

PALAESTRA

APODYTERIUM

bath

(bath?)

douche

FRIGIDARIUM

bath

f

TEPIDARIUM

sudatory

f

CALDARIUM I

bath

f

CALDARIUM II

bath

f

f

N

M.
0   5   10

15. Plan of the public baths, Insula XXXIIIA

afternoons and evenings.[4] The baths of the inn (p. 141) are a rare and interesting case of separate accommodation being provided for the sexes, again as a modification of an existing system.

HYPOCAUSTS

The means of heating the rooms was by hypocaust; and since hypocausts are widely found in houses also, it will be convenient to discuss the system here. A basement cavity, about a metre deep, opened off a furnace constructed in an outer wall at foundation-level. Heat from a fire kindled here circulated under the floor, which was suspended on a forest of small pillars usually made of brick; where less heat was needed, the whole basement was not excavated, a few radiating channels being sufficient to distribute a moderate heat (pl. 37, fig. 17). The heat and gases passed out through small chimney-flues of box-tiles laid flush with the inner surface of the walls and plastered over.

Modern studies of hypocausts depend on the experimental work carried out by the late Fritz Kretzschmer at the Saalburg, where a room containing an installation had been reconstructed in Wilhelminian times. Subsequent observations have extended but modified Kretzschmer's conclusions.[5] There are three salient differences between the hypocaust and any modern method of solid-fuel 'central' heating. In the first place, there generally had to be a furnace for every room, or closely-connected suite; and there was no possibility of the heating being extended to an upper storey, if there was such a thing. In the second place, it may be pointed out that the modern furnace has a grate and a large, tall chimney to provide a strong draught. A modern furnace will therefore burn as much oxygen as the draught will pull through the grate, contact between air and fuel being very intimate. The Roman furnace had no grate, and contact between the air and the fuel was merely superficial, so that the carbon was the dominant partner. In a hypocaust, therefore, the height of the flues had to be carefully adjusted to the requirements of a low but steady fire. Normal living-rooms had four to six chimneys, spaced more or less equidistantly, or in the corners. Their total cross-section was similar to that of a modern domestic chimney. The height of the flues was about 3 to 4 m. above the ground; where rooms were very large, the number of flues and their height was naturally greater. In the *aula Palatina* at Trier, where the walls are 30 m. high, the chimneys are carried up 7.7 m. above the floor, and they then turn at an angle through the walls to debouch some 2.25 m. higher, on the outside. The entire heating-plant is contained below the level of the windows.[6] Another example where traces of the installations have been preserved is the Hunting Baths at Leptis Magna,

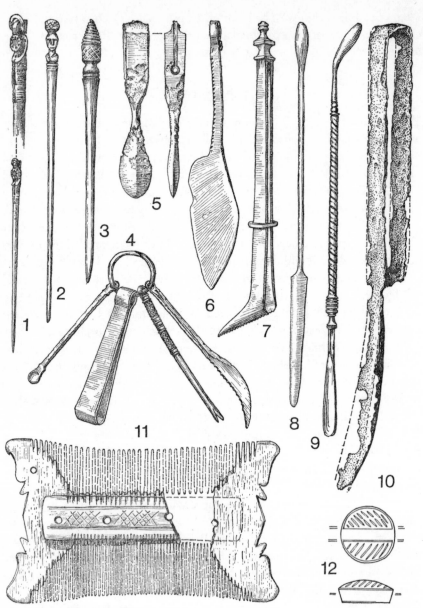

16. Dress, toilet and surgical articles. 1, brass dress-pin, one of a linked pair (with silver ring, see enlarged detail, and red enamel inlay: north British). 2–3, bone hair-pins. 4, bronze toilet-set (ear-pick, tweezers, nail-cleaner, tooth-pick). 5, bronze scalpel-handle with slot for steel blade. 6, bronze razor. 7, bronze artery-forceps. 8, bronze spatula-probe. 9, bronze ligula-probe with stem inlaid with silver wire. 10, iron strigil (blade half-missing). 11, bone comb. 12, jet bead with double perforation. Scales, 5/8, no. 12, 1/1

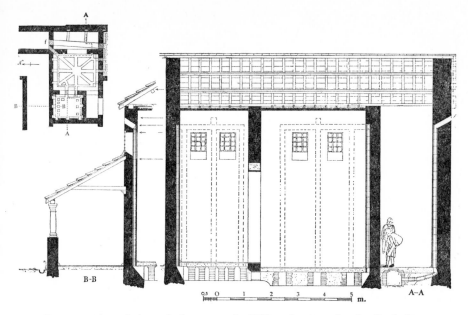

17. Reconstruction of domestic hypocaust in XIX.2, showing also detail of clerestory windows and corridor

where chimneys are vertical throughout, piercing the vaulted roof about 4.5 m. above ground-level.[7] The normal practice was probably to turn the flues through the walls, so that they debouched below the wide eaves of the building. Where flues ran up an internal wall, a duct must have conveyed the gases to an outside wall: a single, fairly large, outlet is shown, for example, above window-level in a relief of a building in the Simpelveld sarcophagus (Leiden Museum).[8] Louvred tiles and chimney-pots are far too rare ever to have had any normal connection with hypocausts.

The third difference with a modern system is that the hypocaust worked within a far smaller temperature-range. Modern radiators are small in relation to the size of the space heated, and are consequently kept very hot: but the hypocaust heated the entire floor, and the walls also contributed. The floor was made of such a thickness that the upper surface became only moderately warm, except in the special conditions of *sudatoria* where ancient writers' expressions such as *fervens pavimentum, cella solearis,* show that slippers had to be worn.[9]

The Saalburg experiments showed that the structure absorbed most of the heat produced in a first firing; but after twelve hours, the temperature in the room began to rise, and ultimately it became clear that a steady 23° could be maintained simply by stoking twice a day, the mouth of the furnace being generally kept closed. After the initial firing, the Saalburg experiment employed charcoal as the fuel, the consumption being about 1 kg./hr. for a room of some 69 cu. m. In many hypocausts, brushwood, heavy timber, rubbish, and even coal (though not at Silchester, where little coal occurred) were used.[10]

Both the Trier basilica and the Leptis installation had walls completely jacketed with columns of flue-tiles, laterally pierced to permit the circulation of heat over the entire wall-area. Such a *tubulatio* is often found in baths, and sometimes served as the main radiant surface.[11] The Saalburg room also had one, though there had not been one originally; and some fault in the construction, or Kretzschmer's blocking of four of the eight chimneys on the grounds that they were too many, resulted in a loss of circulation within the jacketed area. This led to an erroneous deduction that tubulated walls do not heat. In the Leptis baths, an impression in the mortar rendering shows that the upper ends of the jacket were connected by a horizontal duct of the kind discussed above.[12]

In no case did a hypocaust allow of the direct admission of 'hot air', and surviving remains which give an opposite impression have been wrongly interpreted. If the fire was maintained, the gases admitted to the room would have included not only dust and grime, but also carbon monoxide; if, on the other hand, the fire was let out and then rekindled when the temperature had dropped, the whole concept was rendered nonsensical. This section may therefore be closed with reference to a duct embedded in the basement-floor of the second or added *caldarium* at Silchester baths (pl. 21). It led across the room from the stoke-hole, and branched left and right to run to the walls of the alcove opposite. There was a very slight rise over the course of some 15 m. The excavators suggested that the purpose of the flue was to admit warmed, clean air to the room above, by means of vertical flues at the ends of the branches, and this interpretation was adopted by Macdonald in his study of the fort-baths at Chesters. Many such flues have since been recorded or noted in earlier publications. They almost always share with Silchester the fact, inconvenient for the theory expressed, that their intake is in the stoke-hole, amid dirt and ash. Some flues, at Wraxall Roman villa (Som.) and at Zugmantel fort, led into drains and were clearly themselves to be classed as drains. In the subterranean hypocaust-basements, drains were a sensible provision, and in view of the fact that no vertical connection has ever been found, all these flues are so to be described.[13]

DESCRIPTION: PERIOD I (fig. 15)

The portico of the original design was 20 m. long, and had an octastyle façade of Bath stone columns of the usual provincial Tuscan Order, about 3 m. high: stumps of these were preserved under the metalling of the street which was carried past the building (pl. 20, p. 47). The *palaestra* consisted of a gravelled court surrounded by a half-open ambulatory, welcome shade or shelter: not here the covered basilica found in some baths, Caerwent forum-baths among them. The latrine at the north-east corner, approached through a small lobby, has about 11.5 m. run of timber seating over a well-built brick drain 1 m. deep and half as wide, continuously flushed, as we have already seen (p. 89). The accommodation is interestingly compared with the 10.5 m. run provided for two cohorts, or about 960 men, at the legionary fortress of Caerleon.[14] In the middle of the chamber, there would have been a wash-hand basin and a tub to hold the sponges (more probably moss or rags in Britain, perhaps) used in place of toilet-paper.[15]

The undressing-room had a floor of *opus signinum,* white cement into which small pieces of broken brick had been incorporated and brought to a smooth surface to produce an agreeable figured appearance; the plastered walls were painted white. There would have been large, high windows in the east and west walls, above the level of the wooden shelves or lockers provided to hold bathers' clothes.[16] The *frigidarium* was in three divisions: the central part, paved with small bricks set on edge herringbonewise, had as its chief feature the Purbeck marble emplacement for the cold shower, very shallow and about 1.5 m. across;[17] while the eastern division—probably also the western, though all trace had vanished in later work—held a plunge-bath, measuring about 2.5 by 5 m., and no doubt built up, on the side facing the room, to provide a little more than the 1 m. depth otherwise available.[18] The central division would have been rather higher than the others, so that windows could again be provided in the east and west walls.

The *tepidarium* was also divided, but into two. On the west side opened the sudatory suite, the *sudatorium* itself being about 1.8 by 4.3 m., and the antechamber, which existed to conserve the heat of the other, a little larger: both were heated from a furnace to the west. On the east side, there was another small room, perhaps an *unctorium,* or for service. The lighting of the *tepidarium* will have been as before.

Lastly comes the *caldarium,* 6 by 9.5 m., with a large apse on the sunny side, the west: here there will have been a raised *labrum* of cool water for the bathers to refresh themselves, and following normal practice there will have been large windows.[19] At the opposite end, a rectangular alcove held the hot-water bath, built at floor-level just above the inner mouth of the furnace of the hypocaust extending throughout the chamber. Nothing remained of this bath, but discoveries at Pompeii and elsewhere enable us to imagine its character. At the foot of the back wall, there would have been an opening directly into a boiler supported on the side-walls of the furnace, which projected to the rear. The boiler, of lead plates as at Boscoreale, or of bronze as in the Stabian baths, would have been of the semi-circular cross-section which gave rise, together with the joints of the component plates, to the Roman name of *testudo* (tortoise). The bottom of the boiler would have been a trifle lower than that of the bath, so that convection-currents would have carried hot-water into the bath, and allowed cooled water to flow back for re-heating. The installation required an overhead replenishment-tank, possibly a reservoir as well.[20]

On general grounds, we may suppose that the heated rooms were vaulted, with a half-dome in the *caldarium* apse and barrel-vaults elsewhere; or, in the squarish rooms, simple intersected vaults such as may still be seen in the *frigidarium* of the Cluny baths in Paris.[21] If Vitruvian precepts were followed, the vaulting would have sprung above a cornice set at a height equal to the breadth of the chamber, or 6 m. above the floor in the case of the *caldarium*. But the walling of the baths is only 75 cm. thick, and could not have sustained a solid *concameratio*: the vaulting, therefore, would have been of the hollow type found in XXXIV.1 (p. 197) and indeed in the case of the great bath at Bath.[22] Such vaults would have been roofed in tile in our climate, and not left exposed as at Leptis Magna.

Mention was made of windows, and a large piece of fallen masonry from the apse of the second (Period III) *caldarium* preserved part of a jamb and a tiled lintel, with a relieving-arch above: the opening had been over 1 m. in height.[23] Fragments of bluish-green cast window-panes were found here and there (cf. p. 207). The same block of masonry which contained the window-embrasure also showed that the building had been externally rendered in stucco, and of this ample traces were seen, some in position, at various points.[24]

The water supply of the baths has been discussed previously (p. 88).

THE ALTERATIONS

Hope describes some twenty-six substantive changes, and no-one reading his report can fail to be impressed with his handling of a difficult task of interpretation. But it has to be understood that the periods simply represent groups of alterations considered to be mutually complementary, there being no way by which their exact contemporaneity could be decided. A modern account would be full of references to the correspondence of mortars, details of stonework, etc., and would quote datable relics if any occurred in significant places. While we may presume that structural peculiarities were given due weight in his interpretation, little is said of them. Having read the report many times, however, and having checked it against what was, for the time, a lavish photographic coverage, I venture to differ from Hope in only three (or perhaps four) particulars.

Period II saw the remodelling of the porch in response to the laying of the street; the latrine was extended to the street-line also. *Period III* embraced considerable enlargements. The latrine was again rebuilt, and now projected quite as much into the street as the original portico would once have done: we may presume the elapse of a fair period of time before this would have been permitted. The *apodyterium* was divided by a thin partition, and separate entrances into each part contrived; a heated room arose on the west, balanced by another (if we may differ from Hope, who made it part of Period IV) on the east: both were winter *apodyteria,* no doubt. The *frigidarium* was also extended on the west at this time (again a departure from Hope). But the most important alteration was the addition of a second *caldarium* on the south, measuring some 5.8 by 14.3 m.

In *Period IV,* the *palaestra* was widened to align with the *apodyterium,* and the cold bath was doubled in area. In the *tepidarium,* a new *opus signinum* floor was laid, its surface still, when opened, of the original fine, marble-like quality: it was later covered with black and white mosaic (though possibly earlier than Hope believed), which was continued over the lower part of the walls, a very rare feature in Britain, so far as is known.[25] The alcove on the east of this room was given a raised floor, but details are uncertain.

Period V, as arranged by Hope, is dated by a coin of Crispus (317–26) found with others below a new concrete floor in the *apodyterium* (p. 72), but there is no absolute reason to reckon this alteration with the others, so far as is known. The latter included the removal of the cold bath to the west side of the *frigidarium* (pl. 19), where it measured about 5.5 by 8 m., and perhaps 1 m. deep: its drainage has been discussed previously (p. 90). Coins in the waste-pipe—one wonders how they got there—ranged from Antoninus Pius (138–61) to Carausius (286–93), and since coins of the British usurper disappeared at once upon the establishment of central control in 296, we perhaps have a hint here that the alteration in the *apodyterium* is rather later than the generality of Period V work. Further south, the surviving *sudatorium* in the *tepidarium*-range was dispensed with, and in the second *caldarium* an apse was built on the east side to balance that on the west, while the hot bath was removed to the middle of the south wall, where a new central furnace was built. The large furnace-chamber beyond is a prominent feature of the plan.

Period VI was in some degree a return to the days of old. The second *caldarium* was demolished, and its materials were removed,[26] part of the furnace-chamber surviving as a wood-store. The original *caldarium* was extended on the east to an overall length of 17 m., and there terminated in an apse: its furnace was again central, in the south wall. The *tepidarium* was radically altered by the building of a new room, some 6 by 9 m., on the east, heated by a composite hypocaust with both channels and pillars. The cold bath in the *frigidarium* was reduced to permit access to a new range on the west of the *tepidarium,* the partition in the *apodyterium* was removed, and that chamber turned into one large hall floored in tile, over 25 m. long. Lastly, the level of the *palaestra* was raised, with consequential changes in the ambulatory and the latrine.

Presumably the great enlargement of the baths in Period III reflects, at least to some extent, the growth in the population of the town which it seems reasonable to suppose took place in the second century, after the imposition of the street-grid (cf. p. 62). Another point also requires comment: the apparent correspondence, between Periods III and VI, of the erection and demolition of a second *caldarium* and of a partition in the *apodyterium.* Do these features hint at a provision to enable men and women to bath at the same time? Possibly: yet we cannot see how private access to the southern *caldarium* could have been contrived, or how the facilities of the one *frigidarium* and the one *tepidarium,* not to mention the one latrine, could have been shared. No doubt a great deal of evidence has disappeared: but it is safer, perhaps, to take the addition of the second *caldarium* as an index of the growth in population, and the partition in the *apodyterium* as a delimitation of dressing-room space from that allowed for exercise on wet days. Here the turning of the *apodyterium,* in Period VI, into a large, plain hall is not without significance, while the demolition of the Period III *caldarium* could be taken as a measure to conserve fuel.

FINDS FROM THE BATHS

Very few objects are reported from the baths. Of statuary and other adornments, all had gone apart from a small plain altar, incorporated into a filling below a later floor: from analogy, it might have received offerings in honour of Fortuna, who presided not merely over games of chance, such as were often played in such places, but over the well-being of the bathers themselves who, naked as they were, believed themselves to be more subject to the influence of malign spirits than when attired.[27] Personal relics from the baths include a pretty gold earring of the second or third century (fig. 18, 2, seen with another from Silchester); a bone pin with gold foil wrapped round the head; and a large number of ordinary pins from a filling below a Period VI floor, which possibly represent merchandise on sale in the baths.

Such were the Callevan *thermae*. More potent than fancy to repopulate them with their gay and noisy crowd, is a smug passage from one of Seneca's letters: it appears that he had taken rooms over a small bath-house:[28]

> . . . Imagine all sorts of uproar, fit to make you hate your ears! Toughs are put through their paces, they throw their hands about laden with dumb-bells, and I hear their grunts and gasps every time they expel their treasured breath. . . . Then some idle person, content with an ordinary oil-massage, forces himself on my notice, and up comes the smack of the masseur's hand, changing its sound according to whether it is laid on cupped or flat. If the umpire of a ball-game puts in an appearance, and starts to count the tosses, it's all over. The picture is not complete without some quarrelsome fellow, a thief caught in the act, or the man who loves the sound of his own voice in the bath—not to mention those who jump in with a tremendous splash. Besides those whose voices (if nothing else) are good, think of the high, strident call of the depilator, continually advertising his presence, never quiet save when he plucks someone's armpits and makes his customer cry out for him; or the assorted cries of the pastry-cook, the sausage-seller, the confectioner and all the hawkers of refreshment selling their wares, each in his distinctive sing-song . . . But I, of course, pay no more heed to this than to a roaring stream or waterfall. . . .

PERSONALIA FROM VARIOUS SITES IN THE TOWN

Let us now cast our Silchester net a little wider and glance at one or two subjects conveniently brought under this heading. Small toilet-accessories are among the commonest finds on Roman sites and betoken the attention paid to personal cleanliness and appearance (fig. 16). Best-known are the little forked, occasionally claw-shaped, nail-cleaners, tweezers and ear-picks, found singly or in sets. Double-sided bone and boxwood combs and fragments of white-metal mirrors appear. As regards cosmetics, the most interesting relic (fig. 36, 6) is part of a thin-blown glass bird, delicate blue in colour, which once contained white or pink face-powder, heat-sealed in a north Italian factory of the first century.[29] Then there is a shard from a pottery flagon inscriped CARV—, which has been interpreted as (*oleum*) *carvinum*, 'oil of walnuts', used for treating baldness among other complaints:[30] an explanation no more speculative—and perhaps no more correct —than that advanced to account for the seeds of *Atropa belladonna*, the

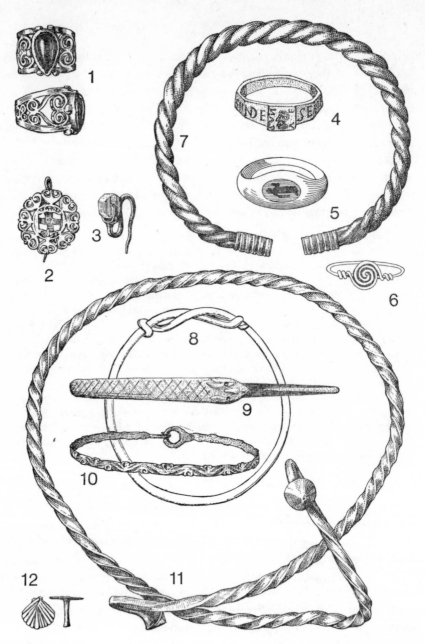

18. Jewellery. 1, filigree gold ring, with garnet setting. 2–3, gold earrings, one with mother-of-emerald setting, the other with setting missing. 4, gold ring with head of Venus, Christianised by inscription *Seniciane, vivas in De(o)* (now at The Vyne, Basingstoke). 5, lost gold ring with cornelian setting, intaglio of Ceres. 6, bronze ring of twisted wire. 7, brass bracelet. 8, bronze expanding bracelet. 9, bronze serpentine bracelet. 10, typical late Roman bronze bracelet. 11, silver collar or torque. 12, silver pin-head. Scale, 1/1

deadly nightshade, found in pits and wells, namely that the berries had been used in a preparation to dilate the pupils of the eyes.[31]

In the first and fourth centuries especially, Callevan menfolk no doubt followed the general custom, and were shaved. It seems that water was the only lotion applied: so that shaving with a bronze razor like that of fig. 16, 6 must have been tedious and uncomfortable, and the steel razor of which the little bronze handle survives, in the form of a bust of Minerva, was not much better.[32]

For dress, the reader must look elsewhere.[33] There is little direct evidence from Calleva: a scrap of late Roman plain-weave linen cloth, part of a jerkin of thin leather, and a number of fragmentary sandals, some with thick studded soles and others more of a mocassin pattern, exhaust the list. On the other hand, the Silchester collection, like most large Roman collections, contains a wealth of articles of personal adornment. The illustrations must speak for themselves (figs. 18–19), though attention may be drawn particularly to the silver torque, a rare find (fig. 18, 11),[34] and the pretty filigree gold ring set with an almandine garnet, certainly meant for a child's finger (fig. 18, 1)[35]—probably the middle finger, for Pliny tells us that in Gaul and Britain, this was the ring-finger.[36] The polygonal gold ring found in ploughing in 1786 (fig. 18,4) is of interest: although it bears a crude intaglio bust labelled as VENVS, it has been Christianised by the addition of an inscription around the hoop SENICIANE VIVAS IIN DE(O) ('Mayest thou live in God, Senicianus'). This is probably the very ring mentioned on a leaden curse-tablet set up in the later fourth century at Lydney temple (Glos.): 'To the god Nodens, Silvianus has lost a ring, he promises half its value to Nodens. Let him not grant health among those of the name Senicianus, until he brings it right back to the Temple of Nodens'.—'[curse] renewed'.[37] Brooches are very common, because cloaks and tunics were fastened by this means, bone and bronze toggles or dress-fasteners being quite rare by comparison. The brooches are of iron or bronze, the latter often tinned or enamelled, occasionally gilt; the pins are very thick, and unless eyelets were provided (p. 285), must have damaged all but the coarsest plaid; and even then, many varieties are so heavy that threads would have been pulled and broken. Very occasionally, a 'crossbow' brooch (cf. fig. 19, 9) was made hollow, to reduce the weight; and in the arm of such a Silchester specimen, badly crushed, is a soldered twist of wire into which the spindle securing the pin was screwed. Brooches were worn with the 'head' either up or down; and when, as was often the case, pairs were linked by a fine chain, they were naturally worn 'head downwards', for the chain-loop is on the 'head'. The penannular brooch was common throughout

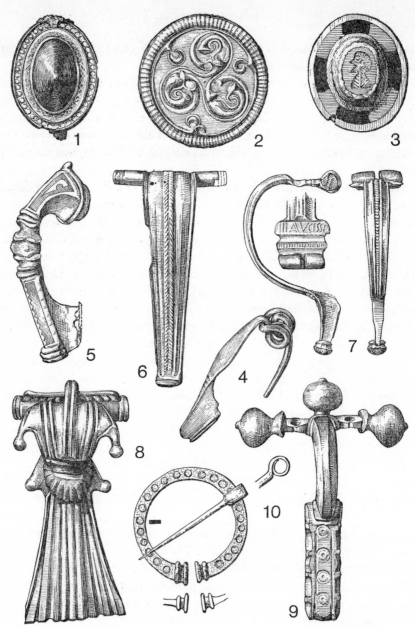

19. Brooches. 1–3, plate brooches, 1, gilt with dark green glass setting, fourth century; 2, with applied repoussé leaf of bronze bearing late Celtic design, third century; 3, enamel (dull opaque red and dark green, with moulded intaglio head), possibly local, fourth century. 4, bronze, simple one-piece type, first century. 5, 'trumpet', bronze formerly enamelled, first century. 6, tinned bronze, continental, first century. 7, brass, with maker's name Aucissa, continental, first century. 8, tinned bronze, continental, first century. 9, 'crossbow', bronze, fourth century. 10, penannular, probably continental, fourth century. Scale, 1/1

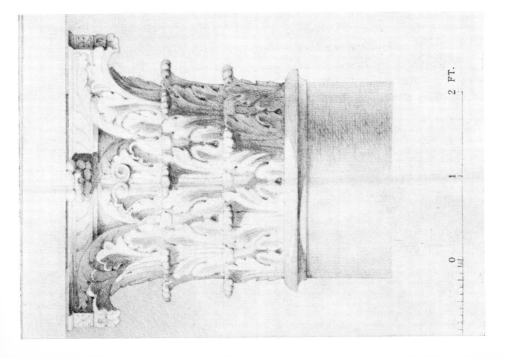

17 Corinthian capital of Bath stone restored, from the basilica

18 Head of Sarapis, Portland stone

19　The public baths. A general view from the west showing the late cold bath and the *tepidarium* range

20　The public baths. The original portico, with stumps of its columns which had survived below street-metalling

21　The public baths. Drainage-duct beneath the basement-floor of the added *caldarium*

the period (fig. 19, 10): when the pin had been pushed through the cloth, the hoop was rotated so that the end of the pin overrode it.

The bracelets include jet, shale and glass examples as well as bronze; the pins are mainly for the coiffure, and include many with large and elaborate heads. Needles, a related item, may be mentioned here: they are astonishingly large and coarse, and the fine sewing-needles must have decayed completely away. The 81 mm. specimen shown in fig. 34, 9 is the finest preserved, and is of bronze.

SURGICAL INSTRUMENTS

There are several bronze surgical instruments in the Silchester collection, and these, with one or two related subjects, may be discussed at this juncture. The most interesting is an artery-forceps with serrated jaws and a sliding ring to retain the pressure (fig. 16, 7). The handle of a scalpel is of typical form, and its blade-like shape was suitable for probing, blunt dissection, or applying ointment. Among the objects not illustrated are a retractor for pulling back the edge of a wound for inspection, and possibly also used in dentistry; and there are simple probes or olivaries, combined either with spatulae or with long, narrow ointment-spoons useful for extracting salves from the long, narrow-necked blown-glass phials frequently in evidence. The dividing-line between surgical and toilet instruments is hard to draw, and was not drawn in antiquity. We may well believe, however, that the ligula-probe of unusually good quality, with a stem inlaid with silver wire (fig. 16, 9) came from a surgeon's trousse. Small bronze balance-arms and stone palettes for grinding medicaments and rolling pills also occur: green and black porphyry, Purbeck marble and fine-grained British greenstone examples are included. A bronze lid from a compartment of a medicine-chest is also to be seen.[38]

As regards the *materia medica* itself, a few tiny lumps of realgar or sandarac, the orange-red crystalline disulphide of arsenic, found in 1895, should be brought under this heading rather than that of pigments, though the substance is the artist's red orpiment: no other British instance is recorded, either of the substance itself, or of its occurrence in the wall-paintings so far analysed chemically. *Summa ejus dos septica,* Pliny remarks: 'its greatest quality is in septic conditions'.[39] Otherwise, we can but assume that the real or fancied medicinal properties of thirty or more plants in the Silchester botanical record would have been known to Callevan leechdom: among them are two which were cultivated in the gardens of the legionary hospital at Neuss—perforate St. John's wort used in the treatment of burns, sciatica, and other troubles, and henbane, decocted as a dangerously powerful anodyne.[40]

The Praetorium *or Inn*

The inn, Insula VIII, measures some 61 by 64 m. Excavation has been incomplete, and a few details are added from aerial photographs (fig. 20).[1] The insula appears to have been formed by suppressing the boundary between two of ordinary size, and the street on the dividing-line may not have been metalled (and then only as far as the main entrance) until the inn was built, possibly in the third century, the date of a close parallel in plan at Richborough.[2] There are few other buildings of consequence in the insula.

There are three ranges of rooms around a courtyard totally enclosed on the fourth side by a wall; if not laid out as a garden, this area may have been provided for soldiers spending the night in tents, or ordinary travellers doing so, as Schleiermacher has suggested in a study of the Kempten building mentioned below.[3] One or two patches of gravel in the outer yard, which was reached by an oblique metalled track leading from the entrance-street, probably mark the sites of timber-built stables and vehicle-sheds. Beyond again is the bath-house, reached by a covered alley at the south side of the outer yard.

In the initial state, the building was composed of three wings of very simple design, containing a row of rooms between outer and inner corridors. Each wing had an entrance upon the court. The most interesting feature is the clear division of the accommodation of each wing into suites, the reception-rooms being confined to the west wing. The arrangement, when taken with the extensive set of baths, fully confirms Fox's interpretation of the building as a whole as an inn.

Joyce comments on the poor state of the remains. The rooms in the south wing appear to have had plain cement floors, and of some only the flint bedding survived.[4] The floor-levels were often covered with a thick bed of yellow clay, which had come from the filling of the half-timbered super-structure (cf. p. 199); only in the west wing, where there were hypocausts,

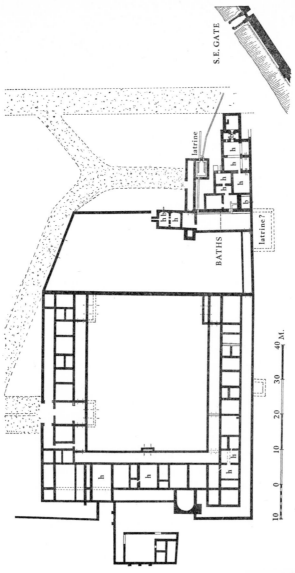

20. Plan of the *praetorium* or inn, Insula VIII
b, baths; *h*, hypocausts

will the flint masonry have continued to the full height of the walls. Apart from the apsidal, probably vaulted room added in the west wing, the walling was in general about 60 cm. thick, corridors and rooms alike, and an upper storey is hardly to be inferred from this evidence, except at one point mentioned below. The elevation will have taken the form of lofty rooms with clerestory windows above the level at which the pentice roofs of the corridors abutted.

The main entrance in the north wing was nearly 6 m. wide, and had columns on piers at either side. A spacious vestibule within gave access to the court and to the inner corridor on either hand. On the west, an isolated room was no doubt a porter's lodge. On the east, there are two suites, the first of four good rooms set two and two on either side of one which has been laterally divided, and the second of one large room only, with another laterally divided annexed to it. Such divided rooms occur also in the southern range and may be taken to have been bedrooms. A room at the east end of the north wing may have been for service use.

At the east end of the south wing, there is a single large room rather than a suite, and since the depth of yellow clay was no less than 86 cm. here, more than double the usual thickness, it seems likely that the superstructure was carried up here to provide a store-room on a second floor. A good deal of rubbish, oyster-shells and so forth lay in the inner corridor hereabouts, and perhaps the kitchen was situated at this end of the building. West of the doorway in the inner corridor, there are two suites, the first double (two pairs of bedrooms flanked on either side by 'sitting-rooms'), and the second possessing a large 'sitting-room' and a pair of bedrooms, one of them heated by 'overflow' from a hypocaust in the west wing. A stub of walling here suggests that there has been some change in the original layout.

As first constructed, the west wing comprised a single admirably-balanced suite arranged about a central room some 5 by over 6.5 m., to which a porch in the garden-court corresponded. On either side were pairs of bedrooms, and a set of symmetrically-disposed chambers of varying size, which terminated in further bedrooms sharing internal walls with the rooms in the ends of the south and north ranges. Alterations have confused this simple layout to some extent. The outer corridor was overbuilt, in order to provide larger rooms on the north (where the 1893 excavators thought the kitchen lay) and on the south, the outer corridor then being carried round these extensions. The apsidal chamber was also added at some period: this room, nearly 6 by 5 m., was perhaps an audience-chamber or at very least a grand dining-room: there is a similar chamber in an inn at Caerwent, and the great villa of Bignor (Sussex) provides another instance.[5] The partition between the rooms in front of this chamber was probably taken down. Now or at another time, the main central room of the range was equipped with a hypocaust, as were two others, all with internal furnaces.

Outside the west wing, and connected to it by a buttressed wall, stood a rectangular annexe containing a building some 15 by 7.5 m. It had two doorways, and partitions at one end; possibly we may see stables, fodder- and tack-rooms here. A second annexe to the north, long and narrow, is more difficult to understand.

The outer corridor of the south wing led to the baths, which form an L-shaped block some 28.7 m. from north to south and 34.7 m. from east to west. Both arms terminated in heated accommodation. The workmanship was throughout of a neat and solid order,[6] but varied in materials, so that there is evidently a difference in date between the wings: the slight divergence of alignment in the northern range also points to this. The public portico and the adjacent latrine were additions to an original southern block, the building at first being intended to be entirely private: the north block, in this case, would form a third period of work. The cold bath in the southern suite, where the skeleton was found (p. 81), seems to have been modified at some period, as do walls at the extremity of the range.

The chief feature of interest is the duplication of *frigidarium, tepidarium* and *caldarium* (cf. p. 121) in the northern arm: in the last of these, there was a hot bath in the apse, and the leaden outlet-pipe remained; but in the *frigidarium* there could only have been a shower. There are also signs that the large *apodyterium* of the main set was also divided, for the floor of the northern part was of plain red tessellation, while that of the southern part— boards laid on joists bedded on brick-mortar sills[7]—represents a later alteration. Thus we have provision for both sexes to bath at the same time; and it is noteworthy that similar arrangements were found in the baths of the Godmanchester inn.[8]

The southern arm of the baths contains the normal sequence of rooms, conceived on a more generous scale. The *frigidarium* possessed a plunge-bath about two-thirds the size of that in the first period of the public baths, east side; the walling of the alcove was painted in 'honeysuckle' pattern.[9] The thick floor of the *piscina* rested on a stratum of box-tiles at the level of the hypocaust-basement to the east, probably a means to prevent the concrete bedding of the floor from becoming waterlogged.[10] Also in the *frigidarium*, as a short branch of the main drain shows, there had been an installation for a shower. On the east side of the room, there was a small sudatory suite, the antechamber also giving access to the *tepidarium* which in turn led into a good-sized *caldarium* (11 by 7.5 m.), where stretches of the *tubulatio* and suspended floor remained when the building was first opened in 1833. The hot bath would have been at the east end, over the inner mouth of the furnace, and one of the alcoves on the south side presumably contained the customary laver of cool water.

The sizeable latrine behind the public porch, preserving elements of its wooden seating, etc., is an addition; the main drain continues beyond the *frigidarium* in the southern arm of the baths, and aerial photographs show a projection on the south side of the building which is probably the original latrine serving baths and inn alike.[11] The water supply and drainage have already been considered, pp. 87, 90. A large collection of relics was amassed during the 1833 excavations, including two gold rings (one possibly that shown in fig. 18, 5, with a cornelian setting engraved with a figure of Ceres),[12] but very little is known of it.

DISCUSSION OF THE PLAN

Fox remarked upon the division into suites and drew attention to the situation of the building close to the south gate and to the temple in Insula VII 'to which there must have been considerable resort on certain festivals'. The inns at Pompeii[13] were 'generally insignificant in size and accommodation, [offering] few points of comparison', but guest-houses adjacent to the Temple of Nodens at Lydney (Glos.) and the great temple at Herbord, Sanxay (near Poitiers) were of very similar design. The latter, the largest of several, was about 43 by 40 m. and, like Lydney, had an enclosed court where wheeled traffic could not enter. To these buildings may now be added those at Heddernheim and Kempten and also Godmanchester, all with enclosed courts, and all possessing baths—at Herbord the baths were elsewhere.[14] At Richborough there was clearly a building of very similar plan to that at Silchester, but only a fragment remains.[15] Various buildings outside forts have been claimed as inns, for example at Caerleon, again lacking baths, but with baths in the vicinity.[16]

So much for general comparisons. Let us turn now to other matters. To be sure of the accommodation which awaited him, the prudent traveller might consult a map of the illuminated type represented by a medieval copy known as the *Tabula Peutingeriana*, whereon standardised symbols, it has been suggested, mark three grades of inn.[17] The commonest is a building with two towers, and it is interesting to see that although most of Britain has been lost from the end of the roll, Richborough, Dover and Lympne remain and so do Canterbury, Caistor St. Edmund and Exeter, three towns of the same standing as Silchester. All these places are marked with two towers, and the close similarity in what is left at Richborough with the great Callevan building suggests that it, too, would have been similarly indicated. There are courtyard buildings on the *Tabula,* but the Richborough comparison is enough to dismiss the notion that the possession of a courtyard qualified for courtyard marking.

Can we proceed from this to determine the ancient name which was applied to the inn? Several of the buildings mentioned have been called *mansiones* by archaeologists. This is a word used of a class of lodging provided mainly for the officials, couriers, and other warrant-holders using the imperial posting-service *(cursus publicus,* cf. p. 144). The *Antonine Itinerary* must record its routes to a very great extent, and there is no doubt that each place named in the *Itinerary* lists was, or contained, a *mansio.*[18] On the other hand, the routes seem to have been worked out in connection originally with special journeys, either imperial progresses or troop-movements, for which the prior collection of food and fodder would have been requisite. Thus the itinerary from Chichester to Silchester runs, not on the direct road,[19] but via Winchester; and some well-marked Roman sites, such as Godmanchester with its inn, do not figure in the *Itinerary* at all, because they were never on such a special route, though very possibly used by the *cursus.*

The *mansiones* were not the only stages. The pilgrim's *Itinerary from Bordeaux to Jerusalem* lists relays *(mutationes)* in addition, but on the other hand—presumably because ordinary travellers were not entitled to use it—omits mention of a special grade of lodging, the *praetorium,* of which we hear from documentary sources and inscriptions. *Praetorium* is a word with a tiresome variety of meanings: commandant's residence in a fort; imperial governor's residence; and headquarters of a large estate, in addition to a type of inn or residency in which, as we learn from the *Antonine Itinerary* reference to Inicerum on the Emona-Sirmium route in the Balkans, the *mansio* might be contained.[20] The *Itinerary* lists only one *praetorium* in Britain, at the Brough-upon-Humber terminus of the first route. There must have been others, at Richborough almost certainly because the crossing to Gaul was made from there; and very likely at Silchester, terminus of Antonine routes and on the way to the Second Augustan Legion at Caerleon and, in the fourth century, to the new provincial capital at Cirencester. On his official progresses, the governor would have many matters to settle and cases to hear, and the addition of the apsidal chamber in the western range of the building might well mark the provision of an audience-chamber for the purpose. A *praetorium* was likely to be large; but although *Praetorium Agrippinae* in Zuid-Holland and two or three others marked on the *Tabula* are given the 'courtyard' symbol, *Ad Praetorium* in Dalmatia has only 'two towers', and another *praetorium* in Gaul has nothing, not even the single building used for the lowest grade of differentiated lodging. It is worth remark that the emperor Julian (355–63) comments on the *basileia* at Batnae, Syria (on the Carrhae-Hierapolis route, marked with 'two towers') as being 'by no means elaborate'—a plain, half-timbered structure with some ornamental cypresses, and fruit-trees and a vegetable-garden in the middle,[21] not very different, perhaps, from Silchester.

As the provision of a public entrance to the baths shows, the building very possibly had to be self-supporting as far as practicable, since its maintenance was a charge on the local authority, whose manager (*manceps*) would have been one of the decurions. The *étape* of the imperial post was no doubt 'in' it as at Inicerum, and as far as possible all kinds of travellers would have been encouraged to stay there except on the rare occasions of an official progress.

TRANSPORT IN ROMAN TIMES

The operations of the *cursus publicus* were strictly regulated, not least in the weight of baggage carried. As we have seen (p. 101), 1500 *librae,* say 500 kg., was the maximum load permitted to the long-distance wagon-service, astonishingly little for ox-drawn wagons. Considerations doubtless included damage to road-surfaces, wear on springless vehicles, and injury to the hooves of oxen pulling heavy carts on metalled roads. The express post, which covered some 80 km. a day, is to be compared with the early posting-services of modern Europe. In Britain, 3 to 5 miles per hour was the usual speed in the sixteenth century, and there was not much improvement until the roads had been brought up to a good standard: little enough even then, until Palmer and his mail-coach system appeared.[22] The Roman post-boys were allowed to carry only 30 *librae* of ordinary baggage or despatches; they rode without stirrups, and the bits were generally simple snaffles (cf. fig. 21, 7).[23] The horses attested at Calleva seem, with one exception, scarcely to have exceeded the stature of an Exmoor or New Forest pony, and a five-year-old immolated at Iron Age Blewburton (Berks.) probably well represents the local breed. A cart-horse of 15 hands (60 cm. to the withers) must have been totally unknown; but cavalry horses at Newstead included some highly-bred animals with more than a touch of the 'Arab' about them, and no doubt imperial couriers rode better horses than the Silchester remains generally indicate.[24] The nailed shoe was almost certainly not in use: the few instances claimed to come from stratified deposits are in no case beyond question, and the absence of shoes in Roman levels of cavalry forts and in sealed fourth-

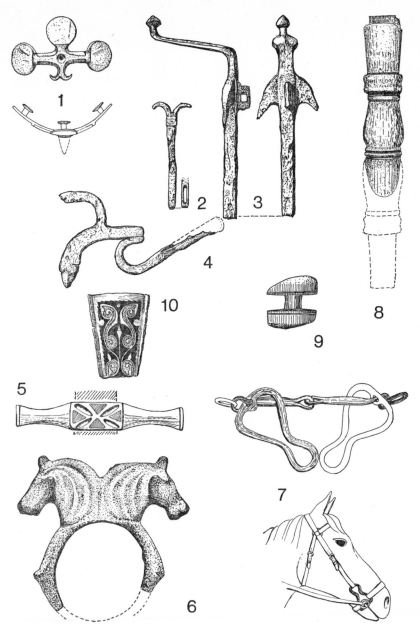

21. Miscellaneous objects. 1, bronze spur, third century. 2–3, iron linch-pins. 4, iron buttrice (farrier's tool). 5, bronze cheek-piece from harness, with red? and blue enamel, first century. 6, bronze harness-ring? 7, iron snaffle with head-stall links. 8, couch- or stool-leg, Kimmeridge shale. 9, bobbin of maple-wood. 10, side of hexagonal bronze inkwell, blue and green enamel. Scales, 1, 5, 10: 1/2. 2, 3, 4: 1/5. 6: 1/1 7, 8, 9: 1/4

century deposits of ironwork (such as ours of 1890 and 1900) combines with the silence of Roman veterinary writers upon the subject. On the other hand, an iron sole, tied on, was widely used, and there are Silchester examples including one from the 1890 'hoard'. Opinion varies as to whether they were worn to protect the hooves, when horses were worked on metalled roads, or whether they were fitted only in case of injury: the former is likely, but does not exclude the latter.[25] The farrier's paring-tool or buttrice (fig. 21, 4) is among the commonest specialised tools surviving from the Romano-British time.[26]

The express post also maintained light curricles and four-wheeled carts with loading-limits of 200 and 1000 *librae* respectively. These were pulled by horses or more often by mules, but the animals were still harnessed by yoke. The typical harness of a two-wheeler is shown on a coin of Nerva (96–8) commemorating the remission of the *vehiculatio*—the tax imposed for the maintenance of the *cursus publicus*—in Italy. It shows a pair of mules grazing; behind appear the rims of the wheels, and the up-ended shaft with its yoke, collars, and reins attached. The collar, as many reliefs also show, is only a neck-band and not at all the rigid, padded, shoulder-bearing collar, which was invented in medieval times. The ancient harness was highly defective. Too great an effort compressed the windpipe and blood-vessels of the neck, and combined with a point of traction rather too high for equids, inhibited the tractive effort.[27]

Roman four-wheelers were all basically similar, consisting of a solid wooden chassis, the floor well above the axles, with fixed front wheels. This 'flat', as it would be known to the Romany, might have box-seats for passengers; a cradle to hold a barrel of wine; or a light canvas, leather or wicker-work body. From Thrace especially comes evidence of an improved design, in which the body was suspended from leather straps; but these were *de luxe* vehicles, often decorated with appliqués and figured bronzes of distinction. The decorative bronze hooks from which the straps were hung have been found in a number of places, but one of similar form from Silchester, terminating in an eagle's head, is far too slight to have served this particular purpose, and may have held the curtains of a litter or light travelling-carriage.[28] We read in the *Theodosian Code* that eight mules were allotted to each four-wheeler in summer, and ten in winter: these figures can only relate to the establishment of beasts in a general sense and cannot be taken to mean that individual vehicles were drawn by so many animals.[29]

The metal parts of wheels are the most readily-recognised surviving parts of vehicles. In the Silchester collection, we can point to iron hub-linings and hub-rings, but the most striking objects are a pair of iron tires from a pit in

Insula XXVII.[30] They are 1.09 m. in diameter, 3 cm. wide, and 2.5 cm. thick; they have no nail-holes, and were thus knocked on to the wheels,[31] following the Iron Age practice. Several Iron Age and Roman wheels have been found in this country, very often displaying a cleverly-formed one-piece felloe doubtless steamed to shape, with a plain scarf or butt joint. There is splendid craftsmanship here: a wheel from Bar Hill had an ash felloe, eleven willow spokes, well-turned and fitted to an elm hub. Carriages fitted with such wheels cost nearly double the price allowed for those with jointed felloes, in Diocletian's maximal edict of 301.[32] Lastly we may allude to what is probably the commonest vehicle-fitting, the linch-pin, those in the collection including an unusually small specimen, and another bent at right-angles to provide a step into the vehicle. (fig. 21, 2–3).[33]

The Amphitheatre

'Tis a most nobl and beautiful concave, but intirely overgrown with thorn-bushes, briars, holly, broom, furze, oak and ash trees &c. and has from times immemorial been a yard for cattle and a watering pond; so that 'tis a wonder their trampling has not defac'd it much more. I examin'd this fine antiquity with all the exactness possbl. the terras at top, the circular walk, the whole form is not obscure. 'tis posited exactly as that before describ'd [Dorchester], with its longest diameter from north-east to south-west. its entrance north-east, tho' farthest from the city. there's an ascent to it from the entrance side, that being upon the lowest ground, at the upper end, the level of the ground is not much below the top of the terras, and vastly above that of the *arena,* so that I conceiv the better sort of the peopl went that way directly from the city into their seats. there is such a gap too in that part, from the ruin of the cave where the wild beasts were kept. an old house standing there with an orchard has forwarded its ruin from that quarter; and they have levell'd some part of the terras for their garden. . . . [pl. 2].

So Stukeley, in 1724, of the still unexcavated amphitheatre,[1] which he was the first to observe.[2] The arena measures about 49 by 40 m. superficially; the ellipsoid banks are about 15 m. wide and 5.5. m. high; both the gaps on the long axis mark entrances. A vignette of Isaac Taylor's *Map of Hampshire* (1759) shows a stretch of ruined walling near the south-west entrance, which has long since disappeared, leaving a scatter of flints and pieces of brick. A large coping-stone found near the spring in the field to the west of the amphitheatre has possibly come from the coping of the outer wall.[3]

It is presumed that the amphitheatre was a product of the intense period of building-activity at the turn of the first and second centuries. The Chichester amphitheatre was built between about 70 and 90; at Cirencester, the early second-century stone amphitheatre had a timber predecessor.[4] The only example in Britain which has been nearly fully excavated is the legionary amphitheatre at Caerleon, built about 80.[5] It had an arena about 56 by 42 m. The upcast from the digging of the arena went to form the banks, which were contained by an inner and an outer wall. Above the ground storey, the superstructure was timber-framed, and vaulting in the eight entrances (two processional on the long axis, two with chambers at arena-level and boxes above, on the short axis, and four subsidiary) suggests that the hope was to complete the building in stone at some date.

The Caerleon amphitheatre is of far too elaborate a design to take as a model for Silchester. The Cirencester amphitheatre, however, appears to have had only the long-axis processional entrances, and the same is true of Dorchester, where a Neolithic earthwork conveniently housed the structure. The Cirencester amphitheatre has an arena a trifle larger than Silchester, perhaps, but the banks are much higher. The seats, of timber, were carried on a series of stepped concentric stone foundations in the banks, and a similar arrangement appears at Carmarthen, where the arena is about 41 by 26 m.[6] Old accounts refer to five 'rows of seats' at Silchester, but nothing of this sort appears in Stukeley's drawing and nothing can be seen there now. In the cases mentioned, the structure was revealed only by excavation, and any effect at Silchester was probably produced by cattle or weathering. The means of access at Cirencester is unknown, as in other cases, and external staircases or ramps on the south-west side are perhaps probable at Silchester. The processional entrances were no doubt lined with masonry, as in the case of the one entrance so far opened at Cirencester; and in that case two small chambers appeared on either side at the arena, possibly dens for beasts or even, in one case, a shrine of the goddess Nemesis.[7] Dens would certainly be expected somewhere along the arena-wall at Silchester, either in the same position or on the short axis as at Dorchester.[8]

Shows were given by magistrates on some of the numerous public holidays. There might be some assistance from the civic chest; and a compulsory fee levied upon election, distinct from any contribution to public works, was devoted to this purpose.[9] What sort of shows would have been exhibited? Firstly, it may be pointed out that the short axis of the arena is three times the diameter of the largest travelling circus-ring in Britain today,[10] so that there was ample scope for all except the most elaborate displays, which would probably have been far too costly for any local purse, even if governmental sanction had been obtained for them.[11] All sorts of blood-sports would unquestionably have been shown: there was no shortage of animals to be hunted, even bears being possibly still to be found in southern England as well as in the remoter west and north.[12] As Camden observed, the poet Claudian has a line on British bull-dogs.[13] Gladiatorial combat would also have figured on the bill from time to time, but perhaps not commonly, for the evidence of gladiators in Britain, though definite, is somewhat meagre.[14]

Gladitorial combats were part of the formal sequence in a spectacle which,

however enjoyable to the audience, had its origin in Italian religious ob-
servance. Very different was the degenerate mode of public execution which
took place in the midday intermission and was not reckoned as part of the
games proper.[15] However, unless the governor or some high official of late
times imposed the death-penalty during an official progress to the town
(p. 143), our ampitheatre is not likely to have witnessed such scenes, for
the local magistrates had no power of inflicting it. The British protomartyrs,
Alban at Verulamium, Julius and Aaron at Caerleon, are connected respectively with a *municipium* and a legionary fortress, and this may be significant.

Nothing has been found to throw light upon what actually took place in
this arena. The section may be closed with reference to an unusual pottery
mould (fig. 40, 5) which was used to form sweetmeats or cakes for a
festive occasion.[16] Imperfect and rough though the impression is, the scene
represented clearly follows the style of the bronze medallions put out by the
Roman mint to mark special occasions: there is a specimen from Silchester.[17]
The mould shows a group of four persons engaged in a sacrifice, three of
them bearded, in tunic and military cloak (*sagum*), and the other a lady.
From what can be seen of the lady's coiffure and of the features, the figures
are plausibly identified as the Emperor Severus, his two sons Caracalla and
Geta, and their mother the Empress Julia Domna, *mater castrorum*. The
mould probably refers to some event between 209, when Geta joined his
father and brother as a third Augustus, and 211 when Severus died at York.
We may imagine, if we will, the townsfolk of Calleva buying and studying
their equivalent of the modern festive chocolate medallion as they bent their
way to the special 'victory games' commemorating some success in Severus'
Scottish war.

OTHER AMUSEMENTS

The objects brought together here include three bone dice, two of the
ordinary cubical form and one of the native, oblong shape spotted only on
the sides. Large numbers of bone, glass, pottery, stone or lead counters in
the collection point to the popularity of board-games, though we should not
forget that the purpose of many of the counters (*calculi*) may have been, or
may also have been, to serve in arithmetical calculation: Roman numerals
are clumsy, and when sums could not be done conveniently on the fingers or
in the head, a board or table-top marked in columns of units, tens, hundreds,
thousands, etc. was employed; long multiplication or division by cumulative
addition or subtraction of counters in these columns thus became a simple

mechanical process. The method survived the introduction of Arabic numerals and still remains in some parts of the world; and it is interesting to reflect that the modern calculating-machine, be it the simple office calculator or the electronic computer, works on a very similar principle.[18]

The bone counters, neatly turned, sometimes bear scratched numerals, letters, or other symbols, and three—clearly for use in a game—are inscribed FVR (thief), MAR (*martialis,* warlike?) and PRIMVS (first).[19] The bun-shaped glass counters are mostly black, but a number are white, and others bright blue or brown, in some cases inlaid with spots of a different colour. The more elaborate specimens are also from gaming-sets: fifteen white and fifteen brown pieces, accompanied by the remains of a gaming-board, were found in the mausoleum at Lullingstone (Kent); and in the absence of a die, it may be concluded that the game was of the nature of draughts rather than backgammon.[20] A larger cylindrical gaming-piece of bone is also in the collection.[21] A few tiles scribed for use as gaming-boards are also to be seen, but in every case they were incised before the tiles were fired, and so relate to leisure moments at the brickyards rather than to recreations in town. Two such tiles, inscribed with five and seven squares a side respectively, appeared in the tile-and-tessera pavement of XXIII.1, and another, much larger, is divided into four compartments of varying size along each side, and diagonally (both ways) as well: this seems to have been a board for a game of nine-men's-morris type, in other words a refined form of noughts-and-crosses.[22] Some of the pieces of bone, glass, or marble inlay in the collection may have come from gaming-boards.

A word on toys must be largely negative. The small metal and terracotta figures are of a religious significance rather than playthings, and the same goes for Joyce's 'quaint little rocking-horse, 4 inches long' (fig. 25) from the forum (p. 167). As far as can be told, the dolls and games of the Callevan children must have been made of perishable or otherwise unrecognisable materials.[23]

13

Temples and Pagan Religion

The temples are now bereft of the personality of god, worshipper and priest alike; and what has survived—sculpture, inscriptions, small accessories— is seldom easily interpreted. Yet we can guess that the religious experience of the Callevans was extensive, pervading, at once primitive and complex. To share it would be to enter a world governed by powers of life and nature, in Roman times at least conceived as deities in human form, equated to the appropriate figures of the Roman pantheon. In these approximations, the native element no doubt remained supreme; and no less than the Roman required due propitiation in return for which beneficence in birth and death, in healing, in the increase of crops and livestock, and in other con- tingencies was assured. Allied but distinct and very Romanised were the honours paid to the Tutela and the imperial power (*numen*) represented by statues in the basilica (p. 119); and on another plane again stand the intro- duced dieties, of which Sarapis is the chief Silchester example (p. 166). We reserve for the next chapter an account of the church, and for the brief succeeding chapter what is known of the Callevan cemeteries and burial- customs.

There is no sign at Calleva of a classical temple such as the Maison Carrée at Nîmes or, for that matter, the 'temple of Claudius' at Camulo- dunum. With one or two possible exceptions, the buildings are all typical Romano-Celtic *fana* consisting of a inner shrine, probably not open to the public, surrounded by a portico; the very simplest type, in Insula XXXVI, lacks even this convenience for worshippers. The plan of such temples is generally square, but in Insula VII there is a sixteen-sided temple, with circular shrine or *cella*. This temple, and those of Insulae XXX and XXXVI, are set within walled precincts.

TEMPLE, INSULA XXXVI

This, the simplest type, may be taken first.[1] It is rather less than 6 m.

square, and only the gravel foundations of the walls were preserved; it lies towards the north-east corner of a precinct some 30 by 35 m., the only other known features of which are two pits, one yielding two little pots, and the other five complete and several broken bone pins and a glass setting from a ring or brooch. To judge by the coins found in the fillings, both pits were filled in during the fourth century, and one of them may not have been dug until the close of the third, for there was a coin of Carausius at the bottom. Pins, of course, are an age-old type of offering, associated with the petitions of women,[2] and their presence here helps to demonstrate the sacred character of the adjacent building, though very similar *cellae*, sometimes demonstrably shrines, are a feature of some temple-complexes, of which that on the Altbachtal at Trier may be mentioned as a supreme example: indeed two of the most important portico-temples there began an existence as simple *cellae*.[3]

22. Imaginative reconstruction of the temple, Insula XXXV, showing offering-altar (also restored) in front

TEMPLE, INSULA XXXV (pl. 23, fig. 22)

This temple[4] is on the 'baths alignment' (p. 47) and is therefore likely to be of first-century origin. It measures 10.7 m. from north to south and 11.1 m from east to west: there is an entrance on the east (the customary siting in temples of this sort), which will have contained two or three steps to a floor-level raised about 60 cm. above the surrounding ground. The *cella* is 3.7 by 4.3 m. internally; its walling, 57 cm. wide, suggests a lofty tower-like superstructure The portico-wall is only 45 cm. wide, and from the discovery of fragments of column and part of a Tuscan capital with an abacus of the same width, it may be presumed to have carried a peristyle with a pentice roof above, resting against the *cella*. The floor of the portico was of plain red tessellation; in the *cella,* only the flint bedding of the *opus signinum* floor remained. On the west side of the *cella,* there was a low plinth edged in brickwork, in all about 1 m. deep and running the full width of the room: here will have stood the statues discussed below. A flint-built altar-base, 80 by 60 cm., was found in an axial position 7.6 m. east of the building, and though no precinct-wall was discovered, it may have existed, or else its place may have been taken by a palisade or hedge.

This temple was the source of the three inscriptions of the *collegium peregrinorum* (p. 58, cf. pl. 11), and also in the *cella* were some fragments of Bath stone statuary. These comprised (a) probably the bent knee of a draped, seated figure; (b) a left hand bent at the wrist, holding the butt of a cornucopiae decorated with a leaf-spray in relief; (c) three pieces of two legs clad in greaves ornamented with lion-masks; and (d) other scraps, such as part of a bearded chin (?) and bits of draperies. Of these, pieces (b) and (c) come from statues rather under life-scale. It may be remembered that in discussing the *collegium peregrinorum* inscriptions, it was pointed out that they recorded, very probably, the dedications of three statues, viz. of Peace, Victory, and Mars; and it seems quite probable that the fragments of sculpture correspond. *Two* statues are certainly indicated on petrological grounds alone, and while it is possible that the Celtic Mars may have been represented, as elsewhere, holding a cornucopiae rather than a more martial emblem,[5] we have too little to be sure of this, and the attribute may well have been that of Peace. For the text of the principal 'Calleva' inscription, see p. 172.

The history of excavation in such temples all over Britain shows that we are fortunate to possess even these pitiful fragments of inscriptions and sculpture. A search was of coure very diligently made for other pieces, but without success, and it is reasonable to conclude, with the excavators, that a destructive agency other than the mere hand of time has been at work here. The emergence of an official Christian cult in the late fourth century (p. 72), having its public church within a very short distance of the temple, is explanation enough of the savage demolition revealed.

From somewhere in Insula XXXV came some pieces of a large white jug with an intriguing graffito sketch which shows a man recoiling before the attack of a large bird; behind him stands a boar or dog. This drawing has been too hastily dismissed as a standard scene of a fight between a pygmy and a crane, such as occurs on samian ware. In terms of its arrangement, it may owe something to this, but the details do not correspond and there remains the question of why such a scene should have been scratched on a jug. It is possible that this was one of the temple vessels, depicting a hunter confronted by an underworld goddess in the guise of a bird.[6]

TEMPLES, INSULA XXX

The space recorded as Insula XXX partly underlies the parish church and extends northwards below farm-premises; the important group of buildings which it contains is therefore incompletely known.[7] The walled precinct of about 1.2 ha. presumably corresponds narrowly to the original *temenos* which appears to have caused problems in the early stages of Romanisation (p. 55). In the north-west corner, there is a rectangular chamber with an apsidal end to the west; and walling to the east may have been that of an *exedra* such as was built along the south side of the temple-enclosure at Caerwent:[8] if so, the apsidal room may have been a *schola* or meeting-place for some religious *collegium*. A short distance to the south, there is a great hall upwards of 21 m. long and 13 m. wide; but its purpose is uncertain.

Two temples are known within the area, both built on the 'baths alignment' with an interval of about 15 m. between them;[9] even allowing for open-air offering-altars as in the case of the Insula XXXV temple, there remains ample room for other temples or buildings, and it has frequently been observed that the present church, 14 or 15 m. east of the more southerly temple, retains the Roman alignment as if its nave and aisles had been constructed on top of a third pagan shrine. It would by no means be the only church established, consciously or not, of set purpose or not, upon a pagan temple.[10]

The northern temple is 22.25 m. square, with an 11 m. *cella,* and is thus the largest of its kind known in Britain.[11] Its floor was raised over 2 m. above the Roman surface, contained by an outer wall 1 m. thick; there would have been a continuous peristyle on this. The *cella* wall was of like thickness, and with equally deep foundations would have been carried up in brick-bonded flintwork to the full height of a light internal dome and external pyramidal roof. The outside of the building was plastered and painted red; the floor of the cella was of *opus signinum* (p. 127) containing chips of grey stone as well as brick, while that of the portico was similar, but lacked the stone chippings. The southern temple was much smaller, 15.25 m. square with a 5.5 m. *cella,* and was raised only about 1 m.; the *cella* wall, however, was of the same gauge as in the northern case, although the outer wall was of the ordinary 60 cm. walling of Silchester buildings. The exterior was again coloured red, but the floors were of red and drab tessellation: nothing remained in place. Among the wreckage common to both buildings appeared fragments of grey-green Purbeck marble wall-lining, red-painted plaster, and a piece of moulded white stucco; a scrap of moulded Egyptian porphyry, found not far distant in XXXIIB.3, may have come from one of the temples. Unfortunately, in neither case could the east side be opened, so we have no clear idea of the entrances, which would have been on this side.

A silver Durotrigian coin found close to the precinct[12] may well indicate the early period at which frequentation of this sacred area began, long before the temples described were built. At the other end of the time-scale, a coin of Valens is the latest recorded: despite the advent of Christianity, the Celtic cults still retained much of their popular appeal.[13] Whether signs of reconstruction noted in the northern temple are to be related to similar work at the adjacent east gate of the town and in the forum-basilica must remain a matter for speculation.

Other buildings outside the precinct-wall include a curious apsidal structure and an adjacent 'portico', both to the south-west in Insula XXXIIB.[14] Both turn their back upon the stream in the little valley just beyond; the apse is about 6 m. in diameter, and seems to have had an arched entrance or columns on piers at either side. Such buildings are not uncommon as *Nymphaea* or shrines of water-deities,[15] and in this case a well only 2 m. from the rear of the structure contained possibly significant finds: two pots, and skulls of a horse, sheep and oxen.[16] The portico is over 17.5 m. long and nearly 2 m. wide; it may be compared with a somewhat similar but larger structure outside the *fanum* of La-mare-du-puits, Normandy,[17] though a far more humdrum explanation is not excluded (p. 259). Finally, and as suggested by the excavators, the house XXXIIB.3 may have been the residence of the chief priest of the temples.

Finds which throw light on the cults are very few. There were two tiny terracotta lamps, of a size suitable for votive offerings; several bronze and bone pins (cf. p. 153), and part of a bone comb which has a similar, feminine connotation as a votive offering. There were also two little talismans in the shape of model bronze axes,[18] and a Neolithic polished flint axehead from Insula XXXII may also have had a votive significance.[19] About a dozen of the little bronze axes, and a votive spear, have been recorded from Calleva generally (cf. fig. 34, 17) and it is worth noting that both axe and spear are carried by a warrior-god carved on a relief found at Chedworth (Glos.) bearing vestiges of an inscription to Mars-Lenus.[20] There is reason to suppose that the Celtic Mars was far from an exclusively warlike deity, and was regarded as the giver of prosperity and health. Thus, the apparent gulf between the axes on the one hand, and the pins on the other, is not unbridge-able. However, there is more than one temple, and caution is obviously necessary in interpreting remains in this way.

TEMPLE, INSULA VII

This temple also stood in a large walled precinct.[21] A small house, VII.4 on the west side, may have been the priest's residence, and there seem to have been cottages on the south wall, near a probable entrance, and on the east, unless the latter was a subsidiary shrine. A large rectangular building, with a door on the north-west, very close to the temple, may have been an assembly-room or a store: it recalls the larger structure in the Insula XXX *temenos*. The rest of the ground seems to have been empty of buildings; a few unproductive pits, one or two earlier than the precinct-wall, may have been dug for the trees of a sacred grove.

As previously stated, the temple is externally sixteen-sided (pl. 22); but the circular interior of the *cella* shows that this shape is a necessary adaptation of the circular, if timber architraves were to span the columns standing on the outer wall as a continuous peristyle. Joyce found a chip from one of these, indicating a height of about 2.4 m. Presumably there were thirty-two, allowing for one at each angle and one midway between. The overall width of the building is nearly 20 m., the *cella* being 10.8 m. in diameter and the portico 2.8 m. wide. The walling is of flint bonded with ironstone rather than brick; but in the absence of any certain indication we can only suppose that the entrance was on the east, or perhaps rather on the south, where it is found in the closest parallel, a fifteen-sided temple at Aquincum (Budapest).[22] The tiled roof of the portico will have rested against the tower-like *cella,* and in good proportion the *cella* would have been about 11 m. high. There was probably an internal vault: in the absence of a hypocaust, Joyce's discovery of a fragment of box-tile suggests as much (cf. p. 197). The outer wall was plastered and painted red, as in other cases at Silchester. As to the flooring, Joyce's notes leave no doubt that it was tessellated: black tesserae from the *cella* and white tesserae from the portico 'well cut and more finely-jointed than usual' are recorded. As we have seen, the floors of *cella* and portico were carefully differentiated in other temples at Silchester.

Joyce mentions a worn *as* of Vespasian embedded in the *cella*-wall, and this discovery carries the erection of the building well into the second century if not to a later date; two unworn *denarii* of 209, found in the excavation of the floor-level, may just possibly have been 'sealed'. A coin of Gallienus' sole reign (260–8) is the only other recorded. On any telling, the temple is not early, and thus the question of whether it had a predecessor is raised. Traces of a bed of pink cement, noted in 1893 just below the footing of the external ring of masonry, suggest as much.

As regards finds, the only objects of note are a triangular iron knife endowed by Joyce with a sacrificial significance which we may take leave to doubt (shown, fig. 34, 13); and, from a trench 'at no great distance', part of a small globular oil-bottle of oriental alabaster which may have held an offering to the god; but who that god was, we have no means of telling. It was in this same insula that the graffito sketch of an ox (fig. 7, 5) was found: but as the sketch was done at the tilery, before the brick in question was fired, it can have no particular reference to the cult.[23]

TEMPLE OR SCHOLA, INSULA XXI

This building (B6) lies in the south-east corner of the insula[24] and stands north and south, its front wall overlapping the line of the street. Little remained: there was a hall 7.5 by 5.8 m., with a rather poorly-built apse at the north end; the doorway, about 1 m. wide, was at the south end of the west wall and not axial. The only other feature recorded, since the floor had perished, is a drain passing obliquely through the west wall.

The lateral entrance suggests that the building was devoted to proceedings of a private character. Temples in London and at Nettleton (Wilts.) are among those which may be adduced as parallels in this respect:[25] the alignment is sufficient to dismiss any thought of its having been a church, and the Sarapeum at York had an axial entrance.[26] A temple of any kind, however, might have been expected to stand back from the street in a precinct of its own, and the prominent siting on a corner of the main east-west street seems to endow the building with an officially-recognised character, perhaps, as the excavators also suggested, the meeting-place of 'some trade guild'. The only *collegium* actually attested epigraphically at Calleva is the *collegium peregrinorum* (p. 58), but there are likely to have been others. A somewhat similar building, with lateral access, was found abutting a public courtyard of the inn at Kempten,[27] and there are numerous other parallels. The proceedings were essentially of a religious nature, for which an apsidal form, where the officers could preside over the rites, was well-adapted.

While considering buildings with apsidal terminations, it crosses one's mind that a room in VII.1, which has an apse facing the street just south of the forum, may also have been the seat of some *collegium,* or a shrine.[28]

TEMPLE, INSULA XIX

This building (B2) lies close to the western boundary-wall of an insula which belonged all to one house (XIX.2). It is a rectangular structure, some 9 by 6.5 m., divided into two chambers, of which the second and more westerly terminates in a rectangular alcove. Such a plan invites comparison with the London temple already mentioned and also with another, outside the Roman fort at Maryport (Cumb.), thought by M. J. T. Lewis to have been a *Mithraeum*: the plan of the Carrawburgh *Mithraeum* is indeed very close in one of its phases.[29] However, the London temple is far too early to be a *Mithraeum*—the worship of Mithras, in Britain, belongs essentially to the third century—and neither at Silchester nor at Maryport were traces of the longitudinal benches, which are a diagnostic feature of mithraic chapels. Even so it must be admitted that both buildings were excavated at a time when a mithraic possibility is unlikely to have been before the minds of those concerned, for there was no good example of a *Mithraeum,* and Cumont's great recension of the texts and monuments appeared only in 1896–8. Furthermore, the benches in British *Mithraea* prove in most cases to be of very insubstantial construction, mere banks of earth revetted by rough stonework or even wattle. That this was a *Mithraeum,* then, is a possibility to be borne in mind. The cult appealed particularly to soldiers, but exercised a parallel attraction for the business-man in its ideals of probity, steadfastness and good companionship: the exception to the otherwise military distribution of known chapels in Britain, not unnaturally, is the London (Walbrook) *Mithraeum*; and given the nodal point of Calleva in the road-system of southern Britain, it is by no means impossible to imagine a situation wherein the numbers of immigrant traders and others had risen to a point when not merely a *collegium peregrinorum* and the worship of Sarapis had taken root, but when a mithraic lodge could also have been formed.[30]

Nothing is recorded from the building, which was in a poor state; and from the environs there is only a cremation-burial in a black urn, found near the curious, canted south-west corner of the insula.[31]

OTHER BUILDINGS

A 'beautiful spring of perennial water' rises in the field next to the amphitheatre; and worked stones turned up nearby suggested to Joyce that there had been a *Nymphaeum,* or shrine of a water-spirit here.[32] The design would have called for the construction of an ornamental well-head or pool, where coping of the sort in evidence (p. 148) would obviously find a place; and there would also have been some sort of containing structure as at Coventina's Well (Northd.) or at Chedworth villa (Glos.).[33] But at present there is no certainty that the stones were not carried there in later times to act as stepping-stones to the spring.

Some thirty or more squarish buildings, of much the same size, in many cases, as the simple *cella* of Insula XXXVI, are dotted about the plan. Some are close to houses, though often on a different alignment; others are quite isolated. The excavators pondered long on the problem of what these buildings could be; and for us, with some knowledge of the plans of other Romano-British towns where comparable numbers of 'squares' do not figure, the problem is even more acute. In the case of the example (B1) near XXIII.2, rather more than 5 m. square, and with an added porch on the east before a wide entrance where blocks of stone seemed to point to a columniated façade, they drew attention to a wall-painting from Herculaneum showing a typical Italian country shrine of apparently similar construction. Inside, the other three walls had a wide ledge on which the floor-joists were set.[34] Below, there emerged an earlier tessellated floor on which a coin of Marcus lay, to give some idea of the date of the later construction. The older floor was not exactly parallel to the later building, and we now know from aerial survey (pl. 8) that it formed part of a suppressed wing of the house. Other examples of 'squares' built on the sites of earlier buildings include one near II.2, one in XXVIII.1, and the free-standing vaulted room in XXXIV.1 could also be adduced.[35] The 'shrine' theory is perhaps not entirely destroyed by these further details, but other explanations could certainly be urged, e.g. that some were granaries (p. 256). Others seem merely to have been parts of houses of which the rest escaped discovery, e.g. the isolated hypocausts of XII.B2 or XXA.B6.[36] And yet it would be foolish to pronounce decisively in all the cases known now merely from the pages of *Archaeologia*: if we have a simple *cella* which seems identifiable as that of a temple principally because it lies within a precinct, some others may also have been temples without a precinct-wall (cf. XXXV). A case in point is possibly the isolated square XXIIB.B2, which belonged to a timber building; for under the floor occurred, centrally, a pit from which six whole pots were exhumed in the middle of a layer of gravel filling. This is not the only instance of pots bestowed thus at Silchester (p. 164), and a votive or ritual explanation of some sort seems requisite.[37]

DOMESTIC SHRINES

The chief subject of this section is the very fine example of a domestic shrine in XIV.2; but by way of transition from the previous remarks, it may be pointed out that certain large houses, notably VIII.1–2, XXVII.1 (east) and XXXIV.1 incorporate square chambers, or in XXI.1 rectangular, clearly distinct in purpose from ordinary rooms because of a situation on the outer side of a corridor, where they project very often into a court or garden. It is worth bearing in mind the possibility that these rooms were domestic shrines.[38]

23. Bronze statuette of a Lar (lost). Scale, 1/1

Room 9 of XIV.2[39] measures about 3.4 by 5.8 m., and is very clearly demarcated in position from the other rooms; probably it represents an alteration. Towards the west side of the room there was a detached structure about 2 m. square, strongly built of flint walling with brick corners and bonding-courses, leaving the east side open (pl. 24). There is some indication that the interior was filled to some depth with flint and mortar suggestive of a raised floor-level or platform-like appearance. The excavators thought that a small Tuscan capital, 16.5 cm. in diameter, might have come from the structure. The room was paved with red tessellation except for a panel of fine mosaic, not preserved, in front of the platform; and fragments of painted plaster showed that the walls had been 'a delicate shade of blue'.

Fox and Hope identified the room as a domestic shrine or *lararium* on the basis of Pompeian parallels, suggesting that an *aedicula*, or house-like structure, had been erected on the platform.[40] The *lararia* of Italy displayed figures of a *Genius familiaris*, in the guise of a *paterfamilias* sacrificing, flanked by *Lares:* these tableaux were often painted as the background in a little niche, leaving a ledge in front where other figurines (*Penates*) could be kept, and in front there might often be an offering-altar or table. It is therefore of interest to find that bronze statuettes answering the description of *Genius* and *Lar familiares* have been found at Silchester (pl. 34e, fig. 23).[41] The *Genius,* from the forum, is hollow at the back and was evidently meant to be fixed to the rear of a niche by the two nail-holes which can be seen. The right hand held a *patera* (handleless offering-dish) and the right still retains part of a rolled napkin. The *Lar* was found in 1824, and was lost in a fire at Wasing House during the late war. It stood about the same height as the *Genius,* 11 or 12 cm., and had silver-inlaid eyes; it wore a wide tunic with a cloak or scarf over the shoulder, tucked into the girdle. The right hand held a gadrooned *patera;* a small *cornucopiae* was missing from the left. Such a representation was quite standard: the *Lar* of the master. There is another type, the dancing *Lar compitalis*, the servants' *lar;* and in the little tableaux mentioned, these are clearly shown in the position of attendants upon the *Genius*.

The natural conclusion therefore is that domestic worship of the Roman pattern had spread to Silchester. Furthermore, two handsome stones from signet-rings seem to underline the notion that Roman religious customs were followed in the town: the plasma intaglio (fig. 24,2) of the *Genius Populi Romani* (p. 68), and a convex brown sard (fig. 24, 5) bearing an augurial wand and a sacrificial ewer. But considerable caution must be exercised in deciding the question. Both *Genius* and *Lar* have occurred in deposits of other bronzes where a Celtic significance is detectable: in a cache of 'Roman' deities corresponding to the favourite *interpretationes Romanae* of the Celts, near the Romano-Celtic hilltop *fanum* of Lamyatt Beacon (Som.); at Felmingham Hall (Norfolk) with ravens and the head of a priestly sceptre, among other objects; and most significantly of all in the strange Devizes find of 1714 recorded in Musgrave's *Belgium Britannicum*. The nineteen figurines included a Genius and some excellent classical deities, again mostly Celtic favourites, others of a very curious rustic type, and some

24. Gems and lead sealing. 1, bloodstone, so-called 'Gnostic' type. 2, plasma, *Genius Populi Romani,* sacrificing. 3, red jasper, gryllus. 4, nicolo, eternity. 5, brown sard, sacrificial implements. 6, bloodstone, sun-god. 7, lead sealing from the basilica, with Christogram. Scales, 1/1; no. 1, 2/1

animals including a recumbent dog (from a rare type of lamp), a horse, a boar, and to clinch the essentially Celtic character of this mid-third century find, a three-horned ox.[42]

When parallels to the platform of XIV.2 are explored, a similar doubt also arises as to whether the shrine standing on that platform witnessed devotions of a Roman domestic kind. At Caerwent, a room in House 8 South, enclosed by a railing, contained a platform about 1 m. square approached by three steps. On it rested a sandstone *tête coupée* of deeply native style: it was clearly the chief object of veneration in a shrine erected upon the platform.[43] In Celtic belief, the head was the seat of the soul,[44] and we shall find an apt demonstration of this in a Callevan funeral rite (p. 185). The commandant's house at Segontium fort contained a similar platform, without steps, and in the third century, to which the structure belonged, the garrison was a Celto-German unit from the Aachen-Köln region.[45] The closest structural parallel, however, occurred at Verulamium, where there were two platforms side-by-side, one a replacement for the other: there was an associated foundation-offering (a worn coin of Vespasian and a pot). The insides of the structures were hollow, but had been filled in: earlier, they had had painted inside walls as if they had formed cupboards for the safe-keeping of sacred or valuable articles, as in a cupboard below a wooden *aedicula* at Herculaneum.[46]

A similar platform existed in XIV.1, but in the open courtyard:[47] it had been demolished when the courtyard was resurfaced, but evidently faced the street-entrance. The excavators thought the position too exposed for a shrine, but the objection vanishes if we think of it as a solidly-constructed, roofed little building. In some of the other houses, notably XXVII.1 (west), Room 9,[48] platforms were found against walls, and in some cases may have been the bases of shrines supporting some sort of house-like model, such as is not seldom encountered in the Rhineland and adjacent areas of northern Gaul, executed in stone.[49] A very fine apsidal construction against the wall of a room in a house at Dorchester (Dorset) lends colour to the suggestion,[50] but other more mundane explanations cannot be excluded.

REMAINS OF PAGAN RELIGION—VOTIVE DEPOSITS

There are some examples of pits apparently dug for votive purposes. The empty pits in Insula VII might so be interpreted, rather than as above; there are some others containing pins, etc. in Insula XXXVI; the well behind the apsidal structure in XXXII, with its animal skulls; and the pit below XXII.B2, with its six pots buried in a layer of gravel. All these have been mentioned in passing, and also (p. 42) the curious pre-Roman deposit in Insula XII,[51] where 'as many as a dozen nearly perfect vessels of pottery [were found] . . . at a depth of [2.54 m.] from the present surface . . . and seemed as if they had been deposited in three distinct layers. There were patches of moss above and about them, and some bones of animals. The pit was dug out to its full depth [4.9 m.]. It had a clay bottom and showed little of the black deposit not uncommon in these rubbish-holes'. The careful bestowal of the vessels, packed about with moss, shows on the contrary that this was not a rubbish-hole, and the accompanying bones suggest the remains of a ritual meal, carefully consigned to the ground: the vessels could have been those actually used in the meal, or else containers for offerings connected with a rite.[52] The orderly arrangement of the vessels in clean layers of filling is the chief clue, found also in XXIIB.B2, and again in XXVII, Pit 22 and perhaps in a well of XXI.[53] These instances must be distinguished from others where the vessels lay in no sort of order.[54]

The two famous 'hoards' of ironwork from a pit or well in Insula I (1890) and a 6.5 m. well in Insula XXIII (1900)[55] are by no means the only deposits of their kind known in Britain or abroad, and a smith-god to whom such offerings were appropriate is widely attested.[56] In the 1890 deposit, the material lay on top of a 'sort of cist of pieces of chalk' containing a pot, resting on the smashed remains of another; two other pots occurred with the material in the 1900 find, which overlay a deep stratum of ash. The pots indicate a late fourth-century date for the deposits, and strongly support the votive explanation of the 'hoards', the contents of which are considered later (p. 268).

Passing to articles of natural origin, three cones of the stone-pine (*Pinus pinea*) are in the collection, and perhaps because they were discovered in Joyce's time or before serious botanical study began in 1898, they are not mentioned in the reports. Such cones had a distinct place in various ancient cults, notably in that of Cybele and Attis (who was turned into a pine-tree), and were also used as altar-fuel. In Britain they have been found in the Verulamium triangular temple and in the Carrawburgh *Mithraeum*.[57] Ours must have come from some deep pit or well; and in this case the parallels lie with others from wells at Lullingstone (Kent) and Low Ham (Somerset) villas, and from the ritual shafts of the Vendée.[58] The cones were primarily symbols of immortality; and, cut in stone, they grace many funerary monuments for that reason: abroad, natural cones have been found in graves.[59] In wells, they were probably offerings to the water-spirit for the benefit of a perennial supply: the Egyptians offered them to the Nile for a like reason.[60] The tree will grow in Britain, though it is tender when young, and there is no reason why the Romans should not have planted it. These cones, however, were imported, for the seeds are fully ripened, and in our climate that is unlikely to have taken place.

Clippings of box (*Buxus sempervirens*) are well-attested in funerary contexts for a similar reason. At Silchester, however, the clippings seem to have occurred with other plant-débris; and although they could possibly be trimmings discarded in the preparation of sepulchral material, they are more likely to have been merely garden-waste. Pliny the Younger, for example, refers to the box-edging in the garden of his Laurentine villa.[61]

INSCRIPTION FROM THE FORUM

To what has already been said of Stair's discovery of 1744 (pp. 22, 110; fig. 1) it may be added that the use of the word *Deo* ('To the God . . .') is a reliable indication that the deity in question was not Roman, whether or not its name was accompanied, as in this case, by a Celtic name or epithet.[62]

THE HEAD OF SARAPIS

With the fine Portland stone head of Sarapis (pl. 18) we enter an entirely different religious sphere.[63] The piece now measures 32 cm. from chin to crown, and the scale is therefore well above the human. The top of the head is slightly flattened, where the *modius*-crown (i.e., in the form of a bushel-measure) would have been set, affixed perhaps by a dowel set in the very hole which later took the clumsy iron bar removed in 1951. The nose has gone, likewise the surface of the chin, where the luxuriant beard would have parted to left and right; but the locks hanging over the forehead make the identification quite certain. The statue or bust, but we cannot tell which, is of an unusually high quality for Roman sculpture in Britain, and as Professor Toynbee suggests, must be the work of a continental, even Mediterranean artist of some competence. In it, and in the stylistically and materially identical Tutela (p. 119) we have a rare proof of an immigrant sculptor working in Britain and, moreover, in an indigenous material which, though of excellent quality for statuary, seems to have been but little employed for works of note.

Sarapis was a syncretistic deity of Ptolemaic Egypt, Zeus-Osiris-Apis, lord of this world and of that to come, hailed as *One Zeus Helios Pantocrator* on an inscription from the Baths of Caracalla in Rome. On the Alexandrian coinage of Roman times he is frequently shown, sometimes with attributes—radiate head, ram's horns of Ammon, trident of Poseidon—which attest and verify that resounding invocation. He was the consort of Isis, whose cult in many lands came to excel his own.

The Silchester portrait is thoroughly typical of the Roman, rather than the Hellenistic period. The earliest representations, on coins and gems, are extraordinarily regal, intent, and vital; under the Empire, however, a change took place in the concept of the deity. 'Impassive' and even 'melancholy' are among the epithets applied to portraits such as this. The absence of detail in the eyes, standard in metropolitan sculpture from the time of Hadrian at least, adds to the aura of remoteness, far-sightedness—indeed foresight—and the slightly-parted lips recall the oracular powers of the god.[64] Representations of Sarapis with full forelocks (which perhaps betoken his marine powers) do not appear before A.D. 174–5, when an unequivocal portrait of the type appears on an Alexandrian coin, as if the principal cult-statue had been changed or modified then, and the facing head of the coin was produced to commemorate the fact.[65] The Silchester head seems somewhat earlier in style than a Severan bust in Prague, and more to be compared with a basalt Antonine head in Alexandria.[66]

It is a puzzle to decide where at Calleva such a figure could have been placed, for the scale demands that we see it as a principal cult-object and not as some secondary inclusion in another shrine, as was the beautiful Sarapis-head in the Walbrook *Mithraeum*. None of the Romano-Celtic *fana* is likely to have housed it,[67] with the exception, perhaps, of the polygonal temple in Insula VII, where the Egyptian *alabastron* could perhaps be regarded as a very tenuous link. The *schola* of Insula XXI is another possibility: it seems unlikely that any major temple can have eluded discovery either by excavation or by aerial survey. It may, however, be conceivable that a bust was set up in the forum or the basilica.

SMALL OBJECTS AND ACCESSORIES—FIGURINES

Passing by scraps of two stone statuettes[68] and coming to those of bronze, bought to stand in domestic shrines or to devote to the deity in one of the temples, we may mention a small Venus and the head of another; a head of Mercury; a small Bacchus, and a Hercules.[69] More interesting that these is the figure from XXIII.2, 12.4 cm. high on a domed base, of a girl attendant at sacred rites, holding a single pipe transversely as if awaiting the signal to begin playing (pl. 34d).[70] She wears a long robe of Greek style, armless; on her head is a diadem of upright leaves. The curious roll at the neck seems meant for a close-fitting necklace of large beads. The workmanship is rough, the modelling poor, but this possibly local production possesses a charm and a freshness denied to the others mentioned. Of animal figurines, we have two goats, a cock and a dog, all attributes of Mercury and either votive offerings or else strays from larger compositions representing that god.[71] There is also a miniature horse, statuesque on a tiny pedestal: but a more famous equine is the attenuated, almost flat 'Silchester horse' from the forum, 10 cm. long (fig. 25) with eye-circles probably once inlaid.[72] The satisfying *triskele* shapes recall the Late Iron Age art from which this figure cannot be far

25. Bronze handle: 'the Silchester horse'. Scale, 1/2

removed, either in time or in feeling. There are signs of attachment at the tips of the legs, and there is some wear discernible: probably the object is a handle from a ritual vessel of some kind, but no very good parallel can be offered. The place of the horse in Celtic symbolism is very well-known, and we have but to turn to British coins (e.g. fig. 4, 1–2) to see it delineated not merely in an elongated, but also a dismembered fashion which bespeaks the intangible quality of the divine solar being which it represented.

The commonplace classical statuettes, turned out by Gaulish factories in large numbers, were inexpensive. A very competent figurine of Mars, found in Lincolnshire, is much larger and far finer than any of the Silchester bronzes under discussion, but its total cost, allowing for the pound of bronze which the *aerarius* himself contributed, was only the nominal equivalent of 28 *denarii,* as the basal inscription informs us.[73] Even less costly, however, must have been the white clay figurines from the Allier or the Rhineland. We have eight or ten fragmentary statuettes of Venus, and two of a mother-goddess seated in a wickerwork chair, suckling infants (pl. 34a).[74] Between them, these outwardly disparate types—the one so classical in pose, the other so homely—denote the two aspects of the female principle. Such figurines, and the cockerel (pl. 34b) which is not a very common type in Britain,[75] are frequent as ex-votos in Gallic temples, and as offerings in graves, where the Venus and mother-goddess illustrate the concept of the earth-mother from which we are born and to which we must return for rebirth into the after-life.[76] In Britain, however, the figurines seem to occur only as isolated domestic finds.

A strange little object in chalk, 63 mm. high, is clearly a candle-holder, for there is a hole at the top, and a slot at the back where the ends could be picked out (fig. 26).[77] The left face bears a serpent wriggling downwards,

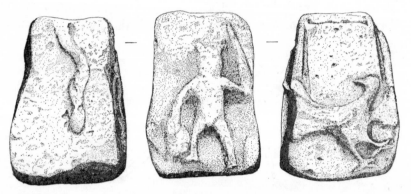

26. Three sides of a chalk candle-holder, showing a deity, etc. Scale, 2/3

the right a bird with spread wings and head turned back; on the front is carved a little male deity, naked, winged or horned, holding what may be a sword upright, and resting the other hand on what may be a shield. There are points of comparison with roughly-cut 'warrior-gods' from Burgh-by-Sands or Maryport (Cumb.),[78] but it would be rash to emphasize a connection, when scarcely a detail is beyond dispute in any of the cases. Within the limits of the Silchester piece, however, it may be pointed out that both the serpent and the bird appear to be in a fleeing or startled attitude. They are probably underworld creatures, in flight from the presence of the deity, who would then be interpretable as a solar being. No doubt this candle-holder stood in a domestic shrine.

27. Terracotta gable-ornament with apotropaic divine face. Scale 1/4

A local deity is surely depicted on the moulded gable-ornaments ('ante-fixes') of the first-century town. All examples are from the same mould (p. 203, fig. 27). The face is male, beardless, and has hair *en brosse* sur-mounted by wings or horns: a somewhat similar Dorchester antefix seems to be winged, and the same may go for a Caerleon example surrounded by 'eternal' firs.[79] They may all be winds-gods, as other Caerleon antefixes seem to be:[80] but whatever the correct interpretation, these alternatives to the classical gorgon's head had the same task of protecting the dwelling, not only against storms, but against evil spirits and the revenant dead whose voices were to be heard in the shriek of the tempest.

POTTERY

Votive lamps and other vessels of small size and sometimes curious shape are in the collection,[81] but whether pedestal-dishes burnt on the basal interior are truly to be described as incense-burners must be very doubtful. They may come to light in circumstances where this explanation suggests itself, as in the triangular temple at Verulamium; but identical vessels have been found in profusion among domestic refuse at Caerleon, and clearly only particular associations will distinguish a ritual vessel from one which is manifestly only a chafing-dish. The specimens from burials are probably chafing-dishes for the foodstuffs left for the journey of the deceased to the after-life.[82]

PRIESTLY GEAR AND PERSONALIA

Several articles in the collection seem to come from priestly crowns or chaplets, such as four thin bronze plates found in the forum, bearing simple repoussé designs: three are semi-elliptical, and one is square.[83] A fragment of bronze with a few crude repoussé letters may belong to a similar category,[84] but the bronze mail mentioned in *Roman Silchester* is definitely of military type.[85] Less convincingly added to the list are a thin leaf cut from sheet-gold, once sewn on to a cloth backing,[86] and a bronze laurel-leaf which recalls the diadem worn by the little 'flute-player'.

Enough has been said for one great fact to have become plain: daily life was deeply penetrated, perhaps dominated, by supernatural considerations: 'il était aussi facile, dans une rue antique, de rencontrer un dieu que de croiser un homme'.[87] In consequence, talismans are common. Particularly obvious examples are two phallic amulets to ward off the evil eye. One is a plain bronze roundel with a phallus in relief, of a type more commonly found fashioned on the roundel sawn from the base of a stag's antler, itself a substance of power;[88] The other is an applique in the form of a bull's head holding a phallus in its mouth: the emblem terminates in a clenched fist with the thumb protruding through the fingers in an age-old and now widely misunderstood apotropaic gesture.[89]

There are many folk today who wear or carry a lucky charm or mascot, sometimes clearly apotropaic,[90] sometimes merely curious, a special coin perhaps, or something else without any external sign in form or decoration of the value which it has for its possessor. The archaeologist cannot of course say very much of corresponding ancient objects, though with greater or lesser confidence he may hazard the opinion that the eye-beads, brooches, rings set with gems, and serpentine bracelets and even pins had a special significance for the wearer (cf. figs. 9, 6; 19, 1; 18, 9 and 12). Possibly the little bronze bells fairly often discovered are to be brought under this heading also,[91] and articles of daily use bearing what we should ourselves regard as mere ornament: key-handles in the form of a lion or panther (fig. 32, 6), for example, may have lent an additional magical defence to locks which were not otherwise very secure.

GEMS

A final word on the gem-stones (fig. 24, 1–6) may bring this chapter to a close. The materials include bloodstone (the *heliotropium,* or 'sun-turner' of the ancients), chalcedony, cornelian, jasper, nicolo, onyx, plasma, prase, sard, sardonyx, and paste mainly imitative of nicolo ('blue paste'). Most subjects are of a simple mythological order, but in many cases, at least, were selected for their 'virtue'. Thus we have, in addition to *Genius Populi Romani* plasma and the sard with augurial wand and ewer, previously mentioned, a Castor and Pollux in dark green prase, similar to that set in a massy gold ring from Pentre, Rhondda;[92] a blue paste with the wrestling of Hercules and Antaeus, symbolic perhaps of the contest between good and evil; an Apollo teaching Hyacinthus; another *Genius* in sardonyx; a Dionysus, perhaps a Jupiter; a Victory, a ship, a dolphin and crayfish cut in cornelian, still set in a simple silver ring; and others of lesser interest. Several gems of importance are shown in the figure. No. 6, appropriately in *heliotropium,* shows a mounted Sun-god, holding a whip; no. 4 is a handsome nicolo showing the crescent moon and stars symbolic of eternity, a frequent device on the imperial coinage commemorating the apotheosis of a ruler or, more often, his consort. No. 3 is certainly the best-cut of all the Silchester gems: a very fine piece in red jasper, showing the oddity known as a *gryllus,* here composed of the conjoined heads of Silenus and a bearded Dionysus (looking downwards, as here shown). Combined with these are a hare, of which the ears are clearly visible, and the snout of a wild boar.

No. 1 is of especial interest, and is again in bloodstone.[93] One side bears a cock-headed, serpent-legged deity in a military kilt, carrying a shield and a whip. The legs suggest the power of earth, the cock's head, shield and whip, that of the sun. The figure is sometimes called *Abrasax* or *Abraxas,* one of the Aeons of the Gnostic sect, which was a strange eclectic mixture of Greek, Hebrew and even of Christian elements. But the identification is unwarranted, since the surviving Gnostic writings contain no reference to a monster like that depicted. On the back of the gem is engraved a word of power, IA Ω, Iaō, one of the commonest incantations in a series which very often includes *Adonai, Eloi, Sabaoth,* and the like, as on the gold-leaf phylactery from Segontium.[94] This gem belongs to a very well-known and large class, and since Iaō is not only engraved from left to right, i.e. to be read on the gem rather than on an impression, but must in fact have been concealed in the mounting, it is clear that the specimen was of a purely amuletic significance.

A final gem is lost, but was recorded by Gough as being in Stair's collection in 1768. Of onyx, it bore 'only the letters ZACP'—possibly another magical word.[95]

Note.—The following is a possible reconstruction of the text of the 'Calleva stone' (pl. 11, p. 22, cf. 58, 154).

[NVM. AVG(G)]
]R[
[SIGN]VM VI[CTO]
[RIAE SINE COLLAT]IONIBV[S]
[COMMISSV]M.SIBI.A CON
[LEGIO PERE]GRINORVM
[CONSISTENTI]VM CALLEVAE
[DONVM]. D. S. D.

'To the Godhead(s) of the Emperor(s) . . . R . . . dedicated from his own resources (this) statue of Victory entrusted to him by the Association of Strangers resident at Calleva, without contributions from (their) resources'

On the other two stones found in the Insula XXXV temple, statues of Peace and of Mars may be mentioned, viz. [SIGNV]M PACIS, [SIGNVM] MARTIS; see note 22, p. 58.

14

The Church

'Close to the south-east corner of the forum in the centre of the city, and in the angle formed by the intersection of two of the main streets, the excavations have disclosed the foundations of a small basilica, which, from its plan and arrangements, there seems every reason to believe was a Romano-British Christian Church!' Hope thus made known the most famous of all the Silchester discoveries, first unearthed in May 1892, carefully covered in at the end of that year's work, and re-examined in 1961 (pls. 26–7, fig. 28).[1] No significant dating-evidence was found upon either occasion, though in 1961 pottery sealed beneath the flooring was able to show that it could hardly have been erected before about 200;[2] and no relics of an indubitably Christian character occurred. The plan alone, therefore, is a guide to the nature of the building. Few who saw it exposed entertained any doubt: but their certainty arose more from a consciousness of what Christian architecture was to become in later Roman times and afterwards than from any detailed awareness of how church-design had developed before and during the reign of Constantine the Great, whose Edict of Toleration for the Christians, the 'Peace of the Church', was promulgated at Milan in 313. A recent study by C. A. Ralegh Radford and a book by H. Kähler have eased the task of tracing this development in the Roman west,[3] but it is thereby swiftly borne upon the enquirer that the little basilica is totally isolated in point of design from any other known fourth-century church nearer than Rome itself. This is a state of affairs which cannot well have corresponded to reality: but neither is it purely accidental, for the discovery followed upon the policy of complete excavation which, for various reasons, has not been or cannot be applied to other towns in the Roman west.

Can the building be shown to be a church? It is like a church in possessing narthex, nave, aisles, and apse; and it faced west, as some early churches did: but, less from disbelief in its Christian character than from a desire to point out that the identification had not been proved, the plan has been compared

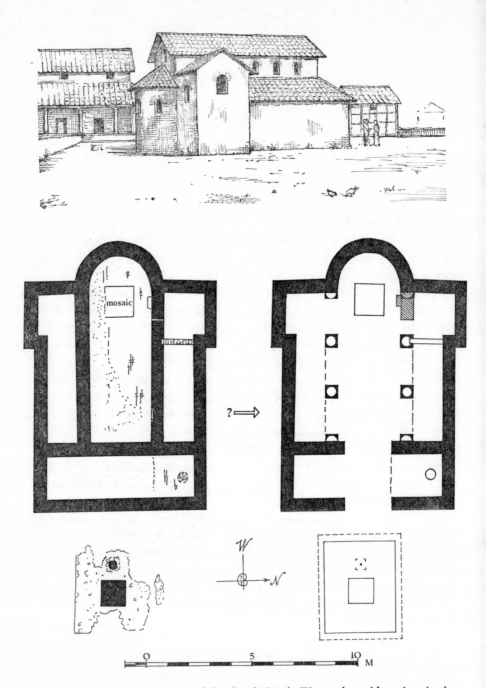

mosaic

W

N

0   5   10 M

28. Excavated and restored plan of the church, Insula IV, together with an imaginative reconstruction of the building from the south-west

with those of pagan mystery-temples in Rome, to which may be added, for example, the Roman reconstruction of the temple of the Pythian Apollo at Gortyna (Crete), for, with narthex, nave, aisles and apse this may stand as a general representative of a whole class of buildings designed for the performance of rites before a congregation.[4] At Silchester itself we have an instance the *schola* of Insula XXI (p. 158). There are Christian buildings of like design: one of the best-known is the *martyrium,* or commemorative chapel with westerly apse erected over holy graves outside the Roman city of Köln, discovered beneath St Severin's church; and at various places (especially in the Rhine-Danube frontier-regions) simple aisle-less buildings, with deep easterly apses, have been detected: they were congregational churches, and have baptisteries annexed.[5] The common ancestor of both pagan and Christian buildings of this type is the long-axis basilica or audience-hall, touched upon in Chapter 9 (p. 113).

All these apparent parallels, however, lack one feature possessed by the Silchester building: a transept. On the excavated plan, this is not perhaps very clear; but the west end of the basilica is distinctly wider than the rest, by the width of a wall upon either side; and when it is realised that the walls extending eastwards from the apse to the narthex or porch were merely substructural, and supported columns, the matter becomes obvious. This is the one particular element of the design which enables us to identify the building beyond doubt as a church: 'seul le transept apparaît comme une nouveauté et comme spécial aux édifices chrétiens'. So Leroux in 1913; and it remains true that no pagan long-axis basilica has ever proved to possess a transept, although the central crossings in some *short*-axis basilicas, such as the Caerleon headquarters-building, had a decided transeptal character.[6]

DESCRIPTION OF CHURCH

The centuries have dealt harshly with the church. Even before soil mantled its ruins, it had been subject to a final, squalid phase of squatter-occupation (p. 82); and prior to 1892 the remains lay so near the surface that untold damage was wrought by the plough. Only around the north-west and north-east corners does anything stand above foundation-level. The building lies in one of the gravelled areas surrounding the forum, delimited on the north by a lane running along the side of that edifice, on the east and south by streets, and on the west by a wall, of which feeble traces were noted in 1892. Apart from a well open in the third century or later, and the foundation-trenches of what I regard as a large early timber building, this space of about 41 by 29 m. is devoid of any known feature other than the church and the brick-built base, set in a square of flint pitching, which stands in front of it. There was no precinct-wall, and if there were subsidiary buildings of the kind to be expected, if not an *atrium* of the usual type, they must have been of the very slight construction which we deduce existed around the square of flint pitching.

The church is very small, barely 13 by 9 m. overall, and is aligned slightly in advance of the east front of the forum near by. It is far from perfectly laid out: in particular, the two stereobates are not parallel. The walls were flint-built with brick quoins, 60 cm. thick; the foundations are solid enough to have carried a superstructure throughout of masonry. The apse is 3 m. in diameter, and the overall length of the apse and nave is 8.9 m., while the aisles are 5 m. long and 1.5 m. wide. The transept is 11.1 m. long and 2 m. wide; the narthex is 7.7 m. long and 2 m. wide. The open character of the interior west of the narthex is fairly apparent, because there is no lateral foundation at the west end of the aisles, as would have been present if the spaces beyond had been conceived as sacristy-like chambers such as are found in various early churches.[7] There is indeed a partition at the west end of the north aisle, but it is not repeated on the south, and it is very slight, being only 30 cm. wide, and at first merely of timber: in fact, it may have been only a railing, the bottom beam of which left its impression in a mortar bedding.[8] The lack of any reserved area which could have been used as a sacristy no doubt accounts for this feature, leading thus to the provision of a *diaconicon* in the usual place, viz. on the left of the sanctuary as one looks towards the nave. Here would have been kept the vestments and liturgical vessels, and here too would have been accepted the gifts of bread and wine for the Eucharist, and other gifts for the maintenance of the clergy; another suggestion, put forward by Radford, is that this may have been a shrine, not necessarily containing any relics, of a martyr whose remains had been destroyed or whose place of sepulture was unknown.[9]

The partition is also important for the light which it throws on the nature of the interior of the building more generally. It is set sufficiently off the inner corner of the transept to require explanation; and this can only be that the inner end was anchored against the middle of the first pier or column upon the northern stereobate. Furthermore, the mortar sill itself projects a little, perhaps 20 cm., over the edge of the stereobate, suggesting that the side of the partition fitted into a chase cut in the upright, more naturally thus a column than a pier, though no scrap of columnar material came to light. Lastly, it will be found that the distance of 2.28 m. between the centre of the mortar sill and the springing-point of the apse is exactly one-third of the distance between the former and the narthex-wall. The measurement suggests that each stereobate carried a row of four columns at 2.28 m. centres, two free-standing, and two half-columns at either end. That there were not more columns between the partition and the narthex seems reasonably clear, because the projecting edge of the red tessellated floor of the nave itself protruded over the edge of the stereobate at a point where the spacing would have required an additional column to stand.

The floor of the nave is continuous into the apse, with no change of level, and its red tessellation is relieved only by a panel of geometric mosaic 1.5 m. square (pl. 27), which projects from the mouth of the apse. The design of black and white chequers on a quarterly counterchanged background of the same, within a border of red and grey-green Purbeck lozenges on white, may have assisted in the centring of some moveable object, presumably an altar, which may have been a simple three-legged table like the Kimmeridge shale specimens described below (p.223);[10] whether the cruciform arrangement is significant in itself is a possibility which may occur to the mind, but cannot be settled. No traces of tessellation, or even of it mortar bed (which would have survived, if only as traces) were to be found in the ends of the transept or in the aisles or in the narthex except, in the last, around a heavy flint foundation exposed in 1961: this must have supported something of massive character, scarcely therefore an offering-table, perhaps a stone *cantharus* of water for ritual ablution. Richmond thought that the lack of evidence for tessellation elsewhere was sufficient to suggest that the flooring, in these other parts, had been of flags or boards, but since flagged floors do not occur at Silchester the second alternative is more probable. Such distinctions of flooring are not unknown in early churches.

ALTERATIONS

There was a subsidence at the north-west corner, which affected the end of the transept and the apse: probably the foundation-trenches of the early timber building adjacent were to blame, though not actually traced below the church. The reconstruction gave a more solid form to the reserved area, the wooden partition being replaced by a narrow central pier of flint-work, with a step in hard chalk blocks on either side to a new floor, again probably of boards. The area was also walled off on the south side towards the apse, except for a narrow doorway: traces remained on the stereobate. Opposite the centre of the mosaic panel there may have been a slight, pilaster-like projection of uncertain character. As for the mosaic itself, it was covered up, probably at this same time: specks of brick-mortar were observed upon it both in 1892 and 1961. Hope thought that the altar had been replaced in masonry, but it seems more likely that the whole area of the apse and projecting panel was raised. If so, we have an explanation of the strangely unworn state of the tessellated pavement west of the panel and to either side (though on the south there was very little left). If the reconstruction took place only a short time after the first erection of the church, these parts would have been protected from the continual tread to which the remainder of the floor was obviously still subject.

COMPARISONS OF PLAN

As it had evolved by 313, the design of urban churches was architecturally undistinguished, despite the occasional richness of mosaic or fresco. It lacked the coherence of a unitary plan, stemming as it did from the simple house-churches of the preceding era, and serves but as a foil to the grand imperial design of the Constantinian basilicas of Christian Rome. Such town-churches in their most elaborate form are exemplified at Aquileia and Trier, where the early cathedrals, in use by the 320's, took the form of parallel linked halls of great size, embracing a baptistery and various subordinate arrangements.[11] The *schola*-like churches of the Rhine and Danube, with a single nave and deep apse, represent a type of 'garrison-church' which may be of parallel development to the Silchester building, but cannot in itself afford a very valuable comparison. In short, it must be concluded—as far as our present knowledge goes—that the transeptal basilicas of Rome are at some unknown remove the model for Silchester.

The earliest building in which a transeptal design is detectable is, however, the double hall-church at Aquileia.[12] Here we have a building nearly 20 by 40 m. at either side of the complex, its superstructure supported by three pairs of widely-spaced columns. But for a slight partition or balustrade, and the disposition of the mosaic flooring, it would be impossible to tell that the east end of either hall was in fact a transverse nave and not a mere continuation of the nave and aisles. The earliest Roman basilica with a transeptal design is S. Giovanni in Laterano, erected under Pope Sylvester (*c.* 313–35): but the transept, as is now known, was not of 'transverse nave' type, but on the contrary took the form, probably, of sacristies which on either side communicated with the side-aisles (there were four aisles).[13] This at present anomalous 'aisle-transept' must have been roofed at a far lower level than the inner pair of aisles and the nave; and this is of interest, for the narrow Silchester transept can hardly have stood as high as the nave.

S. Pietro in Vaticano—Old St. Peter's—was begun about 333, and possessed a fine transept of true 'transverse nave' type;[14] but the *next* dated example is S. Paolo fuori le Mura, begun in 386.[15] In short, it must be doubted whether the Silchester building could possibly have been erected before the very late fourth century, because the slight off-setting of the end-walls of the transept shows that we have to do with a derivative, and not an original, plan. This is the date assigned to the large basilica at Epidaurus in the Peloponnese; another church, at Daphnousi, is very like Silchester, except for its *atrium,* and is of the fifth century.[16] Both are examples of the momentous and surely officially-inspired extension of the transeptal design from Rome to the provinces, a design continuing in favour, though not to the exclusion of the plain basilica, down to Carolingian times.[17]

From the fact that both S. Pietro and S. Paolo housed *memoriae* of saints, it seems probable that the transept may have been devised in connection with the special rites attending the cult of holy martyr-graves or relics; but in point of fact there are other early churches, such as S. Agnese fuori le Mura,[18] and the large Epidaurus church mentioned, which had a transept but no shrine. Thus the transept cannot be associated exclusively with the martyr-cult. At Silchester there were no signs of any reliquary or translated burial. A more general explanation which would account for the facultative character of the transept has to be sought. In the *martyrium*-basilica, its function was essentially to provide additional space for circulation and worship about the focal point, the shrine; in other churches, it is suggested,[19] it gave greater space to the clergy assembled around the ordinary altar, and provided room for the *prothesis* where the bread and wine to be used in the Eucharist were set out when ready. Finally, as has also been pointed out, the seating for clergy in some Greek churches projected beyond the normal confines of the apse; and cases are known where seating on either side of the altar replaced the traditional *synthronos* around the wall of the apse.

The relevance of this material to our little basilica is close. Its apse was so small that seating there would have been very cramped, especially since, in a church aligned to the west, the celebrant stood behind the altar and faced the congregation to the east.[20] The unworn cubes of the flooring extend right up to the wall of the apse, and show that there had been no structural *synthronos.* Thus in the first period of the building at least, it may be suggested, the subordinate clergy, who cannot have been many, took up their position on either side of the altar, leaving room for the celebrant behind it. The projection of the mosaic panel is almost certainly to be explained in this manner.[21] The small amount of room made available by the transeptal design would have been very useful.

RECONSTRUCTED APPEARANCE

The remains are only a 'ground-plan in stone', and to quote Montfaucon in a somewhat similar connection, 'il est aisé de lever le plan sur des mazures: mais ces mazures ne suffisent pas toujours pour donner un profil'. The fifth and sixth century churches of Italy, S. Apollinare in Classe near Ravenna, for example, convey the general style which the Silchester building possessed in much humbler guise. The picture, then, is of a nave carried up into a clerestory, probably with largish windows; a pitched roof above; aisles and narthex with pentice roofs abutting the nave, and an apse with a half-conical roof above an internal light dome. But if pen is to be put to paper, and this image translated into line, there emerge assumptions which have to be examined closely. There is no fragment of evidence to show the height of the building; not a scrap to tell certainly the nature of the roof-cover, whether of tile or, as was ever commoner in the third and fourth centuries, hexagonal stone slabs. Guesswork, informed perhaps but nevertheless guesswork, must enter into our calculations.

Let us look firstly at the skeleton of the building: the two rows of uprights dividing the nave and aisles. We have already guessed that these were columns rather than piers (p. 176); and if they were columns, then most probably they were of the ordinary provincial Tuscan, in Bath stone. Full-size columns of this type were about 30 cm. wide, and on Vitruvian proportions would have stood about eight times this in overall height, or 2.4 m. Granted columns: were they crowned by an architrave, or by arches? There is not so much as a voussoir-brick to prove the latter, but on the other hand, the centre-to-centre intercolumniation would carry the extrados of the arches to 3.54 m. above the floor, and that is about the level of the abutment of a pentice roof on the aisles, supposing that the outer walls were of the same height as the columns, and the roof rested at 30°. A plain architrave with walling above would have made the aisles very dark, unless they had windows; and windows, given the absence of any known kind of enclosure about the church, can probably be ruled out.

So far, so good; but the roofs of the aisles and narthex were very probably continuous; and since the latter is some 46 cm. wider than the former, the east front of the church would then have been only 2.1 m. high. If the east front were made 2.5 m. high, the aisle walls would then be 2.8 m., and the arches of the interior, if they existed, would have been handsomely cleared. This is the solution, speculative as it may be, that is adopted in the drawing (fig. 28).

If the church followed the pattern of St. Peter's, the transept would have been as high as the nave. This is not impossible, but we should have expected a transverse stereobate on the line of the east side of the transept, to carry the weight. Much more probably, the transept was roofed with the nave in the central part, and to either side with a pitched roof at a somewhat higher level than the aisles. Finally, allowing say 1 m. for the height of the clerestory windows, the ridge of the main roof would have been in the region of 6 m. above the pavement.

Very little survived of the interior decoration; and although the 1892 report mentions fragments of plaster, some speckled in imitation of marble, it omits to mention the colouring (probably white and dark red spots on pink, if the usual sort), and the pieces are not now identifiable.

THE BAPTISTERY

Hope regarded the brick base, only 3.5 m. from the front of the church, as clearly being 'the place of the *labrum* or laver in which the faithful used to wash their hands and faces before entering the church, and the shallow pit in front was probably covered by a pierced stone, and served to carry off the waste water. The water itself could be obtained from the well west of the church, to which, as there are no other buildings near, it seems to have belonged'. This explanation has been generally followed, not least by the learned editors of the *Dictionnaire d'archéologie chrétienne et de liturgie,* and it is not indeed impossible that the well was used for church purposes: besides two conical white-metal cups and coins of Victorinus (269–71), it contained a good deal of *opus signinum* flooring, perhaps from the raised floor in the apse, and if so was open during the life of the building.

In 1961 the brick base, 1.2 m. square, and the flint pitching on which it was set were carefully examined under the supervision of Sir Ian Richmond. It was shown that the pitching had originally been rectangular, about 4.1 m. from east to west and 3.5 m. from north to south; it extended within 1.7 m. of the church. The only other detail to be noted concerns the 'pit' on the west side of the base, which turned out to be 50 cm. across and over 1 m. deep.[22] Richmond's conclusion was that the base was that of a baptismal font, perhaps the actual bottom; that the sump acted as a soak-away for the water used in the triple affusion of the candidates; and that the square of pitching had originally been contained by a simple wooden building of sleeper-beam construction. No traces of such a building remained, though sought: but there can hardly be any other explanation to account for the preservation of a straight edge of flintwork on the south and east at least. It remains very curious that a baptistery should not have had the same flint walling possessed by many an isolated square building at Calleva, but perhaps it was erected as a temporary measure, and there was no occasion to reconstruct it more fittingly. More curious, perhaps, is the propinquity of the church: since there was so much apparently open space around the church, why should the baptistery have been placed so near? Again, why should the baptistery have been so small? There is scarcely a 1.2 m. of clearance around the font on any side except the west, where the sump was. Lastly, should not the font have been sunk into the ground, so that the candidates stood at a lower level than the officiating bishop, for convenience at least?

These difficulties can very probably be met. There was indeed very little room in the baptistery, no room for undressing: therefore I am inclined to suggest that the very proximity of the church, in particular the narthex, was deliberate. In this view, the candidates would have been prepared for the ceremony in the narthex, and would thereupon have been led to the baptistery (no doubt wearing a warm wrap or cloak, since Easter, the appointed day, followed by Pentecost as next choice, would have been as often early and chilly as today) across the space, which could easily have been screened.[23] In the baptistery itself, the floor would probably have been of cement laid on the pitching alone extant now: the *cella* of the temple in Insula XXXV similarly preserves only the bedding of its floor (pl. 23). There would have been room enough for three or four to gather and perform the ceremony with perfect seemliness: it may be pointed out that the baptistery at Kaiseraugst, for example, annexed to the north side of the church, is of even slightly smaller dimensions, only about 4 by 2.5 m., 2.5 m. being allowed on the east side of the font.

The construction of fonts somewhat naturally followed that of *piscinae* in bath-houses, and these were often built at floor level. Free-standing fonts were in use at a very early date, as well as sunken *piscinae*.[24] The rubble and tile-built examples recently studied by P. D. C. Brown in his very lucid identification of an undoubted font found, but not recognised, at Richborough in 1923[25] seem not to have been sunken very much below the surrounding ground-level. At Kaiseraugst and Zurzach they were squarish; at Köln and other sites they were polygonal with curved niches in the external faces. In all except Kaiseraugst, there were signs of the outlet-pipes.

Unless more has been lost at Silchester than one would be prepared readily to admit, there was no outlet-pipe, particularly in the brickwork, low as that is. Furthermore, the sump seems strangely large for its supposed purpose as a soakaway, and at an unnecessary distance (70 cm.), if that were its object, from the base. I am inclined to wonder whether the base may not have supported a cylindrical leaden tank of a type occasionally found in Britain, three bearing the sacred monogram of Chi and Rho.[26] Such a tank may have acted as a reservoir rather than as a font proper, and the candidates may have stood on a grille or pierced stone placed over the large, deep sump. Attention is drawn to a very curious installation in a baptistery assigned to the fourth century (how accurately, I know not) at Emmaus in Palestine.[27] On either side of a handsome, quatrefoil *piscina*, there is a shallow sinking in the floor, about 1.5 m. across; and in the centre of each, a narrow drain leads down to the bottom of the *piscina*, so that the water used in the affusion could flow back.

CHRISTIAN OBJECTS FROM CALLEVA

These are few and easily described. Only one can be said to prove the presence of a Christian at Calleva—and not a very honest one at that—namely the *Senicianus* ring already described (fig. 18, 4, p. 133).[28] The others, such as they are, may have come from Christian hands, but are manufactured articles. The most interesting is a leaden sealing found by Joyce in a room of the basilica (fig. 24, 7).[29] It is about 19 mm. in diameter, and has been impressed, by a hinged die, with the Chi-Rho monogram on both sides, flanked by Alpha and Omega. Above, there are two, possibly three, stars on one side, and on the other, the letter M which Joyce thought might stand for the Emperor Magnentius (350–3). But it would be most unusual for an imperial name to be abbreviated so. Possibly the letter should be taken as a numeral, i.e. 40 in Greek or 1000 in Latin. The sealing had evidently been used for a document or packet of some kind, for one can see where the string has lain.

Stamps employing a Chi-Rho, with or without some additional legend such as *Spes in Deo,* are well-known on fourth-century objects, by no means always of a religious nature, most often not: the best examples in Britain occur on pewter ingots found in the Thames.[30] A long search, however, has failed to produce more than a single colourable parallel to the Silchester sealing; and even that parallel is a mysterious item, known only in the pages of Ficoroni's *I piombi antichi* of 1740. One side carries a similar Chi-Rho flanked by A and Ω; on the other is GER/I/MNI, perhaps to be read *Germini* '[sealing of] Germinius'.[31]

Other Christian objects include the north African lamp (pl. 33f, p. 73) and a small piece from the lip of a conical beaker of colourless glass, interesting as being of much earlier date—second or third century—than the openly Christian objects otherwise discussed. Probably of Köln manufacture, it bears as we have it, a fish (in Greek ἰχθύς, standing for the initial letters of

'Jesus Christ Son of God, Saviour'), a palm-branch, and part of the letter C. Several other glasses of the same kind are known in Britain and abroad.[32]

Calleva is not exceptional in the small number of Christian objects of any kind which it has produced.[33] Clearly, the Christian community was very small (p. 72).

15

Cemeteries

Without Col Karslake's researches in Rampier Copse (p. 32), we should know even less than we do of the funeral practices of the Callevans. It seems that the humbler folk used the obsolete bank of the outer earthwork there for burials; all are simple cremations, the rite of Belgic days—as also in contemporary Rome—only slowly being superseded by inhumation towards the close of the second century.[1] Most of the Rampiers burials were disturbed by badgers, rabbits, and 'those who have for many generations endeavoured to dig them out'; but a well-preserved example was found in 1900.

The lower part of the bank was cut back until a vertical face about 1.5 m. high was left. Against this, a pyre of logs was constructed, the body being placed on top, aligned north and south, as could be judged from the position of the nails of the bier scattered over an area of 1.9 by 1.4 m. Sandals had been on the feet, and the studs from their soles lay to the south end of this rectangular space. Probably the corpse was fully clothed. Sustenance for the journey to the after-life was provided in the form of an ox-cheek, and something in a pot, probably a drink. When combustion was complete—it was fanned, no doubt, by the prevailing south-westerly wind, against the face of the earthwork—the ashes were gathered and placed in a grey urn, which was what might be described as a 'second', being somewhat distorted at the rim: it is of late second-century date. This urn was placed on the north side of the area, approximately below, as near as could be judged, the position which had been occupied by the head of the corpse upon the bier. The earth was then thrown back; and all that remained to mark the spot was a small pile of flints, from the revetment of the earthwork, and a piece of a glass bottle which could mark a subsequent libation. If the spot had ever been dignified by a stele, there was no trace. This account goes some way towards demonstrating the point made on an earlier page (p. 163) regarding the Celtic belief that the head was the seat of the soul. Most of the burials, which seem to have been numerous, were on the inner side of the bank; but another on the outer side yielded scraps of fused bronze which might have come from the plating of a casket consigned with its owner to the pyre.[2]

Another cemetery lay north of the town, by the side of the Dorchester road, on the brow of the hill beyond the outer earthwork—possibly within its line also. A Bath stone sarcophagus was found here in 1852, and appears to have lain in a masonry-based tomb of circular plan, about 6 m. across.[3] A pottery sprinkler-bottle, of early third-century date, was the sole object buried with the dead: it is now at Reading.[4] Just as the Rampiers burial described above marks a late stage in the practice of cremation, so this interment reflects an early stage in the spread of inhumation, as far as British evidence goes.

Aerial photographs taken in 1970 by the National Monuments Record reveal small, isolated square markings on either side of the main roads to London and to the west. These are probably masonry tombs or ditched funerary enclosures, as is only likely in view of their completely typical situation (see the folding plan and pl. 9). Some confirmation of the existence of tombs near the London road is afforded by an old record of a great block of stone some 2.1 by 1.2 by 0.6 m., lying on a base of brickwork and rubble, seen in a garden of one of the cottages which stood opposite the amphitheatre. Such a huge block would be unusual, however, anywhere in Britain, and probably a concrete structure might be more readily acceptable.[5]

Only one sepulchral inscription has been preserved entire; it was found as long ago as 1577, and was once in the possession of the great Lord Burghley, Elizabeth's minister. The text reads: MEMORIAE FL.VICTORINAE.T. TAM.VICTOR CONJUNX POSUIT, 'To the Memory of Flavia Victorina. Titus Tammonius Victor, her husband, set up (this monument)' (cf. p. 57). The date is probably in the third, or possibly the fourth century, for the *Memoriae* formula is not an early one. The stone illustrates the prevalent Roman custom of indicating the name and relationship of the person responsible for erecting the monument.[6]

Finally, mention may be made of two unfinished sculptures from Insula V, where, possibly, there was a monumental mason's yard. The material is a drab Greensand. One is a lion, often found in a funerary context to symbolise the consuming power of death; the other is a pedestal-like altar, with a projecting tablet about half-way up, destined no doubt to carry an inscription. These two pieces very probably go together. A monument from Aiud, Romania, shows an open-air offering altar like this, but with a large circular medallion containing family portraits instead of the plain tablet. At the foot there are two funerary lions back to back, and between them a Medusa-head is carved. The Silchester lion is damaged, and this fact may explain why it was never finished. Clearly it would have been accompanied by another, to form an ensemble of the same sort as that described.[7]

16

Houses: Plan and Structure

Most of the houses are widely-spaced: we have already pointed to the contrast between them and the shops ranged along the main east-west street (p. 96). The houses differ greatly from those of our own towns, for the Romano-Britons preferred to align their rooms in a continuous block, with access generally by corridor. All the accommodation could be provided on the ground floor, because there was very little limit to the amount of ground which could be taken, except in the case of the shops. The dominance of the forum-basilica upon a skyline punctuated otherwise mainly by the tower-like *cellae* of the temples, but by few other buildings, would have have been complete.

The typological study of Romano-British houses is artificial, because all the various types existed together from the earliest period, and simplicity or complexity of plan is not necessarily a reflection of relative date. The simplest buildings at Calleva are of course plain rectangles, sometimes containing a hearth to point to their use as workshops, if not as dwellings: we may instance XIII.B2 or B4. The next stage is the rectangle partitioned at one end, such as XIII.B3; but again such a building cannot be positively identified as a dwelling.

SHOPS

Most of the shops along the main street have more elaborate subdivisions. The buildings are aligned so as to present a gable-end to the street, and about half or two-thirds of their area is given to their retail function or, as in about half the examples along the southern margins of Insulae I and IX–XI, to petty manufacturing operations attested by the presence of furnaces which occur either against walls, where a clay hood and chimney could be contrived to carry off smoke and fumes, or in the middle of the spaces, presumably as a precaution against fire: in these cases, the products of combustion must have found their way out through louvres in the roof. If such buildings had upper storeys, it is reasonable to conclude that living-accommodation was confined to the areas above the ground-floor rooms at the rear. Probably, the roof-line would have been continuous, and the upper floor would in consequence have been more like a loft than a full storey.

Perhaps the best example of a shop of this kind is IX.B3 (fig. 29, 2).[1] Here the working-area, some 13.5 by 9.5 m., was open to the street, with columns (or more probably posts) on either side and in the centre.[2] Towards the rear was a brick-built furnace, axially sited. Beyond were four good rooms, including one heated by hypocaust, and a narrow passage which may have held a stair to a loft over the ground-floor accommodation. Whether XXIX.B7 was a shop may be doubted: but if so, the area opening on to a street was much smaller, and a second room behind might have been a restaurant, as in similar cases at Pompeii.[3] Buildings such as those described occur with great frequency in towns and the civil settlements of forts: good examples can still be seen outside the fort of Housesteads, and the *genre* scenes so popular in Roman funerary art readily enable us to repeople them with their hard-working proprietors.[4] The lock-up shops at the north-west corner of Insula VI (fig. 29, 1) and in the middle of the south side of Insula I have already been discussed (pp. 54–5).

SIMPLE HOUSES

XXVIII.1 and 2 (fig. 29, 3) are interesting examples of simple rectangular buildings which have been gradually altered and extended.[5] House 1 is on the 'baths alignment' and is likely therefore to be of early origin; it consists of five rooms in a row, some 24.5 by 6.5 m., and an entrance no doubt on the

---

29. Plans of houses, etc. 1, colonnaded block of shops contemporary with the forum, VI.B1. 2, shop IX.B3, with living-rooms at the rear and furnace in working-space. 3, XXVIII.1-2, strip houses with corridors, etc. added. 4, XXXIIIA.4-5, early double-corridor houses, adapted to the street. 5, VI.2, double-corridor house with western extension over earlier watercourse. 6, small winged house XXVI.1 and ancillary buildings: (a), labourers' dwelling over earlier threshing-floor? (b), granary? (c), drying-chamber for corn? (d), hearth-base for brewing? (e), well. 7, XXIII.2, large house, originally a double-corridor block on the west, extended eastward towards, and adapted by a porch to, the street. 8, XIV.1, double-corridor house with three-sided addition on the west providing a completely enclosed court (with shrine); agricultural buildings in yard to north. 9, VIII.1-2, double-corridor house with three-sided single-corridor addition on the west. A-C, agricultural buildings: A, byre for four pairs of oxen, I.2? B, granary at rear of X.B2. C, large barn attached to XXIV.2. North at top (except C, east at top)

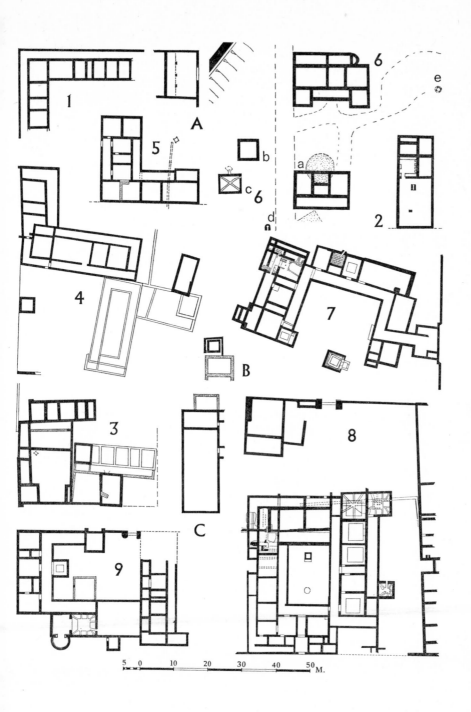

1   A

5

b

c 6

d

a

6

e

2

4

7

B

3

C

8

9

5   0   10   20   30   40   50   M.

east. The first addition was the corridor on the south; then came a large heated room in the courtyard, its furnace being in the corridor, under cover. Eventually, the house was pulled down except for this room, where the hypocaust-basement was filled and a furnace for metallurgical purposes installed; an isolated chamber was also built over the west end of the original block. House 2 also had five rooms; and if there was ever a corridor, it was most probably an addition as in House 1. On the south, a small yard was enclosed, an open shed being built on the west side, and later extended to the street on the south, where there was a rather grand porch or lobby of the kind found in the best houses of the town. Later, an outer yard containing a shed and a well was enclosed also. Walling running north and south was thought by the excavators to be of earlier date, and it may have enclosed a paddock belonging to House 1: it lies some 40 m. from the eastern boundary of the insula, a distance corresponding to the 'unit' of the Silchester cadastre (p. 97).

CORRIDOR-HOUSES

The corridor added to XXVIII.1 gave privacy to the rooms, which could otherwise be reached only from one another. Houses with single corridors are very frequent on the plan: II.2 is a typical specimen, contemporary with the streets, and with further additions, notably a heated room rather more than 3.5 m. square, on the north side. The adjacent isolated square overlies ruins of an earlier building.[6] Equally common are houses with two corridors, front and back; they include one of the earliest identifiable, XXXIIIA.4 (fig. 29, 4). Here the corridor runs around all four sides, and it was certainly an open ambulatory on the south, at least.[7] The main block would have been divided into rooms by timber partitions; the narrowness of the foundations itself shows that the superstructure was substantially timber. A more typical double-corridor house of pre-street days is IX.1, at some 36.5 by 13.5 m. much larger than usual. Another good example is XXIII.2, extended to the street (fig. 29, 7).

The reason for the double-corridor design, and its origin, are obscure. In the inn, or in the case of the largest houses, an outer corridor is explainable on the assumption that it was meant for servants' use; but this is a suspiciously Victorian notion, and it cannot apply, since a double corridor is by no means a universal feature of the plans of the richest houses. Furthermore, the rear corridor is often found to have been partitioned, as if its use as a passage was unimportant (I.2, and in the largest house of all, XIV.1, fig. 29, 8). On the other hand, the existence of the single-corridor type is enough to dismiss any suggestion that corridors helped in some way to buttress the main block. C. A. F. Berry, in a percipient account of Callevan houses,[8] traces the origin of both types of corridor-plan to the basilical or barn type of house with pillared aisles and nave, in which some bays may be partitioned into rooms. In these cases, however, the outer walls are load-bearing, and more important than the inner walls originating in lines of roof-supports: the theory will not do. Possibly the Claudian timber house at Camulodunum may offer a clue.[9] The main supports are posts, and the outer walls are set about 1 m. from them, and were not load-bearing. In this house, the structural importance of the inner and outer elements is exactly the opposite of what is found in the ordinary basilical design, and corresponds to what one may perhaps imagine the prototype of the Callevan dwelling to have been. The existence of signs of partitions and of a single corridor in the Camulodunum house are also significant.

WING-ROOMS

The next development of consequence to require notice—and for what the remark is worth, there do not seem to be any pre-street examples—is the appearance of wing-rooms. XXVI.1 (some 22 by 15.5 m.), with two wing-rooms on the south connected by a corridor is a noticeable example (fig. 29, 6). The metalled track showing on aerial photographs indicates a main entrance in the centre of the façade. Other houses of a similar kind are IX.B1 as completed by aerial survey, III.1 and VI.1 (west wing).[10] The west and south blocks of House 8 North at Caerwent, and a house of Insula V at Verulamium are of the same pattern, but the type is more commonly met in the countryside, where a symmetrical arrangement could be displayed to better effect than in town.[11]

While on the subject of symmetrical façades, attention may be drawn to XXIV.2, described as 'the most peculiar in plan of any yet found at Calleva' in 1900, as in many ways it remained. But when bereft of accretions on the south, it is seen to be composed basically of a double-corridor block lying north and south, and another lying east and west joined to the middle of the former; while to balance the projecting southern arm, a square wing was built at the opposite end of the latter. Here we seem to have a conscious attempt to reproduce the symmetry of a country porticus-villa. The most striking element of the design, however, is the 28 m. entrance-passage running from the middle of the south corridor to the street, and ending in two vestibules or lodges.[12] Wroxeter offers an urban parallel; and another appears at rural Darenth (Kent). It can only be supposed that the passage was half-open on either side, and passed through gardens to the main part of the house.[13]

WINGED HOUSES

In the larger houses, we find a tendency to shut out the streets, other houses, and comings and goings of all sorts as much as possible. Porches or porters' lodges appear, and the best rooms are at the farthest possible distance from the entrance. In the country, the mansion at the centre of a wide and secluded estate could well copy the elegant symmetry of a grand porticus-villa; in town, the loss of symmetry was a small price to pay for seclusion.

The first class of dwellings to be noted now embraces the L-shaped houses, that is with two blocks or wings. Simple forms, adapted to the streets, are XVIIIA.3, where a large hall at right-angles to the original block meets the street at an angle; and XXVI.3, extended by a long corridor at right-angles to a street-porch added at some later period: on the south of the corridor there is another large hall for storage or workaday use, with some divisions.[14] VI.2 (fig. 29, 5) is a good specimen of an L-shaped house contemporary with the streets, displaying a double-corridor wing and a single-corridor extension. XXIX.1 is similar, but both wings have single corridors.[15] Essentially the same in concept are the three-sided houses such as XXIII.2, an original double-corridor block and two added wings of single-corridor type; the porch has been placed at the rear of the east wing, convenient for the street. XXVII.1 (west) had a plain entrance-corridor leading from the street-porch to the main quarters, and other houses of similar design are VIII.1-2, XXIII.1, and smaller, XV.2, XXI.1, and others.[16]

Somewhat surprisingly, there is no example of a house planned *initially* in the form of four wings completely enclosing a courtyard. XIV.1 (fig. 29, 8) *grew* to this so-called 'courtyard' plan by the addition of a three-sided extension to an original double-corridor block of typical simple design.[17] Enclosed courtyards are rare at Silchester, and we may suspect that XIV.1 could not have taken the form it did unless there had been ground to the north which could be turned into a second yard for workaday purposes. Several houses, I.2, VI.1 and XVII.1 among them, offer a kind of half-way stage, where part of a yard has been enclosed for private use, as often in the case of country villas, e.g. Chedworth, on a large scale.[18] Most, if not all the Silchester houses with a single walled court appear to have had a wide entrance into it from the street, e.g. VIII.1–2, XIX.2, and XXXIV.1.[19] We are led to the conclusion that even the largest houses, as well as the smallest, were occupied by folk whose livelihood, in very many instances, depended upon agriculture (Chapter 19); and that what these Silchester house-plans present is an urban adaptation of the country farm-house or villa.

The approximate overall dimensions of some of the large houses are:

I.1 (pl. 25)   Three wings together some 40 by 33.5 m., 10.5 to 12 m. wide; courtyard about 21 by 24.5 m.—about 22 rooms.

VIII.1–2 (fig. 29, 9)   Three wings together about 33.5 by 47 m., 10.7 m. wide; courtyard some 15 by 26 m.—about 20 rooms.

XIV.1 (fig. 29, 8)   Four wings together some 45.5 by 41 m., 12 to 15 m. wide; courtyard about 17 by 12 m.—about 20 rooms.

UPPER STOREYS

The total of rooms would be dramatically increased if it could be shown that upper floors existed. We have already expressed an opinion on this matter; but it must be admitted that clinching evidence does not survive. This is understandable when it is realised that very few Romano-British buildings are preserved to a significant height above their floor-level. In some cases, narrow apartments suitable for stair-case wells have been taken to suggest the existence of an upper storey, and we have already applied this interpretation to one of the shops (IX.B3). In the case of XIV.1, the excavators admitted the possibility that small rooms along the south side could have been 'servants' bedrooms', but concluded that otherwise the plan showed few which were suited, or used, as bedrooms for the family, which occupied, they thought, rooms on an upper floor in the south wing, access being by a stair in the narrow apartment at the end of the same wing. All this, however, is an instance of the nineteenth-century town-dweller speaking *in propria persona;* and John Ward's ambitious reconstruction of a three-flight staircase in XXIV.2—in the chamber facing the end of the long entrance-passage—is another.[20] Again, in VIII.1–2, excavated in 1893, two years before XIV.1, the necessity for an upper storey reached by a stair constructed in a narrow chamber in the east wing would not have sprung to mind if it had been realised that the eastern part of the house was not a separate dwelling but merely the original wing of the house. In short, it is very necessary—here as in many other departments of archaeology—to divest oneself of notions preconceived but sometimes scarcely recognised as such; and to consider these Roman ground-plans for what they do show, rather than for what they do not: and since the older part of XIV.1 remained in use, and moreover contained all the best rooms, there would obviously have been plenty of bedroom-accommodation in the rest of the ground floor of the building.

PRINCIPAL ROOMS AND KITCHENS

Bereft of furnishings, a modern house is an anonymous enough place; and all the more so a Romano-British house, where neither a familiar layout nor a knowledge of customary dispositions serves as a guide. There is some help to be got from the plan; and there are appointments such as hypocausts and mosaics, or bases of what could have been raised cooking-hearths and the like, to enable us to suggest the purpose of some of the rooms.

The general point was made above that the principal rooms are often the farthest from the street-entrance. Nowhere is this clearer than in VIII.1–2 and XXVII.1 (west), both so close in design that we may be forgiven for thinking that the same architect may have been responsible for their erection. In VIII.1–2, the summer reception-room, if such we may call it, opened off the south corridor about 27 m. from the entrance, and was itself some 5 m. square; on the south side was a deep apsidal alcove, defined probably by columns; and on the east, was a heated winter room similarly demarcated, and of considerably larger dimensions (fig. 29, 9). The apse is horseshoe-shaped rather than semicircular, as it is again in XXVII.1 and also in I.2, where it is an addition to the original plan. The floor in the apse of XXVII.1 is believed to be of the second century, so this type of apse may be regarded as being an especial mark of Callevan domestic architecture of about that period. The suite of principal rooms in XXVII.1 lies about 32 m. from the street-door; the first is a heated apartment about 5.5 m. square, but since the floor is of fourth-century date (p. 216) the hypocaust may be an insertion. The original chamber may possibly have extended past free-standing dividing columns to a full length of over 11.5 m. (pl. 30 shows the second-century floor of the eastern part). Late in the history of the building, access was provided to a very large and rambling set of rooms to the east.

In XIV.1, as already remarked, a magnificent series of reception-rooms with mosaic floors of second-century date was contrived in the original eastern range. We surely cannot be far wrong in thinking that this suite was used for the quasi-official receptions and other social occasions which the owner of the largest house in town—a *duovir,* no doubt—would have held. XIV.2, by contrast, is of very different plan.[21] There were two separate wings, that on the west dating back, probably, to pre-street times; the domestic shrine already described lay here (p. 161). The main reception-rooms, however, were in the newer, or east wing, connected to the other by a richly-floored gallery (pl. 32), probably fourth-century in date. The curious banded mosaic of one of the rooms in the east wing suggested to Fox—and we may concur—that here the *triclinium,* or dining-room, was situated.

If it is reasonably clear which were the main reception-rooms in the houses, the occurrence of squalid débris in other rooms with floors of an inferior type may equally well demonstrate the position of the kitchens. The identifications in *Archaeologia* seem very often to rest upon surmise, but in most if not all cases probably arose from the discovery of ashes, bones, shards, shells etc. in the particular rooms concerned. An example of this kind of deduction comes from Joyce, who thought that the room at the east end of XXI.1 was a kitchen, because its floor was merely of clay compared with tessellation elsewhere, and because part of a quern, part of a mended amphora such as might have been used for food-storage, pottery, and bones were found in it.[22] Elsewhere—II.2, V.3 and VIII.4 provide instances—there are raised hearths or platforms upon which charcoal cooking-fires or ovens could have been accommodated.[23] The excellent iron griddle from the 1890 'hoard' of ironwork (fig. 30) would have been used on such a hearth;[24] but for an oven of the sort envisaged, if not built in solid brickwork like those to be seen in many a country *trattoria* in Italy today, we have to turn to an example found in the legionary potteries at Holt (Denbs.).[25] We may also note the occasional appearance of a ledge or stand for a table, working-surface, or dresser, as in XVII.1 and 4 and XIV.2.[26]

Some of the 'furnaces' both outside and inside houses (pl. 35) were possibly for brewing, or in some cases, bake-ovens: in XVI.1, for example, there was such a furnace, and by its side a large earthenware vessel had been sunk into the ground, possibly as a receptacle for the hot ashes raked out of the oven before the food was put in. Another instance lay in the yard of a house near the forum, where several pots were also found.[27]

Mention of these introduces the question of the vessels which were sunk to their rims in the floors of many rooms. In XXVII.1 (west) there were no fewer than six, spaced around the walls; and a brick-built hearth and deposits of lamb and chicken-bones suggest that we are once more in a kitchen. A parallel instance occurred in XXXIIA.1, where there were four pots, two covered, again in a room with a hearth.[28] All these, and the many others found singly, were with one exception—containing the remains of a carp, less head and tail, the scales still preserved in the natural order[29]—empty. If such pots, however, were used for food-storage, it is difficult to see what advantages were gained by countersinking them, especially since they did not exceed the ordinary cooking-pot in capacity, indeed they were ordinary

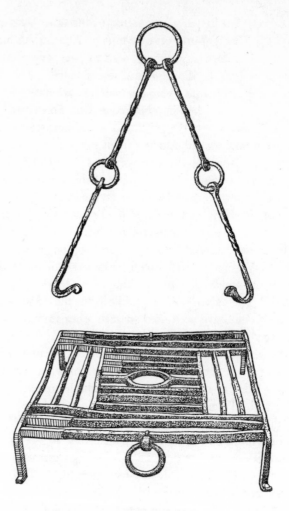

30. Iron pot-hooks from XIX.1; iron gridiron from the 1890 'hoard' of ironwork, Insula
I. Scales, 1/8, 1/6

cooking-pots. Their use as urinals can probably be ruled out, for they were quite perfect, unpierced, and emptying them would have been difficult.[30] In many cases the pots were probably intended for the safe-keeping of valuables, very much smaller versions of the countersunk strong-box mentioned below. Two much larger vessels, however, were no doubt used for food storage: one has already been mentioned (p. 111), the pot walled into a corner of a shop in the forum; the other is the 'Jubilee Pot' of third-fourth century New Forest ware, so-called from its discovery in XVIIIA.2 on the day of Queen

Victoria's Diamond Jubilee in 1897. This vessel bears the graffito VI=, a mark of capacity (6 $\frac{2}{12}$ [*modii*], or about 54 litres).[31]

Prominent among rooms identifiable by permanent fittings in both modern and Roman houses are bath-rooms and privies; but as the Public Baths were popular, only one Silchester house appears to have had a bath-suite (and then only a small one, consisting of *tepidarium* and *caldarium*, in the later XIX.2);[32] and even privies are difficult to identify (p. 90). We must pass, therefore, to other rooms where a specialised function is evident. The first is in XXIII.1, where Joyce found the remains of a strong-box sunk in the middle of the tessellated floor; it would no doubt have been concealed by a mat or fur rug. The cavity measured some 1.8 m. long, 1 m. wide, and was 60 cm. deep (fig. 31), and was roughly walled in flint. An oak frame-

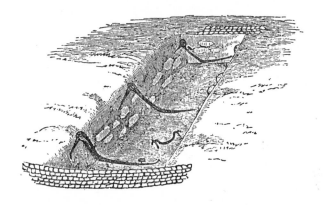

31. Cavity for strong-box in XXIII.1, with remains of hinges and handle. After Joyce

work had been let into the floor, and the chest constructed within it. Three strong strap-hinges turning in loops, the lock-plate, key, and the handle, all of iron, were found in the cavity, and the clenched nails still adherent to the hinges showed that the oaken lid had been about 3 cm. thick.[33] The other may also be interpreted as a strong-room or muniment-room, and was one of the latest alterations at the south end of XXXIV.1. It was a separate unit, rather more than 5 by 6 m. externally, with walls about 90 cm. thick, well-built of flint with brick bonding-courses to support a hollow barrel-vault above. The vault was composed of arches of hollow tiles laid side-by-side in strong brick-mortar; the other side was thickly rendered in brick-mortar brought to a very smooth surface, but it would be a mistake to suppose that there was no tiled roof above. The entrance, in the south-west corner, is also of interest. There was a monolithic sill, a rarity at Silchester, with a slightly countersunk area corresponding to the width of the single door, which turned on pivots as usual. Let into the outer edge of the sill were two iron bolts, which probably held a removable grating in front of the door, an arrangement which seems otherwise unexampled.[34]

GARDENS

Before turning to the structural details we may turn briefly aside to glance at the gardens of Calleva. The open planning, or rather development, of the town was an invitation to turn unused plots into gardens where vegetables could be grown, and fruit-trees raised: on these we comment in Chapter 19. Some of the private courtyards, so-called, were probably laid out in formal parterres of the kind revealed at the Fishbourne villa near Chichester, and again in the small Cotswold villa of Frocester,[35] and the same may be said of the ground in front of houses such as XXIV.2. As yet, there is no example at Silchester of such gardens, and many of the courtyards were devoted to purely practical purposes. Nevertheless, there is evidence that Callevan folk had gardens to tend. The box-clippings mixed with elder, weeds, etc. already mentioned in another context (p. 165) are best explained as garden-waste, and trimmed box-borders, even topiary-work, are likely to have existed.[36] It is also probable that the most highly-prized introduced trees and shrubs in the botanical record—a large plum, a small medlar, black mulberry, vines but not the fig (p. 250)—were planted for their fruit and for shade close to the houses. Ornamental shrubs include the Portugal laurel, to this day a not uncommon sight in gardens and parks. The homely dog-rose, and several showy wild-flowers, can hardly be omitted.[37]

STRUCTURAL DETAILS—WALLS

Walls of rammed clay, or of clay blocks, have been noted on various sites, but not so far at Silchester, where they doubtless existed. Walls of timber-framed construction, filled with wattle-and-daub plastered and lime-washed, sometimes in colour, to protect it, were very common; they are usually marked either by the holes for the uprights or by narrow trenches in which sleeper-beams lay. XXXIV.1 in particular retained interesting traces. One of the main east-west walls of the south wing contained five large oak stumps, 40 to 56 cm. thick, their bottoms cut off square, set in flint-packed post-holes about 3.4 m. apart; the east wall of the adjacent yard had at one time contained two others 2 m. apart. Here we seem to have remains of a timber-built house over 13.5 m. long, on the 'baths alignment'. A cement floor of later date near by overlay a thick bed of clay daub from the filling of the framework of this house, and embedded in it were several of the actual timbers, one of which displayed in its edges chase-mortices for lesser members set an an angle of 17°. Much more of the deposit remains to be excavated, and it would be interesting to do so in order to learn whether any of the timberwork showed on the outside, as a decorative as well as a structural feature: the number and angle of the lesser pieces suggest as much.[38]

The greatest structural improvement, dating from the first century, consisted in raising the entire timber frame clear of the damp ground. XXXIIIA.4 provides a good example of a flint sill, only 30 cm. wide, with brick quoins. In XXXIIA.1, the north wall was 60 cm. thick, and preserved the central chase in which the sole-plate of the timber framework had lain, probably about 30 cm. above the external ground-surface.[39] An indication of the overall height of such walls, indeed of living-rooms generally at Silchester, may be obtainable from XIX.2, where the foundation-trenches, very narrow, alone remained. The room concerned held a fine but ruined mosaic (pl. 28) measuring some 6 by 5 m.; and on the Vitruvian principle of calculating the proper height of a rectangular room by adding length and breadth and then dividing the result by two,[40] we reach a figure of 5.5 m. in the case before us. The result is aesthetically satisfactory, but we do not know whether this formula was applied; if so, the proportions of the best rooms must have been allowed to govern those of subordinate chambers, since the roof-height would have been constant.

Joyce and the Antiquaries frequently mention the beds of yellow clay overlying the floors of many Silchester houses, and in XXVII.1 close attention was paid to the matter. It was noted that over the living-rooms, the bed was about 45 cm. thick, and only 15 cm. in the corridors. Taking their cue from the remains of a cottage which they had come across during a bicycle-ride in the neighbourhood, Hope and Stephenson came to the correct conclusion that this clay represented the infilling of timber framework. In the eastern part of XXVII.1, which had been burnt down, they discovered among the charred timbers many fragments of baked clay daub which on one side bore the impress of wattlework, and on the other a chevron-pattern applied by a roller. As in many other cases since brought to light, this ridged surface was a key for the coat of stucco or plaster, which was sometimes painted externally (as well as internally) white, pink or red.[41]

Walls 60 cm. thick—about the average at Silchester and elsewhere—could obviously have been carried up in stone throughout; and where thicker walling, say 90 cm., occurs, a special reason for its existence must apply, as in the case of the forum, where the chambers were very large and lofty, and in the vaulted room of the inn or that of the strong-room in XXXIV.1. The flint walling usually proves to have suitable foundations: in an example exposed near the church in 1961, there were alternate courses of flint and gravel. The north wall of XXVII.B1 contained a relieving-arch which spanned a soft spot of ground now known to have been the filled ditch of the inner earthwork; and in some cases walling was carried on piles (cf. pl. 16, public baths). Sometimes a spread of gravel was laid to form a solid raft over marshy ground, as Joyce discovered in the north wing of XXXIV.1.[42] Another thick wall to be mentioned is the north wall of the main part of XXXIIA.1, next to that containing the emplacement for a timber sill. A photograph records that it was internally faced for some depth below the ordinary floor-level, and in the absence of a hypocaust it may be suggested that there was a cellar here. The superficial character of much of the exploration of Silchester is probably responsible for a failure to identify cellars more generally, for they are by no means rare in other towns.[43]

Columnar material was somewhat seldom found, in view of the numbers of columns which had existed: much disappeared, no doubt, in post-Roman times when the ruins were looted for stone. Small lathe-turned Bath stone columns from half-open corridors were the commonest discoveries, and occasionally other stones were used, e.g. the Corallian sandstone of the Ogham pillar (p. 77). A good example of a Callevan column is to be seen in Silchester churchyard; it is 18 cm. in diameter and was originally about 1.1 m. high: it came from I.1. It retains its neat Attic base but the corresponding Tuscan capital is missing. Another from the same house was somewhat thicker and may have come from the framing of a doorway rather than a corridor. A half-column from Insula III is a rare example of a full-sized column other than from a public building or temple. Such columns must often have been placed on the piers which project at the sides of the porches of houses such as VIII.1–2 or XXIII.1.[44]

Tools of the mason's craft at Silchester include iron pointing-trowels and pick-pointed hammers used for dressing flint walling, both very similar to those in use today. The fine bronze plumb-bob (fig. 34, 8) may have belonged to a mason or to a carpenter, whose tools are mentioned on another page.

ROOFS

A thatch of straw or reeds no doubt sufficed to cover simple huts. Reid lists

22 (*above left*) Polygonal temple, Insula VII, from the south-west; Silchester parish church in the distance

23 (*below left*) Temple, Insula XXXV, from the south-east

24 (*above right*) Domestic shrine in XIV.2, from the rear or west side

25 (*below right*) I.1, Joyce's excavations, about 1870; from the north-west

26   The church, Insula IV, from the east, 1961; baptistery area in the foreground
27   The church: mosaic pavement towards the west end, 1892

seeds of sedge and other marsh-plants which may have come in with thatching-materials.[45] A crude bone needle or threader may represent the kind of instrument used in sewing thatch; another find is a well-preserved iron hook, described by the excavators as a thatch-hook and perhaps to be compared with the implements once stored, and still occasionally to be seen, in country churches, which were used to pull off burning thatch.[46] Modern thatches project well beyond the walls, the wide eaves enabling the moisture to be shed some distance from the base: the same will have applied in Roman times, and in the case of tiled roofs also, for eaves' guttering was not employed.

The tile bearing the Neronian stamp (fig. 7, 1) shows that tile-making was well advanced by the sixties of the first century. The tiles were of two kinds, used in conjunction: flanged *tegulae* about 45 by 30 cm. or so, and semi-cylindrical *imbrices* which covered the joints between rows of the others. Both types were slightly tapered (and the *tegulae* notched) to allow for the necessary overlapping between one tile and the next below. A series fallen in order, but upside-down, was discovered just outside XIV.2.[47] The tiles were very heavy, a *tegula* weighing up to 9 kg; but they did not have nail-holes or lugs to fit over laths, and the roofs must therefore have been of a low pitch, not more than 30°. They were probably planked underneath, so that the tiles could be set in mortar. The ridges were covered either with *imbrices* or with plain semicylindrical tiles; the gable-ornaments mentioned previously (fig. 27, p. 169) were luted to lengths of such tiles at the manufacturing stage. Hips and valleys were covered with *imbrices,* inverted in the second case; but a mass of lead in the collection, bearing the imprint of the cubes of the mosaic floor on to which it had fallen in a molten state, suggests that sheet-lead was also employed for valleys.

In southern Britain, stone roofing is an especial phenomenon of the third and fourth centuries. Murchison identified Upper Oölitic calcareous grit as the substance employed in the roofs of the later forum-basilica.[48] The slabs were hexagonal, about 40 by 25 cm., and 2.5 cm. thick, weighing thus up to 6 kg. apiece: unlike the tiles, they were fixed by nails, scalewise. The irregular placing of the nail-holes again suggests that the roofs were planked. Slabs fitting along the ridge or the eaves were of course cut square. The ridges of stone-roofed buildings were usually covered with Bath stone blocks, but only one piece seems to have been recorded, and perhaps tiles were more often used at Silchester. There are a few specimens of lantern-like, or perhaps rather temple-like, gable-finials of Bath stone in the collection.[49] The point has already been made that vaults at Silchester were internal, and most probably roofed over.

CEILINGS

We naturally imagine that there were ceilings in most of the rooms, but this is because we have ceilings ourselves. There is little evidence of them at Silchester; but in one room a thin layer of fine white plaster directly on top of a mosaic floor was interpreted as a fallen ceiling. Where there were lofts, we should expect there to have been ceilings below. At Verulamium and elsewhere, elaborate painted ceilings have been discovered, and Dr David Smith has suggested that the panelled arrangement of mosaic floors (e.g. pl. 30) may have been repeated in the ceilings above.[50]

DOORWAYS

The monolithic threshold of the vaulted room in XXXIV.1 is very exceptional at Silchester, where there is no good local stone to be used for the purpose. Other examples are known only in an outer doorway of XIX.2 and in XV.3, a curiously lightly-built early house. Normally, door-sills were of cement, set with tiles or bricks, or else with tessellation continuous with that of the rooms on either side: in such cases, there may have been curtains across the opening. Other thresholds had wooden sills, which in XXVII.1 left an impression 1.4 m. wide in the mortar bedding. Outer doors were generally double, as is shown by the width of the thresholds, and were frequently heavily panelled; they were normally pivoted rather than hung on hinges, and iron pivot-shoes and sockets similar in all but size to those of the gates in the town-wall are to be seen in the collection.[51]

LOCKS

There are about 150 or more keys in the Silchester collection, representing types of lock which range from a simple latch to complicated tumbler-locks and lever-locks of the sort in use today. Padlocks are also common (fig. 32).

A key is a means of withdrawing a bolt from the outside. Strings would do this, but a key offers greater security. In the simplest lock, there is a hole in the door near the bolt, through which a hooked bar can be inserted: its tip engages a hole in the bolt, which can thus be prised back. Penelope is aptly described in the *Odyssey* as 'aiming' the ivory-handled key of Odysseus' strong-room door.[52] The same sort of key would fit the simplest kind of tumbler-lock; for, as Pitt Rivers put it, a tumbler is 'the bolt of a bolt', i.e. a small sliding bar which fits into a slot or mortise in the bolt proper.[53] The key raised the tumbler and the bolt could be drawn by a string. Most

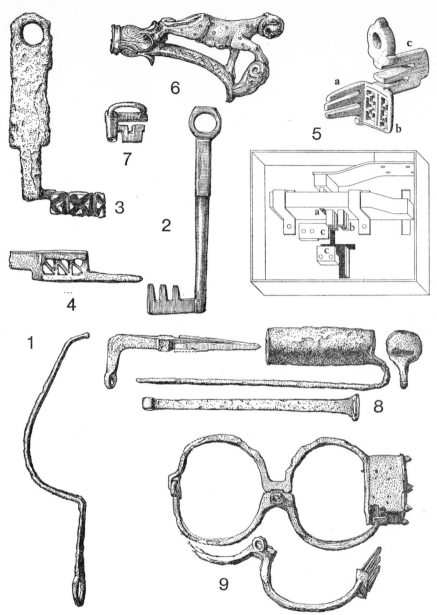

32. Locks and keys. 1, iron latch-puller. 2, bronze key for simple tumbler-lock. 3, iron key for tumbler-lock (cupboard). 4, bronze bolt showing holes for tumbler-pins. 5, bronze key for complex tumbler-lock (reconstruction of lock below, where the pins (a) fitted into the tumbler-holes when the wards on the bolt (b) had been passed, but only if the wards on the lock-plate (c) had also been passed; note elaborate key-hole required). 6, bronze handle for key, in the form of a panther with its paw on a ram's head: the panther is inlaid with copper spots. 7, bronze rotary key for a casket, shaped as a finger-ring. 8, iron padlock with barbed bolt and key (different locks). 9, handcuffs with triple barbed bolt. Scales, 1, 8, 9: 5/16. 2–7, 1/2

tumbler-locks, however, had at least two tumblers, calling thus for pronged keys.[54] This was the sort of lock fitted to most Callevan front-doors, and in the most elaborate varieties required an L-shaped keyhole. One or two keys have elaborate handles modelled as a lion or panther, bronze inlaid with copper spots. The strong-box found by Joyce in the floor of a room in XXIII.1 (p. 197) also had such a lock, but since the action was horizontal, the tumblers must have been spring-loaded.

Smaller and more elaborate tumbler-locks were worked by the upward pressure of the key, the pins of which were therefore set at right-angles to the shank. Sometimes there were wards on the bolt or the lock-case, so that only the proper key would pass. The more complex the wards, the larger and more elaborate the key-hole, leading eventually to the possibility that ingenuity would defeat its own end, and the consequent triumph of the rotary-lock (though not in Roman times). Fig. 32, 5 is an unusually complex tumbler-lock key, to which indeed only one lost parallel is known.[55] A little tinkering with pieces of stout card showed how the lock must have been constructed, and this is shown below. There was so much play in the mechanism that the pins of the key have become bent and one, owing to a flaw in the casting, at last broke away.

All these more complicated patterns of tumbler-lock were never fitted to house-doors, only to cupboards[56] and caskets, because the key could not be withdrawn until the bolt had been shot into the 'locked' position. This deficiency did not affect the rotary-locks, but Roman examples are usually very simple and again seem always to have been fitted to cupboards and chests rather than house-doors, or else took the form of padlocks.[57] One of the keys illustrated is shaped as a finger-ring and no doubt belonged to a lady's jewel-case. Another type of padlock, very much commoner, had a barbed bolt, the side-springs expanding within the case and preventing the withdrawal of the bolt until they had been compressed by a slotted key inserted at the other end (fig. 32, 8). A lock of this kind, no less than 53 cm. long, was found in the 1900 'hoard' of ironwork.[58] I believe it may have belonged to slave-shackles. The lock of the handcuffs (fig. 32, 9) worked on the same principle,[59] as did a flimsy bronze padlock of misleadingly modern appearance.

WINDOWS

A few window-embrasures have survived in Romano-British buildings, but mainly in cellars. There is none at Silchester apart from the detached piece of masonry mentioned in our chapter on the public baths (p. 128). The only ground-floor windows occur in a room of the fort-baths at Chesters (Northd.) and in living-rooms of a house at Dorchester (Dorset).[60] In the latter case, the sills were about 75 cm. from the floor, and about 1 m. wide, with splayed sides: the height is unknown. The embrasures (one of which can be seen reconstructed on the site) belonged to rooms not flanked by corridors: where there were corridors on both sides, windows were probably confined to clerestory level, above the abutment of the pentice roofs over the corridors.

The gay colouring of walls and floors in the best rooms demanded a flood of light, and it is hence mistaken to suppose that windows were few and small: they will, as the Dorchester instances suggest, have been few and large, or alternatively many and small. Sculptured elevations of part of a house, in the Simpelveld sarcophagus (Leiden Museum), show good-sized windows divided by glazing-bars, and they could be protected or covered by heavy wooden shutters sliding to either side.[61] There was a provision for a stout frame, flush with the outer surface of the walls, at Dorchester, and here, doubtless, there would have been shutters of a similar kind.

Many of the windows were glazed. Until the third and fourth centuries, the panes were very crudely cast, and the glass itself has a bluish-green tint due to the presence of iron in the sand supplying the silica. Sometimes nearly colourless fragments are found, but are never frequent enough to suggest that decolorisation of the mix was specifically undertaken. Most probably, panes were made on the spot, and as some Silchester evidence (p. 281) suggests, not from primary ingredients but from scrap. The worst roughnesses of the underside were sometimes removed, probably, by grinding two sheets together with an abrasive. The largest pane recorded from Roman Britain is 60 cm. square, but panes of the order of 20 by 25 or 30 cm. are likely to have been much more common.[62]

In the late Roman period, another kind of window-glass is found. This is the so-called 'muff' glass, made by blowing a cylinder, slitting it, and allowing it to open out in a muff-kiln: this mode of manufacture has continued until fairly recent times, and many of the windows in my own house are fitted with such panes. Late Roman material is easily distinguished from the earlier, cast type by its shiny surface on both sides, and more particularly by the elongated shape and parallel alignment of included bubbles; it is also much thinner than the cast type, which may be several millimetres thick, especially at the edges.[63]

A fragment of a grooved wooden glazing-bar was found at the Saalburg. Traces of a red cement fixative appear on the edge of a fragment of window-pane from Insula XIII; but, as there is also white cement on the back, this may have been a wall-tile.[64] But whether they were glazed or not, windows were sometimes protected not by shutters but by metal or stout wooden grilles, having stars or crosses of iron at the corners and elsewhere.[65] Several crosses have been found at Silchester, mainly in the forum-basilica; some complete grilles have been found elsewhere, and are of interest as showing the size of windows. The largest British example measured 55 by 61 cm, but a grille rather more than 1 m. square comes from a Swiss villa, where it had been fitted to the ground-floor window of a wing-room.

FLOORS

As has been noted in passing, floors were of various materials: rammed gravel, chalk or clay; cement, either brick-mortar or its more decorative variety, *opus signinum* (p. 127); tiles, tessellation or mosaic, which we consider from the decorative point of view in the next chapter, and timber.

Indications of a timber floor laid on joists have already been mentioned, in the case of the *apodyterium* of the inn (p. 141). Another example occurred in Insula XVI, where a stretch of rammed gravel contained slots 15 cm. wide at intervals of about 45 cm., again the site of floor-joists.[66] Such a method of construction was bad, for the joists would speedily have rotted. Boarded floors must have been very common: there are many cases, for example, of rooms whose walls stood well above the floor-level, without a sign remaining of the nature of the floor; and in such circumstances a wooden floor must almost certainly have existed. As an indication of the planks or boards available, there is no better guide than the oaken timbers actually preserved in the lining of a water-trough in Insula VI (cf. p. 88). Particularly noteworthy are two planks sawn apparently from the same tree, measuring some 7.6 m. in length, 38 cm. wide, and 7.5 cm. thick.[67]

Tile floors were also very common; and to pass over those of ordinary type, we may pause at examples in XXIII.1, XXIV.2 and another building not now identifiable[68] in which hexagonal or octagonal tiles were used. In the first two cases, square tiles were used in the borders, but the main areas were paved in the others, the spaces between tiles being filled either with small diamond-shaped tiles or else with black and drab tessellation. In these two cases, the floors had been laid in porches, where they were well-adapted to the hard use expected in such positions. Joyce's coin-list from XXIII.1 suggests a main incidence of occupation in the later third and fourth centuries, and the floor may be of that period. In XXIV.2, the floor was laid over earlier red tessellation and is also probably late. Floors of polygonal tiles are not very common in Britain—there was one of small hexagonal tiles in the baths at Caersws fort (Mont.)—but are commoner abroad, perhaps especially in the Danubian regions where tiles of fancy shapes frequently occur. The origin of these floors is no doubt to be found in the *opus sectile* or cut-stone floors which are also rare in Britain.[69] A floor of small bricks laid herringbone-wise in the public baths (p. 127) represents a type well-known on other sites.[70]

On first looking through the Silchester reports, the reader may be surprised to discover how frequent floors of plain red brick tessellation were. There is scarcely a building, where flooring survives, that does not produce an example. Yet to cover long stretches of corridor or large expanses of rooms with small pieces of brick knapped to about 25 mm. cube on the spot was an extremely laborious occupation, justified only by the very hard-wearing quality of the result, and the ability of the surface to follow any slight sinkage of the ground without becoming dangerously disarranged or presenting edges which could be kicked up. Most tessellated floors of this description have a rather slight mortar bedding, but for fine mosaic it was necessary to provide a secure foundation, the thickness and character of which would depend on the nature of the ground beneath. At Silchester, the natural gravel was so close to the Roman surface that few mosaics had thick foundations. The cubes themselves were generally laid in brick-mortar spread over one or two layers of cement or concrete, and this again—though not invariably—on a flint base. The best-laid floor occurred in XIV.1: 2.5 cm., pink cement for cubes; 10 cm., white cement; 18 cm., concrete; 20 cm., mortar and gravel; then a stratum of flints. But another floor in the same house was only 15 cm. thick over the channels of a hypocaust, not counting the thickness of the tiles which spanned them.[71]

HEATING

Hypocausts, generally of the channelled or 'composite' variety were often found in the houses (cf. pl. 37, fig. 17). This, however, is a subject exhaustively discussed earlier (p. 123) and no more need be said of hypocausts here. Fireplaces were found in several rooms,[72] and in the example illustrated (pl. 4) it can be seen that the installation is secondary, having been built over the cubes of the tessellated floor. It measures about 90 by 60 cm. and had a half-hexagonal back let into the party-wall; there would probably have been a clay hood above the part which projected into the room. It may be true to add that the appearance of this form of heating in the houses of the rich is 'late', and may possibly reflect a shortage of hypocaust-fuel or a desire to economise in the quantities used; the infilling and supersession of hypocausts is a familiar phenomenon of late Roman times. The two best-preserved fireplaces in Roman buildings—at the Newport villa, Isle of Wight, and at the Star villa, Somerset—are clearly secondary; and as Dr. Joan Liversidge has reminded us, it is to the late Sidonius Apollinaris that we turn for a heart-warming description of a really festive blaze in a fireplace.[73] In the simpler houses and huts, fireplaces were of course always to be found, and a small and rather poor iron ox-head in the collection comes from a fire-dog of Belgic pattern. As for fuel, coal was little used, if at all, for domestic fires at Silchester,[74] but there is a possibility that peat may have been obtained occasionally from deposits in the Kennet valley (cf. p. 356).

The only other form of heating was the portable brazier, the repeated use of which in XIV.1, for example, can fairly be deduced from the discoloured patches and repairs visible on the mosaic floors.[75] In a room tightly closed against the cold, such a means of heating was not without danger, and lofty ceilings were little protection against it. On one occasion, the emperor Julian (355–63) was overcome by what he called 'fumes from the walls' after a charcoal fire had been introduced into his bedroom during a bitter Parisian winter night:[76] a clear case of carbon-monoxide poisoning from a brazier.

17

Houses: Interior Decoration

WALL DECORATION

Vitruvius wrote that 'colour, when carefully applied to the damp plaster surface, does not fade, but lasts forever',[1] but the Augustan architect would surely have been astonished to see how bright and gay the fragments of painted wall-plaster still lie amid the débris of Roman homes. The reason is that the colours were generally of mineral origin. Vitruvius was thinking of 'good' fresco-painting, in which the colours are applied with great dexterity and speed before the plaster dries. 'Dry' fresco, which requires the plaster to be moistened before the colours are laid on, was probably always commoner. The existence of scratched guide-lines on the dado from XIV.1 (pl. 29) is an instance of this type of decoration at Silchester.

The plaster surfacing of the walls was normally in three coats, the last of these being a very thin layer of lime-plaster. The colours were prepared on the spot, as is shown by a Purbeck marble mortarium in which red ochre has been ground, and a pot of the same; and by little balls of blue frit (*caeruleum*).[2] Also in the collection is a rectangular marble rubber, about 15 by 10 cm., with an iron strap-handle on the back, which was used for grinding and mixing colours on a flat slab. There are traces of red, yellow, blue and green paint upon its polished surface.[3] The pigments were applied to the walls in an organic medium; and in addition to those named, and varieties of them, there are purple and black and white, the last being mixed when required with other colours to make pink, grey, etc. Linear borders and details were generally indicated in a thick impasto, calling for brushes of different width.[4] With such a palette at their disposal, the Callevans fully indulged a love of bright colour: even the walls of a guard-house at the west gate were painted in pink stripes on white.[5] The wall-paintings, of course, are only part of the décor: ceilings were painted, sometimes—on

Verulamium evidence—in colour; floors were finished very often in red or drab tessellation or in mosaic, mainly polychrome. The total effect in the best rooms was thus one of richness and brilliancy, though it was in practice somewhat subdued by the bluish-green light admitted by the coarse window-panes (p. 207).

It is difficult to judge directly of the designs of Callevan wall-paintings, and indeed the small pieces of plaster retrieved tend to give an impression of garishness and sketchy detail. But the rooms were larger and loftier than our own; the areas of colour were wide; and from discoveries on other sites it is clear that the architectural compositions generally favoured were not ill-balanced in any respect,[6] however bright or dim their reflection of Roman mural art.[7] In general, there was reliance upon large panelled areas framed in contrasting colours and divided by vertical bands or pilasters: a stretch remained in the baths of the inn.[8] Below, there might be further architectural treatment, as at Caerwent,[9] or some other kind of dado; above, there would have been a frieze. The panels were executed in plain colour, yellow or red very often, or else figured in imitation of marbles: yellow with red streaks for *giallo antico,* red or pink with darker spots, dark red with white spots for porphyry. In the later XIX.2, for example, there were panels of grey veined in blue, and others of yellow blotched with pink and dark red veins, between vertical bands coloured in imitation of porphyry;[10] and in XXIV.2 there were brilliant red panels with dark red borders, and other areas painted in golden yellow, blue, and green.[11] A lighter scheme in a corridor of XXVII.1 displayed panels of yellow alternating with white, in which there had been painted draperies; below, there was a dado of marbled pink, and the frieze above contained green circles. The floor was of drab tessellation, so that the wall received complete attention.[12] The apse in the same house had white walls marbled with thin yellow lines; and here the polychrome mosaic of the floor was the dominant feature.[13]

The best-known of the Silchester paintings, however, is the dado reconstructed by Fox from fragments found in the heated room with a mosaic floor at the north end of the great suite of reception-rooms in XIV.1 (pl. 29);[14] it is of the second century. On a dark red band some 39 cm. wide, between black and green bands respectively below and above, there are hollow circles and squares of grey, from which yellow barley-ears and green leaves sprout; there are intermediate centres of blue rosettes, and lilac-coloured quatrefoils ('corn-cockle') and green berries in the field.

With passing mention of the brilliant red walls of V.B3, scattered with small white, yellow and blue flowers,[15] the anthemion-pattern already referred to in our discussion of the baths of the inn (p. 141), and the solitary mention of a figural element—a dolphin[16]—we may conclude this short account.

Fragments of wall-linings of white, green-and-white (two sorts), and pink-and-white marbles were found here and there, notably in the vicinity of the forum-basilica, from which they were no doubt derived (p. 115): there is little indication that such exotic materials appeared at a domestic level, for even the largest houses produced none. In Insula V some scraps of thin imperial red porphyry sheets, 5 or 6 mm. thick, were found, as well as another in Insula XXXV.[17] The destination of these pieces is uncertain: they may have been intended for *opus sectile* flooring, though they retain no shape definitely indicative of such a use; or they may have been used in inlay-work for furniture rather than as wall-lining material. The native Purbeck marble was by far the commonest material employed for wall-cladding and interior moulded work, but again the evidence for its use in houses is very meagre. A simple sandstone panel came from II.1.[18] In short, it is clear that the decoration of houses relied almost exclusively upon colour for its effect, perhaps with some crude attempt at perspective, such as we see at Caerwent.[19] No use was made either of terracotta or of stucco mouldings, except the quarter-round cement fillet usually placed at the junction of wall and floor.[20]

MOSAICS

There is perhaps nothing in the realm of archaeological excavation to compare with the excitement of uncovering a mosaic floor—the gradual revelation of the lines of tesserae, the first hint of a pattern in colours fresh from long concealment, the hope that the pavement may be a figured one, or will at least not abruptly disappear into a chaos of displaced and missing cubes. A Cirencester floor was actually reproduced in the useful medium of floor-cloth by an enterprising Bristol manufacturer in the middle of last century, and another floor was carted about from place to place, with a note from the incumbent of the parish in which it was found, to attest its authenticity.[21]

About thirty Callevan houses possessed mosaics, some but one and others several.[22] The surrounds at least were laid before the walls were plastered, as the relationship of the edges to the wall-plaster shows; but otherwise we know little of the way in which they were laid. The simpler parts were probably set direct, cube by cube; and simple calculation shows that a pavement measuring some 5 by 3 m. would contain about 120,000 cubes of 1 cm. tesserae, allowing for the mortar between. The more complex parts of the design were probably prefabricated and brought to position glued to sheets of cloth: so much is suggested by the detection of patches of differently-coloured mortar backings when the Hinton St. Mary pavement was lifted upon removal to the British Museum.[23]

With the exception of glass, the cubes contain no exotic materials, and their bright appearance, especially when damp, is due mainly to the careful juxtaposition of tile and natural stone of contrasting shades. The following have been identified:

black	Kimmeridge beds, Dorset
buff or drab	sandstone
grey-green	Purbeck marble, Dorset
lime-green	Rhaetic sandstone, west country
pink	limestone, Dorset; samian-ware
purple	burnt tile
reds	tile or brick
yellow	Lias limestone; tile
white	Lias limestone, west country; hard chalk, chalk.

Intermediate shades were sometimes obtained by burning some of these materials. Glass tesserae appear, but very rarely: they provided royal blue, jade-green, and colourless or blue-green tints.[24] With only one exception (XIX.2, see below), the patterned areas were set within a margin of coarse tessellation, on which furniture, probably, was placed. The marginal cubes were 2.5 to 4 cm. across, and most of the patterned work was executed in cubes of 1 cm. gauge, or slightly less or more; the cubes were knapped on the spot in many cases.[25] Since we have already described the foundations laid for mosaics, it remains merely to draw attention at this stage to the small tile-drain which sometimes appears in a corner of a room, clearly designed to carry off washing-water.[26]

With few exceptions, the Silchester mosaics are devoid of figure-subjects and are often purely geometric. The majority are polychromes of red, yellow, grey and perhaps one or two other shades, outlined in black on a white ground, all within the coarse margin which was generally brick-red, sometimes drab. The different elements which enter into the compositions—the guilloche or rope-pattern and other borderings,[27] the main motifs such as *canthari* or two-handled wine-mixing bowls,[28] rosettes, knots, and so forth—are such as can be found across the length and breadth of the Roman Empire. The only one of our mosaics which stands apart from the general series was found in the house underlying XIX.2, and is described and discussed below.

The study of Romano-British mosaics has received a considerable impetus in recent years as the result of the discovery of first-century examples on the one hand,[29] and of the patient collation and interpretation of earlier discoveries on the other, for which Dr David Smith has been largely responsible.[30] It is now a little easier than formerly to determine the period of a floor from stylistic criteria, and the work of second and fourth century 'schools' is now also being identified in various parts of Britain.[31] Here we must content ourselves with a brief sketch of the Silchester material. As far as is known, there are no first-century floors; the second century is well represented, and the fourth also, but not to the same extent. Throughout Britain, few mosaics seem to have been laid in the earlier part of the third century, no doubt for economic reasons, for this was the time when a good deal of money had to be found for the walled defences of the towns. Such, at least, is the present picture.

A glance at second-century floors may begin with a plain black-and-white pavement from Room 23 of XIV.1: it is presumably of about the same date as the polychrome mosaics in adjoining rooms, described below, i.e. between 140 and 160. This floor, which was removed to Reading and can be seen there, measures about 4.7 by 4.3 m., and has an all-over fret or key pattern alternating with squares filled with simple geometric motifs.[32] This is a slightly evolved version of a floor laid in the dressing-room of the women's baths at Pompeii and may well be a late representative of the Italianate black-and-white style which, as the first-century Fishbourne examples prove, exerted a strong influence on the first stages of Romano-British mosaic art.[33]

The floors of Rooms 22 and 27 are polychrome.[34] They too have been lifted and can be studied at Reading. They are of similar size to the floor just described. In the first case, the design consists of five circular medallions containing formal rosettes, counterchanged diagonally—enough is left to show this—by way of diversification. The central medallion has gone. The medallions are all outlined in an octagon of black lines, forming the border of a supporting framework of lozenges also outlined in black on the white ground, enclosing small polychrome motifs. This lozengular construction was a favourite, and in favourable circumstances lent an illusion of three-dimensional quality to the design. An unpublished mosaic from XXI.4, unfortunately very fragmentary, was probably laid by the same firm, and also the *cantharus*-panel in the earlier I.1, now at Stratfield Saye.[35] Returning to the rosettes, the inturned form of one is again a favourite, and there is a close parallel, extending also to the basic essentials of the whole design, at Verulamium.[36] The other rosette has outward-pointing petals vertically divided by unusually delicate shading, and has been dubbed by Dr David Smith 'the Silchester rosette'. In point of date, the double braided guilloche of the outer enclosing border is enough to show that the floor cannot well have been laid before about the middle of the second century.

The other floor mentioned, from Room 27, has a design of nine elongated hexagons outlined variously in wave-pattern, in guilloche, in scroll-patterns, or in small motifs, again diagonally counterchanged. The *cantharus* in the centre is closely matched for design by others on second-century floors at Verulamium and Colchester, and further correspondences can be seen in the case of some of the details.[37] The hexagonal medallions are at present otherwise unexampled elsewhere in Britain, but the contents of two, one on either side of the *cantharus,* are typical of mid- and late second century floors in south and south-east Britain, though rare elsewhere and on the continent: this is the simple device of enclosing the rosette, which is admirably designed for the purpose, in a square.[38] In sum, we begin to see how comparison of motifs and details between floors of approximately the same date can indicate the sphere of activity of a particular 'school' of mosaicists, or at least the area in which a particular pattern-book may have circulated.

Other second-century floors occur in XXIII.2, with a *cantharus* and a dolphin as the subjects of two of its four panels,[39] and the horseshoe-shaped pavement in XXVII.1 (west), notable for the excellent adaptation of its fret border to the curvature: this is also at Reading,[40] but unfortunately its centrepiece had gone. The floor in front of this alcove is shown in pl. 30, previously unpublished.[41] The strong cruciform design, formed by the semi-circular side-medallions and the corner quadrants together enclosing a central circle, is in the main a second-century motif, though later instances are known. The striped margin may possibly afford the hint that this floor is later than the others previously described, for it seems to carry us on towards the fourth-century series.[42]

With the possible exception of a floor in XIV.2 (pl. 4), similar to an example dated c. 220–80 at the Rapsley villa (Surrey),[43] there is no mosaic at Silchester which can be placed between the main second and fourth century groups. Unfortunately, the latter is not well-represented in the *Archaeologia* illustrations. A pavement from XXXIV.1, now at Stratfield Saye, typifies the banal quality and coarse execution of some late floors.[44] The design, very closely matched at the Cotswold villa of Tockington Park,[45] is assignable to the 'Corinium' school, as indeed is the poor, rough bust of Ceres from XXVII.1 (pl. 31):[46] in the late period, therefore, we find Silchester drawn into altogether another orbit from that of earlier days. The XXXIV.1 design is based on a St. Andrew's Cross, with a circular medallion of singular unattractiveness and lightweight effect in the centre. The shaded lozenges, the *peltae* and leaves with attached curlicue tendrils, and the piled triangles appearing upon this floor are all characteristic of late times in Britain.

By far the most interesting of the late floors is that of the long gallery connecting the two wings of XIV.2; part is shown in pl. 32.[47] We find a somewhat random assortment of squares and oblongs, including guilloche mats and rosettes, quite typical of late work when used by themselves; a square containing the remains of a bust within a circular medallion, a square with quadrant corners; and an oblong preserving one of a pair of baskets of flowers unparalleled in Britain: the basket is mainly in warm, dark colours, while the flowers are largely in blue glass cubes (p. 214).[48] These panels of fine work are set within very wide coarse margins of red and buff, unusual in that they contain various striped and lozenge-filled bands. In the western part of the floor these surround a very plain area completely devoted to simple buff stripes in a red ground. Fox pointed out that this coarse work 'lessened the size of the more finely-worked panels and was a cheap expedient for giving effect', and one may readily agree. Other floors in the house, unfortunately much ruined, employ the same device and it is to be found again in the north or later wing of XXIII.2.[49] Similarly, there are coarse chequered bands around a destroyed panel of fine mosaic, of reduced size, in II.2.[50] A whole room (20) in XIV.2, east wing, is devoted to coarse banded work in red and buff, and from the arrangement of the bands Fox was inclined to identify it as the *triclinium*. A small oblong panel towards the centre would indicate the position of the table; three sides of the double surrounding square would show where the couches were to be placed, and additional stripes on the west or entrance-side would mark the space reserved for service (p. 223).[51]

Among the corridor pavements, mostly plain though not entirely so,[52] that of the north side of I.2 is interesting. It has a 'runner' of drab cubes within the usual red margin; an inner border, forming a rectangle some 24 by 1.5 m., encloses a medial line of red on which are set, towards each end, an octagon and a hexagon respectively, with their centres marked.[53] The centres are 18.75 m. apart; and unless this odd design can mark the pitch of some game to be played under cover on wet days, it seems difficult to explain. It is possibly to be compared with a floor at Chilgrove villa (Sussex), which displayed a row of two sets of three roundels of different patterns, and at some distance to one side, another single one.[54]

The last pavement to be described occurred in what was thought, on its evidence, to be an early house beneath XIX.2.[55] It is quite distinct in style from all other Silchester floors, and although the basic arrangement is paralleled in various second-century examples,[56] the content is far from being so (pl. 28). The building concerned, which otherwise had plain red tessellated floors, is aligned with the street-grid and can hence hardly be earlier than the second century. It may be much later: as Dr David Smith observed some years ago, one of the panels of the mosaic under notice appears to contain the remains of a hunting-scene, characteristic of floors laid in the late third and fourth centuries, as at Frampton, for example.[57]

This badly-damaged floor was taken to Reading. It measured 5.3 by 4.6 m., and shared with few other British pavements the continental peculiarity of having been laid without a margin of coarse tessellation.[58] Such margins seem very often to have been intended, not merely to set off the more finely-worked patterned areas but equally, and more practically, to provide room for furniture which might otherwise damage the finer work. A dining-suite could certainly have been arranged on the oblong panel flanking the main square of the design. This oblong contains a great spray of smilax in unrelieved black, neither florets nor red berries being shown: it is not ivy, for, as Fox remarked, ivy has no tendrils. *Smilax aspera* was much used in the ancient world for festive chaplets, and here the spray might certainly be taken to identify the dining-room. No precise parallel for the Silchester spray has been found, though at Caerleon and at Lyon there are floors with monochrome borders of basically similar type, and of fairly late date.[59]

The adjoining square is in polychrome work, and in its fussiness of detail at first sight contrasts awkwardly with the boldness of the oblong. Next to the smilax spray, there is an elegant design of florets, mainly red-and-yellow or black-and-grey, enclosed by looped ribbons respectively dark-red-and-red and grey-and-white. Again, a similar border is not easy to find: a floor at Italica (near Seville) has perhaps the nearest, but lacks the looped ribbons.[60] On the left or north side, the great acanthus-scroll (which would have been balanced opposite) cannot be very closely matched either, although it may at least be said, on the basis of a Verulamium example, that not all fourth-century scrolls were of the heavy Chedworth or Woodchester pattern, nor were as crude as the Bignor specimen.[61] The Silchester scroll parts on either side of a small Genius worked mainly in pink, standing on a pedestal; the acanthus is not, perhaps, well-done, but the general construction is clear, with reasonably good frontal and perspective views of the flowers, and fantastic tendrils in red. Fox linked this design with Pompeian painted and mosaic scrolls, and certainly it is more reminiscent of painted work than anything else.[62]

The hunting-scene at the east end of the pavement is very fragmentary. On one side there are the black, brown and yellow leaves of a conventional tree, and on the other side just two leaves remain of the corresponding tree. The red-and-grey shape next to the tree is taken by Dr Smith to be the flying cloak of a huntsman, red with a grey lining showing: the frieze of mounted huntsmen in the Virgilian mosaic at Low Ham provides an apt

28 Mosaic pavement, in remains of house found below XIX.2.

29 Fresco in XIV.1, restored by G. E. Fox

30 Mosaic pavement in XXVII.1
31 Mosaic pavement, detail: head of Ceres (from XXVII.1)
32 Part of the mosaic in the gallery of XIV.2

illustration,[63] though in our case the figure can hardly have exceeded the height of the *Genius* in the north border and must have been on foot, as on the Frampton pavement.

Within these borders, there was a square (about 2.85 by 2.75 m.) outlined in a mainly red-and-grey guilloche, which further divides the area into a central compartment probably enclosing a circular medallion (destroyed)[64] flanked by nearly square corner compartments, with rectangles between. Busts had occupied the corners, and, to judge by the better of the two partial survivors, were in profile rather than the almost universal full-face view. One, worked mainly in grey and black, is winged; the other is a curious jumble of mainly red and black, as preserved, and also seems winged: I incline to believe that they were Winds.[65] In the surviving rectangle, there are parts of two beasts, perhaps panthers, sejeant regardant: of one, there is only part of the tail. There is some tendril-work between them, but space would not allow for the inclusion of a *cantharus* of normal proportions, as is often found in such compositions. Pavements at Wellow (Som.), of late date, show confronted beasts with tendril-work behind, and no *cantharus*.[66]

In sum, we evidently had here a mosaic of ambitious and (surely as regards the original cartoon) even exquisite design; for as one studies it in detail, one sees that the apparent conflict between the oblong with its bold *smilax* spray and the main square is very satisfactorily resolved. Yet, in execution, there are astonishing deficiencies. The surface was so uneven that there could not have been a proper foundation, such as is recorded for the second-century pavements in XIV.1 (p. 209); and the two busts in the corners seem to have been surprisingly ill-centred, while the florets of the ribbon-border are irregular. Furthermore, although very small cubes (5 mm. or less) are used here and there in the more intricate parts of the design, they are often poorly-shaped and sometimes mere chips of stone or tile.

It cannot be said that the poorness of execution points at all certainly to a late date: indeed, the majority of fourth-century floors in Britain are well-made, though not always well-founded. But for the 'huntsman' border, we should be inclined to relegate this mosaic to the second century: the grid-like design of the square panel, Fox's parallels for the great scroll, and several of the other details urge as much, though a still earlier date is ruled out by the alignment of the house with the streets. Whether a fragmentary hunting-scene can really bear the weight which a late dating would impose, is an enigma for the present.

18

Houses: Furniture and Equipment

FURNITURE

It is very fortunate that the *ébénistes* of Roman Britain hit upon a substance less subject to decay than the woods which must have been used for the great majority of pieces of furniture. This is the Kimmeridge shale of south Dorset, a dark bituminous material which, when freshly quarried, can be carved and turned with facility and at its best is very like jet in appearance; but the gradual oxidation of its oily content during burial, and its replacement with water, have ensured that most pieces excavated up to very recent years have flaked and split upon drying to such a degree that their original smoothness, enhanced no doubt by the wax-polishing which would have lent them a jet-like quality, is now difficult to envisage. The impregnation of shale objects with a water-miscible wax now ensures proper conservation, provided only that they were kept thoroughly damp ever since the moment of discovery.

The Silchester collection contains important fragments of shale furniture.[1] The first is an incomplete turned leg about 23 cm. long, with traces of a tenon at one end (fig. 21, 8),[2] either from a stool or from a couch—perhaps more probably the latter; the general shape is well paralleled in the scenes of funerary repasts depicted on gravestones.[3] Supposing, therefore, that the leg came from a couch, it is likely that the main frame would have been of timber, perhaps painted in a similar or contrasting colour, or inlaid with bone, glass, metal or porphyry plaques[4] or sheathed in bronze. Stuffed furniture was a rarity,[5] but leather upholstery, conceivably textile as well, is attested by the extremely numerous bronze tacks in the collection, many with wide or otherwise decorative heads. The mattress of the couch would have been supported underneath by straps or cords, as we are reminded by a passage in the *Saturae* of Petronius, where one of the disreputable characters is told to hide under the bed, and by holding on with hands and feet to the cords 'as Ulixes of old clung to the Cyclops' ram', so elude detection; but is eventually betrayed by sneezing, and revealed when the mattress is stripped back.[6]

The form of couch shown in the reliefs usually has high sides and a back: it is in fact a bed—the death-bed, and not a dining-couch except in a much smaller number of instances. One of the best sculptural parallels occurs in the Simpelveld sarcophagus in Leiden Museum; another, interesting for detail, occurs on a stele from Caşei (Romania): here the deceased, warmly clad in a thick sleeved garment and covered in a fleecy blanket, reclines on a thick but hard-looking mattress, and receives a wreath from his widow, seated in a high-backed chair by his side; in front is one of the little three-legged tables which we shall mention below. Double beds were of the same type, as a terracotta from Bordeaux shows;[7] but whether beds were always of this pattern, we may take leave to doubt. The dining-couches of the Roman *triclinium* differed only in having a single side-piece —the central one of the three, none; for, on formal occasions, three persons were supposed to recline to their meal upon each.[8] It is again questionable, whether the dining-rooms of the Callevan houses were all equipped in metropolitan fashion, rather than with chairs: the evidence of provincial reliefs suggests that sitting to meals, rather than reclining to them, was commonplace.[9]

The other fragments of shale furniture may be taken together, since one is a carved claw-foot from a small dining-table or *delphica* with three legs, and the others parts of circular tops from such tables. This was a normal form for dining-tables, as ubiquitous reliefs, and also frescoes and mosaics, in addition to actual examples, well show;[10] though once again, it was not the only form, for some of the Gallic reliefs depict rectangular, four-legged tables of solid wooden construction, generally covered by a rough, thick cloth, but also of no great size.[11] However, our evidence relates to the much more elegant *delphica*. The Silchester foot is similar to that of a complete leg 47 cm. high to the tenon, from Dorchester (Dorset); otherwise, only fragments are known, albeit in some number. The paw of the Dorchester leg is continued to the hock, where a stylised moulding supports a feline head at the front or 'knee': here the craftsman modified the classical prototype to his taste and the demands of the material.[12] A small curved fragment in the collection, with a bone peg let into it, comes from another leg ineffectually repaired by that means.

The lathe-turned top was about 39 cm. across; the broad rim of the underside reveals two of the tapered dovetail housing-joints for the legs. Another fragment is from a larger top, and the bevelled rim carries simple chevron and ring ornament: since the tables were not very high, this could not be seen unless the top was removable, and in this case at least we may perhaps imagine the top as a kind of tray which could be placed on legs fixed together by stretcher-bars.[13] Pieces of other shale discs, thinner and with beaded mouldings, certainly come from trays up to 45 cm. or so in diameter.[14] They have no joint-sockets on the underside, and could have been mounted on tripods of the folding type, feet for which have been found at Caerwent and elsewhere.[15] We have already mentioned the monolithic side-table tops from the forum-basilica (p. 116), and there is another from VII.3.[16]

As regards other furniture, we can but guess at the wide range of simple, serviceable, though perhaps occasionally ornate, pieces which must have existed in wood. There must have been basket-chairs, 'meuble à la fois solennel et familial'[17] (cf. pl. 34a); cupboards; and chests and caskets often metal-bound and studded: pieces of tubular bone hinges survive for them,[18] and there is a plate for a rotary-lock, in the usual thin bronze, with the marks of the prominent studs (often fashioned as lion-masks) which had fixed it into place. The locks have already been discussed (p. 206). One item is missing from the list: the drawer. The single relief known to me, which shows a drawer—that of a till on the monument of a cutler at Rome[19]— seems to give prominence to this detail, as if it were unusual or novel. Some of the plain bronze rings in the collection could have been curtain-rings.[20]

LIGHTING

The ordinary oil-lamp needs no description, and the various types need not be gone into in detail here. The earliest lamp, of Italian or perhaps central Gaulish make, is represented by a portion of the *discus* (or circular area on top of the reservoir) which carries a figure of Fortuna holding a *cornucopiae*. It is interesting because a lamp from the same mould was found at the Swiss legionary fortress of Vindonissa.[21] Most of the other lamps are of local, or certainly British, manufacture and the Silchester series is rather a poor one.

Such lamps, as interruptions to the public electricity-supply in recent winters enabled me to prove for myself, gave about as much light as an ordinary candle, and with about a tablespoonful of oil in the reservoir, burnt for about two hours, given a twist of linen fibre for wick. If the flame was too high, heavy oily smuts were given off; and even when no smoke was evolved, the wick soaked up far more oil than it burnt. Hence, perhaps, arose the crucial episode in the tale of Cupid and Psyche, when the sleeping god is awakened by a drop of hot oil from the lamp held over him by the girl. A drip-tray was necessary, and there are examples of these in nearly every Roman collection, either of pottery or lead, in the form of 'open lamps', for which they no doubt also served from time to time. Many lamps were needed to light a room satisfactorily; alternatively, lamps with multiple burners were used. Fragments of two uncommon ring-lamps, with eight and possibly twelve burners, are unaccountably omitted from May's *Pottery* (fig. 33). One at least is designed for suspension from a candelabrum or bracket. They are of the second century and come, probably, from north-east Gaul. Moulds for such lamps have been found in the potteries of the Tenth Legion at Holdeurn near Nijmegen,[22] but the Silchester lamps have not been moulded.

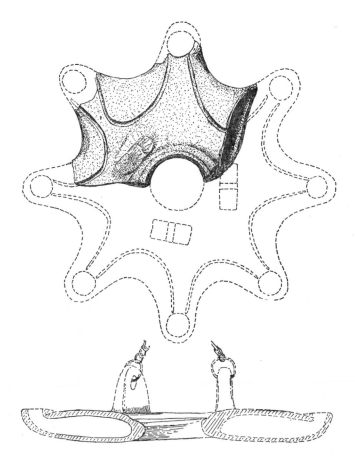

33. Terracotta hanging-lamp with eight burners (restored); continental. Scale, 1/2

There are only a few scraps of bronze lamps, notably a handle-terminal in the form of a half-length figure of a satyr holding a bunch of grapes. This bronze was found in the garden at Stratfield Saye, where it is preserved, but probably came from Silchester.[23] Two iron lamps of the usual form may be mentioned, and a combined open lamp and candle-holder from the fourth-century deposit of ironwork in Insula I; it stands on a tripod foot.[24]

A chalk candle-holder has been mentioned previously (p. 168; fig. 26), and there is another, of plain cylindrical form, as well as sundry stumpy pottery types, some with flat bases, and others apparently designed to be fixed on to pegs; most have grease-trays.[25] In iron, there are several patterns of sconce, designed to be driven into masonry or into a beam or a wooden block. There is also a four-socketed 'caltrop' type, three of the sockets acting as legs while the fourth, containing the candle, was upright. The intention was evidently to provide fresh sockets for a total of four candles, say two-hours' burning-time, without there being a need to clear out the stumps.[26] The size of the sockets generally shows that the candles, no doubt mere dips made by plunging a strip of reed-pith into melted tallow or beeswax, were much thinner than the standard moulded candles of today.[27]

Fire would have been kindled with flint and pyrites or iron: there are probable (but no certain) examples of this equipment in the collection. In any case, care would have been taken not to let the kitchen fire go out.

DINING-ROOM EQUIPMENT

The small size of the dining-tables brought about a requirement not only for sideboards and dumb-waiters such as we see in reliefs, but also for the active ministrations of servants, who are also represented upon such works of art.[28] In itself, however, the refinement of many of the vessels used at table suggests that the Romano-Britons of the upper classes, at least, dined according to a polite and well-established ritual, and a Winchester discovery throws light on the matter: in a well-furnished grave containing various pottery vessels, there was a 'place-setting' for the deceased, consisting of a rectangular Kimmeridge shale plaque or tray about 50 by 40 cm., on which a samian cup and dish, two iron knives, a bronze spoon, and the remains of what might be called a Bath chap had been arranged.[29] Many other trays of this kind are known, among them fragments of two from Silchester; their carefully-finished upper surfaces carry simple geometrical ornament. Knife-cuts on many encourage their identification as trenchers on which portions of meat or fish would be cut up and distributed to the diners by the servants.[30]

Dining-forks were not used. The knives require little description (fig. 34,

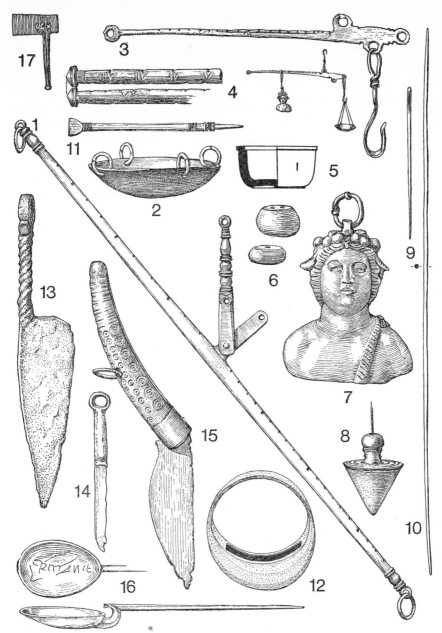

34. Miscellaneous objects. 1, bronze scale-beam (1890 'hoard'). 2, scale-pan 3, small bronze steelyard. 4, part of steelyard-arm, graduated. 5, bronze weight (*quadrans*) from nested set. 6. bronze weights (*uncia, sextans*). 7, bronze steelyard weight in the form of a bust of Bacchus (1900 'hoard'). 8, bronze plumb-bob. 9, bronze sewing-needle, the finest surviving. 10, bronze knitting-pin. 11, iron stilus. 12, bronze arm-purse (lid missing). 13, 14, iron knives. 15, clasp-knife with antler handle, bronze-mounted. 16, silver spoon, fourth century, inscribed *L(igula) Primanie* 'Primania's spoon'. 17, votive bronze axe, with numerical? symbols. Scales, 1/2, no. 12, 1/4

13–15), but it may be suggested that the rather flimsy folding kind, including some which had openwork bronze handles in the form of a hound chasing a hare, were probably dinner-knives, for there are also folding bronze spoons; and as in later centuries guests may have been expected to bring their own. The spoons were much lighter than ours, and seldom exceeded a modern teaspoon in capacity: the stems are rounded and pointed, the bowls round, oval, or lyre-shaped, and in some cases (such as the fine fourth-century silver example inscribed *L(igula) Primanie*, 'Primania's spoon', (fig. 34, 16)[31] are joined to the stem in an elegant stepped moulding. The pointed ends of the stems were employed to eat snails* or shellfish. Some of the bronze spoons are tinned in imitation of silver; there are also iron spoons, and many of bone with round bowls, probably egg-spoons.

Space forbids all but the briefest account of table-wares. Imported bronze vessels are well-represented, if mainly by fragments and handles, feet, etc. The first to be noticed is a mere wreck, a Campanian or Gaulish bowl which has lost its cylindrical handle, which would have terminated, no doubt, as usual in a ram's head (fig. 35, 2). Poor as the specimen is, it is a first-century example of one of the most widespread types, and since its true purpose has only recently been realised as the result of research by Dr H. U. Nuber of Frankfurt, a little time may be spent upon it. In sealed deposits, such as graves, this *trulleus*[32] is very often accompanied by a trefoil-mouthed ewer or *urceus* forming a pair with it, and they also appear carved on the sides of stone altars: in particular, one from Stockstadt in the Saalburg-Museum, where the ewer is shown tilted above the horizontal dish, and liquid is depicted flowing from it into the latter. There happens to be, in the British Museum, a late antique ivory with a scene of Pilate washing his hands, in which a servant pours water from a ewer over the hands and collects it in a handled dish held below: hence, indeed, the handle. Various other representations confirm the identification of this pair of vessels as a hand-washing set.[33]

Other imported bronze vessels of similar date include the amphora previously mentioned (p. 86; fig. 35, 3), its one surviving handle bearing a mask of Silenus;[34] and pieces of a handled wine-strainer, the bowl perforated in a delicate fret-pattern.[35] Since the military mess-can with the stamp of a Campanian manufacturer does not belong to the category of vessels under discussion (p. 47), we may turn without more ado to the pewter which came into fashion in the late third and fourth centuries, as a substitute for

* 'Fox reintroduced *escargots* to their old haunts; but the birds speedily made an end of them'—note by J. Challenor Smith, F.S.A. In point of fact, *Helix pomatia* is not among the Silchester fauna.

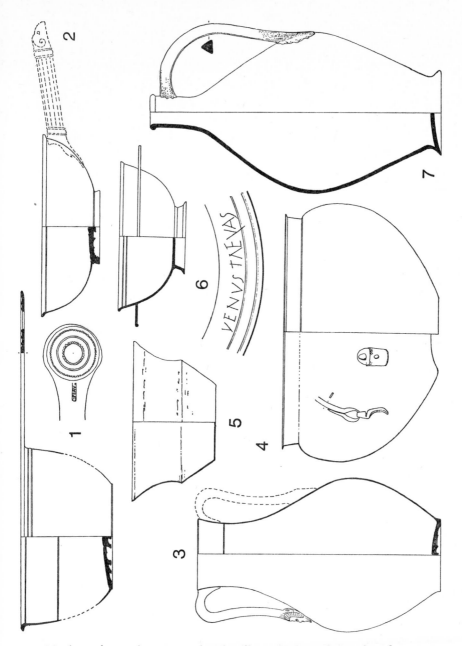

35. Metal vessels. 1–5 bronze: 1, tinned military mess-can, Campanian, first century
A.D. with stamp CIPI AVG(*ustalis* or *-ustani*); note graduation-line on interior.
2, *trulleus* from hand-washing set, handle restored, first century. 3, amphora, mended,
one handle missing, Gaulish, first century. 4, cauldron, with detail of handle, restored,
perhaps third century. 5, hammered tinned bronze bowl, fourth century. 6–7, pewter,
fourth century: 6, flanged bowl with inscription 'Venusta's bowl' on the flange, scale
1/2. 7, Flagon, restored, found below Ogham stone in a well, Insula IX. Scale, 1/4

the precious silver-plate which no Callevan seems to have left behind. Pewter dishes were undoubtedly made in the town (p. 274), but no examples are preserved. The most important piece is the flanged bowl (fig. 35, 6) inscribed *Venustae vas* 'Venusta's bowl'.[36] A restoration of the biconical flagon found crushed beneath the Ogham stone (p. 77)—a common type of vessel, of which there are other representatives in the collection—is shown in the same figure.

The sometimes patronising attitude which modern man adopts towards many of the antiquities displayed in museums must melt before the glassware of Roman times, the most remarkable of all the articles of everyday use to have come down to us. Generally there are only fragments, sometimes tiny ones: complete vessels come mostly from graves, where they have been protected by careful burial. Thus, there are few in the Silchester collection at all entire, and on these we may concentrate attention. Early polychrome mould-pressed wares, of which there are about a score of specimens, include the ribbed bowl shown in pl. 33b, 11 cm. in diameter, of royal translucent blue with opaque white and yellow marbling:[37] others, fragmentary, are marbled brown with blue and white florets. The same form is common in naturally-coloured, blue-green glass, occasionally in royal blue or brown: there are about sixteen examples. The most important *millefiori* piece, however, is the handled bowl (fig. 36, 1), unique in this material; the matrix is brown, with yellow, green and red florets.[38] The dish (fig. 36, 2) has an emerald matrix with tubular yellow florets, and like the specimen just described derives its shape from a metal prototype, seen also in pottery. It is interesting to note that the total of similar polychrome vessels from Wales, definitively occupied by the Roman army only in 74–8, is only about fourteen, so that the fashion for this type of glass was evidently then fast disappearing: in northern Britain, there are even fewer.[39]

---

36. Glassware. 1, mould-pressed and ground *trulleus,* polychrome (opaque green, red and yellow flowers in deep brown matrix), first century A.D. 2, dish, same technique, opaque yellow florets in emerald matrix, first century. 3, mould-blown and ground colourless cup, second century. 4, blown colourless cup with wheel-ground decoration, third century. 5, mould- and free-blown jar, amber, first-second century. 6, free-blown bird for face-powder, light blue, first century. 7, flanged free-blown and tooled bowl, natural-coloured (blue-green), third century. 8, free-blown beaker, sharp rim, fourth century. 9, thick blue-green free-blown oil-bottle, with 'dolphin' handles, from a companion-set for the public baths. 10, mould-blown bottle with 'celery' handle and pattern of circles on the base, second century. 11–13, bottle-bases: 11–12, with elements of abbreviated name *C(olonia) C(laudia) A(grippinensis)* (Cologne). 13, from a barrel-shaped wine-bottle, with letters standing for the Frontinian glassworks of northern Gaul, second-third and third-fourth centuries. Scales, 1/3; nos. 11–13, 1/4

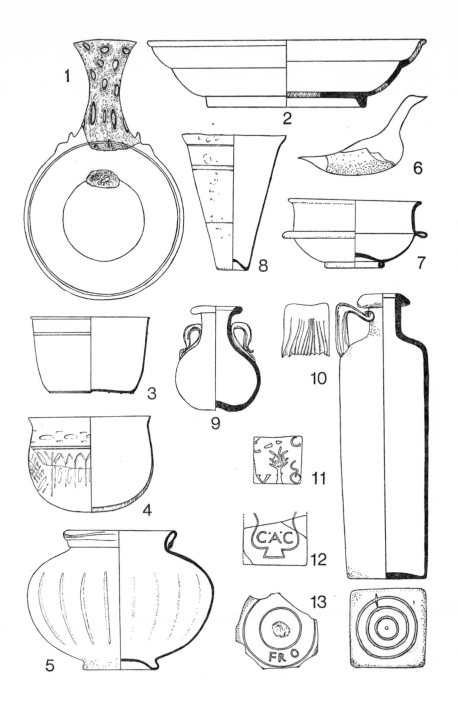

Mould-pressed and ground colourless pieces of about the same date or a little later are represented by one or two examples of dishes somewhat of the form of a modern soup-plate: there is, however, curiously little of this glass, common for example at Caerleon; and there is no example of the conical facet-cut beaker, though a fragment of colourless glass from a similarly shaped vessel, formed by abrasion from a mould-blown blank, displays almond-shaped relief ornament.[40] The drinking-cup (fig. 36, 3), also colourless, is a ground variety of a type often found in free-blown ware.[41]

The glory of Roman glassware, however, lies less in all these items, where the material is treated as no more than a substitute for coloured agates and rock-crystal, than in the wide range of blown forms, sometimes as thin as an electric lamp-bulb and strongly or delicately coloured with metallic oxides. The soda-lime-silica mixture had particularly ductile qualities, seen still in some of the fantastic creations of Murano; and these qualities were fully exploited for both the forms and the ornamentation of vessels. The technique of mould-blowing, used for the common cylindrical or square containers (fig. 36, 10), was also adapted to produce more decorative forms, but of these there is at Silchester only a tiny amber-coloured scrap bearing a moulded leaf-pattern, probably from the lid of an early Syrian cosmetic-jar.[42] The original which the artist had in mind was of metal or pottery, and throughout the Roman industry we continue to find shapes derived from other media, while the opposite is not unknown.[43] The third-century free-blown and tooled blue-green flanged bowl (fig. 36, 7) might claim a pottery original. Typical of a range of blown flagons and jars of first to second century date is that shown in fig. 36, 5, light amber in colour; the ribbing was produced by an initial mould-blowing process followed by free inflation. Some of the drawings show very well how the rims and bases were fashioned; and the flanged bowl bears on its basal underside a small scar left by the pontil-rod to which the bubble was transferred for tooling-operations from the blow-pipe. The late fourth-century beaker (fig. 36, 8) with pushed-in base and slight engraved decoration is of poor, bubbly, olive-green 'metal'; and its rim is so sharply knocked off, and left unground, that we might possibly regard it as a lamp rather than a drinking-vessel.[44] The round-bottomed colourless cup (fig. 36, 4) is typical of third to fourth century table-ware: it is free-blown, and has simple ground or 'cut' decoration.[45] Not shown are many fragments illustrating a wide range of decorative work: trailed threads or applied spots, in relief or marvered flat with the body; rounded points pulled out from the body; applied 'prunts'. A fragment of delicate colourless stemmed glass, Rhenish, with hatched serpentine trails in white and yellow, represents a very popular type of the second and third centuries—the so-called 'snake-thread' glass.[46] A last fragment to be mentioned is a rare scrap from a cage-cup in colourless glass; as the name implies, the vessel had an outer cage of network or possibly figured design, attached at the necessary points to the inner core. Such vessels, cut and ground from solid bell-shaped castings, belong to the late luxury trade, and only one other piece is known in Britain.[47] Unlike most of the earlier cut glass, the cage-cups were fully polished.

Kimmeridge shale, already discussed in another connection, supplied a score of turned dishes and bowls of various sizes, and simple forms: the most interesting is the handle of a *trulleus*.[48] The mere fact that such vessels could successfully be fashioned in shale, and put to use, shows that the material was very much more serviceable than surviving remains seem to suggest: like the glass *trulleus* illustrated, the handle projected at right-angles to the rim and, in the absence of any kind of thickening or bracket below, the strain applied to that thin line of junction would have been considerable.

Turning to pottery table-ware, the dominant type is the glossy red samian —very occasionally black, or red-and-yellow marbled—produced in south, central and east Gaul from the early first century onwards.[49] We have already written of the Italic ware, which served the early samian potters as model (p. 40); and of the last stages of the samian-industry represented by the roulette-patterned Argonne ware (p. 73). The forms of samian vessels found include cups, dishes, bowls and jars; many of the plain forms have such fine and sharp contours that a template must have been used to produce them as the clay was spun on the wheel. The methods of decoration include, besides rouletting and moulding—bowls with moulded decoration are perhaps the most characteristic product of the industry (pl. 33)—trailing liquid clay to form 'ivy' leaves or more extensive work *en barbotine,* and 'cut-glass' patterning incised at the air-dry stage before firing. May's *Silchester Pottery* lists some 330 potter's stamps on samian-ware from the site, mostly on plain forms, and from all the principal areas of manufacture. By ancient standards, the process of manufacture was exacting. Not all clays were suitable: in Britain, for example, the industry never flourished. There is a single piece of British samian in the collection, of poor quality both as a ceramic and an artistic production. The gloss was obtained by dipping the air-dry vessel into an infinitely fine watery suspension of clay particles containing a good deal of the natural iron present in the clay; firing took place at about 950°. If oxygen was admitted to the kiln during the final stage of firing, the iron-content was turned to red oxide; if oxygen was excluded, the far less common black ware resulted. There are several examples of this in the collection, most notably two heads in high relief which had been applied to a globular vessel, one of Mercury, the other perhaps Rosmerta, his Gallic consort.[50] Marbled ware is comparatively rare, and also in the main of early date: it was produced by the use of a slip very poor in iron, to which an iron-rich slip was added at the moment of dipping the vessel.

The moulded bowls illustrated include two of standard form. Pl. 33d (Form 29) is a vessel of a shape which passed out of favour almost entirely by about A.D. 85. On the basal interior is the stamp of the potter *Primus* of La Graufesenque, south Gaul. The other (pl. 33c) comes most probably from the Heiligenberg pottery, east Gaul, but is a most unusual piece (Form 30).

Not all the pottery made in the samian factories was of the type discussed. Early on, there was a certain amount of experimentation with lead-glazed ware, some moulded: Silchester has the base of a small early Lezoux (central Gaulish) *trulleus* with a greenish-yellow glaze and the soft micaceous paste characteristic of the area and date,[51] while pl. 33a is another early Lezoux piece in a more rustic style, the base kicked. The scale-pattern, applied, is found on a great variety of pottery and is probably derived from the pine-cone. The colour of this bowl is olive green, with a single row of the scales in brown.[52] Fig. 37 is also Lezoux ware, black gloss; it belongs to about the

37. Black-gloss beaker with decoration *en barbotine;* Lezoux, central Gaul, second century. Scale, 1/2

middle of the second century. The decoration *en barbotine* is delightfully elegant, and characteristic of the refined taste informing Roman provincial art at its best.[53]

The long tradition of Gallo-Belgic black wares (cf. p. 40, fig. 6, 4–6) was maintained in northern Gaul and the Rhineland, and many of the second and third century products are found in Britain. The little grey-gloss beaker, with decoration *en barbotine* (pl. 33e) is an example. Gayer are black-gloss beakers with overglaze mottoes or floral designs in white or ochre; Silchester pieces include one inscribed VITAM TIBI '[long] life to thee'. From the same region, but earlier, comes a range of 'bronzed' (mica-dusted) ware.[54] Among highly specialised vessels, the cream-coloured filter-bowl for spiced wine and the like is an interesting piece (fig. 38, 9).[55]

The Lezoux or Rhenish beakers were much admired in Britain and gave rise to imitations, especially in the Castor district of Northamptonshire. The flowing scenes of hares and hounds *en barbotine* produced there are justly famous, and the beakers bearing them were exported to the continent in some number.[56]

After the precipitous decline of the samian industry in the third century (probably as a result of the civil war of 196–7), British potters began to supply local requirements for red-surfaced table-wares, although never able to reproduce the quality of the continental material, and scarcely ever attempting moulded wares. Much late pottery of this sort at Silchester came from Oxfordshire, and some from the New Forest.[57] Large numbers of rosette-stamped, mainly Oxfordshire red-coated bowls are represented in the collection; the beaker, with white-painted decoration (fig. 38, 10) is also typical, as are white or cream basins with simple peasant patterns in brown or red.[58] The best-known New Forest wares are indented beakers ('thumb-pots') in a hard maroon-glazed stoneware; there are many of these, and a few other forms.[59]

It is impossible to give more than a summary indication of the table-pottery, and the same applies to the culinary wares discussed briefly below. We conclude by mention of the baby's feeding-bottle (*titina* or—onomatopœic?—*ubuppa*), used for administering water or watered wine rather than milk (fig. 38, 6).[60]

KITCHEN EQUIPMENT

Pride of place goes here to the fourth-century gridiron (*craticula*) with drop-handles, about 45 by 43 cm. and 10 cm. high, from the Insula I deposit of ironwork (fig. 30).[61] It was designed for use on a charcoal hearth, probably

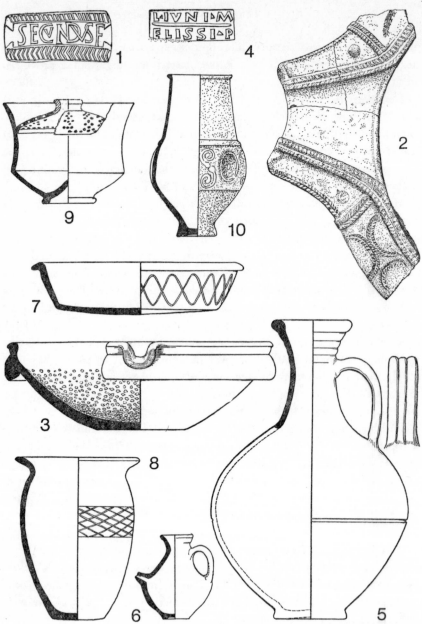

38. Roman pottery. 1, mortarium-stamp, *Secundus F(ecit)*, Verulamium region, first century A.D. 2, 'boar-snout' spout of very large local? mortarium. 3, mortarium, second century. 4, amphora-stamp *L. Juni Melissi P*(. . .) '(bailiff) *x* of L. Junius Melissus,' south Spanish, second century. 5, cream-surfaced orange-ware flagon, first century. 6, baby's bottle for wine-and-water, first-second century. 7, dish in black-burnished ware, Dorset, second century. 8, cooking-pot, same ware, third-fourth century. 9, strainer for spiced wine, north Gaulish, first-second century. 10, red colour-coated beaker, with cream-painted decoration, fourth century. Scales, 1, 4: 1/2; others, 1/4

of the raised type already discussed (p. 195). Meat and fish, perhaps cakes, could be grilled on it, or vessels placed on it to simmer. An iron tripod[62] was no doubt used on a similar hearth, as were pottery bowls standing on three feet.[63] There are parts of an iron ladle and flesh-hooks in the collection.

Metal cooking-pans were somewhat rare. Four shallow bronze pans were found in the Insula XXIII deposit of ironwork; two may have been frying-pans.[64] There is also a paper-thin bronze cauldron, raised from a single piece of metal, with iron rim-binding,[65] and the unusual cauldron shown in fig. 35, 4. For these vessels, there were pothooks and chains.[66] Two tinned bronze vessels found in XXXVIA.1 include that shown in fig. 35, 5, and another with a flat rim, which may have been used as the inner container in *bain-marie* cooking.[67]

Pottery was much more commonly used for cooking than metal-ware. A ubiquitous early Silchester type of cooking-pot, hand-made, is shown (fig. 6, 9); its coarse paste is tempered with pounded flint. From about the year 100 or a little later, a hand- or wheel-made black-burnished ware appears: fig. 38, 8 shows a third or fourth century variety of cooking pot in this fabric; the latticed zone around the middle provided a good grip when the pot was lifted from the fire. Lime or fur in many examples shows that they were used for boiling water. Bowls of plain or flanged type also occur in this fabric (fig. 38, 7, second century). The other culinary vessel (fig. 38, 5) is a typical jug or flagon of somewhat earlier date.[68]

Perhaps the most characteristically Roman culinary vessel is the mortarium.[69] There are some stone specimens, of Purbeck marble, and L-shaped rubbers for them; but the pottery examples are in overwhelming majority. They are generally in strong, light-coloured wares, and there are quartz-grits in the inner surface to assist in the mixing and trituration of food (fig. 38, 3, a small second-century piece). Another, of the same date but different form, still contains traces of a pulp of fruit-stones and pips from the last dish prepared in it: two varieties of cherry and two of plum were identified, but if this is correct, one or other of these fruits must have been preserved, since they ripen at different times of year.[70] The very worn state of some of the mortaria proves that they were used for the purpose indicated, but somewhat similar bowls were employed in rural France until recently in cheese-making; their rough interiors assisted in the curdling of the milk without the need to add fresh whey to each batch. It is suggested that mortaria were also used for this purpose: their grits would have retained bacteria, and their spouts would have been well-adapted to drain off the whey.[71] The thin walls of most such vessels have led some writers to believe that they could not have been used for pounding foodstuffs; but the rims, on the other hand, are very stout

S.—P

and rubbing, rather than pounding, may have been the usual procedure. Enormous fragmentary mortaria up to 90 cm. across (the spout of one is shown to common scale in fig. 38, 2) were found in an outhouse of XIV.2,[72] and may have had this function: the building, with its three divisions and yard attached, could be interpreted as a dairy, with milking-parlour at the rear, and a central cool room where big stone supports indicate the existence of a heavy table-slab. These very large mortaria could be of local make; others, however, bear potter's stamps which indicate manufacture principally in Kent and the Verulamium region (fig. 38, 1 shows the stamp of *Secundus*, from the latter area). Later mortaria were made in the Oxfordshire or New Forest kilns.

An indispensable article in the Roman kitchen was the quern or rotary hand-mill. Those from Calleva include many—perhaps a quarter of the total—made of lava from the Rhineland, quarried in the hills west of Koblenz.[73] In British stones, we have evidence of production in the west country or Welsh borderland, many examples of Old Red sandstone and quartz-pebble conglomerate of similar geological date being known; a few are of Greensand from a less distant source. The querns are usually about 33 to 48 cm. in diameter. The ordinary domestic model consisted of two stones set one on the other, the lower stone having a metal pivot around which the upper stone rotated. There is no evidence in these examples of a metal bearing, and the central orifice had to be large enough to admit the grain. The grinding surfaces, slightly conical, are radially striated to assist the movement of the grain towards the edge, where it would emerge as a rather coarse flour. The upper stone was turned by means of an iron ring in its edge, or an inserted wooden handle: an example from Insula XIX actually retained its oaken handle, which was fortunately copied in modern wood before it shrank to its present deformed state. The handle, with a comfortable T-shaped head, has a tapering shank which enabled it to be driven tightly home in the chase cut for it in the stone.[74]

Some of the domestic querns may have been kept on tables or placed on a clean cloth where the flour could easily be gathered up; but often they were set on the ground. In X.B5, a lower stone was found in place upon a brick plinth; pieces of charred wood around it suggested to the excavators that there had been some sort of wooden frame as well. Fragments of the upper stone lay nearby.[75]

Some years ago, the leading authority on ancient hand-mills, the late E. C. Curwen, carried out an experiment with a rotary quern, which I was able to witness. The flour produced, though coarse, was surprisingly free from grit, though a lifetime intake did not fail to wear down the teeth considerably, as the skull of an elderly Callevan shows. The absence of caries in the dentition, normal in ancient skulls, implies a diet infinitely poorer in sugars than our own, and all the better for that (see further, p. 262).

Flour was probably ground domestically as required, but there must have been some means of storing grain, flour, and other dry goods. Returning therefore to the subject of containers, we refer to a bentwood tub about 30 cm. in diameter and 18 cm. deep, formed of a thin strip of oak no doubt steamed to shape, and fitted with a thin bottom. This could well have been a flour-bin.[76] Carved and turned wooden vessels, and basketry in osier and other pliable twigs or in rushes must have been everywhere in evidence: a fragment of basketry survives, made of peeled withies, some entire and some split, but now much shrunken.[77] The question of the pots, large and small, found sunk to their rims in the floors of various rooms has already been discussed, and the great 'Jubilee pot' singled out as a likely example of a food-storage vessel (p. 196). In this chapter, therefore, we need only add mention of an amphora of Spanish origin, from which the neck had been removed for a similar purpose: the surviving shard is inscribed AVIIN, i.e. *Aven(ae)* 'Oats'.[78]

PART THREE

ECONOMIC

19

Agriculture and Food

THE LANDS OF THE CALLEVANS

Emerging from its Cogidubnian chrysalid, Roman Calleva stood directly on the site of the autonomous Belgic *oppidum,* unlike some other towns which were Roman creations or grew from the civil settlements of early Roman forts. Thus there is no reason to question the assumption that the descendants of the original Belgic land-owners continued to occupy the soil on which their basic livelihood depended. In chapter 3, we suggested that the second to fourth century population of Calleva might have been about 1200 souls, though it could have been smaller. Taking the larger figure, it is clear that the cultivated land, pasturage, etc. attached to the town must have been extensive, and must have been augmented in response to the demands of the *annona* (p. 60). Unfortunately, we have no means of telling what the total area of agricultural land actually was.

A starting-point in the following sketch of Callevan agriculture[1] is the name, which suggests an original settlement founded deep in woodland, though on a spur bearing a much lighter type of vegetation than encumbered the surrounding clay (p. 36). The earliest cultivation will have taken place to the west and north-west of the walled town, where the scrub of the gravel plateau was easily cleared. But we can also suggest that the heavier, richer slopes south of the town were also tilled to some extent before Roman times, because the dykes which traverse them (fig. 5) were necessary only where there was cleared or open ground across which a hostile advance might occur. The longest dyke stretches for some 2.4 km., and apparently ends on the far side of the valley of the Silchester brook, where, presumably, heavy forest intervened. A very short distance to the south-west lies the hamlet of Little London, where evidence of Roman tile-manufacture occurs, doubtfully claimed as an imperial enterprise (p. 277).

Although the Silchester area has been archaeologically 'sensitive' for well over a century, singularly few sites of Romano-British occupation have been reported near the town; and indeed we should not expect many. The nearest are on the south, and like the tilery appear on the far side of the Silchester brook—perhaps significantly, since this may have been the limit, in this direction, of lands farmed directly from the town. Traces of a building or buildings have been recorded at a spot just to the east of the junction of the Winchester and Chichester roads (as we now know);[2] and some 800 m. eastward again, 1.5 km., from the town, part of a typically Romano-British field-system has been revealed during aerial survey by the National Monuments Record during the favourable summer of 1970.[3] The fields are marked by their ditches, and are of squarish shape with sides up to about 150 m. in length; they are fairly regularly laid out on either side of a main droveway, which probably ran back to join the main road. Several of the fields are divided by lesser droveways, and one takes the form of a concentric double rectangle. There, if anywhere, excavation might reveal the remains of a timber-built farmstead. It is now generally accepted that this type of layout, with droveways and linear pens around the main enclosure, was associated with animal husbandry, in particular with cattle. The system as a whole seems to have replaced an earlier and less regular one; and though the matter remains to be ascertained, it may well be that we have evidence here of the Romanisation of an original Belgic farm.[4]

Apart from these discoveries, the nearest known settlements south of Calleva are considerably more distant, over 6 km. from the walled town. Several sites, presumed to be villas, occur on the lighter soils beginning with the rise of the ground towards the chalk downs above Basingstoke.[5] Further south-west, Pamber Forest seems to have remained inviolate throughout the Roman period: the steep slopes at the edge of the gravel plateau and the frequent marshy spots below, sufficiently account for this. The forest was in itself very valuable, for it supplied building-timber, fuel, bark for tanning, and forage for pigs; there, too, the huntsman found his prey.

The nearest known sign of occupation on the west of Calleva is at Crookham, over 11 km. distant. North-west and north of the town runs the Kennet valley, where settlement centred upon Thatcham Newtown near Newbury, but stretched thereafter discontinuously downstream towards Reading and the Thames. Very probably, the Kennet was the boundary of Callevan lands in this direction; and close to the Roman road to Dorchester-upon-Thames, on the north side of the river, a small Belgic and Roman agricultural settlement has been excavated. At Theale, Southcote, Prospect Park and Reading itself, particularly on the south side of the Kennet, evidence of Romano-British occupation is profuse and long-continued, and A. L. F. Rivet has suggested that there may have been a river-port for Silchester at Reading.[6] Finally, to the east of Calleva, nothing has been recorded before we reach the Loddon, a distance of 6.5 km; and that lazy stream may well be taken as the boundary of Callevan lands here. The varied terrain around the town, therefore, offered the farmer light, well-drained but poor gravel soils to the west and north-west, for cultivation or for pasturage; and fertile arable slopes to the south, south-east and east running down to well-watered pasture-meadows terminating in reed-beds for thatch and withy-groves. Here, wild fowl will have abounded, and fishing was to be had.

The area contemplated, however, is large, amounting to over 180,000 hectares, and the suggestion has been made that the Silchester brook, only 1.5 km. from the town, might have been the effective limit of lands farmed directly. To the north-west, across 3 km. of very much poorer land in the main, there is Grim's Bank (fig. 5, p. 79), the late Roman earthwork which may well have delimited the irreducible minimum of cultivated ground in that quarter; while the far outlying cross-ridge dykes on Crookham and Greenham commons (p. 78) may possibly mark successive stages in the clearance of pasture. The main arable will have lain closer to the town, within a reasonable distance for the slow-plodding oxen which drew both plough and cart, although the possibility that there were byres in the cultivated areas distant from the town cannot be overlooked.

Some of the remarkable aerial photographs taken by the National Monuments Record in 1970 show the boundary-ditches of ancient fields aligned with the Roman highways both east and west of the town (folding plan)— basically contemporary with the roads, therefore, and Callevan. The interpretation of the markings on the east side is difficult, and some there are clearly post-Roman or even recent. About 500 m. from the east gate of Calleva, however, the existence of metalled accommodation-ways, necessitated perhaps by the heavier ground encountered as the valley of the Silchester brook is reached, is discernible on either side of the road: most clearly, one at right-angles to the road and another parallel to the road at a distance of about 135 m.

On the west side, the ditch-markings are very much clearer (pl. 9) and are definitely antecedent, in the main, to the present field-pattern. The system is not traceable within the line of the reduced outer earthwork, and understandably so, since this was the boundary of the urban plan (p. 46). Beyond the earthwork, immediately north of the Roman road to the west, there are three small enclosures, perhaps four, up to about 50 by 60 m. in size: they seem to have been laid out at different times, since their northern boundaries are not precisely aligned. To the north again, there is a much larger field about 90 by 105 m., and another, wedge-shaped, to the west: their common northern boundary can be traced running further to the west at a constant distance of some 140 m. from the road: this may or may not have any connection with a dimension of four *actus* (4 × 120 *pedes* of 0.296 m.); in any case, no precise deductions are practicable until the system has been planned and studied properly. Marks to the west of the wedge-shaped field are indistinct, with the exception of a long droveway, apparently ancient, on the far side of the Silchester-Reading road, and ending about 620 m. from the walls. The *agger* of the Roman highway to the west, some 145 m. to the south, was identified by Mr. J. Balderstone in 1968, without side-ditches, and a boundary-ditch of the road-zone 12 m. from the crest: just to the north, post-holes and black soil marked a mid fourth-century hut. On the south side of the highway, and returning very much closer to the town, we find a band of enclosures about 105 m. wide, with further traces west and south. The boundaries pay little attention to the original course of the earthwork (p. 46) and to some extent also ignore the metalled track which had led to a causeway built across its ditch in the third century.[7] Though the field-system may include earlier elements, it is, in the main, clearly of the later third or fourth century, as indeed relics from the limited excavations of 1956 suggest. At first, the area enclosed by the primary line of the outer earthwork may have been devoted to other purposes. There were probably tombs along the road, as on the east side of the town, and two or three small buildings certainly stood along the road also: one of timber construction has been partly excavated.[8] The earliest features known from excavation are traces of rough sheds built into the rear of the rampart before it was demolished, and it seems possible that a good deal of the area between the original and reduced lines had at one time been devoted to cattle-pounds connected with the tanning-industry (p. 290).[9]

Subject to the findings of excavation, it can otherwise be suggested that the small plots enclosed piecemeal on either side of the Roman road are more suited to the purposes of market-gardening than to ordinary tillage. The close and not altogether random grouping of small dark spots in one or two places on the photograph suggests that the tree-pits or orchards may be identifiable.[10] Many of the spots elsewhere, however, are probably nothing more than the marks of pits or wells, and one of large size was tested in 1956. An extensive exploration of the area might prove that it was a suburb of small-holdings with houses (mostly timber-built) attached, rather than composed merely of fields, gardens and orchards.

Returning to the question of arable land at Calleva, can we form even the most blurred impression of its extent? An answer must depend in part upon the average consumption of grain; in part upon the yield; and in part upon the imponderable, the incidence of the *annona*.

In modern times, the annual consumption per head is placed at over 160 litres; but this is too small an allowance for our purposes, because it excludes other staple carbohydrates, mainly the potato, and the heavy intake of sugar which in ancient times was not available except in the form of honey or decoctions of wine, and was really no more than a flavouring. The Roman legionary consumed about 415 litres, and had a varied diet in other respects.[11] In civilian circumstances, more meat and dairy produce may have been eaten, though it would be difficult to prove the point; and if we reduced the average annual consumption of the Callevans to 300 litres, with allowance thus for children's smaller intake, this would probably be a minimal figure. In 1807, Middleton estimated that the annual average consumption of wheat in all forms of food was 288 litres, 'about equivalent to the average net produce of half an acre of land [0.2 ha.], that is, after deducting seed, loss by vermin, accidents, etc'.[12]

Did the Callevans expect to average a harvest of 1440 litres per hectare, net? Applebaum, indeed, has suggested that the villa-system, under good management, was capable of producing between 1350 and 1800 litres 'where we can check granary capacity with ox-stalls and estate boundaries',[13] but it is difficult to believe that this estimate is other than highly optimistic. Peasant agriculture at Figheldean Down, also studied by Applebaum, would present the striking contrast of no more than 450 litres,[14] but to reach this figure Applebaum has applied the thirteenth-fourteenth century average yields—net or otherwise—of granges of the Bishops of Winchester. Here the return for wheat is less than four for one, and, derisory though this figure may seem, it is curiously close to that recorded for estates of the Knights Hospitallers in Provence about the same time; and almost the same as that officially reported for the same region in 1812.[15] Agricultural conditions in Provence differed in no essential way from those of Italy; and for Roman Italy we have the surprising statement of the first-century agronomist Columella, who can 'scarcely remember' a time when the yield—whether as the result of poor seed, inadequate manuring, imperfect cultivation or unsuitable land—was as much as fourfold.[16] I do not see how it can be maintained that medieval agriculture was less efficient than Romano-British. No doubt there were many occasions when a Romano-British yield, in favourable areas and under the best management, far exceeded the fourfold: but these would have been particular circumstances upon which a sound economy could hardly be formed. Bearing in mind the very small fields which alone are as yet discernible at and near Silchester—fields of the same dimensions as can be seen to this day in parts of western Ireland—and the known extremely weedy state of the crop,[17] it would be rash to assume that less than half an hectare was reaped for every inhabitant of the town, allowing for seed and waste. If our estimate of the population of Calleva (p. 62) is correct, therefore, we have to assume that the minimal annual harvest amounted to 600 hectares.

Only the problem of the *annona* can be sketched. Under Hadrian, the army of occupation was in the region of 50,000 strong; and at the legionary rate of diet, nearly 21 million litres of corn would have been annually required. Some came from fields near the forts, no doubt; more, perhaps, from imperial domains. The residue remained a heavy burden to be shared among the local authorities occupying corn-growing areas, and Silchester lay in such an area.[18]

From the dawn of settled agriculture in the west, the desirability of allowing ground to lie fallow (or in the most advanced ancient practice, sometimes to bear a leguminous crop which could be ploughed in for green manure rich in nitrogen) has been appreciated; and some kind of two-field rotation was the ancient norm.[19] Thus the *minimal* Callevan arable would have amounted to 1800 hectares on the basis suggested, and to include the *annona*-land we should think in terms, perhaps—who can tell?—of a total of 2400.[20] But these are minimal figures, and the comfortable life of the town was not based on a subsistence-economy as far as the larger houses were concerned. An agricultural surplus, in part no doubt arising from animal husbandry and not by any means confined to the growing of crops, must have been substantial. On an earlier page the possibility that the Silchester brook represented the limit of the ground that could be farmed *directly* from the town was considered. A circle of 1.5 km. radius of Calleva would contain something over 705 ha., but would include much land useless for arable purposes.

CROPS

The actual evidence of crops is meagre. Carbonised grains of wheat were identified,[21] and oats were grown, on the evidence of the cut-down amphora labelled AVIIN (p. 239); the presence of barley, likely enough, is suggested by the ears on the painted dado from XIV.1 (pl. 29); and if corn-cockle is also depicted, it is among the score of weeds recorded, and may be particularly associated with rye.[22] Legumes are represented by a single green pea, fortuitously carbonised: most vegetables are consumed when their seeds, if present at all, are soft and immature, and their survival into the palaeobotanical record is very hazardous.[23] On the other hand, the plant-list is firmly based where fruits are concerned, and the pea may stand for other legumes—beans, etc.—well-known for the period in other contexts.[24] The brassicas found, black and white mustard,[25] may have been grown for fodder or manure, and may stand for others unrepresented, such as cabbage.[26] Of roots, we have carrot, radish, the beginnings of a cultivated parsnip, perhaps turnip, all very poor by our standards.[27] Other vegetables in the Callevan record include celery and those long-forgotten standbys of the past, corn-salad and good-king-Henry.[28] The principal crop other than food-stuffs seems to have been flax.[29] Of the plants mentioned in a listing which, we may repeat, is incomplete and dependent on the wholly fortuitous survival of some rather than all the evidence, it is of interest to note that the carrot, radish, turnip, pea and corn-salad are regarded as Roman introductions, and possibly flax as a cultivated plant.

Before turning to the fruits, the pot-herbs and other useful plants require mention. Chervil, coriander and dill are there, Roman introductions all three,[30] as likewise is the opium-poppy, the seeds of which, dried and harmless, were dusted on to bread, then as now.[31] All these were garden-plants: wild, there grew others of lesser note. Wild, too, in all probability, are three dye-plants—gipsy-wort for black, a bedstraw for a superior red, saw-wort for yellow. Only the last of these bears the Linnaean accolade *tinctoria*,[32] but it may be presumed that the value of the others was recognised as well. Some medicinal herbs have been mentioned above (p. 137).

And so to the fruits. First come wild strawberry, raspberry, and blackberry;[33] the elder too, of which Reid observed that the seeds were so abundant in the samples, and so often present in a crushed state, as to show that the berries were commonly eaten; and an elderberry dish is included among Apicius' more homely receipts.[34] Elderberry-wine does not seem to be mentioned as such in the ancient sources, but the making of 'wine from apples', 'pears' and various other 'factitious' wines[35] suggests that a brew still so widely enjoyed was made and appreciated in Roman times: certainly the medicinal properties of the elderberry were well-known.[36] Wild stone-fruits include the cherry: Pliny's statement that the tree was introduced in Roman times must refer to a cultivated variety possibly glimpsed in the Silchester record.[37] Then there are the sloe and the bullace, and in another family the apple (were they always crabs?). Hips and haws should probably be admitted to the total.[38]

Evidence of cultivated fruits is much more meagre. There were a cultivated bullace 'in every respect identical with the form . . . still cultivated in cottage gardens in Wales';[39] a large plum, very like an old black variety grown in Cornwall;[40] and, finally in this group, the damson—Pliny's Damascus plum, often dried.[41]

A small medlar not much larger than a cherry, like one known in Germany, is an interesting find,[42] but the greatest interest attaches to the black mulberry, the grape, and the fig. Of these three, the first was probably grown in gardens, being an exotic introduction;[43] as for the other two, both are available in varieties which grow perfectly well outdoors in southern Britain today, and there is much evidence to show that the vine was cultivated in Roman Britain, as in later times.[44] Whether wine was made from Callevan grapes must remain doubtful, for there was none of the residue associated with wine-making; and bearing in mind the fact that the vine is not a reliable cropper in these islands, it must remain an open question as to whether the pips may not relate rather to imported produce, fresh or dried.[45] The fig is the most intriguing of all: the Emperor Julian mentions that figs were raised even as far north as Paris, where in winter they were protected by 'straw cloaks' and by other means against the inclemency of the weather.[46] There would thus appear to be no reason why the devoted gardener could not have raised figs at Silchester also. Alas! there is one very important reason why the fruits denoted by the finds of seeds cannot possibly have been locally grown. The varieties of figs raised in Britain are parthenocarpic: that is, bear fruit without pollination, and consequently have no hard seeds. The tiny hard seeds of fertilised figs, which we have in these ancient deposits, betoken cultivation in a warmer clime where the caprificatory wasp, *Blastophaga grossorum,* may live. The Silchester figs may have come fresh, or more probably dried like the Smyrna figs of today, from lands bordering the Mediterranean.[47]

Since there was evidently a traffic of this kind, it is perhaps a little strange that similar goods, such as the olive, are not known from Roman contexts in Britain; and indeed only one almond is known in this country.[48] The only nut directly in evidence at Calleva is the hazel-nut; walnuts have been found elsewhere, and it is possible that a graffito on a jug may refer to an oil expressed from this nut (p. 131). The sweet chestnut was also known in Roman Britain.[49]

FARM ANIMALS

That 'grass-burning engine', the ox,[50] was the foundation of ancient agricultural economy. It was the principal beast of burden, for, as we have seen previously (p. 146), a harness which took advantage of the quicker pace of horses had yet to be devised. Thus, oxen pulled the plough and hauled the cart. Their manure, in common with that of other animals and of man himself (p. 90) enriched the fallow and improved the meadow. Oxen provided dairy products: milk, cheese, perhaps butter in this peripheral region (it was a curiosity further south);[51] the ox gave meat, leather, bone, horn, and glue. By comparison, the horse was economically a light-weight. Sheep, goats, pigs, and barn-door fowl complete the list. Unfortunately, very little can be said directly of the varieties (p. 31).

The first report on animal remains, that of 1891, describes the ox under the heading of *Bos longifrons,* the Celtic short-horn, which undoubtedly composed the greater proportion of the finds; but it was suggested—though the matter was not developed—that two sub-varieties were in evidence.[52] Another important notice, that of 1902, refers to the predominance in that year's finds of animals 'of moderate size, which cannot be distinguished from some of our modern cattle, *Bos taurus'*. An admixture of breeds is to be expected, on the basis of the skilled investigation of the osseous remains from Newstead fort,[53] where the larger kinds probably resembled the wild white Chillingham cattle. To some close relative of these may have belonged the original of the Silchester sketch (fig. 7, 5),[54] for the horns point forward and are fairly large, and the coat is clearly very shaggy. The Celtic shorthorn was small, the equivalent of the Kerry or Alderney cow, according to Pitt Rivers' comparative studies;[55] and the small size even of plough-oxen is amply confirmed by statuettes, notably the Piercebridge (Durham) group in the British Museum.[56] These animals can have stood only 1.0 to 1.2 m. at the shoulder. Lastly, mention may be made of one or two iron goad-tips in the collection, spirals of iron with a short point. As regards sheep, the Romano-British breed was of light build, and has been likened to the Soay or St. Kilda type.[57] Little can be said of the pig or goat: boar's tusks are always common on Roman sites, but the goat is seldom encountered.

Among the avian remains, those of domestic fowl vastly predominate, and there were apparently two varieties, one small with leg-bones displaying the well-developed spur of the game-cock. Otherwise, the commonest birds about the houses of Calleva were ravens and crows, which no doubt picked a living from the many open rubbish-pits.

Some doubt may adhere to the identification, given without comment in *Archaeologia,* of the pheasant *(Phasianus colchicus,* not the game-bird subgroup *torquatus,* which is an eighteenth-century introduction).[58] The evidence of a wall-painting and a mosaic suggests that the pheasant was not unknown in Britain,[59] but its remains are only with difficulty distinguished from those of the common fowl. But both reared and wild birds are listed in Diocletian's maximal edict of 301—*fasianus pastus* (crammed) and *non pastus, agrestis,* with prices in line with those fixed for geese: so it was a bird not uncommonly bred for the table in late times, though a luxury in earlier days.[60] Palladius, alone of the agronomists, discusses its management, and among other advice suggests setting hens to hatch the eggs, as is the usual practice for *torquatus* today.[61]

DOMESTIC ANIMALS

The bones of dog[62] especially, but also of cat,[63] occurred and their paw-marks are visible on tiles laid out to dry before firing. Over twenty dog-skulls were found in 1891 alone; but a skeleton recovered nearly complete in that year, whether 'just dog'[64] or not, received less attention than could be wished. Judging by the remains, about three breeds of dog ran about the town; they ranged in size from terrier to stag-hound. The greater number of skulls are like that of poor Laddie, the greyhound, which has joined them in the collection. Among all the permutations and combinations of which dog-kind is naturally so prolific, a breed with very bowed legs appears more than once, and was encountered by Pitt Rivers at Cranbourne Chase.[65] Whether this was a bull-dog, an otter-dog or a corgi-like animal, we can scarcely tell: Pitt Rivers' specimen was of slender build, and made him think of a dachshund.

The cat has a far shorter history of domestication than the dog, and its bones resemble those of its wild counterpart. The domestic cat, indeed, is supposed to be a Roman introduction,[66] and the Silchester cats would have compared well in size and build with those of today; and at least we know that they had house-mice to stalk.[67]

FARM TOOLS AND IMPLEMENTS

The ploughs in use by the Callevans, as far as we can judge from their surviving metal parts, were of two kinds. The first is represented by a small iron share-tip, flat, about 6 cm. wide, and with turned-up or flanged sides which fitted over the wooden share (fig. 39, 9): the type is well-known in Iron Age and Roman contexts.[68] The second is represented by material in the two fourth-century 'hoards' of ironwork, namely the well-known coulters (fig. 39, 10) or heavy knives, up to 4.5 kg. and 74 cm. long, with a 23 cm. cutting-edge, set vertically in the plough-beam to slice through the ground ahead of the share; and also the heavy iron bars well-worn at the tip, clearly metal versions of the wholly wooden 'fore-share' of the famous Danish Iron

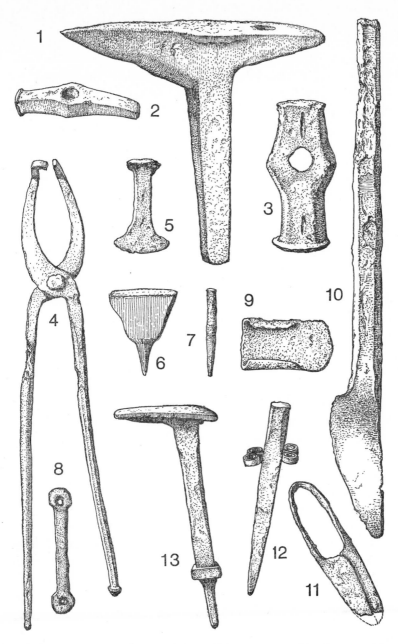

39. Smith's tools, etc. 1, beaked anvil. 2, small hammer. 3, striking-hammer. 4, tongs.
5, chisel or set (sate). 6, punch. 7, drift. 8, nail-heading tool. 9, plough-share tip or
peat-cutter iron. 10, coulter, 11, shears. 12, field-anvil. 13, cobbler's foot, Mostly from
the 1890 and 1900 'hoards' of ironwork. Scale: 1/5

Age plough *(ard—aratrum)* from Donneruplund: the comparison, which pl.
38 shows is very just, was made by W. H. Manning in 1964.[69] Thus we have
a 'light early plough' and a 'heavy later plough', but both basically of the
simple Iron Age design equipped with metal parts, in the second case also
with an iron coulter.[70]

These ploughs would have been drawn by a brace of oxen in yoked harness
attached to the plough-beam by a rope, probably of twisted withy.[71] There
is evidence from Denmark that the simple *ard* was capable of working heavy
land,[72] but the later Roman pattern equipped with a coulter would have been
much more effective. The light plough was capable only of burrowing
through the ground to make a V-shaped furrow; but by tilting it, the soil
could be shifted preferentially to one side. In the case of the heavy plough,
we naturally wonder whether other features—ground-wrests, mould-board,
wheels—were incorporated, so bringing the implement into line with the
kind of plough used until recent times. There is no direct evidence here.
The ground-wrests, amounting to wide, lateral extensions of the main 'share',
however appear on the Sussex and Cologne plough-models,[73] their function
being to push aside the soil with greater effect. As in the case of the light
plough, much could be achieved by tilting the implement, and the existence
of a coulter does not presuppose that of a mould-board to turn the furrow
over.[74] Pliny refers to a plate *(tabula)* which was fitted to the plough
when seed was to be turned in, and this is a mould-board.[75] Evidence for
wheels is also from Pliny, who writes of a type of plough recently invented in
Raetia, which possessed 'little wheels'.[76] This plough must have been of a
very different design from those which we have considered, and its beam
must have been kept close to the ground, as many medieval illuminations
show; the structure, probably, would have required a rectangular frame in
place of the curved beam of the *ard*. The medieval plough-coulter was set
in a large mortise, and its rake and splay could be altered at will by wedges
or other simple means, so that it might cut preferentially to one side or the
other; unless the Roman coulter could be adjusted similarly, the fields must
have been ploughed either in 'lands' or strips, or else round and round.[77]

Other agricultural gear in the Silchester collection includes spade- and
shovel-irons, indeed part of an oaken blade,[78] and several other types of
tool mentioned briefly below. That spades, particularly, were made of wood
and had only an iron rim or edge is due not to any consideration of cost or
scarcity of the metal, but to the difficulty of making the blades rigid enough,
at a desirable thickness, to withstand the leverage applied in use. Both
square-ended and round-ended varieties appear.[79] Other digging-tools, from
their size more appropriate to the kitchen-garden than to the field, are a

small mattock and a two-tined hoe, as well as the wreck of what may per-haps have been a crescentic turf-cutter.[80] Rakes are evidenced by iron tines which had been clenched over the wooden cross-piece or clog;[81] two forks from one of the 'hoards' are too narrow for any use except baling, and the type with prongs at right-angles to the haft, occasionally found in Roman Britain and well-known as one of the chief implements of Roman cultivation, the *bidens*,[82] does not appear. Many commonplace tools, then as in recent years, were completely of wood where that material was suitable, and have perished.[83]

Edged tools embrace pruning-hooks, sickles (the largest small by modern standards), and portions of scythe-blades with a stout rib to counter-act any tendency to bend. Nicks in the edge of these implements were re-moved by hammering, and there are numerous mower's anvils in the col-lection (fig. 39, 12), mainly from the hoards: they prove that scythes were much more numerous, perhaps mainly in the later Roman period, than the actual traces of the blades themselves might imply. The anvil consists merely of a short, pointed iron bar, which was driven into the earth as far as the curved brackets or stops on either side; when Sir John Evans wrote his account of the Insula I 'hoard' of ironwork in 1894, he was able to comment that very similar anvils were still in use in parts of France, Spain and Italy, and were even made in Birmingham for export to South America: there are some of these comparative modern specimens at Reading.[84] Scythes may have been used—presumably were used—for mowing hay; but they may have found equal employment in the corn-harvest, the speed and progress of which would have been improved thereby.[85] The straw would have been used to augment other supplies of winter fodder and as bedding for animals in addition to bracken;[86] some may have been used for thatching.

FARM-BUILDINGS AND OTHER INSTALLATIONS

There have been several opportunities in this book to point out the agri-cultural basis of the Callevan economy in Roman times. The great rarity of known sites of farmsteads within some kilometres' radius of the town, and the uncrowded spacing of most of the houses within large insulae, some with walled yards attached, and the repeated discovery of seeds of weeds of cultivation suggesting the cleaning of corn,[87] are all important indications. But if the economy was in fact so firmly attached to agriculture, it must follow that farm-buildings and other installations remain in an identifiable form. To discover the extent of this evidence, we must turn for comparison to the country farmsteads and villas, where certain buildings and installations appear, of which the agricultural purpose can hardly be denied.

A start can be made with XXIV.2, prominent on the plan, and enclosed by a special extension of the inner defences, as mentioned above (p. 50): the full expansion of this house and its appurtenances, it must seem, was complete by about 200. At the north-west corner of this house, there is a large building some 30 m. long and 10.5 m. wide, exclusive of a later addition.[88] Within, a narrow partition at one end can be seen (fig. 29,c). Other houses which have similar buildings attached to them, or in some way incorporated into their plan, are XIV.1 (north-west corner of the outer yard, fig. 29, 8),[89] XVII.2 (closing the courtyard on the south);[90] XIX.2 (later: south wing);[91] and XXIII.1 (north-east corner).[92] Buildings of the same design occur at Gadebridge Park (Herts.), Bignor (Sussex), Great Wheldon (Notts.) and Hartlip (Kent) among other villas.[93] The great size of most examples suggests that their purpose was to contain hay, fodder, or—since granaries are otherwise exampled—the unthreshed corn-harvest; the small partitioned areas may have been for handling. On the other hand, Applebaum traces the origin of the plan to primitive farmsteads where the family dwelt in the larger portion, and their cattle in the smaller; and as adjuncts to more evolved types of dwelling, they may have continued to serve for farm-hands in some cases. In parenthesis, we may add that an ankle-shackle in the collection, and probably the large padlock already noticed (p. 206), if not the handcuffs (which are more probably ascribed to the *gendarmerie*, p. 66), point as likely as not to a labour-force which embraced non-free elements.[94] Some of the plain rectangular buildings, for example the two blocks in Insula XXV facing XXIV.2,[95] in I.1 (east side of the courtyard)[96] and XXXV.2 (projecting from the east side of the house)[97] might be described as barns, as in the villas of Barnsley Park (Glos.), Cox Green (Berks.) and Bignor.[98] XIX.1 is a very stoutly-walled example, to which external rooms have been added, perhaps for labourers: it was here that the pothooks (fig. 30) were found.[99] Other examples, such as XIII.B2,[100] contain flues which may have been connected with the processing of corn. The plan of the last, with an area partitioned, is reminiscent of a barn at Langton villa (Yorks.), where a corner was walled off to serve as a wheat-store, and there was a corn-drying plant outside.[101]

The bulk storage of grain is the next matter to concern us, and has already been introduced in our discussion (p. 160) of the square buildings dotted about the plan. Behind one of the shops on the main street (X.B2, fig. 29B),[102] there is a chamber measuring internally some 4.5 m. square, with a narrow entrance: the interesting feature is the inner square of stonework enclosed concentrically, which places this chamber clearly in the same category as the granaries of tower-like form, found at Iwerne (Dorset) and Stroud villa (Hants.), the function of the inner foundation being to provide for the circulation of air beneath the floor, which was also thus raised above the damp.[103] The square building erected concentrically round an earlier and suppressed part of XXIII.2, some 4.5 by 4.0 m. internally, might be interpreted similarly; it had a wide easterly entrance and a porch, and was thought by the excavators to have been a shrine (fig. 29, 7).[104] In this case, it is doubtful whether the inner square of walling played any part in supporting the later floor, though it may have done: it is clear, however, that the later floor was carried on joists bearing upon a wide offset. This is a feature noticeable in the case of a slightly smaller isolated square in XVII.2,[105] and again in a larger instance, XXXVII.1.[106] The possibility is, therefore, that some of the isolated squares with very thick foundation-walling, such as that just south of I.2,[107] were originally of a similar character. Although the explanation cannot well apply to all the isolated squares, unless we are prepared to countenance *une Callève des fées* it must seem likely that a great many of them were tower-granaries.[108]

There is one installation which can probably be interpreted with some assurance as a threshing floor; the work was otherwise, presumably, carried out in the barns. The building in question occurs to the south of XXVI.1; it was circular, about 8 m. in diameter, with a good concrete floor laid on flint pitching, but the walls were of timber-framed construction filled in with clay, a bank of which occurred around the outside of the trench which had contained the uprights.[109] On the east side, there was provision for an entrance nearly 2.5 m. wide. Similar installations occur at Ditchley (Oxon.) and other villas, sometimes with an indication of a central post to support the roof, as at Langton; one of octagonal plan, convenient for roofing in other materials than thatch, occurred at Stroud (Hants.).[110] Later, the building was superseded by another, probably a small house, though accommodation for animals cannot be excluded. Probably beasts were admitted to tread out the grain, unless some simple device, such as a sledge, was in use: the jointed flail is a medieval invention.[111]

Yet even before the grain was threshed and winnowed, it was sometimes necessary to 'dry' it. Under this term, two distinct processes are involved. On the one hand, there is evidence to suggest that the British climate was deteriorating—growing cooler and wetter—during the Roman period,[112] and this is probably the explanation of the fact that most of the corn-drying plant identified is of the third and fourth centuries, the T-shaped furnace being entirely typical of installations of that date (pl. 36). The provision of corn-dryers might therefore enable the farmer to snatch his grain-harvest from ruin. On the other hand, the drying, or rather parching, of the crop was necessary when it consisted of spelt, a form of wheat to which the husk adheres very firmly unless embrittled by heat.[113] Spelt was extremely widely grown, and probably most corn-dryers were installed to handle it rather than for any climatic reason. When mixed grains were grown together, as was very often the case, the entire crop would have been treated in this way, the seed-corn alone excepted.[114]

The T-shaped corn-drying furnace installed in XXXIIIA.B3 has a main flue about 3.7 m. long, and two short cross-flues which project beyond the wall of the building and served as outlets. The best-preserved example of an installation of this kind was found, as a late insertion, in a villa at Atworth (Wilts.).[115] Here there were traces not only of a covering to the flues, but of a separate floor of stone flags raised about 15 cm. above it, the air-space serving to distribute the heat more evenly and gently. A similar T-shaped furnace at Caerwent[116] was inserted into the middle of a large room which gave space, as at Silchester, for the corn scattered on the pavement to be turned at intervals; and the type of installation reminds one of the Faeroe kiln constructed at one end of a barn, described by Sir Lindsay Scott;[117] the smoke in that case found its way out through the roof, though at Silchester it was clearly discharged outside.

The ostensibly late date of the Silchester furnace just considered leads one to ask whether other types of furnace, of earlier date perhaps in some cases, were used for corn-drying. There is a multiplicity of different types at Silchester, and as the many curiously-shaped examples in the yard of the Hambleden villa (Bucks.) well show, corn-drying plant was by no means always of the T-shaped design.[118] Very much more sophisticated examples may be represented by the isolated hypocausts such as those of XII.B2, XXA.B6, or XXIII.B2,[119] and by furnaces in the yard of later XIX.2 or inside a room of XXXI.1.[120] A hypocaust with traces of a double floor, probably a corn-dryer, was found at Park Street villa, St. Albans, and was dated to the second century; elsewhere, circular structures with flues beneath, in one case yielding carbonised grain, have been discovered.[121]

The simple 'long hearth' consisting of a single, narrow flue a metre or more in length, found in great numbers all over the plan of Calleva and both inside and outside buildings (occasionally in close association with round furnaces or oven-bottoms as in X.B3, a matter which we must discuss in the next chapter) is perhaps of too little specialised a type to have had only one purpose;[122] yet similar flues associated with burnt grain were found in an out-building of a Roman villa near Bawdrip (Som.).[123] Sir Lindsay Scott describes a very similar single-flue corn-dryer in Shetland, which consisted of an open trench within a block of masonry about 1.5 by 0.9 m., when in use covered by sticks upon which straw was laid, and then the ears of corn to be dried; a simple baffle at one end kept the flames away from this combustible bed.[124] No signs of baffles were recorded in any of the Silchester cases, but clearly the flues could have been bridged in the same way and used for the same purpose. The obvious dangers and disadvantages of such a primitive contrivance, virtually useless except on a domestic scale, may have led to the development of safer and larger plant such as that described in the preceding paragraphs.

Having considered the storage and treatment of corn, we may now turn to the accommodation for beasts. Some of the rectangular 'barns' mentioned may have been byres, or cart-houses for that matter; but byres and other quarters for animals can be perceived a little more distinctly here and there. Perhaps the most interesting possibility of all is the small, partly-roofed yard measuring about 13 by 8.8 m. at the north-east corner of I.2, with an entry from the street on the east almost 4 m. wide (fig. 29A).[125] On the west side, a strip 3 m. deep was roofed, the roof being supported by three posts at like intervals, providing four bays in which horses, oxen, or possibly carts could have been kept; but the measurement of the bays corresponds well with Columella's prescription for double ox-stalls,[126] and since there would not appear to be very much point in providing a narrow yard for carts, we may conclude that the building could well have been a byre. Another example of similar dimensions, abutting upon a wider yard approached through a narrower entrance, is seen at the east end of XXIIA.1,[127] but the central post-hole appears to have been missed in excavation. The 'portico' XXXIIB.B2 (cf. p. 156), with its six bays again of similar size, may also have been a row of ox-stalls, if it is conceded that there was a yard to the east which was not detected.[128]

Another type of accommodation is probably to be recognised in XXVII.B1, near XXVII.2.[129] The block is divided into two rooms, each about 6 by 5 m.; in one, there is a shelf or ledge rather like that in the 'barn' attached to XXI.3,[130] which could have been used for grain or other provender stored in sacks; in the other, divided by piers, there are stalls perhaps for two yokes of oxen.[131] Another chamber divided by piers is in XVI.3,[132] but in that case another explanation may be preferable.

Another kind of building of which several examples can be perceived is the rectangular 'barn' flanked by a narrower building possibly roofed in common with it. Examples are in XV.B2,[133] XXVII.B3 near XXVII.2,[134] and at the south-east corner of Insula II.[135] A villa at Thurnham (Kent) possessed a similar outbuilding, where the 'barn' was floored in clay, and the 'strip' in cobble, and Pitney villa (Som.) provides another example, which Applebaum believes may have been a barn for fodder, with a pigsty on one side.[136] The long, narrow building (35 by 2.7 m.) which fills the south side of the main yard of XXXIV.1 may also have been devoted to pigsties; but the western yard contained a large timber-built steeping-tank, with which were associated some skulls of horses and oxen without lower jaws, suggestive of tanning-operations (cf. p. 290): the long shed may perhaps have been quarters for beasts destined for slaughter.[137] The small chambers added on the south side of the barn of XXIII.1 seem more likely to have been pigsties.[138] In XIV.2, there appears to be reason to identify a dairy (p. 238); and these notes may close with reference to the very large walled compound near the east gate of the town, upwards of 56 by 32 m. aligned with the angular length of street running down to the gate. No internal appointments are recorded: possibly this was either a cattle-market or a government magazine similar to that still partly visible at Caernarvon-Segontium (Hen Waliau), though hardly to be described as fortified:[139] other explanations are obviously of equal validity.

To draw these various threads together, we may briefly list the principal groups of dwellings and agricultural buildings mostly considered individually above.

1. I.2[140] Rich house; partly-roofed yard at north-east corner containing four double ox-stalls; large enclosed yard to the west, where traces of other buildings occurred; to the south, tower-granary; near by, Pit N with the '1890' hoard' of ironwork including various agricultural items.

2. XIV.1[141] Rich dwelling with totally-enclosed garden-court; large yard to north, extending round to east, containing barn or hands' quarters; watering-trough? near entrance-gateway on north side. Fig. 29, 8.

3. XIV.2[142] Rich dwelling with large yard on north, and two subsidiary yards each with a well, one probably a stock-yard, dairy attached.

4. XVII.2[143] Complex house of different periods; barn on south, agricultural buildings on east?—isolated tower-granary.

5. XIX.2[144] House in walled insula; barn in south wing; industrial and corn-drying plant in walled yard to the south; granary to west projecting into large yard containing barn or labourers' accommodation (XIX.1) and second barn? to the south (for possible temple in this yard, see p. 159).

6. XXB.2[145] Small house with attached yard near the inner defences: in front, isolated square drying-floor and granary?, perhaps also barn with traces of yard, B4.

7. XXIII.1[146] Large house with added barn and pigsties.

8. XXIII.2[147] Large house with granary to south; blocks to north, including a drying-floor may belong; also Well no. 2, with the '1900 hoard' of ironwork including agricultural pieces.

9. XXIV.2[148] Large house; big barn with handling area and addition to the east; to the west, in XXV, sheds may belong.

10. XXVI.1[149] Small house of markedly 'rural' plan (cf. p. 191); small dwelling in front superseding circular threshing-floor; granary, drying-floor and hearth in XII, to the west, seem to belong. Fig. 29, 6.

11. XXVII.2[150] Large complex house; barn, byre, fodder-store and pigsties.

12. XXXIV.1[151] Large complex house in walled insula; main yard with accommodation for beasts; small yard near east entrance; western yard with installation for tanning.

The reader will require no reminder that a great deal of what has been suggested above is highly speculative. Had we been in the fortunate position of possessing a full record of the finds made in all these buildings, matters might in some cases be different; but it can at least be said that the buildings and installations described can reasonably be interpreted in the way suggested, and can furthermore be paralleled in the surroundings of country villas where agricultural purposes can confidently be assumed and in a few cases particularised.

VARIOUS FOODSTUFFS AND DRINK

Under this heading may be assembled summarily the remaining evidence for articles of food and drink not already mentioned.

The hunter's prey included red deer, roebuck, and perhaps fallow-deer, hare and wild boar; the wild-fowler's, swan, wild goose, wild duck, teal, widgeon, woodcock, grey plover, crane, and stork (the latter is attested merely by one utilised bone); the fisherman provided eel, dace, perch and pike, no doubt mainly from the Loddon and the Kennet;[152] there is a bronze fish-hook in the collection, but probably nets were also used. Other fish represented are grey mullet, herring and sea-bream, which show that there was a market for the produce of coastal fisheries far inland; since there is no shortage of coarse fish in the rivers, the sea-fish are likely to have been dried, salted or smoked.[153] Shellfish reached Calleva in large quantities, above all the oyster, from the Thames estuary perhaps, or the Hampshire coast (cf. p. 90). Mussels were very common; cockles, periwinkles, scallops and whelks also appear,[154] and an adequate system of transportation had evidently been devised: Juvenal, for example, refers to oysters from the Richborough fishery.[155] The edible frog was also identified.[156]

Two other essential articles of diet were salt and honey. Salterns existed in many coastal areas of Britain[157] and the trade in this commodity must have been important throughout the country, especially for preserving the meat of the animals slaughtered in autumn, and for the carcase-trade which we can glimpse at Silchester (p. 291). Honey was the prinicpal sweetening-agent, though decoctions of wine were also used for this purpose;[158] Columella and Palladius tell how wild swarms are to be trapped in empty hives or pots placed near the observed watering-places of the bees; the colonies were then installed at the farm.[159] Very few ancient hives have been discovered, no doubt because they were mostly made of perishable materials; pottery hives— considered by the ancient writers to be the worst sort, owing to the extremes of temperature to which the bees would have been subjected—have been found, however, at Casterley Camp (Wilts.; Iron Age) and Rockbourne villa (Hants.), in either case taking the form of an ordinary large jar suitably pierced with holes.[160] Two-handled jars in the collection may have been honey-pots.[161]

OIL AND WINE

The two principal imports are well-represented archaeologically by amphorae, glass bottles, and barrels subsequently used as well-linings (p. 86). It may be pointed out, however, that since these objects are all merely containers, other commodities may have been conveyed in them to Silchester. In particular, we know from inscriptions upon them, and from actual finds, that amphorae were used for a wide variety of substances, dry goods as well as liquids—olives, dried fruit, honey, lentils and so on, and the curious, strong-flavoured fish-sauces then so popular.[162]

The Silchester amphorae include parts of long-bodied and globular types, the former possibly mounting in date to the pre-Roman period, and Italian: these and later long-bodied varieties, all fragmentary, were principally for wine. Elsewhere some (like the Harelbeke barrel mentioned below) have been found to bear an internal resinous or pitchy coat, applied to render the surface impermeable, and to impart a special flavour to the wine, as well as helping to preserve it.[163] The globular amphorae are from southern Spain, quite typical of the first to early third century production; it may be taken very nearly for granted that they were oil-amphorae.[164] Many of them bear stamps on the handles, in some cases referring to the potteries where they were made, such as F(iglino) Scimniano 'From the Scimnian estate' near Écija, represented in the collection among some sixty amphora-stamps,[165] and in other cases naming the owners of estates in the valley of the river Baetis or Guadalquivir where the oil was produced, and who either manufactured their own containers or else had close links with potting-concerns. Such was L. Junius Melissus (fig. 38, 4), one of the household names of the second century, who had such links with the Scimnian *figlinum,* since examples are known of the two names being stamped on the handles of the same amphora. Another widely-occurring name, of rather earlier date, is *G. Antonius Quietus,* and there are other very common names in the oil-trade to be found among the Silchester stamps, such as the 'Three *Ennii'.*

The amphorae were sealed with a cork or wooden bung, pitched or plastered over. There is an oak bung, now 11 cm. across, in the Silchester collection: on the top is the gash made by some tool to prise it out, and on the underside there is still a speck or two of pitch or resin.[166] The globular amphorae were better shaped for transport by water than by land, and the principal route into north-west Europe was the Rhône and its tributaries. Reliefs and carvings show that the amphorae were often protected by wicker or plaited cases for the journey,[167] and for short stages they could be carried by two men, slung by ropes through their handles from a pole, as a fresco at Augst shows.[168]

The glass bottles, mainly of the first and second centuries, were of variable size despite the mould-blowing process used in manufacture: four bottles in the British Museum, clearly from the same mould, were measured and found to vary between 440 and 510 ml. Cylindrical bottles holding as much as 4 or 5 l., with a single ridged or 'celery' handle, have plain bases; but the very common square (occasionally rectangular or hexagonal) bottles are rarely of anything like that capacity, and usually bear simple moulded devices on the base (fig. 36, 10). Rarely, there is lettering; and fig. 36, 11–12, shows two Köln 'trademarks' including the letters CCA for *Colonia Claudia Agrippinensis,* that city's official name.[169] The other base illustrated, from a smallish cylindrical bottle of third or fourth century date, bears the letters FRO, one of the marks of the large Frontinian glassworks somewhere in the Seine-Rhine area (fig. 36, 13). This bottle would have had circumferential ribbing reminiscent of the bands of a barrel, and would doubtless have held a superior wine from one of the northern vineyards.[170] A few reliefs show large square bottles in wicker cases, in which they were brought to table. There is an interesting distinction here between the large cylinders and squares of all sizes, for the latter never exhibit the mass of fine vertical scratches seen almost always on the former, merging into rubbed bands at shoulder and base. These scratches could not arise from wicker casing, but rather from the rubbing together of bottles packed in crates, with or without divisions.[171]

About fifteen Silchester barrels are recorded. Two exhumed in 1897 from wells in Insulae XVII and XVIII were finely preserved; one at least still had its hazel bands, which extended for a third of the distance top and bottom.

There was a 5 cm. bung-hole in the middle of both barrels, and near it a 13 mm. vent-plug hole. A groove for the seating of the ends, knocked out when the barrels were put to their final use, was present but only at one end of the Insula XVII example, which had been slightly shortened.[172]

Well over eighty barrels have been listed by Ulbert, mainly from the Rhine-Danube frontier and Britain—the end of the water-borne trade.[173] Stamped, branded or scratched inscriptions are frequent, both inside (where they must relate to the manufacture) and outside (where they probably relate to the shipper, consignee, or stages of the route which the commerce followed). These markings are seldom very informative. A rare exception is the stamp interpretable as 'duty-free on the hospital account of the Second Legion Adjutrix' found at Budapest, where this legion, once at Chester, had its quarters. The Insula XVII barrel is a fair case. On the inside, all the staves had been numbered I—XVIII, as in a London example; and the name VERCTISSAE, 'of Vercetissa' had been stamped on seven staves; other internal stamps read DO and NIO. On the outside, GI had been stamped near the bung-hole, and various letters, upright (but in two cases upside-down) when the barrel was on its side, had been scratched stave by stave.[174] On top of this barrel, there had been another, of which about half survived; the name *Sualinos* had been traced externally upon it. The use of the Gaulish termination *-os* for the Latin *-us* is an interesting index of early date.[175] The Insula XVIII barrel had AR stamped small on two staves near the bung-hole;[176] and a barrel from Insula XV was stamped HERM externally several times.[177]

Vercetissa is likely to have been a master-cooper. Since the barrel has clearly been re-assembled at some time—the external scratched letters make no sense as arranged in the order of the numbered staves—the other two internal stamps could have been on staves re-used. GI on the outside, to judge by its position close to the bung, should refer to the contents: perhaps an abbreviated estate-name, but I can trace no colourable expansion; AR on the other barrel, similarly.[178] HERM(ogenes, or the like) will have been a shipper, of the Greek extraction so common among Roman businessmen; but Sualinos, probably another shipper, was a Gaul.

The vent-plug holes are a good indication that the contents of the barrels were liquids, and thus wine, since beer was everywhere locally-made, and oil came in amphorae. Wine has been positively identified by the detection of a tartrate adherent to a stave from Oberaden, and the resinous coating of a barrel from Harelbeke, Belgium, points in the same direction—not improbably, as the report suggests, this barrel had held the famous Allobrogian *picatum* from the Viennois.[179]

The timber of the Callevan barrels was identified as silver fir.[180] The natural habitat of this tree lies between 400 and 1300 m. in the Alps, the Pyrenees, and elsewhere, and lower in Normandy. But a point arising from the highly-detailed study of the Harelbeke barrel requires emphasis. We do not know whether all the staves of the Silchester barrels were examined, and would suppose the contrary; and at Harelbeke, and in another case, some turned out to be of silver fir, and others of larch. The value of the determination is shown by the fact that the natural occurrence of larch is much more restricted—as far as we are concerned, the Alps between 1000 and 1800 m.[181] Vines may ripen up to 500 m. in the Alps and 900 m. in Piedmont, thus well towards the lower limit of the larch. Lowland producers of wine, it is argued, would scarcely have sent to the Alps for barrels when perfectly good oak grew near at hand: hence the tentative conclusion regarding the contents of the Harelbeke barrel, to some slight degree borne out by a hint, from its internal inscriptions, that the vessel had passed through the hands of a Lyon shipper.

On the other hand, oak barrels seem to have been extremely rare. Ulbert mentions only two, whereas various coniferous woods have been identified much more commonly. We know from Pliny that it was the custom, in Alpine regions, *to store* wine in stave-built vessels,[182] but it seems improbable that barrels were used for the first stages of an upland wine's journey to its market. Most of our evidence for barrels and their manufacture (not only actual discoveries, but epigraphical references to coopers and the axe-hammers with lettered cross-panes used to apply the marks) relates to places with access to river-routes and the possibility of long-distance bulk-transportation. An interesting case in point is the axe-hammer from Epfach on the Lech, Upper Bavaria, not a wine-producing area; and in this instance it is suggested that Italian wine, brought over the Alps by pack-animals, was transhipped into barrels for the last stage of its journey.[183] The multiplicity of internal markings on staves might well be explainable on the assumption that rough-outs manufactured in the Alpine areas by peasant industry were finished and assembled at such riverine entrepôts. Certainly there was an Alpine industry in its richest natural product, timber: the ubiquitous writing-tablets are of silver fir or larch, or at least are recognisably of some coniferous timber from the uplands.[184]

The dimensions of the two barrels from Insulae XVII and XVIII are similar and may be contrasted with those of the Insula XV specimen, and with another from Insula VI (*in situ*, pl. 40).[185]

	Insula VI	Insula XV	Insula XVII	Insula XVIII
Height	190 cm.	152 cm.	197 cm.	194 cm.
Diameter (max.)			84 cm.	86 cm.
Diameter (min.)		91 cm.	66 cm.	72 cm.
Staves (no.)	25	16	18	19
Capacity (approx.)			880 l.	930 l.

The gross weight of the Insula XVII and XVIII barrels would have been about 880 and 930 kg., approaching double the maximum load permitted in the long-distance imperial transport-service (p. 144). Though some reliefs show barrels being transported singly on carts, or in twos and threes when of small size, as on Trajan's Column, it is not surprising that other reliefs show barrels on river-craft.[186] In the case of the Silchester barrels, it seems likely that they would have been transferred into lighters in London and conveyed upstream, and so via the Kennet or the Loddon to a landing-stage by the side of the Roman road only 6 km. or so from the town. In view of the lesser gradient, the Loddon route would have been preferable.[187]

BEER

A last beverage and a last subject for this chapter is the favourite drink of western Europe and elsewhere from a remote period. Positive indication of manufacture is rare. One of the motto-bowls made at Banassac is inscribed CERVESA R[EPLE]: it may come as something of a surprise to find that samian bowls of considerable size were used for consuming beer.[188] The beer will not have resembled our own barley and hop-flavoured brew very closely. Such finds as there are suggest a concoction of mixed grains with or without the peculiar local taste imparted by added herbs or fortuitously-included weed-seeds.[189]

It is uncertain whether any particular building at Calleva was a brewery; but it is suggested on a later page (p. 286) that many of the 'round furnaces' scattered about the plan were the bases of brewing-vats. If so, the other installations which one would expect to find have left no trace, and may indeed not have been permanent or substantial enough to do so.

20

Industry, Crafts and Trade

METALLURGICAL INDUSTRY

Since Calleva lies far from substantial sources of ore, metal-working in the town was of a minor order, and with the exception of a certain amount of smelting of iron derived from the 'pan' formed in the gravel by percolation and concretion, depended wholly on imported supplies of raw metals and upon scrap. The working of iron, copper, bronze, lead, pewter and silver is attested, the last-named being of particular interest inasmuch as there is evidence of refining the precious metal from a base alloy or an argentiferous copper-ore. It would be hazardous, however, to conclude that even this operation was of any greater scope than may have satisfied the needs of manufacturing jewellers in the town, indeed it may have been carried on by them.

IRON

The commanding superiority of iron over other metals which have been used for edged tools and for structural purposes lies less, perhaps, in its physical nature than in the ubiquity of the deposits of ore, and the ease whereby the metal can be smelted; though, as is well-known, the temperature of the simple furnaces employed was seldom high enough to result in the liquefaction of the metal, and cast iron almost never occurs in ancient times. The ore was heated with charcoal in a small bowl- or shaft-furnace and was reduced to metal; at about 1050° much of the dross became fluid and could be tapped off, leaving the residue in a spongy condition which required repeated hammering before it could be consolidated into a useful bar, or bloom, of iron. When decayed ancient ironwork is stripped of corrosion-products in the laboratory, its fibrous nature and its numerous inclusions of dross become very evident.[1] A certain amount of furnace-slag was found in the Claudio-Neronian filling of the inner earthwork ditch, and points to the exploitation of local sources of ore as described above; there is also an iron bloom (nearly 11 kg.) in the collection.[2] On the whole, however, there is only a small amount of furnace-slag from Silchester, and furnaces have never been identified. Much commoner is smith's slag, which is of a much more porous consistency.

The presence of impurities in wrought iron makes it possible to see how some tools in the collection were forged. Thus an axe-head was made by bending a bar of wrought iron double, and welding it into a strip; the strip was then bent in half and a mandril was inserted between, to allow for the shaft-hole or eye, and the whole welded again by beating out at the proper temperature. The final smithing, which gave the tool its form, necessitated several heatings in the charcoal forge, and in the course of these a certain amount of carbon became engrained in the metal, especially towards the cutting-edge, turning the iron into a mild or medium steel. A metallographic examination of one of the axes[3] showed that there had been no further attempt to harden the edge by tempering (heating and quenching). None of the other tools in the collection has been examined, but it is highly probable that the technique of carburisation was applied to the cutting-edges of chisels, gouges, and the like, as in the case of a specimen found at Caerleon, which was examined by Dr R. F. Tylecote.[4] The metallic structure at the cutting edge of this gouge could have been produced by putting charcoal on the inner side and heating to over 900°, while the outer side was protected by clay; and then by quenching and tempering at 650° for half an hour. The hardness, British Standard 329, is far less than that of the edge of a modern tool, which would be in the region of 413.

The Callevan blacksmith, like his country successor of recent times, was a most versatile craftsman, and probably combined the trades not only of iron-worker (and bronze-worker: it is noteworthy how frequently the débris of smithing and bronze-founding occur together),[5] but of wheel-wright, plough-wright, wagon-maker, locksmith and others, perhaps including farriery. Some of his tools are shown in fig. 39, mainly from the two great fourth-century ironwork 'hoards' of 1890 (Insula I) and 1900 (Insula XXIII) (p. 164).[6] Both 'hoards' probably belonged to blacksmiths—indeed possibly to one blacksmith, since the contents are to some extent complementary, and occurred only about 140 m. apart; but they do not collectively present a complete set of blacksmith's tools.[7] In the following list, illustrated articles are marked by an asterisk (see figs. 8, 21, 30, 34, 39, and 41; pl. 38).

33 Pottery, glass, and lamp. (*a*) Lead-glazed bowl, green with a row of brown scales, mid-first century, central Gaul (Lezoux), d. 24 cm. (*b*) marbled glass bowl, ribbed, yellow and white streaks in royal blue, mid-first century, perhaps Italian, d. 9·6 cm. (*c*) red-gloss samian bowl, east Gaul (Heiligenberg?), mid-second century, h. 10·5 cm. (*d*) red-gloss samian bowl, south Gaul (la Graufesenque), internally stamped by the potter Primus, third quarter, first century, d. 22 cm. (*e*) grey-gloss beaker, Rhenish, second half, second century, h. 12·3 cm. (*f*) lamp, red gloss (mostly gone), with figure of a horse, north African, fourth–early fifth century, 12 cm.

34 Figurines, etc. (*a*) 'Pipe-clay' mother-goddess in basket-chair, central Gaul, second century A.D., h. 13 cm. (*b*) 'pipe-clay' cockerel, central Gaul, second century, l. 12·6 cm. (*c*) bronze eagle from the basilica ('the Silchester eagle'), first century? l. 23 cm. (*d*) bronze figurine of a pipe-player, second–third century, h. 12·5 cm. (*e*) bronze figurine of a *Genius familiaris*, first–second century? h. 11 cm. (*f*) silver-plated bronze band from a statue-pedestal, basilica, first–second century? w. 7·5 cm. (*g*) bronze lappet from a cuirassed statue, basilica, first century? w. 6·5 cm. (*h*) bronze coin in the name of 'Carausius II', overstruck on a Constantinian coin, *c.* A.D. 354–8

	1890	*1900*
Blacksmith's Tools		
* beaked anvil, wt. 9.3 kg.[8]	I	—
* tongs	I	2
* striking-hammers	—	2
* hammers (some carpenter's?)	3	10
cold chisel	—	I
* sets	—	2
* drift	—	I
* nail heading tools[9]	—	2
* files (4 with saw-setting notches)	2	4
tool for turning iron	I	—
hand-levers (short bars)	—	2
Farrier's Tools		
* buttrice (p. 146)	—	I
* rasp	I	—
Carpenter's Tools		
* axes	8	I
hammer-adze	I	I
* cooper's adze (p. 282)	I	—
* mortise chisels (8 socketed; p. 270)	6	3
* gouges (socketed; p. 284)	5	—
* iron-cased jack-plane (p. 282)	I	—
* centre-bit	—	I
* compasses	—	2
Shoemaker's Tools		
* lasts or feet (p. 290)	2	I
Agricultural Tools, etc.		
* coulters (p. 252)	2	3(4?)
* bar-shares (p. 252)	2	4
* mower's anvils (2 unfinished; p. 255)	4	8
baling forks	—	2
hipposandal (scrap; p. 146)	I	—
Miscellaneous Ironwork		
mill-stone pivot (p. 289)	I	—
* sword-blade (scrap; p. 68)	I	—
spear-head	—	I
* cook's gridiron (scrap; p. 195)	I	—
candlestick-lamp (p. 226)	I	—
* linch-pin (stepped)	—	I
cotter	—	I
knives	—	?
choppers	—	?
* pocket-knife (p. 228)	—	I
bucket-handles	—	?

cauldron-chains (scrap; p. 237)	–	3
large padlock (p. 206)	–	1
parts of padlocks (scrap)	1	2
strap (scrap)	–	1
cart-pole shoes (scrap)	–	?
other scrap unspecified	?	?
Bronze Objects		
* scale beam (p. 292)	1	–
* steelyard-weight (scrap? p. 292)	–	1
cooking-pans (scrap, one fused)	–	5
	48+	70+

Totals given in *Archaeologia*: '1890', nearly 60 objects; '1900', over 100 objects.

BRONZE, ETC.

The refining of copper is attested, though apparently on a small scale;[10] bronze-working, again of limited scope, is attested by the presence of crucibles, spoilt work, droplets of metal and casting-waste from moulds. In a pit excavated in 1955, there was a small crucible of about 6 ml. capacity, shaped like a modern laboratory evaporating-basin; parts of a large crucible or crucibles; and part of a thin clay slab with a lug to provide purchase at one side. This material was associated with much ash, smith's slag, and snippets of bronze, evidently raw-material for the operations: scrap and filings, it would appear from another discovery in 1961, were carefully kept.[11] A clay mould for a finger-ring is in the collection, and it is probably indicative of the sort of trinket which, rather than anything larger or more complex, marked the usual limits of the founder's work. Certainly, the fine bronze statuary and figurines mentioned on an earlier page were not of local manufacture, though it is probable that the crude repairs to the eagle (p. 119) were executed by a local craftsman.

The very small size of the crucible mentioned is worthy of comment. Such crucibles, however, are commonplace. In a parallel instance at Whitchurch (Som.), where small castings, in point of fact counterfeit coins, were made,[12] there was a similar association of small with fragments of larger crucibles and with small scrap. Now if the little crucibles had been employed for pouring direct into moulds, difficulty would have arisen, because of the rapid loss of heat occurring when once they had been lifted from the fire. R. F. Tylecote, writing of crucibles ten times as large, indeed 'wondered how the pouring was done at all'.[13] The truth of the matter may be that the

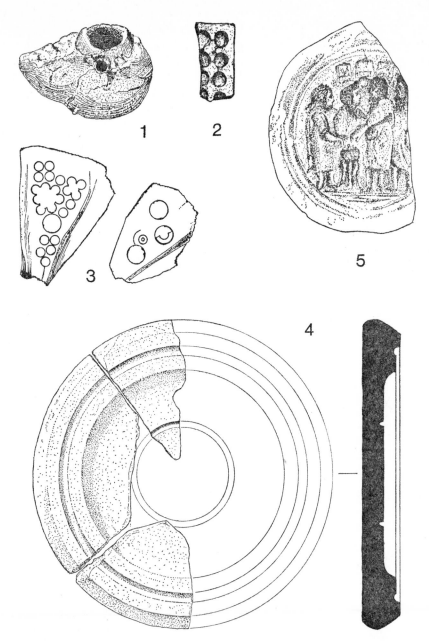

40. Industrial remains, etc. 1, small crucible with clay envelope (once going over the missing lid) and piercing (once bunged). 2, fragment of Belgic coin-flan mould. 3, sheep's shoulder-blades utilised for making eyelets. 4, fragments of Bath stone mould, turned, for making pewter plates. 5, cake-mould with Severan sacrificial scene. Scales, 1, 5: 1/2. 2, 3/8. 3, 4: 1/6

small crucibles were not used for direct pouring, but solely for melting scrap; charged with the snippets of metal, they may have been heated on a charcoal hearth and their contents transferred to the larger crucibles when ready: fragments indicative of a 15–20 cm. diameter are in the collection at Reading. The exclusion of air from the small crucibles would have reduced losses by oxidation, and among the other material in the collection there is a specimen (10 ml. capacity) which had been cased in clay, which had been formed into a lug at one side (fig. 40, 1). A curious collection of neatly broken-off flagon-necks in pottery, from a pit or well, may have been intended to serve as the nozzles of bellows, but if so the objects were never used.[14]

LEAD

The working of lead was of great practical importance. The Callevan plumber, utilising imported raw material,[15] supplied sheeting for tanks, including the 'tortoises' of the baths (p. 128), piping, and various small objects such as weights. Skilled metallurgy is evident in the addition of about 1% of tin to the piping used for the cylinders of the pump from Insula XIV (p. 86); soft-solder was also in use, the first British finds being made at Silchester.[16] The piping was made by wrapping sheet-lead round a mandril, the edges being brought together with an outward turn, forming a channel along which superheated lead could be poured to 'burn' the joint; one pipe, however, of the usual somewhat pear-shaped section, had been sealed with an alloy containing 4.5% of tin, which could be applied at a temperature considerably lower than that of the lead usually employed.[17]

PEWTER

The production of pewter plates may be reckoned among the later industries of the town, for discs of Bath stone (fig. 40, 4) similar in every way to pewter-moulds found at Lansdown near Bath and elsewhere were discovered, in a fragmentary state, in the forum;[18] some years ago I discovered them in store at Reading. From the fact that one or two have lathe-turned depressions on both sides, it may be deduced that the moulds were packed together in rows or blocks, and the dishes cast several at a time. No examples of plates formed in the moulds have come to light.

Cakes of pewter containing 70 or 80% of lead and 30 or 20% of tin have been found in the Thames at Battersea and are now in the British Museum; they bear typical stamps of the late Roman period, including the Christogram. They show that there was a trade in raw pewter from the areas of production in the west country—Cornish tin and Mendip lead—to other parts of the country, where vessels might be manufactured.[19]

SILVER

Silver-working at Calleva appears to have been of much the same order as bronze-working: it is denoted by an unfinished ring, a small, partly-used strip from one of the forum shops (p. 111), and droplets. Among the few objects of silver in the collection, that with the greatest claim to have been made at Silchester is the torque from Insula XXXII, for it is of very unusual form (fig. 18, 11).[20] The metal, as already suggested, may have been derived from the refining of argentiferous copper, which is well-attested on four sites within the town.

The material consists of a number of cakes of a metallic substance, dull and uninformative in outward appearance, but upon analysis yielding information of considerable interest for the history of metallurgy in Britain, though similar finds have been studied since.

The first discovery was made in VIII.4, a small house near the south gate; the débris occurred in one of the living rooms, perhaps representing a late conversion of use, as a furnace or long hearth in a room of an older wing near the street also suggested.[21] The remains were studied by Professor Roberts-Austen, who reported that one sample consisted of lead with silver in the proportion of about 0.015%, probably from the smelting of argentiferous lead-ore, and a second, of a complex lead-copper alloy containing oxides of both metals, silver sulphide, and 0.138% of silver. The first sample could have come from the direct smelting of a normal argentiferous lead-ore, and certainly a little galena has been found at Silchester, most probably of Mendip or south Wales origin.[22] The second sample points distinctly to a cupellation-process such as was deduced by Gowland in connection with the other Silchester discoveries; the first sample may have been related to it also.

The other discoveries were made in IX.3, XI.B1, and Insula V–VI.[23] The first was a house adapted to the main east-west street; the second, craftsman's premises containing a long hearth, also on this street. The specimens, which had been discarded, had evidently been formed at the bottoms of hearths about 30 cm. across; the remains from the third site indicated a 90 cm. hearth. The hearths would have been enclosed and provided with a means of forced draught so that the necessary high temperature for cupellation could be achieved, for the process involves the complete oxidation of the lead added to the material requiring treatment. The silver is, as it were, leached out of the alloy, and then left behind in the metallic state as heat and oxygen turn the lead to litharge. The lead can be reduced to metal again if desired: this is the process which has resulted in the numerous pigs of lead, marked *Ex Arg(entariis)* 'from the silver-works', found in Britain.[24] Unless the operation was to be conducted on a very important scale, as was the case in the official silver-works, where much lead was consumed, it would have been carried out in a number of convenient stages, and this is the case at Silchester.

Material from the first hearth contained 2.98% of silver, 78.13% of copper and 16.14% of lead; and from the second, 32.61% of silver, 56.64% of copper and 8.81% of lead, as well as 0.39% of gold, which suffices to show that the second hearth cannot well have formed a second stage of primary material represented in the first. Gowland was of the belief that a further cupellation of the second hearth sample would have completed the process; that it was completed is proved by the occurrence of a pellet of silver in a mass of pure litharge. Gowland suggested two possible sources of the argentiferous copper which was refined: (a) argentiferous lead ores and copper ores; and (b) the imperial coinage of the later third and fourth centuries. There is a degree of correspondence between the silver in the first hearth and the low silver-content of coins of that period, though for various reasons the matter cannot be pressed; but if coins really did supply the primary material, we should probably have expected tin to figure in the analysis, since it figures in the coinage to about the same proportion as silver, in very many cases at least.[25] Gold, however, certainly does not appear in third-fourth century coins of base alloy, and its presence in hearth no. two leads us back to the first of Gowland's alternatives. In later years, he was concerned with the analysis of similar slightly auriferous material from Hengistbury Head (Hants.) and in that instance suggested ore from Callington, near Tavistock, as the most probable source.[26]

Without precise information as to the origin of the specimens in two distinct localities within the town, and apparently without knowledge of Roberts-Austen's contribution of 1893, Gowland felt free to speculate that the remains indicated 'operations of a considerable magnitude, such . . . as would be carried on in a public or government establishment, or for the work of a small mint'. There is no evidence whatever for an official mint at Silchester, and what we know of the occurrence of the specimens does not encourage any suggestion that they were connected with the British mint (p. 42). There is some slight, obscure possibility that cupellation of official coins was carried out at Whitchurch (Som.) largely in connection with the production of base counterfeits,[27] and this is a possibility to be borne in mind in the Silchester case.

A final feature of Gowland's work remains to be mentioned. The identification of phosphate of lime in the hearth-bottoms is proof that they had been lined with calcined bone, a substance which has the important properties not merely of resisting the corrosive action of molten litharge, but of absorbing it 'as readily as blotting-paper absorbs water': it is the best of all materials for use in silver-refining furnaces, though now superseded, as is the method of cupellation itself as far as the commercial refining of silver is concerned (though it remained the only method in use as late as 1833). From Gowland's work we see how the Callevan metallurgist, applying information which for some strange reason never seems to have been set down by any ancient writer whose works are now extant, was able to apply the most efficient means for the successful completion of his work. We also see that the Silchester excavations of the nineties were able once again to demonstrate their wide interest and value to historical technology; and if the story is deficient in any way, it is, as so often, in respect of the inadequate means of archaeological recording which persisted throughout the campaign.

OTHER INDUSTRIES AND CRAFTS—STONE

Enough has been said in connection with the structural details of buildings to demonstrate fully the aptitudes of the mason and builder. It does not seem likely that the columns and other architectural details were turned and carved on the spot; and if an exception is to be made, it may concern immigrant craftsmen's work on the Corinthian capitals of the basilica, perhaps too delicate to be transported from the Bath region (pl. 17). Even so, it seems preferable to regard the numerous chisel-sharpening stones which came to light when the forum-mounds were being levelled in 1908–9[28] not as evidence of the carving of the original capitals on the spot, but rather as indicative of the extensive repairs, and replacements of capitals, necessary when the building was restored. There is, of course, perfect evidence of the local production of monumental sculpture, in the unfinished carvings from Insula V (p. 186). For the working of shale at Silchester, see below.

TILE-MAKING

Bricks and tiles were beyond question locally made: many of them contain pieces of flint or small pebbles which it would be almost supererogatory to assign to a source more distant than some neighbouring brickfield. Karslake's discovery of the Roman (and later) brickfield at Little London about 3 km. south of the town has already been mentioned, together with a word of caution on its imperial character.[29] Here he found 'broken bricks and all the usual forms of roofing and box tiles covering the ground about 8 ft. 10 in. [2.68 m.!] below the present surface . . . broken up wasters . . . soft, friable, overfired. . . . Among these fragments was part of a tile of which sufficient remained to preserve a round stamp in the centre with the legend NER.CL.CAE.AVG.GR. of much the same form but not identical with the stamp . . . discovered . . . in the baths of Calleva'. This tile is a mystery: no illustration was published, and it was not among the small collection of objects which had belonged to Col Karslake and which were handed over to me in 1951 by the late Mrs Leonora Karslake to form the nucleus of the Calleva Museum; neither in conversation, nor in a subsequent search at Acre House and elsewhere was any further information regarding it brought to light; and to make matters more confused, the tile illustrated by S. E. Winbolt in an article mentioning the Little London site is the Silchester tile (fig. 7, 1).[30] One may be forgiven for wondering whether the supposed 'stamp' may not have been a somewhat optimistic interpretation of a scar upon the surface of a fragment of tile, left by the detachment of a flake or spall during firing.

I myself have never found anything but eighteenth-century material on the site, and it is to this period that the large clay-pit in the field opposite the Plough Inn belongs. Taking Karslake's depth-measurement literally, therefore, it must appear that his material occurred on the flat floor of this pit; but perhaps the measurement includes a printer's error for what was written as 8"–10" [20–25 cm.]. In the Willis Museum, Basingstoke, however, there is a small collection of material from Little London which does include a piece of a grey, overfired Roman flue-tile and a piece of a small tegula, as well as fragments which in some cases may be Roman, but in others are certainly of the later period—pantiles, plain tiles, and bricks.[31] The flue-tile is particularly valuable, for it belongs to the class which bears patterns applied by a roller in place of the hand-drawn combings usually found. Relief-patterned flue-tiles have been studied by A. W. G. Lowther, and several of his varieties appear at Silchester, though in very small numbers: no. 3, found also in London; no. 38, perhaps the same as at Hartlip (Kent); no. 27, found in London and Dover; and no. 39, which is the type found at Little London, known only at Silchester. The general dating of these tiles is between A.D. 80 and 150, and possibly 200.[32]

Lowther has suggested that the relief-patterned tiles may have been made at different places by itinerant craftsmen; but it is known that stamped tiles apparently produced at Cirencester occur as far afield as Hucclecote villa on the outskirts of Gloucester, and even at Lydney temple, a distance of 22 and 45 km.[33] Some of the Silchester tiles may therefore have been imported from a distance. The Nero tile may be such a one, despite the pebble embedded in it. The historical significance of the tile, clouded as it is by the uncertainty of Karslake's record, has already been noted (p. 44).

No kilns have been identified at Little London. Tile-kilns were generally of a massive square or rectangular construction, appropriate to the dimensions and weight of the charge. Best-known in this country are those of the Twentieth Legion at Holt-on-Dee; civil kilns were no less solidly built, but tiles were sometimes fired in clamps.[34]

The various types of tiles and bricks were first prepared in wetted wooden moulds dusted over with sand to prevent the adherence of the clay; their upper surfaces were formed by hand or by drawing a strip of wood across the mould. At a suitable moment, the consistency of the clay was tested by the tile-maker, who drew the tips of his fingers across the surface in a rapid curve or loop, probably a trademark recognisable as his within the tilery, if not further afield. When judged ready, the products were turned out of the moulds to dry thoroughly under cover. It was then, if not before, that many received the marks which so intrigue the modern eye: the paw-marks, the footprints—once, a baby's (pl. 39)[35]—or quickly scrawled inscriptions (fig. 7, p. 64). A few of these are of a personal nature, but there can be very little doubt that the appearance of names, with or without further indication (e.g. *fecit tubul*[*os*] *Clementinus*), relates to individual stints, whatever they may have been: the word *Satis* 'enough', appearing on a large brick (see the tailpiece of this book, fig. 42) is also to be reckoned as a case in point.[36] As previously remarked, it seems that it was regarded as necessary that the workmen should be able to write in order to record their production, and one of the tiles (fig. 7, 4) is regarded as a writing-lesson given in some moment of leisure on the spot. The tile bearing a date—VI KAL OCTOB[RES]—equivalent to 26 September (fig. 7, 2) is of especial interest. Dated tiles are not uncommonly found, either in tileries or elsewhere, occasionally also giving the name of the operative (as here, *Icc*—) and a total. They were probably either part of a system of control, or else a kind of memorandum helpful in determining the proper sequence of batches for the kiln. Tile-making was a seasonal activity, owing to the dangers of frost; and it so happens that the Silchester tile bears the latest known date of any tile in the western part of the Empire.[37]

POTTERY

Two very small pottery-kilns, about 80 cm. and 60 by 40 cm. across internally, were found in 1906 a short distance beyond the north gate.[38] They dated from the end of the first century and were of typical design, in which heat and gases from a combustion-chamber were carried through the perforated floor of the oven, or kiln proper, and passed out through a vent in the top of a temporary dome.[39] No doubt others remain to be found in the same vicinity or elsewhere.

Each kiln consisted of a sunken combustion-chamber approached by a narrow firing-flue worked from the same stoking-pit. The flues and chambers were lined with clay stiffened with grass and ling; and in the chamber there was an axial fin projecting as far as the centre from the back, clay-built, and serving to support a radial arrangement of prefabricated terracotta bars, on which the clay of the oven-floor, pierced at intervals, was laid. All the underground parts were probably subjected to a preliminary firing to consolidate them, and would have survived several chargings. The domes, on the other hand, had to be constructed (on some kind of light frame of sticks) for each firing, once the charge had been packed into position. The domes were made of clay and broken pottery. Articles found in the excavation included two supports for vessels and some lumps of burnt clay which had probably served a similar purpose; otherwise there was only a brooch and half a quern.

Pottery from the first, or larger, kiln included some grey jars; to produce ware of this description, it would have been necessary to close the vent and block the stoke-hole towards the end of the firing, in order to exclude oxygen. A carinated jar and a dish from the firing-flue of the second kiln are now in a buff-coloured or oxidised fabric, but were no doubt black or grey originally.

It is possible that the very coarse, flint-gritted hand-made 'Silchester' ware —so-named from its ubiquity in first and early second-century levels—was fired in clamps and not kilns (fig. 6, 9).

GLASS

A fragment from the base of a large pottery jar, heavily burnt, is coated on the inside with a layer of blue-green glass; and another specimen shows similar glass heavily encrusted upon a hard-burnt clay which is evidently the base of a furnace, or siege. Although the exact provenance of these two objects within the walled area is not known, it appeared that they might point to the manufacture of glass at Calleva, and they were accordingly submitted for examination to Mr Henry Cole, Deputy-Director of the Research and Development Laboratories of Pilkington Bros. Ltd., who had on an earlier occasion undertaken some analyses of Roman window-glass from Caerleon (p. 207).[40] A second, larger fragment of 'siege' has since come to light at Reading.

Chemical and physical studies showed that both the specimens were derived from a glass-smelting operation. Thus Silchester can in fact be added, some sixty to eighty years after the discovery of these fragments, to the growing list of sites in Britain and abroad where glass was manufactured in Roman times. As far as the glass itself is concerned—a typical Roman silica-soda-lime mix containing also both manganese and antimony among minor constituents[41]—it could have been prepared fairly easily from the required batch materials at around 1150–1200°; and there is plenty of suitable sand beneath the gravel capping of the site, which would have needed a simple washing and perhaps burning process to rid it of unwanted clay and other matter. The soda would probably have been obtained from seaweed-ash imported from the coast; the lime was probably present to sufficient quantity in the sand, or the ash, but could have been added.

This, however, is not the end of the story. The mineralogical study of the crucible showed that this vessel had not been at temperatures even above 1100° for any appreciable time, and this result was confirmed by the determination of the expansion-contraction characteristics of the shard, which proved that it had never been heated above 1000°, approximately.[42] Attempts to make glass to the formula indicated were fruitless at this temperature, and the conclusion therefore was that the glass had been prepared from scrap, or cullet.

Unless a considerable body of glass was melted, it would not have been practicable to pour it satisfactorily. At 1000°, the viscosity of the melt was extremely high, and the further cooling which would have taken place during the pouring would have prevented the flow otherwise. The size of the vessel used as a crucible, however, was large: the basal diameter is about 18 cm., giving in ordinary proportion a height in the region of 30 cm.: it would thus have held at least 15 kg. of glass. It seems most probable that the end-product would have been cast sheets of window-glass (cf. p. 207). We can see very well from fragments that the glass was highly viscous when poured —cool enough not to scorch the mould, which was often of wood, as the undeniable imprint of its grain upon the underside of panes well proves, and solidifying rapidly enough to require spreading by a tool into the corners, as marks on the upper surface again attest. It is no wonder that this Roman window-glass retains, in the break, clear signs of the layered structure (or 'ream', as it is known in the trade) common to any poured viscous liquid; momentarily visible, for instance, when one pours treacle on to a plate, but here petrified for ever. A piece of ordinary modern plate-glass, if placed edge-wise to the eye and moved a fraction vertically, will reveal the same inhomo-geneity, but the Roman panes are so crude that the phenomenon is very much more obvious.[43]

WOODWORKING

The wealth of woodworking tools in the two 'hoards' of ironwork (cf. fig. 41) encourages us to pause for a moment upon this subject. Many of the forms are identical, or nearly so, with those in use today,[44] though some, such as the axe and adze, are no longer a regular part of the carpenter's tool-chest. The so-called cooper's adze may have been used in making stave-built vessels, but would have been employed for any hollow work, as in making troughs and the like. Saws, however, are very rare. Only two saw-blades were found at Silchester—such blades were too thin to stand a very good chance of survival, except in unusual circumstances. One, with an iron handle, is a small hand-tool with fine teeth, probably more suited to use upon bone than ordinary timber; the other is part of the blade of a frame- or bow-saw, the most practical form until high-carbon steels became available, for a blade kept in tension would be far less likely to buckle than otherwise. Pliny is the first writer to mention the setting of the teeth of saws, and some of the files in the 'hoards' had saw-setting notches. Large frame-saws were used for cutting logs into planks or boards; the logs were commonly raised on trestles for the purpose. A sawyer's line-hook is in the collection.[45]

Reference was made earlier to planks as much as 7.6 m. long, sawn from the same tree, which had been used in the construction of a timber water-channel (p. 88). There are several recorded instances of planks or boards in excess of 5.5 m., all of oak.[46]

The plane (fig. 41, 10) from the 1890 'hoard' is a particularly interesting object, and fairly rare.[47] As preserved, it gives the impression of a design very similar to the modern all-metal smoothing-plane, such as a Stanley or Record plane, but this is accidental: it is nothing but a wooden plane with an iron sole and partial casing. The sole is 13.5 cm. long and 5.7 cm. wide, and is turned up at either end to grip the wooden body, probably oak, secured by four vertical bolts; two other bolts on either side of the blade pass horizontally. One is coated with lead, as if for a bearing for the blade, but this is now rusted at an angle of 67°.[48] The wedge would have been inserted in front, and would have borne against the horizontal bolt there. Judging by other evidence, the stock would have had hollowed grips on either side of the blade. The blade is 11.5 cm. long and only 2.5 cm. wide; the cutting-edge

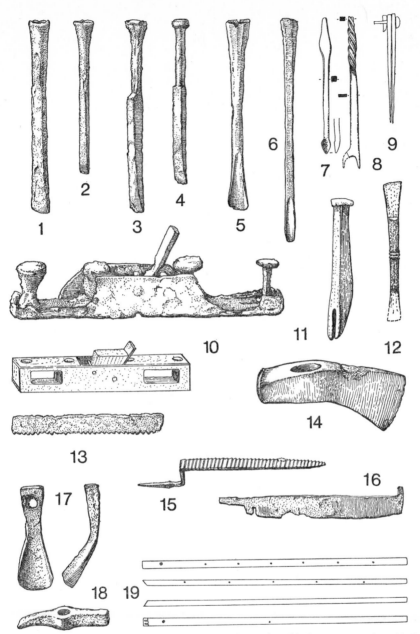

41. Carpenter's tools. 1–2, socketed paring and mortise chisels. 3–4, mortise chisels. 5–6, socketed gouges (the first, for lathe-work). 7–8, iron spoon and centre-bits. 9, compasses. 10, iron-cased jack-plane (with reconstruction below). 11, nail-claw. 12, potter's or plasterer's spatula. 13, fragment of frame-saw blade. 14, axe-head. 15, rasp. 16, file with saw-setting notch. 17, hollow or cooper's adze. 18, hammer-head. 19, views of half of a folding bronze rule, graduated in *digiti* (top), *unciae* (right side), *semis* (left side), *palmi* (underside); hinge at left. Scales, 1/5; no. 19, 1/2

was presumably carburised (p. 268). Such a tool could only have been intended for finishing surfaces already dressed fairly smooth, or for accurate fitting of edges, as in joinery or coopers' work.

There can be no doubt that the lathe—probably a pole-lathe of the kind still used by Chiltern 'chair-bodgers' for making chair-legs—was in wide use in Roman Britain. Handsome turned woodwork survives from Iron Age Glastonbury and in favourable circumstances elsewhere, as at Vindonissa in Switzerland; and although the only surviving turned wooden object from Silchester is a maple-wood bobbin (fig. 21, 9),[49] one of the gouges in the 1890 'hoard' of ironwork has been ground on the inside rather than the outside of the edge, and was almost certainly destined for the lathe, as Sir John Evans pointed out.[50]

SHALE

The working of Kimmeridge shale is attested at Silchester by the presence of two cores from the manufacture of lathe-turned armlets,[51] and local manufacture may have extended to other articles, possibly the turned furniture-leg (p. 222, fig. 21, 8) which is at present unexampled elsewhere. It is, however, fairly clear that shale was mostly worked close to the site of the quarries in Dorset, remains of its manufacture elsewhere being somewhat few.[52]

BONE

Bone, horn and antler were valuable raw-materials for the craftsman until very recent times, when moulded plastics completely destroyed the trade. Offcuts and unfinished articles show that these materials were worked at Silchester, producing handles for knives and other tools, pins, pegs, toggles, needles, counters, frames, inlay, spindle-whorls, spindles, dice, labels, hinges, and a whistle. Some of these things are roughly-made, but others are finely finished; a few are so well-preserved that they might almost be taken for ivory: ivory, however, is a very rare material in Roman Britain generally, being confined to imported objects,[53] and there is none in the Silchester collection.

The refuse of a worker in bone was found in a pit of Insula XVI,[54] and consists of numerous shoulder-blades of sheep from which flat rings have been cut by means of a centre-bit. The rings are of two sizes, 2.8 and 1.3 cm. across, the central perforation of the bit being about 0.6 cm. wide (fig. 40, 3). Another shoulder-blade, from which rings 0.8 cm. in diameter had been cut, was found in a first-century filling of the inner earthwork[55] and may probably show that this industry was of early date. It is difficult, however, to be sure of the function of the rings. They were certainly rings and not counters; but they would have exhibited a central layer of cancellous tissue, which is not seen in the majority of pieces of inlay, etc., cut from much thicker bone. It may be concluded that they were eyelets; but their small size precludes their use on rick-sheets, cart-covers and the like, and there is no proof that they were sewn into clothing. On the other hand, as was pointed out on an earlier page (p. 133), the pins of many of the brooches are so thick that they would have damaged any but the coarsest plaid; and since brooches were used to fasten garments and not merely for ornament, and would have been inserted in the same place time after time, it would have been advantageous to incorporate eyelets for the purpose.

CLOTH

Bone spindles, spindle-whorls of bone, shale, jet, pottery, stone and glass, and fragments of jet distaffs indicate the production of thread and yarn on a domestic scale, the more valuable objects in jet pointing to the participation of the ladies of the household in this work. On the other hand, there is a singular absence of loom-weights, only one small pyramidal example, of terracotta, being recorded. On sites where cloth-manufacture was practised, loom-weights occur with some frequency, for example at Glastonbury in the late Iron Age, and many Saxon huts also yield them.[56] In Roman Britain they are not found very commonly, and it must in consequence seem likely that the two-beam loom was in general use.[57] No weaving-combs, frequent on Iron Age sites, occur at Silchester: some small, rather sharp plates of bronze with teeth may have served as such, but the teeth are rather too small and too sharp for the purpose, and they were more probably used to mark out the holes for stitches in fine leatherwork.[58]

Turning to connected subjects, tablet-weaving for the manufacture of braid is attested by triangular bone plaques, pierced at the angles to hold the threads equidistant;[59] but more intriguing is the likelihood that knitting was practised at Calleva: it is difficult to see what purpose the thin, carefully-finished bronze rod, 29 cm. long and bluntly-pointed at both ends, can have had unless it was, in Dickensian parlance, a knitting-wire (fig. 34, 10). The earliest-known specimens of knitted fabric, highly elaborate and thus attesting the long previous history of the craft, are of the third century A.D., and were found at Dura-Europos on the Euphrates.[60]

BREWING

It is possible, indeed likely, that yarn produced at Silchester was dyed there, and we have drawn attention to three dye-plants in the botanical remains (p. 249). The excavators, however, went much farther than this, and proposed that the circular 'furnaces' found throughout the town, and especially in Insulae X and XI, were the bases of dyeing-vats. The matter is discussed at length in *Archaeologia*,[61] where several possibilities were considered. 'A very slight examination' proved that the structures could not have been the bases of bread-ovens; pottery-kilns and metal-working furnaces were also ruled out by the absence of characteristic débris. Fulling and tanning were discounted, because there was no adequate water supply in the one case, and because there were no tanks in the other. The identification of the bases as those of dyers' boilers was derived from a Pompeian parallel described and illustrated in the report:[62] the peristyle of a house had been given over to the industry, and the vats, missing, had been set in masonry bases not unlike those in evidence at Silchester, much resembling old-fashioned domestic coppers. There is, however, a difference between the Pompeian and the Silchester remains to which attention was not drawn. At Pompeii, the fires were lit directly under the boilers; at Silchester, there was nearly always a short flue leading into what was evidently a combustion-chamber (pl. 35).

It must be conceded that any industry requiring abundant water supplies —and dyeing is one of these—would have been sited, by preference, in the lower or south-easterly part of the town near the public baths, or in a valley outside; and when it is remembered that the identification of the furnaces was proposed at a time when three-quarters of the walled area remained unexplored, that many more examples would come to light, often isolated, in other insulae,[63] and that the area of Insulae X–XI was not quite so open as was thought (cf. p. 49), a sceptical view is not unjustified. The frequent association of the round 'furnaces' with long hearths of a type which may often have been primitive corn-dryers (p. 258) is noteworthy, and suggests a connection not with dyeing, but with the processing of grain. The excavators noted that the number of querns found in Insulae X–XI, about a score,[64] 'would not have furnished a quarter of the workshops along the main street, had they been bakeries', and we should not expect ordinary bake-ovens to have been equipped with fire-flues, however short (p. 195). Sir Ian Richmond, indeed, stated that the bases were 'manifestly' quite different from those of 'such structures as bread-ovens.'[65] The only serious possibility to be canvassed, therefore, is that the bases were indeed bases of vats, but of vats used for brewing and not dyeing: an even, controlled temperature is vital for this pur-

35 Furnace-
bottom with
circular
combustion-
chamber,
perhaps for
brewing;
courtyard,
XXI,3
36 T-shaped
corn-drying
furnace with
outlets pro-
jecting
beyond the
wall of
XXXIIIA.B3
37 Domestic
channelled
hypocaust,
XIX.2

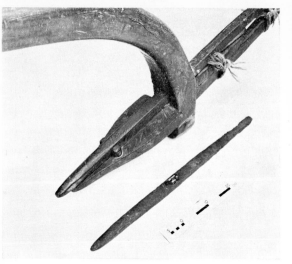

CMS.

38 Model of Danish Iron Age plough with wooden fore- and main-shares, with Silchester iron bar-share shown for comparison
39 Baby's footprint, 5·5 cm. across the toes, on a tile laid out to dry before firing
40 Well in Insula VI, showing square oak curb at the bottom, and the lower part of a barrel used as lining

pose, and would explain the presence of the fire-flues. It is of interest to note that in a barn at Shakenoak or Wilcote villa (Oxon.), there was not only a granary, but at a safe distance from it a very similar round furnace with fire-flue, in or near which a mass of lead was found, possibly the actual remains of the brewing-vat.[66] Although there was no sign of a tank, tubs and vessels could have been set on, rather than into, the ground. It would thus seem that some of the shops along the main east-west street were taverns catering, no doubt, for the through-traffic.

MILLING

Flour was generally ground at home, as we have seen (p. 238), but there is one establishment, XVIIIA.3,[67] which was thought to have been devoted to flour-milling on a commercial scale. The building, early to judge by its alignment, was extended to the street at right-angles in the form of a hall some 13.5 m. long and 10 m. wide internally. Along either side, and about 1.5 m. from the walls, there was a series of three circular masonry 'platforms' about 1.2 to 1.4 m. across and 60 cm. high above the floor: they can thus hardly have been the post-hole packings for roof-supports that the plan suggests, unless the floor-level had been mistakenly excavated to far too great a depth. Fox suggested that these bases supported large querns. Very similar bases appear at Pompeii and Ostia and are surmounted by the 'hour-glass' type of mill, which is extremely rare in Britain.[68] The upper stone of a very heavy quern of the normal discoidal shape was found in Insula XIV; and at 71 cm. in diameter and 19 cm. thick it would certainly appear to be too heavy for normal domestic use,[69] and could have been employed in the way envisaged above.

Flour-milling on a large scale is more certainly indicated by a spindle from a mechanical mill among the articles in the 1890 'hoard' of ironwork.[70] It is an iron bar about 91 cm. long, drawn out to a point at one end to act as a bearing, and at the other end squared to take the rynd, or piece of metal, which fitted into a slot cut in the upper stone, having passed through a hole in the lower. Just above the bearing, there is a swaged collar and a squared portion of shaft, where a drum-shaped cog would have been fitted. An appliance of the type to which this spindle was fitted is described by Vitruvius,[71] and a reconstruction can be seen at the Saalburg; it is designed to be turned by a cranked handle.

LEATHER

It is scarcely possible to over-emphasize the importance of leather in Roman times. The army alone made huge calls upon supplies, using sheep- or goat-skin and occasionally, calf-skin for tents (p. 48), and ox-hide for boots and harness; civilian demands were of a similar order: cart-covers, rick-covers, boots and shoes (p. 133), clothing (p. 133), harness, and much else. Three shoemaker's feet in the ironwork 'hoards' are especially interesting (cf. fig. 39, 13) and recall a relief which shows a shoemaker sitting astride a bench in which a foot is fixed:[72] undoubtedly a scene often to have been glimpsed at Calleva. Some needles and awls, and perhaps the small bronze plates mentioned above (p. 285) are also among the tools of the Callevan leather-worker.

The leather-industry appears to have been of particular importance, and the chief economic activity of more than local significance. The extensive deposit of ox-jaws in the north-west corner of Insula VI[73] may be regarded as stratigraphically earlier than the establishment of the forum and the block of shops, VI.B1, upon the forum-alignment (p. 55), and among the few datable relics found in the bed of jaws, pottery of early appearance, including samian-ware, is mentioned, together with an iron ring containing a paste intaglio, itself indicative of a first-century date. Another deposit of at least sixty horn-cores of ox, associated with a coin of Domitian, occurred in a pit of Insula XXXVI.[74] No date can be given to the apparently large number of deer-antlers in the space immediately east of the forum,[75] but since these remains lay on the Roman ground-surface, they must be late. The horse- and ox-crania found above the boarding extending over one end of the tank in XXXIV.1 are also presumably late.[76]

The deposit of ox-jaws in Insula VI was regarded as most remarkable by all who saw it, and indeed it is so. Lyell's conservative estimate of the number of animals represented is 2,500. Of an area about 1 m. square and 35 cm. thick, E. T. Newton says '. . . scarcely any bones but the lower jaws of small oxen were turned out, and these in such numbers as practically to constitute the mass of the deposit. A few portions of *scapulae* were noticed, but no other parts of oxen. One or two bones of horse, sheep, pig and dog were found. No fewer than 71 *rami* were counted, dug out in my presence from this small area'.

None of the bones appears to have been utilised, and in the complete absence of other parts of the skeleton beyond a few pieces of scapulae, it can only be suggested that large numbers of flayed hides, with the heads attached, were prepared for steeping prior to tanning near this spot, the useless lower jaws being wrenched off and thrown down here; the fact that the crania discovered near the tank in XXXIV.1 (see below) lacked lower jaws adds some colour to this belief, though that deposit is of much later date.

It is worth reflecting also upon the carcase-meat which these 2,500 beasts would have provided. Most of this would have been available for sale, either to the army (when it would have been salted) or to markets in London. In this deposit we thus have a very interesting demonstration of the agricultural surplus produced in the town, and mentioned on an earlier page as the basis of the prosperity of the leading citizens (p. 248).

The vast spread of oyster-shells which underlies part of the east range of the forum and extends over 30 m. eastwards to disappear beneath the street in a bed 15 or 18 m. wide and at least 15 cm. thick is of about the same date, stratigraphically, as the deposit of bones just mentioned.[77] Hope thought that this immense number of shells, probably over a million, had been brought to this spot to be burnt into fine lime for the plasterwork of the forum-basilica; but it must seem that the foundations cut through the bed, and some other explanation is demanded. The steeping of hides in a solution of slaked lime is one of the standard stages in tanning,[78] and serves to loosen hair and epidermis. Whether liming was a technique practised by the ancient tanner is unknown, but it seems possible that this was the purpose in collecting such an immense number of shells, presumably brought expressly from the coast rather than the assembled débris of meals. No very good parellel exists: shells were found in the Caerwent forum, curiously enough, but the deposit was superficial; and considerable obscurity surrounds the very large bed said to have been found at Clermont-Ferrand,[79] 10 to 12 cm. thick over an area of about 80 sq. m.

It may well be that some of the tanks and wood-lined pits of Silchester were used for tanning, in which the bark of young oak-trees was no doubt employed. On the other hand, there are other steeping-processes, e.g. for flax, which it would be difficult to distinguish archaeologically from tanning, in the absence of clinching details. Analysis would be of little value, for the oak used for the tanks would itself reveal tannin. The most likely case is the tank in the western yard of XXXIV.1, where horse and ox skulls may well suggest that clinching evidence: it measured about 19 m. in length and 1 to 1.5 m. in breadth, with a clay bottom about 38 cm. deep below a timber stage built over one end. A drain from the house debouched into it, and an effluent-channel led away south-eastwards.[80]

WEIGHTS AND MEASURES

The final subject of this chapter is one which is intimately bound up with many others which we have discussed, and forms therefore a fitting tail-piece to the whole work.

There are several examples of balances and weights in the Silchester collection. The best of the former is the bronze balance-arm found in the 1890 'hoard' of ironwork: it is about 33.5 cm. in length (fig. 34, 1). Balance-pans suitable for this kind of instrument, with rings for suspension by four chains, were found on other occasions. The scale-beam is graduated by punched dots, and could also have been used as a steelyard.

The weights in the collection are problematical. There are four typical, well-made cheese-shaped bronze examples, marked with one or two dots (in two cases inlaid with silver, fig. 34, 6) to denote their values. We should expect these weights to answer either to the Roman *libra* (327.45 g., traditional value; 322.56 g. according to Naville's estimate, which has much to recommend it); or to the Celtic pound of *c.* 309 g., found at Neath and matched at Mainz.[81] A third possibility is a local standard. However, the weights with a single spot weigh 19.22 and 22.52 g.; and those with two spots, 48.65 and 52.97 g. Only the last is at all close to the value of two Roman ounces (53.76 g., Naville). Otherwise no relationship is readily detectable, and none within the group itself. This is by no means a new problem, and has generally been dismissed on the supposition that provincial Roman weights were very carelessly adjusted.

Another weight, of lathe-turned yellow bronze, is an import, and comes from a nest of weights fitting into one another. At 69.66 g., having lost perhaps 0.5 g., it presents much the same difficulty as the others (fig. 34, 5), unless we reckon it at 2½ Roman *unciae,* which seems an unlikely expedient; but, being imported, it is more likely than the others to correspond to a widely-accepted standard.[82]

Other weights include a large discoid stone example, unfortunately broken, and several of lead, which need not detain us: one of the latter, however, is perfectly cylindrical and has traces of an iron loop; possibly it is a pump-piston rather than a weight of between four and five Roman pounds (p. 86).

There are several bronze and iron steelyards in the collection, mostly small and flimsy (fig. 34, 3–4). The commodity to be weighed could be suspended in different positions according to whether it was light or heavy, the position of the fulcrum-hook being varied accordingly. The inscribed fragment shown is numbered along two edges, to weigh up to the final figure indicated (IX and XV *librae* respectively). Steelyard-weights were often of a decorative form, at some cost, probably, to their accuracy. A large example from the 1900 'hoard' (fig. 34, 7) is in the shape of a bust of Bacchus; a very tiny specimen is in the form of a bust of Apollo, with silver-inlaid eyes.[83]

As far as I am aware, there is nothing in the collection which may be described as a measure of capacity, unless the hollow, nested weight mentioned above was intended for this additional purpose. We turn therefore to the half of a folding foot-rule mentioned on a previous page (p. 97). Many examples of such rules are known, and they were probably a specialised manufacture of a Gaulish or north Italian firm. The two halves were held in the open position by a pivoted catch (the Silchester rule retains the hole for the stud which it engaged). The rules are seldom, if ever, of the exact length of a Roman foot or *pes monetalis* (296 mm.). The following examples illustrate the variation found:[84] Silchester (291 mm. when complete); London (294 mm.); British Museum (292 and 294 mm.); Caerleon (294.5 mm.). Furthermore, as can be seen from the illustration (fig. 41, 19), the marking of the subdivisions is irregular. The *unciae* or inches vary between 23 and 26 mm., the *digiti* between 17 and 19.75 mm., and the *palmi* between 70.5 and 76.5. This is not at all unusual; and it hints at a reason for the difficulty encountered over the weights, for if the foot might vary by about 1.7%, and the subdivisions by more, then the *libra,* as witnessed by finds, might vary by a similar amount, and the subdivisions, more widely still. It was the large unit that mattered; and in mason's or carpenter's work, where measurements of less than half a *pes* were in question, the pieces concerned were probably matched edge-to-edge rather than measured.

COINAGE

This important subject, essential for a full understanding of economic conditions, cannot be sketched adequately here. Briefly, the early imperial system was remarkably stable down to the early third century. There was a gold piece (*aureus*) worth 25 silver *denarii*; and the nominal equivalent of a *denarius* was 16 copper *asses,* with larger denominations in the form of brass *dupondii* (2 *asses*) and *sestertii* (4 *asses*), the last a very handsome coin 30 to 35 mm. in diameter. Occasionally fractions of the *as* (*quadrans, semis*) were issued, but seldom sufficient, and sometimes early *asses* have been cut in half to serve the purpose of *semisses.* The *denarius* and the *aureus* were struck to a standard fairly close to the intrinsic purchasing-power of the metal, allowing for the costs of minting and issuing, so that coined metal was then generally more valuable than uncoined, weight for weight. But since the currency, in these respects, was a 'value currency', any official reduction in the purity or weight of the maid of all work, the *denarius,* was bound to upset the system. The silver-content was in fact reduced, to meet all kinds of government expenditure—i.e., so that more *denarii* could be produced from a given amount of silver, by the addition of alloy—and by the time of Septimius Severus, about A.D. 200, it averaged only about 50% of that in first-century *denarii.*

The relationship of the *denarius* to the *aureus* was upset, and the introduction of a new coin, the *antoninianus*, in 214 may have been intended to redress the balance. It was of the same alloy as the contemporary *denarius* but larger, worth about 1½ *denarii*, and probably tariffed at two denarii. This over-valuation led inevitably to a fall in its value over the years, and by A.D. 250 old *denarii* were being restruck as *antoniniani*. Very swiftly thereafter the silver-content of the *antoninianus* was reduced, and by about 270 it contained little more than a few per cent, beneath a silvery surface. Gold was very sparingly issued at this period, and since the relationship of the hitherto fiduciary bronze coinage to the silver had been destroyed, it too was no longer issued in any quantity, and in Britain at least had been somewhat rare since the early part of the century. There were attempts to restore the *antoninianus* about 274, but the main reform was that of Diocletian in 294, when a new large silvered coin of *antoninianus*-alloy, the *follis,* appeared together with several subdivisions, a reasonable amount of gold, and a good silver *argenteus,* in effect the Neronian *denarius* restored. But *argentei* were too small in number to guarantee success, and the monetary history of the fourth century reflects the gradual decay of the *follis,* punctuated by attempts to restore a better denomination. Until the reign of Valentinian I and Valens (364) the government maintained the fiction that the *follis* was a 'silver denomination' by reason of its small content of bullion, and truly enormous amounts of hard-won silver were frittered away in these poor overvalued alloys. By that date, however, good silver and gold coins were becoming freely available, and although the problem of the small denominations was never really mastered and their decline in value continued, the situation was in general less wretched than it had been for a century or more.

About 12,500 coins have been listed in the Silchester Catalogue at Reading Museum. The content is quite typical of site-finds, high denominations being less well-represented than low, for it must always be remembered that such finds do not truly reflect the proportions of coins in general circulation at any time, with the exception probably of the crisis-period in the years around 270. We can say little here of individual pieces, however interesting some of them may be—the early silver *denarius of* Carausius, for example, produced soon after his arrival in Britain *c.* 286 when, presumably, the Dolaucothi gold-mine was unable to supply the necessary gold for the high denomination of the coinage, a matter which was soon put to rights. It is more interesting to mention the large numbers of counterfeits which form part of the finds. Counterfeiting is an endemic disease of coinage, and at times reaches epidemic proportions owing to a scarcity of true coin. These waves occurred immediately upon the Roman invasion and at later dates: there are only 10 orthodox Claudian coins, for example, and 75 copies, including 2 counterfeit *sestertii* stamped officially PROB (seemingly, a British mark) to show that upon some inspection they passed muster: similarly, a local issue of Lyons, much worn, had been approved in Germany by the countermark AVG. Most of the counterfeits belong to the third and fourth centuries—a curious light-weight series produced when official bronze had become short, and large numbers of copies of the radiate *antoniniani* of the period around A.D. 270, and of *folles* of the period around A.D. 360, to choose the most prominent peaks: there are some 950 radiate copies to 650 orthodox *antoniniani,* and some 475 'falling horseman' copies to 84 orthodox, including one of the rare pieces bearing the probably fictitious name of Carausius 'II', *Domino Carausius Ces* 'To our lord Carausius Caesar', with the imperial name of Constantius II on the other side (pl. 34 h). Some of these third and fourth century counter-feits are very small, absurdly so to the modern eye: but counterfeits are either smaller or baser than originals, and a steady decline in size will come about if they, rather than originals, are taken as models for further imitations. But it can be demonstrated that the reformed *antoniniani* of the 274 standard were not regarded in Britain as more valuable than the bad coinage which pre-ceded their issue; and they were copied to minuscule size themselves. Even quite small copies are likely to have been accepted as being of equal value with originals, and were certainly not worth less than a quarter on any show-ing. Counterfeiting in quantity is always a mark of insufficient orthodox coin, and although there were vast numbers of official products available about 270–80, prices had probably risen so high in terms of this bad coinage that a considerable augmentation of the supply was locally necessary. By 282, however, and end had been put to this wave, and the numerous barbarous coins of Carausius (*c.* 286–90) are not of the minim size: many are over-struck on orthodox coins and require another explanation, which is found in the *desirability* of coins of the new emperor, who was a usurper: this in turn points to insufficient official production at the start of the reign in 286. Overstriking is again found in about 354, when a financial enactment had demonetised earlier varieties of coins and created a scarcity which was at first met in this way and, as it continued, by coining ever smaller versions of the 'falling horseman' type introduced in that year. The 'Carausius II' piece is one of these overstrikes, dating between *c.* 354 and 358.[85] A final object to close these pages is the bronze arm-purse (fig. 34, 12).[86]

Quicquid ames, cupias non placuisse nimis

MARTIAL, VI, 29

42. Complete brick with finger-drawn inscription 'Enough'. Measures about 40 by
27 cm

Notes and References

Volumes of *Archaeologia* are denoted by Italic figures. Volumes of other periodicals are given in Roman numerals and plates in Arabic. Dates of publication are given only to distinguish a particular edition or for other specific reasons. The following abbreviated titles are used. Other abbreviations are, it is hoped, intelligible as they stand.

AA	*Archaeologia Aeliana,* series 1–4.
AC	*Archaeologia Cambrensis.*
ACt	*Archaeologia Cantiana.*
AJ	*The Antiquaries Journal*
Allen	Derek Allen, 'The origins of coinage in Britain; a reappraisal' in S. S. Frere (ed.) *Problems of the Iron Age in southern Britain.*
Ant	*Antiquity.*
Applebaum	S. Applebaum, 'Roman Britain', in H. P. R. Finberg (ed.) *The Agrarian History of England and Wales* I, pt. ii.
ARB	R. G. Collingwood, *The Archaeology of Roman Britain* (ed. I. A. Richmond).
ArJ	*The Archaeological Journal.*
ASPSE	J. N. L. Myres, *Anglo-Saxon Pottery and the Settlement of England.*
B	*Britannia.*
BAJ	*Berkshire Archaeological Journal.*
BBCS	*Bulletin of the Board of Celtic Studies,* University of Wales.
Ber.RGK	*Bericht, Römisch-germanische Kommission.*
Ber.ROB	*Bericht, Rijksdient voor het oudheidkundige Bodemonderzoek.*
BHMG	*Bulletin of the Historical Metallurgy Group.*
BJ	*Bonner Jahrbücher.*

BMC . . .	*British Museum Catalogue . . .*
BMGGRL	*British Museum Guide to Greek and Roman Life.*
BMGRB	*British Museum Guide to the Antiquaries of Roman Britain* (1922).
BMQ	*British Museum Quarterly.*
CA	*Current Archaeology.*
Cabrol-Leclercq	F. Cabrol and H. Leclercq, *Dictionnaire d'archéologie chrétienne et de liturgie.*
Callender	M. H. Callender, *Roman Amphorae.*
Camden	W. Camden, *Britannia, sive Florentissimorum Regnorum . . . chorographica Descriptio* (1586).
Camulodunum	C. F. C. Hawkes and M. R. Hull, *Camulodunum, first report on Excavations at Colchester 1930–1939* (Res. Rept. Soc. Ant. Lond. XIV).
CB	M. W. Barley and R. P. C. Hanson (edd.), *Christianity in Britain, 300–700.*
CC	J. S. Wacher (ed.), *The Civitas Capitals of Roman Britain.*
CIL	*Corpus Inscriptionum Latinarum.*
CK	W. Schleiermacher, *Cambodunum-Kempten, eine römische Stadt im Allgäu.*
Columella	*L. Junii Moderati Columellae de Re Rustica* (ed. J. M. Gesner, 1735).
DAB	D. B. Harden (ed.), *Dark-Age Britain: Studies pres. to E. T. Leeds.*
ECC	A. Pitt Rivers, *Excavations in Cranbourne Chase.*
EE	*Ephemeris Epigraphica.*
EHR	*The English Historical Review.*
Esp.	É. Espérandieu, *Recueil général des Bas-reliefs, Statues et Bustes de la Gaule romaine.*
Fishbourne	B. W. Cunliffe *et al.*, *Excavations at Fishbourne 1961–1969* (Res. Rept. Soc. Ant. Lond. XXVI).
Fox Coll.	(Boxes of drawings presented by G. E. Fox to the Society of Antiquaries of London).
Frere	S. S. Frere, *Britannia, a history of Roman Britain.*
G	*Germania.*
Gillam	J. P. Gillam, *Types of Roman Coarse Pottery Vessels in Northern Britain* (1968).
GM	*The Gentleman's Magazine.*
Godwin	H. Godwin, *History of the British Flora.*

Grenier	A. Grenier, *Manuel d'archéologie gallo-romaine.*
GV	K. Lachmann, *Gromatici Veteres, Die Schriften der römischen Feldmesser* I (1848).
Hearne	*Remarks and Collections of Thomas Hearne* (ed. Oxford Historical Society).
Hengistbury	J. P. Bushe-Fox, *Excavations at Hengistbury Head* (Res. Rept. Soc. Ant. Lond. III).
HG	C. Jullian, *Histoire de la Gaule.*
ILS	H. Dessau, *Inscriptiones Latinae Selectae.*
It.Ant.	P. Wesseling (ed.) *Vetera Romanorum Itineraria, sive Antonini Augusti Itinerarium, Itinerarium Hierosolymitanum;* (1735).
JBAA	*Journal of the British Archaeological Association,* series 1–3.
JGS	*Journal of Glass Studies.*
Journal	J. G. Joyce, Journal of Excavations at Silchester (Reading Museum).
JRGZ	*Jahrbuch des römish-germanischen Zentralmuseums, Mainz.*
JRS	*Journal of Roman Studies.*
Lewis	M. J. T. Lewis, *Temples in Roman Britain.*
Liversidge	J. Liversidge, *Furniture in Roman Britain.*
LRT	R. E. M. Wheeler, *London in Roman Times* (London Museum Cat. no. 3).
Lydney	R. E. M. and T. V. Wheeler, *Report on the Excavation of the Prehistoric, Roman and Post-Roman Site in Lydney Park, Glos.* (Res. Rept. Soc. Ant. Lond. IX).
MA	*Medieval Archaeology.*
MAAR	*Memoirs of the American Academy in Rome.*
May	T. May, *The Pottery found at Silchester.*
MGR	H. Stern *(ed.), La Mosaïque gréco-romaine.*
NC	*The Numismatic Chronicle.*
Neue Ausgrabungen	W. Krämer *(ed.), Neue Ausgrabungen in Deutschland.*
Newstead	J. Curle, *A Roman Frontier Post and its People: the Fort of Newstead in the Parish of Melrose.*
ORL	*Der obergermanisch-raetische Limes des Römerreichs.*
Oxon	*Oxoniensia.*
PCAS	*Proceedings of the Cambridge Antiquarian Society.*

PDAS	*Proceedings of the Dorset Natural History and Archaeological Society.*
PF	F. Baudry and L. Ballereau, *Puits funéraires gallo-romains du Bernard (Vendée)* (1873).
PHFC	*Proceedings of the Hampshire Field Club and Archaeological Society.*
Phil.Trans.	*The Philosophical Transactions of the Royal Society.*
Pliny	*C. Plinii Secundi Historia Naturalis* (Leiden 1669).
PPS	*Proceedings of the Prehistoric Society.*
PSAL	*Proceedings of the Society of Antiquaries of London,* ser. 2.
PSAS	*Proceedings of the Somersetshire Archaeological and Natural History Society.*
PSASc	*Proceedings of the Society of Antiquaries of Scotland.*
PUBSS	*Proceedings of the University of Bristol Spelaeological Society.*
PW	*Paulys Realencyclopädie der klassischen Altertums-wissenschaft,* ed. G. Wissowa.
RA	*Revue Archéologique.*
RAC	*Revue Archéologique du Centre.*
RAE	*Revue Archéologique de l'Est.*
RCHM . . .	Royal Commission on Historical Monuments (England). . . .
RIB	R. G. Collingwood and R. P. Wright, *The Roman Inscriptions of Britain,* I.
Richborough	J. P. Bushe-Fox *et al. Excavations of the Roman Fort at Richborough, Kent* (Res. Repts. Soc. Ant. Lond. VI, VII, X, XVI, XXIII).
Richter	G. M. A. Richter, *The Furniture of the Greeks Etruscans and Romans* (1966).
RLÖ	*Der römische Limes in Oesterreich.*
Roman Bath	B. W. Cunliffe *et al., Roman Bath* (Res. Rept. Soc. Ant. Lond. XXIV).
Roman Colchester	M. R. Hull, *Roman Colchester* (Res. Rept. Soc. Ant. Lond. XX).
Ross	Anne Ross, *Pagan Celtic Britain: Studies in Iconography and Tradition.*
RS	G. C. Boon, *Roman Silchester.*
RVB	A. L. F. Rivet (ed.), *The Roman Villa in Britain.*
SHA . . .	*Scriptores Historiae Augustae . . .* (Loeb).

Shakenoak	A. C. Brodribb *et al.*, *Excavations at Shakenoak Farm, Wilcote, Oxon.*
SJ	*Saalburg-Jahrbuch.*
Stukeley	W. Stukeley, *Itinerarium Curiosum. Or, an Account of the Antiquitys and remarkable Curiositys in Nature or Art . . ., Centuria I* (1724).
TBGAS	*Transactions of the Bristol and Gloucestershire Archaeological Society.*
TSAS	*Transactions of the Shropshire Archaeological Society.*
TZ	*Trierer Zeitschrift.*
VCH . . .	*Victoria History of the Counties of England . . .*
Verulamium	R. E. M. and T. W. Wheeler, *Verulamium: a Belgic and Two Roman Cities* (Res. Rept. Soc. Ant. Lond. XI).
Verulamium Excav.	Sheppard Frere *et al.*, *Verulamium Excavations,* I (Res. Rept. Soc. Ant. Lond. XXVIII).
Vitruvius	M. *Vitruvii Pollionis de Architectura* (Amsterdam 1649).
WAM	*Wiltshire Archaeological Magazine.*
Wild	J. P. Wild, *Textile Manufacture in the Northern Roman Provinces.*
Wroxeter 1923–7	D. Atkinson, *Excavations at Wroxeter 1923–7.*

CHAPTER 1 *(Silchester: A Mirror of British Archaeology)*

1. Calleva, Calleva Atrebatum, *It.Ant.* 478.3, 485.7, 486.7.8; cf. Ptolemy, *Geogr.* II, 3.26, Καλκούα ἤ Κάληούα; *Anon. Ravennatis Cosmographia,* 67. On the name see K. Jackson, *B* 1, 70.

2. J. Aubrey, *Monumenta Britannica* (MS Bodl. Top. Gen. C24, f.214); T. Hearne (ed.), *Itin. of John Leland the Antiquary* VIII, 8; *Camden,* 135.

3. First Duke, *GM* 1863; 490; second, *40, 403*; third, PSAL XIII, 92.

4. Forum, *46, 349*; density and houses, *PSAL* XIII, 89; quotations, *ib.,* 92 and Sir M. Wheeler, *Archaeology from the Earth,* 127.

5. Devil's Highway: the antiquity of the name is perhaps doubtful. The late Mr Francis Needham drew my attention to a deed of 1442 at S. Saye, naming the stretch from Stanford End (p. 362) eastwards to Riseley as *Parkestrete.* Grim is better rendered, Woden. Onion, *Camden,* 134; cf. *Hearne* IV, 360. Imp Stone, *Stukeley,* 171; cf. PRO Misc. Chancery Bundle XI, 3 (a ref. owed to the late O. G. S. Crawford);

RIB 2221 accepts IMP without due authority: the stone was dug up in 1890–1909 and found not to be inscribed. The road was sectioned in 1957 by Mr E. J. Larbey at SU 610635: 7.3 m. wide with side-ditches, and boundary-ditches 26.8 m. apart centre-to-centre. Another section nearer the town at SU 620631 revealed no side-ditches, cf. p. 246. Sparrows. *Stukeley*, 171, embroidered by T. Kempe, *GM* 1833, 124.

6. Horsley, *Britannia Romana*, 458; Halley, *Hearne* VI, 175, VII, 350. Vindomis may be Neatham, see A. L. F. Rivet, *B* I, 60, and cf. *B* III, 348. Lhuyd, *Commentarioli descriptionis Britanniae Fragmentum* (1572), f. 14^r, cf. 53^v; *Camden*, 132, cf. 387. Henry of Huntingdon, *Historia Anglorum*, 3: the appearance of this name so early must surely suggest that another inscription to Hercules *Saegontius* had been turned up. Nennius, *Historia Brittonum* (ed. Lot), 208; Caesar, *De Bello Gallico* V, 21. Inscription, J. Ward, *Phil. Trans.* XLIII, 200, *RIB* 67. *Sego—*, most recently K. Jackson, *B* I, 79. Derivation of modern name, Ekwall, *Dict. English Place-Names* (1960), *s.v.*

7. Inscription, Haverfield *61*, 215, cf. 207; *RIB* 70, cf. our p. 154. Colt Hoare, quoted by A. Stradling, *PSAS* 1849–50, 56.

8. Sources: Silchester and Aldermaston parish registers; chance refs. by Hearne, Gough (*Tours*, MS Bodl. Top. Gen. E 16, f. 162^r), etc. Letters and plans, BM Add. MSS 6181 ff. 9, 11, 13, 15; 6210, f. 44; 6211, f. 183; 6212, f. 37 [quoted here]; BM K. Top. XIV, 8 b-d [pl. 1].

9. Villa, *27, 418; 50, 272*, with refs. Maclauchlan, *ArJ* VIII, 227 ff.

10. Joyce, mainly from obit., *PSAL* VIII, 106; also Foster, *Alumni Oxon.; Crockford*, 1878; *Hampshire Chronicle* 6 July 1878. I acknowledge gratefully the help of the Hampshire County Record Office, the Bodleian Library, the Office of the Chief Herald, Dublin, and, for the photograph pl. 3, Lord Dynevor, who found it in a family album. Quotations following, *46, 332, 336*. Pottery, Roach Smith, *JBAA* IV, 1; Fox, *57, 101* (*May* makes an interesting comparison with the latter, for his bibliography cites early French and German work on sigillata and seminal British work on coarse pottery).

11. Pitt Rivers' letter is published by permission of the late Duke of Wellington; it is at Apsley House. Quotation, *PSAL* XIII, 85. Characterisations mainly from obits., *PSAL* XXII, 471 (Price), XXXII, 168 (Hope); *ArJ* LXV, 338 (Fox)—his gift of drawings, *PSAL* XVI, 419—*AJ* II, 390 (Gowland), XVII, 449 (Stephenson). Details of work from surviving chance mentions and from the recollections of the late Mr Fred Smith, who had been employed. The late Duke of

Wellington told me that the rich soil from pits and wells was sometimes sold. Photographs suggest that marrows were sometimes grown on the spoil-heaps.

12. Quotation, *PSAL* XIII, 94. Tour de force, *50, 265*. Models: west gate (1890); I.1 (1890); II.2 (1891); church (1892); temple, Insula XXXV (1907). Pitt Rivers' work interpreted by C. F. C. Hawkes, *ArJ* CIV. Haverfield, *VCH Hants.* I, 275; see n. 15.

13. Silver-refining, *57, 113*. *Godwin*, 343. Seeds, *57, 252* and later. Lake-dwellings, O. Heer, abstract in F. Keller (trans. J. E. Lee) *Lake Dwellings of Switzerland and other Parts of Europe* (1866), 336 ff. Bartlow Hills, *28, 5*. Insects, cf. *62, 445*: determinations otherwise very rare at this period; earliest *use* of such was by Pigorini and Strobel, 1864, cf. R. Munro, *Lake Dwellings of Europe* (1890), 275. Mammalian remains, fish, birds, *53, 285* (H. Jones); *58, 423* (E. T. Newton). The first substantial work on animal bones was that of L. Rütimeyer, 1861, abstracted in Keller-Lee, *o.c.*

14. Quotation, F. Brunton, *Year's Work in Class. Stud. 1925–6*, 94. *The Book of Silchester* was not reviewed in any national archaeological periodical.

15. Stephenson and Haverfield, *PSAL* XXII, 323.

16. Karslake, *62, 330*; *PHFC* VII, 43; tilery, *AJ* VI, 75; Sarapis, *57, 110*. He published numerous more or less speculative papers, but his 'Little London' enquiries are unfortunately not among them; I learnt of them from the late Mrs Leonora Karslake.

17. 1938–9, *92, 121* ff.; 1954–8, *102, 1* ff.; 1961, *JRS* LII, 185; defences, *JRS* LIX, 231.

18. Third Duke's letter, Reading Museum; details following from memo taken by Stevens of his visit (with Mr W. I. Palmer, Chairman of the Museum Committee and a member of the biscuit-manufacturing firm of Huntley and Palmer) to Stratfield Saye.

CHAPTER 2 *(Early Settlement and the Establishment of the Town)*

1. Nothing is known of the Mortimer barrows. The relics mentioned include a Neolithic polished flint axe (*58, 423*; our p. 156) and another in chert (J. S. Eyton Coll., Silchester); a flaked lance-head (Reading Mus.); a Middle Bronze Age flanged axe (*ibid.*); and a small Late Bronze Age 'Wilburton' sword now at Stratfield Saye (*JBAA* I, 147, not illus.). Bead, very rare type in Britain, turquoise opaque base, three 'eyes' containing blue spots outlined in white all within a brown

matrix outlined in white, in all but size identical with two, cf. J. Keller, *Das keltische Fürstengrab von Reinheim* I, 49, Taf. 26a–b, 1–2; see T. E. Haevernick, *Prähistorische Zeitschrift* XLVII, 78 ff. on the type. Cheek-piece (*102*, 45, no. 14): cf. P. Jacobsthal, *Early Celtic Art* nos. 146–7, etc. Only 88 mm. long; the cheek-pieces of the Ciumeşti helmet (I. Rusu, *Ber. RGK* L, 269, Abb. 2) are also small. Brooch, imperfect, seen by me 1951, and photographed: Mr A. M. ApSimon likens it (*in litt.* 1973) to the Münsingen IB series, but adds that it is insular; fourth-third cent. B.C.

2. All the British coins mentioned are listed in *Allen*. The total of coins of Caratacus is now five or six, see Boon, *BBCS* XXV, 243–5, incl. another recently in the London coin-trade, seen 1973. The Pond Farm stater is in the J. S. Eyton Coll. at Silchester, and I am indebted to Capt Eyton for permission to illustrate it. Pond Farm and 'salient', *102*, 22.

3. A. L. F. Rivet, *Town & Country in R. B.* (1964), 89 suggests that already in Roman times the centre of trade was moving to Reading; and *ib.* 140 that there was a kind of river-port here for Silchester; but cf. our p. 266.

4. Commius, Caesar, *De Bello Gallico* IV–VIII *passim;* Frontinus, *Stratagemata* II, 13. Sons, chronology, Allen 90, 4 (but rejecting doubts over identification of the 'numismatic' Commius); Epaticcus, *ib.*, 24; relations with Rome, C. E. Stevens in *Aspects of Archaeology*, 332.

5. Flex-ditch probably so named because flax was steeped there. The bank has almost gone. Dykes, see *102*, 24, 35–6. Belgic *oppida, Camulo-dunum*, 8 ff.

6. Arretine etc., *102*, 25. Dannell's attempt in *Fishbourne* II, 262 to date Arretine there to the early Roman military occupation is not felicitous: there is none at Richborough or Valkenburg; and the Belgic occupation at Fishbourne is side-stepped in the report. Gallic wares, *102*, 29 and Boon, *RAC* VII, 321. The early *Acutus* stamps may be La Graufesenque as easily as Montans, see Balsan, *ib.* IX, 101 for examples similar to Montans shown by A. Oxé, *Archäologischer Anzeiger* 1914, 70.

7. Cf. D. Peacock in *The Iron Age & its Hill Forts* esp. 181; cf. *May*, pl. 67.

8. *102*, 34, cf. *55*, 430 for the inlay (dark blue matrix, yellow plant, yellow and red flowers, probably Alexandrian).

9. *102*, 29.

10. *102*, 31, cf. *55*, 248 and *May*, 186, correcting pit-number to A.

11. *102,* 35; also listed by Allen, *l.c.* note 2.
12. Allen, *l.c.* note 4.
13. *Ib.*
14. *102,* 25, cf. *AJ* XXXIV, 68; mode of use, R. F. Tylecote, *NC* 1962, 101.
15. *102,* 13, fig. 15.
16. Verica-Berikos, Dio, *Hist.* LX, 19. Selsey, *AJ* XIV, 49, fig. 15, 14.
17. General source: *Frere,* ch. 5.
18. Tacitus, *Agricola,* 14.
19. *RIB* 91.
20. Josephus, *Bellum Judaicum* I, 399. Incidentally, Herod's kingdom was also extended.
21. K. Jackson, *B* I, 78.
22. *Legati juridici,* E. Birley, *Prosopographia Imp. Rom.* IV.3, 108, 14, cf. *102,* 38. Tile, our n. 26; royal estate taken over, *Applebaum,* 15, 29 (but only one tile is certain; and not the Little London one).
23. BM Add. MS 33658, f. 126.
24. Inner earthwork, *102,* 3 ff. Type, Wheeler-Richardson, *Hill Forts of Northern France,* 8 ff. British examples, M. A. Cotton, *Celticum* LXXIII–LXXV, 104; Danebury, B. Cunliffe, *AJ* LI, 246, fig. 5. Chichester road, A. Clarke, *PHFC* XXI, 82.
25. Outer earthwork, *102,* 15 ff. and illus. Winchester had a first-second cent. bank: *AJ* L, 284.
26. *59,* 355; tile, 366, fig. 13. The lettering is clearer on the drawing than on the original because a workman had stretched sacking over the die to prevent clogging; but because of this the ligature of ER in GERM is not certain. See p. 278.
27. *Ant* XXII, 172 (the discussion of house-types is now obsolete).
28. As a possible instance of a regular layout on the baths-alignment, take XXXIIIA.4—XXXV.2 (south wing) and XVII.3 parallel with the direct route east-west; XVIIIA.3 on a line at right-angles. The public baths are about 240 Roman ft. from the direct route; there is a block in Insula I about the same distance on the north side. Other instances may 'fit', e.g. XXI.B4, but pattern-making is deceptive. Streets were often long left unmetalled, cf. *Roman Colchester,* 180 and F. Fremersdorf, *Topographie des römischen Köln,* 32, with ref. to Augsburg.
29. Tacitus, *Annales* XII, 31: . . . *socialis copias.* . . .
30. G. Webster, *B* I, 183, note 26 suggests that the amount of early material points to a fort on the site; he envisaged the short angular length of street between the east gate and Insula XXVII perhaps

marking it. But the topography of Calleva would naturally result in a choice of site further west; and the main lot of material is Flavian, see next note. For the explanation of the angular length, see p. 55.

31. *57*, 244 with analysis by Gowland. *Lorica segmentata:* cf. the full-size figure in the Legionary Museum of Caerleon, made after the most modern findings by H. Russell Robinson of H. M. Tower of London. The *trulleus* is graduated on the inside for the measuring of rations. The late Dr Aladar Radnóti kindly confirmed my reading of the stamp with reference to three similar collected by Mme. Susanne Tassinari of Paris from Pompeii (unpublished). The *cognomen* is uncertain: *Augustalis* or *Augustanus* probably. Among other Flavian military objects is a fragment of a field-flask in terra sigillata by *Mommo* of La Graufesenque, very rare.

32. *102*, 49, fig. 7, c3. Sheep or goatskin according to the late J. MacIntyre, as at Valkenburg, W. Groenman-van Waateringe, *Nederlandse Oudheden* II. Tents as restored by Richmond and MacIntyre, cf. G. Webster, *The Roman Imp. Army,* fig. 26. *Sub pellibus,* 'under the skins', corresponds to our 'under canvas'.

CHAPTER 3 *(The Success of Urbanisation)*

1. Some huts have of course been found, e.g. *92, 124; 102, 12.*
2. Some earlier buildings underlie later and were sealed by gravel levelling, e.g. I.1 *(46, 332),* III.1 *(54, 424)* and others.
3. Cf. M. Todd, *B* I, 118.
4. Summary, *102, 39.* Flavian, main north-south and next street E.; peripheral Hadrianic, cf. *92,* 135, *127* fig. 2, *159,* fig. 13, 20, 39, N. of XXIIA. At Camulodunum, streets are Neronian, at Verulamium, pre-Flavian; at Canterbury, Claudian; at Winchester, probably regularised at the same time as Silchester and for the same reason so late, M. Biddle, *AJ* XLV, 240.
5. For the polygonal outline of the truncated area, Chichester is the best parallel, *CC* 110; Caistor St. Edmund was reduced, *ib.* pl. 3.
6. *Ancient Town Planning,* 129; cf. *Applebaum,* 34, who puts the matter in a nutshell. An interesting comparison is offered of areas likely to have been controlled and partly worked from hillforts, A. H. A. Hogg in *The Iron Age & its Hill Forts,* 118 ff.
7. *53,* pl. 32, thought to have been a bath-house, but evidence elusive.
8. *53,* pl. 21.

9. I.1, I.2, VI.B1, XIII.1, XV.2, XXIV.2? XXVII.B3, XXXII.3(?).

10. *53, 543,* pl. 41.

11. *102,* 41. Aerial survey on the E. shows the road S. of the suspected line.

12. *60,* 155, 165, pl. 21.

13. *80,* pl. 85; newest plan, O. E. Craster, *Official Guide* (1971).

14. *Verulamium Excav.* I, fig. 147; Wroxeter, *Official Guide;* Caistor, see n. 5.

15. See p. 317, n. 26.

16. *Roman Colchester,* 80, fig. 36 (two large semi-detached, in grounds, later thrown into one).

17. Gallic town-sizes, *ArJ* CXVI, 48; cf. Rivet, *CC,* 105, fig. 2.

18. *Grenier* III, fig. 48; Laur-Belart, *Führer durch Augusta Raurica* (1966), plan 3; J. Szilágyi, *Aquincum* (1956), Beilage 1; *CK,* Abb. 2.

19. Auxiliary soldiers' citizenship, G. R. Watson, *The Roman Soldier,* 136; *Constitutio Antoniniana,* cf. A. H. M. Jones, *JRS* XXVI, 223.

20. The arguments are summed up by J. E. Bogaers in a review, *JRS* LVII, 231–3.

21. Brough, *RIB* 707; Sens, *ILS* 7049; Wroxeter and Caerwent, *RIB* 288, 311.

22. *Ib.* 69–71; illus., *60,* pl. 24; Boon, *B* IV, 107–14, n. 51.

23. *CIL* XIII, 4679, a simple dedication by 'strangers' to the *Genius* of a village.

24. See Boon, *B* IV.

25. *HG* IV, ch. 8.

26. Caerwent, *RIB* 311; Chichester, 92.

27. Compare the north African situation, M. G. Jarrett, *Amer. Journ. Philology* XCII, 513 ff.

28. Corinium *duovir, B* II, 289 no. 3; Glevum tilery, E. M. Clifford, *JRS* XLV, 68 ff. Aedile of *vicus, RIB* 707; *questorius,* 933.

29. Cf. A. H. M. Jones, *Later Roman Emp.,* 755.

30. Ogilvie-Richmond, *Cornelii Taciti de vita Agricolae,* 215–16.

31. Ulpian, *Digest* XXXV, 2.68; cf. Gregory King's figure of 32 at birth, cited by P. Laslett, *The World we have Lost,* 93.

32. Cf. A. R. Burn, *Past & Present* IV, 14; Acsádi-Nemeskéri, *Life Span & Mortality,* ch. 6; K. Éry, *Alba Regia* X, 51. As late as 1907, the infant mortality-rate in rural England and Wales, for example, was 11.6%.

33. Cf. *62,* 447.

34. L. P. Wenham *et al., The R.B. Cemetery at Trentholme Drive,* pt. ii.

35. Ninety-seven infant-burials were discovered at Hambleden villa (Bucks.), *71*, 150. Lesser numbers, usually about one to four, frequently appear.

36. *59*, 369. Otherwise, infant-remains are somewhat few, even allowing for the fact that it was permissible to inter infants within a town: *52*, 743 (two, one in a pot); *53*, 572; *61*, 214 (two).

37. Cf. *ARB*, fig. 38. I have toyed with the idea of correlating seating-accommodation in the public baths latrine with that in military latrines provided for a known number of troops. At Silchester, the 11.5 m. run answers well to the Caerleon 10.5 m. run serving two cohorts: giving thus a population of around 2,000 since men and women bathed at different times. This promising line of approach ends, however, with recognition of the fact that the Housesteads latrine serving a milliary regiment (= two legionary cohorts) has almost twice the Caerleon seating.

38. *62*, 325. No trace of writing remains. Later identified as *Abies alba,* confirmed recently by my colleague Mr R. Perry from a separate splinter.

39. Ink-writing on tablets, e.g. from Chew Park, Som., *JRS* XLVI, 115, pl. 12. Pens were mostly of reeds and had wide, split nibs to judge by metal counterparts, not at Silchester. Inkwells, *May,* pl. 31, 25; *56*, 124, fig. 3; for a complete example of the type to which our fig. 21, 10 belonged, cf. F. Henry, *Préhistoire* II, 142, fig. facing.

40. *Puellam, 46,* 341, fig., *CIL* VII, 1259. A vulgar remark, *EE* IX, 1292A.

41. *EE* IX, 1223, a stray find of about 1850 (perhaps doubtful). For tags from Virgil and Horace, probably a calligrapher practising, *JRS* LVII, 60, pls. 1–2, on Egyptian papyrus; names on a thin sheet of lead, Leintwardine, *ib.* LIX, 241.

42. *58*, 30, fig. 3; *EE* IX, 1292B. Another occurrence of the word, plus a number indicative of the batch, Wiggonholt (Sussex), *JRS* XX, 187: *Pi(lares)* . . . *XX/Cuniati IV Tubu(li) N(umero) DLX. Pilares:* bricks for hypocaust pillars; *cuniati:* voussoirs. A third occurrence was at Barnsley Park villa (Glos.), 1972.

43. In *Confessions* VI, 3, St. Augustine records it as a notable fact, calling for comment, that St. Ambrose read to himself silently. If this was unusual in the cultivated circles of the late fourth century, it must have been equally so earlier, and more so among the lower classes.

44. Latin loan-words in Welsh, K. Jackson, *Language & History in Early Britain,* 78; take with D. Greene in *CB,* 76.

CHAPTER 4 *(Change in the Third and Fourth Centuries)*

1. *62*, 321, 325–6; *92*, 129, 132. Latest sigillata below the bank, *ib*. pl. 37A, 3, style of *Cettus, c.* A.D. 135/40–160.

2. *ArJ* CXVI, 26.

3. *AJ* XLI, 65. Timber gate at Winchester, *B* III, 348–9, fig. 19, late second century, soon superseded.

4. *Digest* L, 10.6; 1, 8.9.4. Unrest, Jarrett and Mann, *BJ* CLXX, 186; Boon, *Isca* (1972), 36. It is possible to over-estimate the effect of building the wall on agricultural production. In the Great War, Russian peasant agriculture actually flourished despite the departure of men to the Colours, though the far more scientific farming of the large estates suffered; cf. M. T. Florinsky, *The End of the Russian Empire* (1961), 35.

5. Coin, *62*, 325, at Reading. In pottery from the 'wall-trench' filling, *92*, 164–5, there is nothing necessarily later; the additions to the bank are however later; cf. Rhenish ware, *92*, fig. 15, 12–13, and cf. *JRS* LIX, 231 'late third century'.

6. Cf. *HG* IV, 274, 288, and notes; and the Urso (Spain) charter *ILS* 6087. (Indeed the 'man of tribunicial power' who met S. Germanus at Verulamium in 429 might have derived his authority from the provisions of such a charter, which gave civil magistrates the power of military tribunes in an emergency.)

7. *53*, 268, fig. There is a completed set from Zugmantel, *SJ* I, 48, Abb. 19, Taf. 8; component badges are widely scattered: in Britain, High Rochester (Northd.), J. C. Bruce, *Lapidarium Septentrionale,* 303; Aldborough, *AA* ser. 4 VII, 178, fig. 10—[*numerum*] *omnium* upside-down, one *militantium* only a scrap.

8. *54*, 470, fig. 6; cf. from Vechten the identical piece ('silver'), *Archaeologia Trajectina* III, pl. 2, 2; cf. in general A.Alföldi, *Amer. Journ. Arch.* LXIII, 1, figs.

9. Shows the *Genius Populi Romani,* the standard, and a long trumpet; cf. *BMC Gems* 3710 with plainer spearhead between trumpet and javelin-head *(pilum).* A *beneficiarius consularis* at Dorchester-on-Thames, *RIB* 235, conjectured by Richmond (*Roman Britain* (1963), 96) to have been connected with road and river transport and/or tax-collecting; late second, or more probably third, century.

10. Bow-tip, *52*, 757 ('netting-peg'), cf. Boon, *Isca* (1972), fig. 30—a common type, e.g. also at Bar Hill (Antonine Wall) where the garrison was a Syrian regt. of archers. For the type of bow, see G. Rausing,

The Bow, 137, fig. 52. Chapes, *Isca, ib.,* again a common type, at Richborough, etc. One chape and the backs of two others are in the collection. The complete chape came from the inn or *praetorium,* probably, since it is not among the many illustrations in the earlier part of the *Journal.*

11. Boon, *BAJ* LXIV, 38, refs.: the best parallel is at Carnuntum.

12. *54,* 140; *JRS* XLIV, 108; cf. *Notitia Dignitatum, Occidentis,* IX, 16 ff., e.g. *fabrica Ambiensis spatharia et scutaria* 'broadsword and shield manufactory at Amiens'.

13. See *102,* 21 for the negative result of excavation at a site where Aubrey appeared to indicate a tower. Caerwent, *80,* 251, figs., pls., for the south side: five are now known on the north, see *Official Guide* (1971), plan: spacing of these hollow towers is curiously irregular and none is known on the east or west walls despite recent clearance. Cardiff, *ARB,* fig. 20b; J. Ward, *57,* 335 ff., figs., pls.; etc. There is insufficient space to discuss the function of the towers in detail here. A *bastion* is of course altogether larger than a *tower,* as any manual of fortification will show, and did not exist *sensu stricto* in ancient times. There is no evidence that the towers of Romano-British town-walls were designed for, or contained, even from time to time, *ballistae* (though this latter possibility may be admitted). The theory that they were so designed was largely popularised by the late Philip Corder on the basis of Richmond's appraisal of the Aurelianic defences of Rome *(City Wall of Imp. Rome,* 80, cf. 67). It has been thought that the solid pear-shaped towers at Burgh Castle, 4.5 m. in greatest width, held *ballistae* mounted on heavy posts or turn-tables fixed in square central holes (about 60 × 60 cm.) still visible. But as G. E. Fox saw *(ArJ* XLVI, 348), when allowance is made for the side-walls, the available space is reduced to about 3 m. The smallest *ballista* in use measured about 1.3 m. in the stock and 1 m. across the arm and weighed only 50 kg. It required two highly-trained men to operate it and discharged 1 aimed shot per minute (E. W. Marsden, *Greek and Roman Artillery,* fig. 8, 1). Thus it could have been placed in such a tower, but there would not have been room for two to provide the necessary cross-fire (to cover the bases of adjacent towers, since the *ballista* could not be usefully depressed to discharge below the horizontal). Furthermore, there would have been no need or advantage in having a fixed upright or turn-table. The towers could scarcely have held larger *ballistae,* and are of course quite unsuitable for the stone-firing *onagri* with their high trajectory of shot: at High Rochester the emplacements for these are behind the ramparts and very

large. Thus there was no advantage in having *ballistae* in the towers as a regular part of the system of defence. Archers were more readily recruited (Marsden *o.c.*, 197 points out the extreme scarcity of artillerymen in the late Imperial army) and fired more easily and quickly. Even at Rome, and supposing Richmond's theory is correct, the towers were modified by the end of the fourth century for the use of archers. Artillery-defence on the Hellenistic pattern was rare in the late empire, cf. Aurelian's own letter on the difficult siege of Palmyra (*SHA Aurelian*, 26).

14. S. Hawkes and G. C. Dunning, *MA* V, I ff.; countryside, S. Hawkes, *Shakenoak* III, 74 ff. Winchester, Larkhills Cemetery, G. Clarke, *AJ* L, 295, fig. 4. Dorchester, Hawkes-Dunning, *l.c.*, fig. 1. Lydney and other comparisons, Boon, *MA* III, 79. Reading, Hawkes-Dunning, 45, fig. 14; date, *ASPSE*, 91. Blewburton, Hawkes-Dunning, fig. 14; beads, Boon, 81.

15. *VCH Hants.* I, 275.

16. In general, *Frere*, 335 etc.; strategy, D. Eicholz, *JRS* XLIII, 41.

17. Carausius, *NC* 1902, 360–1, pl. 19, 9; *Lockett Sale* lot 152 (Herzfelder). Allectus, *Phil. Trans.* XLV, 610, pl. 4, 5, clearly the same as in B.M. ex Wigan; cf. *NC* 1865, 106, no. 179.

18. *46, 367.*

19. *Frere*, 375; *CC*, 87.

20. *59, 354.*

21. *46*, 364 (hoard, omitted by me in *NC* 1960, 24): Theodosian bronze ending with Arcadius, *Journal* 21 Sept. 1869. Inn, *Journal* 31 March 1876; temple, *52, 747.*

22. *Cabrol-Leclercq* III.2, 2519; cf. II.1, fig. 1287. It cannot be quite excluded that the bishop was a visitor, esp. as ancillary buildings are unknown, cf. Radford, *MA* XV, 3.

23. Arles bishops, conveniently, *Ant* XXXV, 317. The bishops of the British and Gallic provinces are mentioned together in the dedication of Hilary of Poitiers' *De Synodis*. . . of 358 against the Arians, written in exile (text, E. Griffe, *La Gaule chrétienne* I, 177, n. 26). I owed this reference to Mr Francis Needham. It would be difficult to say that any Gallic church except Lyons and Arles had a resident territorial bishop before 313, cf. R. Louis, *S. Germain d'Auxerre et son temps* (Soc. des Sciences de l'Yonne, 1950), 43. Spread of bishoprics, Griffe *o.c.*, 123.

24. *JRS* LII, 186, gives Richmond's preliminary view. One or two subsequent writers have mistakenly stated as a fact that the coins came from the bedding of the floor. This is false; and nothing can be made of

their stratification. Nothing of datable value was found in the bedding, which was entirely dug up in 1961.

A handful of mostly early Roman shards came from the surface of the gravel metalling around the forum, where it remained under the church, and from a thin layer of spoil spread on top of it from the foundation-trenches of the church walls. The latest certain identifiable piece was a small fragment of late Antonine samian Form 79. That all the 'dating material' should come from a single source—a squatter's hollow—and nothing whatever should remain sealed in the actual bedding, is the chief of several improbabilities. Three of the coins were said to have mortar on them. Richmond agreed eventually to have these scientifically examined. I am indebted to Professor Frere for permission to refer here to the results of the examination, which was carried out at the British Museum Research Laboratory. Two of the three were examined spectrographically and the crust was found to be composed mainly of lead phosphate and not mortar. Probably we have traces here of a cupellation-process designed to extract silver from coins (cf. p. 275), though hardly on the spot. In *PSAL* XX, 214 Gowland refers verbally to cupellation-remains in the area excavated in 1905, i.e. Insulae V–VI opposite the forum. The coins with the incrustation were an early Constantine, of A.D. 309–10, almost unworn, and Urbs Roma and 'falling horseman' copies of *c.* 340 and *c.* 360. No coins later than Constantine were found in the church.

25. *58*, pl. 2; XIV.2 mosaic with cement upon it, *55*, 242; other mosaics, p. 213 below.

26. *40*, pl. 24; *57*, pl. 31—centre entirely tiled, border of soft white chalk cubes. Some Italian floors, e.g. at Pompeii (M. E. Blake, *MAAR* VIII, pl. 8) have tesserae around central marble panels, but at Silchester a repair of former tessellation is more likely.

27. *46*, 340; *Journal* 7 Feb. 1874 and 16 July for scattered hoard (also omitted from my *NC* 1960 list): pre-330 (8); 330–41 (88); 341–8 (6); Gratian (1). Cf. the Insula I hoard ending with a solitary Valentinianic, my list no. 7.

28. *Hearne* IV, 360. Presumably a silver piece *(siliqua)*: these are the commonest.

29. Apart from the forum hoard, n. 21, they appear to be separate finds, not as at Caerwent. In *GM* 1792, 529, pl. 3, 5 a very odd gold piece *(solidus,* 4.34 g.) of Arcadius is mentioned.

30. Verulamium, A. Ravetz, *NC* 1964, 202, fig. 1a.

31. Late objects, *MA* III, 81. Argonne fragment, *May* pl. 38, 9, with Chenet's molette 132; cf. Hübener *BJ* CLXVIII, 241, Group 7. There

are shards of fourteen bowls of Form 37 (Chenet 320), mostly Group I, *c.* 325–50; and Forms 31 and 45, identified by P.-H. Mitard. Lamp, 57, 110, after *c.* 390; cf. M. Ponsich, *Lampes de la Maurétanie tingitane,* cf. 370, Type IV, fig. 4. There is a mould from Forlì showing that the type was copied (*surmoulage*) in Europe (G. Ballardini, *L'Eredità ceramistica dell'antico mondo romano,* figs. 14–15) but ours is of true north African fabric. A very similar lamp, save that the palms were 'one sided', was shown in 1969 at the National Museum of Wales as a tourist's find near Tripoli. On the Christian significance of the horse, see M. G. Abbiani, *Lucerne fittili paleocristiane nell'Italia settentrionale,* 184, citing *II Timothy* 4, vv. 7–8.

CHAPTER 5 (*The End: A Problem*)

1. Zosimus, *Hist.* VI, 10.
2. J. Morris in Dobson and Jarrett, *Britain & Rome,* 145: I have followed his account generally. J. N. L. Myres, *JRS* L, 21, and *ASPSE;* Frere in *CC,* 87; and L. Alcock, *Arthur's Britain* may also be consulted. A. H. M. Jones, *Later R. Emp.,* 190 maintained that Britain was briefly re-occupied after 410, but Procopius, *Vandalic War* I, 2 seems sufficient to dismiss the possibility.
3. J. P. C. Kent in M. Dolley, *Anglo-Saxon Coins,* 5.
4. *MA* III, 82, 86; *RS* fig. 15, 1; cf. E. Fowler, *ArJ* CXX, 122, n. 5 (late dating); third is probably J. Ward, *The Roman Era in Britain,* 247, top row.
5. *Newstead* 337, pl. 92, 11; Boon, *Isca* (1972), fig. 18, note 104. Another from Silchester might be a local copy, the head being curiously formed, and lacking enamel. None has provision for a chain.
6. Caerwent, e.g. H. N. Savory in *DAB,* pl. 5g; fig. 10 for distribution (except Silchester). Anglo-Saxon graves, Bifrons and Nassington, Northants, *ArJ* CXX, fig. 6, 7 and *AJ* XXIV, pl. 30, 11a. Friesland, *MA* III, 87; cf. Fowler *l.c.,* fig. 3, 2. Scotland, Longfaugh, *PSASc* II, 237. Holyhead, *ArJ* XXXIII, 131. Kingsweston, *TBGAS* LXXXVI, 195.
7. *MA* III, 82, refs. Mendip, *PUBSS* XIII, 67, no. 1, fig. 22. Poor parallel? Harnham, Salisbury, *30,* pl. 19, 6.
8. Killescragh, Co. Galway, E. Rynne, *Trans. Dumfries & Galloway Antiq. Soc.* ser. 3 XLII, 102, fig. 2. Pembrokeshire, Savory, *l.c.,* fig. 11, 5; a variety of a common type in the west.
9. Alcock, *o.c.,* 201 for the most recent discussion of this pottery.

10. *MA* III, 83 and one or two other objects, including a bronze pin with faceted head from a linked pair, typically Saxon with its conical expansion of the lower stem (our fig. 9, 5); and an 'upsilon' bucket-binding as e.g. Baldwin Brown, *Arts in Early England,* pls. 112–13. The eighth-century Byzantine follis mentioned *RS,* 80 and *MA* III, 84 has no place here and no proper link with Silchester. It came with Roman and English coins bought by the Duke from the farmer in 1864; only the Roman ones need have come from Silchester, the medieval English groats, etc. might be a hoard. I have recorded now some 120 Byzantine coppers in Britain and in no case with the possible exception of a pierced follis of Anastasius from Ilchester, Som.—i.e. not used as currency, but as ornament—is it possible to maintain that the coins are anything but recent losses.

11. Cf. the name *weala brucge*—'Welsh', i.e. 'British bridge' given to the bridge carrying the western highway over the Kennet, later known as Quaking Bridge for obvious reasons (Birch, *Cartularium Sax.,* 802, *BAJ* XXIX, 207).

12. 54, 233, 441; stone, *MA* III, 87.

13. Cf. R. A. S. Macalister, *Corpus Inscript. Insular. Celtic.* I, xi, xvii (overstated).

14. V. E. Nash-Williams, *The Early Christian Monuments of Wales,* nos. 43, 288, Crickhowell and Loughor, for the nearest with and without a parallel Latin text.

15. Dorchester, occupation in town later than cemetery outside, Frere, *ArJ* CXIX, 123; Winchester, *ASPSE,* 112; *AJ* LII, 101–2.

16. *Ant* XVIII, 114, n. 3; *AJ* XLVIII, 299, cf. *MA* III, 87.

17. In *Custom is King,* 188.

18. *Ant* XVII, 188; XVIII, 113; *ArJ* C, 178, with H. Peake; cf. also R. Gilyard-Beer, *BAJ* LIV, 56.

19. *ASPSE,* 89; J. R. Kirk, *DAB,* fig. 24.

20. *ASPSE,* 91; two late coin-hoards, Boon, *Oxon* XIX, 41–2.

21. Ekwall, *Dict. Eng. Place-Names* (1960), but see Dodgson, *MA* X, 1 on *-inga* names.

22. Anglo-Saxon remains in Hants. are recently mapped by A. Meaney and S. Hawkes, *The A.-S. Cemeteries at Winnal,* fig. 1, but the inhumation at Basingstoke is Viking (Shetelig, *Viking Antiqs. of Gt. Britain,* 11). A fine late Saxon sword dredged from the Loddon near Stratfield Saye a few years ago (Reading Museum: Thames Conservancy Board loan) exemplifies the use of the river as a highway and helps to explain the Basingstoke burial.

23. *ASPSE,* 91.
24. *ArJ* CIV, 26.
25. *ArJ* C, 180, fig. 3; *Gillam,* nos. 102 (roughly) and 147.
26. *JRS* LIII, pl. 14, 2.
27. *ASPSE,* 114; cf. Map 8.
28. *The Practice of History* (1969), 20.
29. *De Excidio Britanniae,* 24–5; cf. 19, not actually naming Vortigern except by a periphrasis; cf. Nennius, *Historia Brittonum* 31.
30. *EHR* XIX, 628. Noricum, details from Eugippius, *Vita S. Severini.*
31. *CC,* 98.
32. *Reading Mercury* 18 Feb. 1833, quoted 50, 274. Cf. Wroxeter, Anderson, *Uriconium* 23, 108. A Caistor St. Edmund find is obscure: *JRS* XXI, 232.
33. 57, 111.
34. 60, 164.
35. *Journal,* 16 May 1867, cf. 53, 572.
36. 52, 755. Other human bones came from the outer ditch, *53, 572, 62, 325, Hearne* IV, 363: but caution is needed in assessing stray finds of this kind, which could have been redeposited from earlier levels; cf. *102, 52.*
37. Cf. *46, 330, 333,* where the dilapidated state of the floor beneath the upper ash is mentioned.
38. *De Excidio,* 22; cf. C. E. Stevens, *EHR* LVI, 363 and Myres in *Aspects of Arch.,* 228.
39. See n. 2.

CHAPTER 6 *(Water Supply and Drainage)*

1. *61, 213* for a possible 'British water-hole', wicker-lined; cf. *AJ* L, pl. 31a (Dragonby, Lincs.). Other wicker linings, Roman, *54, 444, 57, 94;* cf. *AJ* L, pl. 31b.
2. Extremes, 2.5 and 9 m., *58, 424, 55, 245.*
3. *57, 244.* Inclined oak sides and five (surviving) fir rungs fixed with wedges at 35 cm. intervals; cf. R. Merrifield, *Roman London,* pl. 113. Ladder-making on a Pompeian fresco, A. Maiuri, *Pompeii* (1960), fig. 88.
4. *60, 161.* A good tool for work in confined spaces, as both the Neolithic flint- and Roman copper-miners (of the Great Orme) found.
5. Alder for the usual oak, *58, 421.* Good drawing of struts ('rungs') in a Wickford, Essex example, *B* I, 291. Barrels, fifteen: *54, 447; 55, 245*

(two), 414,418; *56,* 107, 108, 121 (two), 238 (two wells); *58,* 415, 423; *60,* 152, 161. Similar linings on many other sites; cf. G. Ulbert, *Bayerische Vorgeschichtsblätter* XXIV, 6–29. Flint lining, *60,* 160; brick, *PSAL* XX, 339.

6. *52,* 743. There is an oak pulley-wheel, 11 cm. diam., in the collection.

7. Fir bucket, *54,* 222, pewter bucket, *58,* 32; amphora, *55,* 418 (crack repaired with resinous compound). Bark rope, *61,* 481.

8. *Vitruvius* X, 12. Bolsena, *55,* 254 (British Museum). Sotiel, G. Gossé, *Ampurias* IV, pl. 14; M. Luzon, *Archivo esp. de Arqueológia* XLI, 119, fig. 16, does not show the squirt from the side. Trier, *Ber. RGK* XXVI, 128. See also now *TZ* XXXV,109–21.

9. *57,* 415 (Gowland). Tin occurs with lead ores in Britain only in a few Cornish localities (information kindly supplied by Dr E. H. Beard, Institute of Geological Sciences). But no Roman pig from Britain contains tin, as Gowland pointed out, and a deliberate addition seems likely. (Seventeenth–eighteenth century pipes from Liège, however, contained 0.7% tin, Buffet-Evrard, *L'eau potable à travers les ages,* 149.)

10. *ArJ* CI, 124, envisaging the use of such a pump on the Lincoln aqueduct.

11. *53,* 570; cf. *60,* 155.

12. *50,* 276, pl. 17; *54,* 321, pl. 17.

13. *59,* 363, pl. 73.

14. *60,* 160, pl. 21.

15. *55,* 522, fig. 2 (but section on south side of gateway: line only of pipes, not of base, projected on to it).

16. Fixing of collars, Buffet-Evrard, *o.c.,* 149, fig. 139. Caerwent, *57,* 300, 309; *59,* 93, pl. 9; *60,* 122, 126; *61,* 566, pl. 91, 426, pl. 60. Probably fed from the Troggy brook tapped 2 km. NW of the town via a *castellum aquae* just outside the walls. Other Roman pipes, rectangular section, *LRT,* pl. 12. Cf. Plommer, *Vitr. & later R. Bdg. Manuals,* 50, 52.

17. See *102,* 10, pl. 7K. Central gutters are well-known in other towns.

18. *53,* 544. On the analogy of the third-century central gutters elsewhere in the town, this should also be 'late', but no earlier arrangements came to light.

19. Cicero, *De Oratore* I, 38.173; and *Digest* VIII.2.21 [20], 6.8.

20. The excavators made an exaggerated case of this, *59,* 363.

21. *59,* 343.

22. Stream: 'Roman fountain' is marked on 1st ed. O.S. plan and on excavation-plans to 1899: it depends on the Collet letter otherwise quoted above, p. 23, largely repeated in *Phil. Trans.* 1748, that 'this good

spring of water, generally running & but seldom dry in a hot Summer' was cleared out in 1741, and several large stones were found in it 'which inclin'd them to think a Conduit or some such building was erected over it'. Nothing was reported in the 1906 excavation of the area. All may have gone when Chalk Meadow was enlarged in the late eighteenth or early nineteenth century. Culvert in wall, *58*, 419.

23. *59*, 364, figs. 12, 7.
24. *54*, 229f., pls. 17, 20.
25. *55*, 235, pl. 15; Boon, *Isca* (1972), fig. 53.
26. The brick-built drain adjacent to XXVII.B1–2 is puzzling, for it begins below the modern track. It is the only one of its kind on the site except at the baths, and might have served a latrine flushed by water brought from a spring to the north, by pipe-line. See *61*, 201–2, figs. 1–2, pl. 22.
27. Caerwent, *57*, 301, pl. 40. Ho. 3S; cf. also 12S (inns?). Wroxeter, I. A. Richmond, *Roman Britain* (1963), 107. The provision of decent sewerage depended on there being plenty of surplus water, either a stream, or piped. Such drainage is typical of the more 'Roman' side of Roman Britain and is best exemplified in the legionary fortress of Caerleon and at Lincoln *colonia*, Boon *o.c.* 25, n. 61; J. B. Whitwell, *Roman Lincs.*, 31, reproduces a nineteenth-century engraving of the main sewer with branches. Rarity of flushed privies in cities generally, cf. J. Carcopino, *Daily Life in Ancient Rome* (1956), 48.
28. *Columella* II, 15; XI, 2.12. Modern, J. Loudon, *Encyl. Cottage Farm and Villa Archit.* (1833), 249, no. 502 is an instance.
29. *61*, 212 (house wrongly numbered 3); cf. 203.
30. *53*, 562, 573 (for 'thick', read 'deep from surface').
31. *60*, 165.

CHAPTER 7 *(In the Steps of the Roman Street-Surveyor)*

1. A denarius of Julia Maesa, struck under Elagabalus *c.* 218–22, slightly worn, was found in silt on the surface next below the uppermost which contained the drain (unpublished section of 1961, east of the forum).
2. Throughout this book, Imperial measure as used in the reports has been converted to metric by a British Standard conversion-slide, decimal places being rounded off as appropriate; similarly the nearest round number has been taken when desirable.
3. Cf. *57*, pl. 32; *54*, 450; *60*, 149.
4. *Vitruvius* I, 6. Caerleon (aligned north-west/south-east) is a better case, and much more densely built up: here the surveyor anticipated development, which never occurred.

5. *Ibid.* and *GV* I, 188.
6. M. della Corte, *Monumenti Antichi* XXVIII, 5 ff.
7. G. de Montauzan, *La science et l'art de l'ingénieur aux premiers siècles de l'empire romain,* 46; O. A. W. Dilke, *Roman Land Surveyors* for procedures.
8. M. Green, *CA* II, 134.
9. J. Wacher, *AJ* XLIII, 25; XLIV, 18.
10. RCHM *Dorset* II.3, 589.
11. *53,* pl. 41.
12. *53,* pl. 21; for Insulae X–XI, *54,* pl. 46. The urban divisions *(merides)* at Orange were let by foot-frontage, the depth not being given, presumably because it was constant: A. Piganiol, *Les documents cadastraux d'Orange,* 333.
13. *Ancient Town Planning,* 129 n. 1.
14. *ARB,* figs. 33–4; Wroxeter may have parcels 120 by 360 *pedes* in one part only, *TSAS* LVII, fig. 29.
15. Haverfield, *o.c.,* 111 (*70 pedes*). His statement, *ib.,* 79, that 'in most towns, though not in all, the dimensions approximate to 120 ft. or some multiple' never was really acceptable.
16. J. Ewald on Insula XXX at Augst, *Provincialia* 96, Abb. 11; referring to Laur-Belart's work on Insula XXIV, suggests for the first, squares of 38 *pedes,* and for XXIV, rectangles of 30 by 70 *pedes,* both within a 10 *pedes* border.
17. J. E. Lee, *Isca Silurum* (1862), 68, pl. 35, 11, opened and cleaned by myself. The Silchester rule was of the same kind; I found it in a box of miscellaneous scraps.
18. *GV* I, 123.
19. *Grenier* III.1, 37 mentions a few other measures instanced in Gaul.
20. Cf. *58,* pl. 2.
21. *54,* pl. 17; p. 210 gives the north-south dimension as 470 ft. (143.26 m.) but the insula-plan gives less; the 1908 plan, *61,* pl. 85, gives about 128 m.
22. *102, 20.*

CHAPTER 8 *(The Town Wall: An Expensive Undertaking)*

1. Caerwent, *AC* ser. 6 XVI, 16; York, I. A. Richmond, *Proc. Brit. Acad.* XLI, 311, fig. 3.
2. *54,* 231; *58,* 419 (for 'west' read 'south'); *62,* 322; *102,* 3.

3. J. Ward, *AC l.c.*, 12, fig. 2; also e.g. at Segontium midway between south-west gate and corner turrets. At Silchester only one is in an angle (north-east) and others are merely near.

4. Melville, 92, 143. Some Corallian Jurassic from north-west Berks., Hawkins, *MA* III, 87. The traditional mode of hand-quarrying probably reflects Roman practice well; cf. *Country Life* 21 Oct. 1971, 1082. A diorama in Bonn, Landesmuseum, shows the Roman mode of working a large quarry. (We may add here that some Roman lime-kilns are known in Britain; but the best-studied are in a row at Iversheim; cf. W. Sölter, *Römische Kalkbrenner im Rheinland* for details).

5. *AJ* VI, 75–6.

6. Ptolemy, *Geogr.* II, 3.28, 'Hydata therma'.

7. *RIB*, 179; *Applebaum*, 29.

8. 52, 757; Fox Coll. IV, 38: 86 × 48 cm., fillet at the edges, lewis-hole; but short (?complete), 70 cm. long.

9. R. Florescu, *Trajanssäule* Taff. 36, 38; E. Nash, *Pictorial Dict. Ancient Rome* I, 221, fig. 254. Embrasures in Aurelian's Wall vary from 1.5 to 2.7 m. wide with 1 m. merlons; the spacing is equal in the Maxentian work: see I. A. Richmond, *City Wall of Imperial Rome,* 59, figs. 7, 69.

10. The maximum cart-load permitted for the (long-distance) government transport, to save the road-surfaces probably, was 1500 *librae, Cod. Theod.* VIII, 3.8. The main road to the west, sectioned near the town, was only 30–40 cm. thick, *102,* 21, pl. 10.

11. These figures depend on the following calculation:

    (1) *Volume of wall.* Average area of parapet is $[(1.8 \times 0.75) + (1.1 \times 0.75)] \div 2 = 1.09$ m². Area of upper wall is $(3.4 \times 2.3) = 7.82$ m², and area of lower wall is $(2.6 \times 2.9) = 7.54$ m². Total area thus 16.45 m². Length of wall is taken as 2430 m. Volume therefore $(16.45 \times 2430) = 39973.5$ m³.

    (2) *Bonding-stone.* Allow three courses and a plinth in the lower wall and four courses in the upper, each 0.25 m. thick. Volume is therefore $[(4.0 \times 0.25 \times 2.9) + (4.0 \times 0.25 \times 2.3)] \times 2430 = 12636$ m³; but of this allow 25% for mortar, result 9477, say 9500 m³. Taking weight of Oölite as 2480 kg/m³ and dividing the product into cart-loads of 500 kg., the *number of loads* is $(9500 \times 2480) \div 500 = 47120$, say 45000.

    (3) *Flint.* Volume by difference $(39973.5 - 12636.0) \times 0.75 = 20503.13$ m³, say 20500. Taking the weight of flint as 2560 kg/m³, and dividing into cartloads of 500 kg., the *number of loads* is $(20500 \times 2560) \div 500 = 104960$, say 105000.

(4) *Mortar*, volume is $(39973.5 \times 0.25) = 9993.375$, say 10000 m³.

12. *46*, 345, pl. 15, 1; *61*, 474, pl. 84, details restored after west gate.
13. *52*, 753, pl. 31, 2 as reinterpreted.
14. *52*, pl. 31. Oakwood, *PSASc* LXXXVI, 89, fig. 5; Haltwhistle, *AA* ser, 3 V, pl. 2; Portchester, B. Cunliffe, *AJ* XLIII, pl. 34, LII, 78 fig. 9.
15. Cf. T. Bechert, *BJ* CLXXI, 240; H. v. Petrikovits, *JRS* LXI, 201 points to the long continuance of the 'forecourt' type.
16. *AC* CIII, 54; *BBCS* XV, 235. Caerwent wall need not be much earlier than the towers added to it *c.* 340.
17. *52*, 757, pls. 31, 3, 33.
18. See note 12. Repairs to S. tower, *61*, 475.
19. *Verulamium*, pls. 22–3; Cirencester, *AJ* XLI, 66, fig. 1; London, RCHM *London* III, fig. 24.
20. Richmond explained when considering the towers of gateways of Hadrian's Wall forts that the ridge of the roof would have lain parallel with the line of the defences so that missiles hitting it would roll harmlessly to front or back, and not on to defenders as might occur in the contrary case. Such a roof would not be practicable in the case of rectangular towers.
21. *Journal* 16 and 24 Sept. 1873; *52*, 750, pl. 31, 1; *46*, 348, pl. 15, 2; *52*, 753, pl. 31, 2; at both gates, the roadway was of pitched flints, and the side-walls stand on it; it therefore served an earlier structure. Similar gate with guard-rooms, Caistor St. Edmund, *JRS* XXV, 213.
22. *AC* ser. 6 XVI, 17, fig. 10.
23. *55*, 425, pls. 23–5; *40*, 416; *54*, 237; *61*, pl. 83, 92, 130, fig. 4 (misleading as to thickness of the town-wall), pl. 32D.
24. *92*, 131, pl. 33; cf. pls. 33A, 31, which contrast the character of the bank behind very neatly: at the gate there is no sign of the 'wall-trench' filling, the gravel running right up to the wall: probably there was a 'bank period' gateway here.
25. *54*, 230, pls. 17, 20; culvert for public baths and stream, *58*, 419.
26. *92*, 133, pl. 30, 198 m. NW of the amphitheatre gate, apparently. Largely open, *102*, 10 and n. 4; pl. 8; road, *62*, 323.
27. *92*, 135, *RS* 85; cf. Wroxeter, *TSAS* LVIII, 216; visible at Caistor St. Edmund and probably quite common in town-defences.
28. *92*, 135. Petrikovits *l.c.*, 197, says that the earliest known instance of a wide outer ditch is of the time of Postumus, A.D. 260–9.
29. *Journal*, 24 Sept. 1873; *62*, 319 fig. 2.
30. See p. 310, n. 13.

31. *59, 90,* figs. 4–5 (note lintel formed of coping-stone for the sallyport); *80,* 259, fig. 7, pl. 81, 2. For a military gateway of the period, cf. the north gate of Cardiff: a photograph showing both towers before the Bute restoration is in my article in *Glam. Historian* I (1963), pl. 1B.

32. *52,* 754, pl. 34; *52,* 750, cf. *46,* pl. 15, 2; *RIB,* 68; *55,* 424, pls. 24–5; *54,* 230, pl. 20; *40,* 416.

CHAPTER 9 *(The Forum-Basilica)*

1. *ArJ* XXX, 21; *46,* 349; *53,* 540; *61,* 474.

2. Shard, *Journal* 16 July 1867: Form 27, now at Reading; coins, *ArJ* XXX, 26; *46,* 374. Winchester and Chichester. *Frere,* 204.

3. H. Kähler, *Röm.-germ. Forschungen* XIII, 27, 32; Bath, *JRS* XLV, pl. 23; Caerwent, *61,* 573.

4. Xanten (Neronian) and other legionary *principia:* see verso of Nat. Museum of Wales, *Plan of Caerleon* (1967); Caerleon, *AC* CXIX, 14, fig. 2: a close relationship is evident with Caerwent, *61,* 91.

5. Rodenwaldt, *Gnomon* II, 339; *Wroxeter 1923–7,* Appendix C. Cf. Tacitus, *Agricola,* 21 and in this connexion *ILS* 5795 (Atkinson).

6. J. B. Ward Perkins, *JRS* LX, 6.

7. M. R. Hull, *Roman Colchester,* fig. 81. Lincoln is doubtful. Verulamium, cf. my note in *AC* CXIX, 20, n. 30.

8. The overall measurements of 84.43 × 95.50 m. correspond to 319, say 320 × 356, say 355 *pedes monetarii* and 256 × 288 *pedes Drusiani.*

9. *JRS* LX, 7; *Grenier* III.1, 344.

10. Kempten, W. Kleiss, *Die öffentlichen Bauten von Cambodunum,* Beilage 3; Cyrene, *JRS* XXXVIII, 62, fig. 7; Corinium, *PSAL* XVII, 203 with *AJ* XLII, 7, fig. 3; Basilica Ulpia, e.g. Banister Fletcher, *Hist. of Archit.,* 143B, 165B.

11. A partial parallel (square and apsidal) at Doclea, P. Sticotti, *Schriften der Balkankommission* VI, 107, fig. 57; apse omitted by Wilkes, *Dalmatia.*

12. BM Add. MS 6181, f. 15; J. Driehaus, *BJ* CLXIX, 424 for more elaborate types; also n. 36.

13. Misleadingly called 'a shallow pan' in *46,* 355: see *Journal* 30 Jan. 1867 for sketch. Cf. A. Maiuri, *Pompeii* (1960), fig. 95, etc. and in general T. Kléberg, *Hôtels restaurants et cabarets dans l'antiquité romaine,* 16.

14. Coins, *Journal* 27 Feb. 1868: radiates (7), Constantinian (28), Valentinianic (4), rest 'worthless'. A silver Licinius is a rare piece. Banking, exchange, purchase: cf. M. Crawford, *JRS* LX, 43; J. R.

Melville Jones, *Bull. Inst. Classical Stud.* XVIII, 99–105; J. P. C. Kent in *Essays pres. to H. Mattingly,* 191.

15. *Richter,* fig. 505; H. Lamer, *Röm. Kultur in Bilde,* Abb. 117— unfortunately the wife doing the accounts is cut off in A. Birley, *Life in R.B.,* 109. See also n. 18 and our p. 339, n. 4.

16. *53,* 545 ff. and *The Builder* 7 April 1894, 264, illus. after 272.

17. Based on a 56 cm. basal diameter and proportions according to *Vitruvius* IV, 7.

18. M. Rostovtzeff, *Social and Econ. Hist. Rom. Emp.* (1957), pl. 30, 2; Lamer, *o.c.* Abb. 115.

19. *Basilica principiorum* and *thermarum* at Caerleon, for example, 66.2 × 29 and 62 × 23.7 m.; civil basilica at Caerwent, 63.3 × 18.3 m.

20. Trier, W. Reusch, *G* XXXIII, 184, fig. Cf. timber-lengths in a fragment of Diocletian's maximal edict of 301, *JRS* LX, 124: oak is quoted in beams only 6.4 × 0.9 m., but fir goes to 22.8 × 1.8 m. Cf. lengths of Silchester oak planks, our p. 208.

21. If an original western stereobate had been grubbed up and another laid exactly by the side, the weight imposed upon it would have caused subsidence into the softer filling of the old trench. If there were separate pier-foundations as at Caerleon *(basilica thermarum)* they would have been about 1.5 m. square and deep and could hardly have been missed. Magnesia, Priene: Wymer, *Marktplatzanlagen* Abb. 1–3; Pompeii, Abb. 8; Rome, Banister Fletcher *o.c.* 143B; Zuglio, G. Mansuelli, *Urbanistica cisalpina,* tav. 29; Vidy, *Grenier* III.1, fig. 172; Caistor, *B* II, 4, fig. 2; fortresses, see n. 4 above; auxiliary forts, *AA* ser. 2 XXV, pl. 15, XLVI, pl. 1.

22. Rome, Banister Fletcher *l.c.;* Augst, R. Laur-Belart, *Führer durch Augusta Raurica* (1966), Abb. 16, 22 (not 17, which shows later arrangement, despite caption). *Vitruvius'* own basilica at Fano (V, 1) was of the short-axis type, with a temple of Augustus corresponding to our *aedes* at Silchester.

23. *JBAA* XVI, 92: 76 cm. diam. and hence not belonging to any other building, even if found in the garden of a (vanished) cottage near the amphitheatre. Not mentioned by Joyce or Fox.

24. Augst, Laur-Belart *o.c.,* Plan 1; reconstruction in 1948 ed. only, Abb. 17. Caerwent, *61,* 576, fig. 3, pl. 91.

25. *54,* 443, 90 × 60 × 12 cm.; mouldings, *53,* pl. 39, key overleaf; chalk strips wrongly thought by Joyce to be intended for tesserae, *Journal* 8 Oct. 1866; cf. *57,* 241, n.*b.*

26. 'Campan vert from quarries at Bagnières de Bigorre', *53,* 265, 270.

27. Cf. the richly-painted room at Caerwent basilica, 60, pl. 19. There is much good plaster at Caerwent, including figured work, mostly unpublished.

28. Fox Coll. IV, 67 for the Purbeck slab (with corner ornament as crossed shields, probably early) and IV, 37 for the Bath stone slab. Another top of this kind from VII.3, 50, pl. 16. Such tops are common in the west country, rarely as far east as Silchester (cf. *JRS* LII, 185, fig. 29, pl. 24, 2, West Park villa). It is hoped that Mr W. Solley of Bristol will shortly publish his corpus of examples.

29. Cf. *monopodia* with rectangular tops from Mont Auxois *(Esp. 7126)* and elsewhere, e.g. Pompeii, G. Boyce, *MAAR* XIV, pls. 32, 2, 33, 2.

30. *Esp.* 5156 shows a solid jointed chair with cushion, perhaps the type in use here; 5140 for a famous banking-scene of the sort of payment which must often have been made in the basilica; 5176 for the equally famous lost relief of a bookcase with rolls of documents, better in Sandys, *Companion to Latin Stud.,* fig. 24.

31. *RIB,* 84–5, probably *not* from separate inscriptions; 86 (for a leaf-stop in bronze, J. E. Lee, *Isca Silurum* (1862), pl. 37, 2); *Civitas Atrebatum,* 73. Some fragments are shown in photographs, *VCH Hants. I,* facing 280, 282.

32. *ArJ* XXX, 24; *53,* 558; Boon, *B* IV 107–14 (identification of the stone, by Dr F. G. Dimes of the Institute of Geological Sciences). Origin of such statues, G. Ferguson, *Religions of the R. Emp.,* 84; see also *PW* 2.VII, 1599 for examples, and J. Toutain, *Cultes païens* I, 448.

33. *Add. to Journal,* 27 Nov. 1882; Fox Coll. IV, 57. Statues of private persons were not over life-size.

34. *53,* 557; I. A. Richmond, *AJ* XXIV, 7, with sketch of evolution; Caerleon, *AC* CXIX, 41, figs., pl. 13; Segontium, *AJ* LII, 332. In general, G. Gamer, *G* XLVI, 53 ff. Manufacture, Ch. Boube-Piccot, *Bronzes antiques du Maroc* I, 33.

35. *Journal,* 9 Oct. 1866, section at 27 Sept.; *GM* 1866, 776; *46, 363,* pl. 17 in colour; Toynbee, *Art in R.B.,* no. 60. No exact parallel exists. Some small figures of Jupiter, copied from some large original, show an eagle at the feet or on the arm (S. Reinach, *Répertoire de la statuaire gr. et rom., passim; ib.* IV, 9 for an eagle as the base of a bust). The wing from Lons-le-Saunier *(RS,* 100) was rightly republished by P. Lebel as that of a Victory. The London bird *(JBAA* XXIX, 183) was a pigeon: another, L. Coutil, *Archéologie gauloise-carolingienne* IV, fig. 101. In the Landesmuseum at Mainz is the foot of a much larger bronze eagle, another is at Speyer, see H. Menzel, *Die römischen Bronzen aus*

Deutschland I, Taf. 32, no. 28—'from large Jupiter statue', and another was found at Jupille, Belgium. Another eagle, improbably said to be of *steel*, was exhibited as a Silchester find to the Society of Antiquaries in 1788, *9*, 370. A few bits of feathering and hair in the collection belonged to the statues discussed or to others, but little can be made of them.

36. *53*, 558: 7.5 cm. wide and 3 to 5 mm. thick; cf. n. 12 above.

CHAPTER 10 *(The Public Baths)*

1. *59*, 341 ff.
2. *Wroxeter* 1923–7, Appendix B. Types, Krencker-Krüger, *Die Trierer Kaisertheremen,* 177 (Reihentyp, as here), 178 (Ringtyp). The baths at Castell Collen fort are about the same size as those of Silchester, initial state, 40 × 20 m. *(ARB,* fig. 38).
3. The iron strigil came from the stoke-hole of XXI.1 *(Journal,* 6 April 1865). Otherwise there are a few bits of blades and enamelled handles; types as *JRS* LVII, pl. 16, 6 and E. Bónis, *Folia Archaeologica* XIX, 32, Abb. 13 (in a good study of sets); dipper, cf. M. H. P. den Boesterd, *Bronze Vessels in the Rijksmuseum Kam,* xxi, 13–15. See J. Carcopino, *Daily Life in Ancient Rome,* or J. P. V. D. Balsdon, *Life and Leisure in Ancient Rome,* for accounts of bathing procedures.
4. Hours, cf. the mine-regulations at Vipasca, Spain, *ILS* 6891.
5. *SJ* XII, 8 ff.; cf. *G* XXII, 200 ff., still maintaining that *tubulatio* was for heat-insulation; but W. Huber, *SJ* XV, 38 ff. adduces it as a main radiant surface.
6. W. Reusch, *G* XXXIII, 187, Abb. 3–4. G. E. Fox mentions in *52*, 663 chimney-stacks on a four or five storey house shown on a destroyed Algerian mosaic: I have been unable to trace the illustration. They cannot be hypocaust-chimneys, being far too high.
7. J. B. Ward Perkins, *93*, pls. 48, 51.
8. *Esp.* 7795. Not all reproductions show this lightly-incised feature well. Its significance was first recognised, in part, by Richmond, *Arch. and the After Life,* 19.
9. Pliny, *Epistulae* III, 14; *SHA Caracalla,* 9. Badly translated by Lewis and Short, and not to be emended to *solaris.*
10. Coal, G. Webster, *AJ* XXXV, 204 ff., Boon *et al., Geol. Mag.* CII, 469. Rare at Silchester, *60*, 449; *102*, 52. Soot-rake from hypocaust, *ArJ* CII, 68, fig. 10, 13.
11. See n. 5. There is a form of insulation with box-tiles or *tegulae mammatae* (tiles with lugs raising them from a surface). As pointed out

by Kretzschmer, the rows of flue-tiles meet overhead in the *tepidarium* of the Stabian Baths at Pompeii, and hot gases would have stagnated there. But he erred in thinking this was the only *tubulatio*-type.

12. *93*, pl. 39B.

13. Wraxall, *PSAS* CV, 44, not made clear (but clear upon personal inspection). Zugmantel, *SJ* XII, 12 Abb. 4. Kretzschmer's discussion of 'warm air' heating, *ib.* 36–7. Macdonald, *AA* ser. 4 VIII, 284 ff. Other drains at Silchester, *56*, 109 pl. 6; *60*, 434.

14. Boon, *Isca* (1972), fig. 51.

15. Seneca, *Epistulae Morales,* 70; cf. R. Davies, *SJ* XXVII, 85, fig. 1 (Housesteads).

16. A. Maiuri, *Pompeii* (1960), fig. 53; cf. Chesters, *AA* ser. 4 VIII, pl. 45.

17. The centre would have been pierced for the escape of the water, cf. Boon, *Isca* (1972), 102. Fragment of similar type, *Fishbourne* II, 39, fig. 22, 2.

18. Hope thought that the western division, about 8 m. long, was primary but details suggest an original alcove of smaller size. There might well have been a *piscina* here, as the one on the east side is so small: the symmetrical arrangement is common, cf. Krencker-Krüger *o.c., passim.*

19. *Vitruvius* V, 10. *Labrum,* e.g. Maiuri, *o.c.,* fig. 56. The finest British example is from Caerleon, *Isca,* fig 70.

20. Krencker-Krüger, *o.c.,* 303, Abb. 348; *93,* 176, fig. 3. Since the temperature of boiling water is 100°, lead could be used safely.

21. P.-M. Duval, *Paris antique,* fig. 66.

22. *Roman Bath,* pls. 20B, 21. But the reconstruction (fig. 37, left) would not have stood, and in the British climate, the vault would have been roofed.

23. *59,* 360, fig. 10: jamb in shadow in the foreground.

24. *59,* pl. 80, last period of original *caldarium.*

25. Hope notes examples at Wroxeter and Wingham villa, Kent (*ACt.* XIV, 135). We are told (*59,* 352) that the floor-tesserae were oblong (about 7.5 × 7.5 × 15 mm.) but such cubes are characteristic of early floors, as at Caerleon (Fortress Baths). Perhaps the division into periods is not very reliable here, but at the same time it must be noted that this floor was the third on the spot.

26. *59,* pl. 80 shows the levelled site (Hope standing L., Stephenson R.).

27. I. A. Richmond, *Roman Britain* (1963), 205; at Caerleon, cf. *RIB* 317–18, *Isca* fig. 71.

28. *Epistulae Morales,* 56.

29. C. Isings, *Roman Glass from Dated Finds,* Form 61: three in colour, P. la Baume, *Römisches Kunstgewerbe,* Taf. iii.

30. *102,* 68.
31. *58,* 427, questioned by Will in Jacobi, *Das Römerkastell Saalburg* (1897), 541.
32. Shaving, Carcopino, *o.c.,* 163. Another bronze razor, Wiggonholt baths, *SAC* LXXVIII, 36, fig. 10. Minerva, wrongly interpreted in *RS,* 127, cf. *ACt.* XXXVI, 66, pl.; and in general Walton, *Trans. Woolhope Nats. Soc.* XXXIII, 190. The usual form of razors is rather different, however; cf. M. E. Mariën, *Helinium* XI, 213 ff., XIII, 71ff. Both types are shown on terracotta, R. Meiggs, *Ostia,* pl. 27A.
33. J. P. Wild, *BJ* CLXVIII, 166 ff, an important article, in English; J. Liversidge, *Britain in the Roman Empire,* 121 ff.
34. *58,* 422.
35. *55,* 468, found crushed and expertly restored.
36. *Pliny* XXXVI, 1.
37. *8,* 449. Curse, *RIB* 306. An earlier Senecianus at Caerleon (*ib.* 367) suggests that the family may have originated in the civil settlement of the legionary fortress.
38. The only general work on surgical instruments is J. S. Milne, *Surgical Instr. in Greek and Roman Times* (1907); but see also R. W. Davies, *SJ* XXVII, 89–91, figs; R. Caton Thompson, *Journ. Hellenic Stud.* XXXIV, 114–18, fine set from Colophon; and (on trephining instruments) J. A. Brongers, *Ber. ROB* XIX, 7–16. British material is usually very simple, the most interesting being a uvula-forceps from Caerwent, P. H. Thomas, *Journ. Coll. Gen. Practitioners* 1963–6, 497–8, pls. 3–4. A retractable iron or steel blade in a bronze cylindrical handle from Silchester may have been surgical; I know no parallel. A *cucurbita* or cupping-vessel, bronze, was found in the Verulamium car-park excavations, when I saw and identified it, but cannot now be traced in the museum. Palettes, see a short incomplete list by M. G. Jarrett, *Trans. Durham & Northd. Archit. and Arch. Soc.* XI, 121 ff. Lid of chest, cf. J. Szilágyi, *Aquincum* (1956), Taf. 1 and various other examples.
39. Realgar, *55,* 252, cf. *Pliny* XXXIV, 18 *ad fin.;* Dioscourides, *Mat. Med.* V, 122; R. W. Davies, *Medical History* XIV.1, 101. Colourant, *Vitruvius* VII, 7; cf. S. Augusti, *I colori pompeiani,* 98–9.
40. Plant-remains, *57,* 252–6; *58,* 34–6, 426–8; *59,* 367–8; *60,* 164, 449; *61,* 210–13, 485. The lists may be run through with the help of e.g. R. T. Gunther's *The Greek Herbal of Dioscorides* and, in general, J. C. Th. Uphoff's *Dict. Economic Plants.* Neuss, K.-H. Knörzer, *Novaesium* IV, 137, listing five *sichere Heilkräuter,* among them *Hypericum perforatum* and *Hyoscyamus niger* represented at Silchester.

CHAPTER 11 *(The* Praetorium *or Inn)*

1. *Reading Mercury* 11, 18 Feb. 1833, *GM* 1833, both quoted *50, 271;
   27, 418; S. Chandler, *Hist. Silchester* (1837), 36; *JBAA* XVI, 92;
   50, 271–80; *54, 222; Journal* 23 Aug. 1875—14 June 1876 and
   Additions; accretions to published plan from Cambridge aerial view,
   JRS LV, pl. 13, 1, which also shows that the building has been planned
   3 m. too far E.

2. Joyce mentions coins of Nerva and Trajan in 'low levels' but they may
   have belonged to an earlier building. Richborough, see n. 15.

3. *CK,* 40.

4. As in the *cella* of the Insula XXXV temple; cf. our pl. 23.

5. Caerwent, *59,* pl. 66, mosaic, pl. 68; Bignor, e.g. *JRS* LIII, 156. It is
   likely that a large mosaic found near the south gate not long before
   1714, 'miserably broken', belonged either to this room or to another
   in the western range: *Hearne* IV, 361.

6. See Hodge's perspective views, *50,* pls. 18–19.

7. Described as 'eleven bands of rammed tile'.

8. M. Green, *CA* II, 136, fig.

9. *JBAA* XVI, 92, probably much as Caerwent, *60,* pl. 43.

10. *50,* pl. 19: it cannot have warmed the bath, for there is no exit for the
    gases.

11. Cf. the latrine attached to an inn at Caerwent, *57,* pl. 40, similar size.

12. W. Fairholt, *Rambles of an Archaeologist* (1871), 84, fig. 89 (I owe
    this reference to Mr M. Henig; the drawing, to Dr. H. Schönberger,
    derived from *Illustrirte Zeitung* 12 April 1879).

13. Pompeii, T. Kléberg, *Hôtels restaurants et cabarets dans l'antiquité
    romaine.*

14. *Lydney,* pl. 52; C. de la Croix, *Mém. sur les découvertes d'Herbord,* pl.
    2, scale 1:2500 and not as printed. The *hôtelleries* were destroyed after
    excavation. Plan without scale, *Grenier* IV, fig. 170. Heddernheim and
    Kempten, *CK,* 36 ff., Taff. 17–19 including Silchester; W. Kleiss, *Die
    öffentlichen Bauten von C.,* 60. Godmanchester, cf. note 8. Cambo-
    dunum has no symbol on the *Tabula Peutingeriana.*

15. *Richborough* II, 13, pl. 39, Site 3; V, 240, fig. 28, 241, figs. 29–30.

16. *JRS* XLVI, 119, fig. 20; cf. my *Isca* (1972), 60, fig. 35.

17. *Tab. Peut.* ed. Miller 1888, repr. 1962; A. and M. Levi, *Itineraria
    Picta* (1967). The interpretation of the symbols was proposed by A.
    Levi and Bluma Trell, *Archaeology* XVII, 227.

18. Both Wesseling's 1735 and Cuntz's 1929 ed. of the *Itinerarium Antonini Aug.* contain the *Itinerarium Hierosolymitanum* mentioned in the text. The essentially official character of the lodgings is shown by expressions such as *mansiones nunc institutae* and by Wess. 260.5, the Inicerum instance mentioned later (*mansio Augusti in praetorio est*). *Cursus publicus,* see A. H. M. Jones, *Later Roman Emp.* II, 830, III, 271; H-G. Pflaum, *Le cursus publicus sous le haut-empire romain.*

19. Direct road, A. Clarke, *PHFC* XXI, 82 ff. D. van Berchem's thesis that the routes mark the establishment of a regular tax-in-kind system, *annona militaris,* under Severus has been adversely criticised by G. E. Rickman, *Roman Granaries,* 278.

20. See prev. note. On the civil *praetoria,* see R. Egger, Österreichische Akademie der Wissenschaften, Philosophisch-Historische Klasse, *Sitzungsberichte,* CCL, *Abh.* 4, 'Das Praetorium als Amtssitz und Quartier römischer Spitzenfunctionäre' (officials carrying a spear as emblem of office, i.e. *beneficiarii* and others). See also J. E. Bogaers, *Bull. koninkl. ned. oudheidkundige Bond* ser. 6 XVII, 209 ff., on Praetorium Agrippinae. Brough: I see no reason to emend the text of *It. Ant.* 466.4 to 'Petuaria', as is often done.

21. *Ep. 27, ad Libanium.*

22. Speed, cf. A. M. Ramsay, *JRS* XV, 60 ff. Modern details, cf. Howard Robinson, *Britain's Post Office* (1953).

23. Stirrups, cf. P. Vigneron, *Le cheval dans l'antiquité,* 86; Lynn S. White Jnr., *Medieval Technology and Social Change,* 14. *Esp.* 2771 shows a civilian's saddle-horse. Bits: the figure-of-eight link, our fig. 21, 7, is uncommon. Manning, *Verulamium Excav.* I, 171 quotes examples from Caerwent and Caistor St. Edmund; cf. also *Oxon.* XVI, 26 (Harpsden villa). The cheek-piece shown, fig. 21, 5, is an Iron Age type, and one from Highclere (Hants.) in Reading Museum is red-enamelled in that tradition (*BAJ* LXI, 103). The horse-head fitting in our fig. 21, 6 is presumably from harness, but no parallel has come to light; it is at Stratfield Saye.

24. Exceptional horse, *58,* 244; cf. *ECC* II, 213 and J. C. Ewart in *Newstead,* 362. A donkey mentioned *ib.* 371 is as far as I know the only Romano-British identification of an animal commonly shown on Trajan's Column. No remains of mule have been recognised (or sought?). Blewburton, J. King, *BAJ* LIII, 59.

25. Nailed shoe, cf. Vigneron, *o.c.,* 44; White, *o.c.* 57. Simple shoes said to be stratified, *Camulodunum,* 342; Wheeler, *Maiden Castle,* 290; *Ant.* XL, 306. 'Hipposandals', Vigneron, 44; L. de Noëttes, *L'Attelage, le*

cheval de selle, 142, for experiment with a *solea* attached to an injured hoof, which healed while it was worn; the *solea* came loose only at speed. It is worth noting that there was a curious correspondence in *The Times* in 1878, in which it was suggested that shoeing was not the necessity it was usually believed to be. Donkeys in rural Ireland are rarely shod, even if they could frequently be found to benefit from a farrier's attention as the result of being worked on metalled roads.

26. *57, 248,* cf. fig. 7, with bronze handle, showing a farrier at work (Pompeii). Other examples in Britain, cf. W. Manning, *Beds. Arch. Journ.* II, 53 (also at Caerwent, Housesteads; and cf. G. Webster, *AJ* XLVIII, 303).

27. The best coin is shown by O. Keller, *Die antike Tierwelt* I, Taf. 2, 5; poorer, BMC *Coins R. Emp.* III, pl. 16. Some Rhenish carts had shafts, e.g. Vigneron, *o.c.* pls. 54–5, but again used in conjunction with yokes! De Noëttes, *o.c.,* 162 mentions an experiment with a Roman type of harness, successful with light loads (as those of the *cursus publicus*) but prevented animals exercising their full power.

28. Vehicles, e.g. Vigneron *o.c.* pl. 62A, (barrel); 65A (covered); these and many others in *Esp.* and other collections, e.g. S. Ferri, *Arte romana sul Danubio.* Thrace, I. Venedikov, *Trakiyskata kolesnitsa,* esp. pls. 97–8; cf. L. Tarr, *Hist. of the Carriage,* figs. 199–200. Hook, *56,* 124, fig. 5.

29. Cf. Vigneron, *o.c.,* 117, n. 3.

30. *58,* 32; cf. *JRS* LI, *162* (Inchtuthil). *Esp.* 5159 shows tires.

31. One James Hunt received a sixty-guinea prize as recently as 1769 for devising the method of shrinking on tires, which of course greatly improved the strength of the wheel and led to a better development of the dished wheel: see A. Bird, *Roads and Vehicles,* 74. The earlier dished wheel was weak and inefficient (see e.g. 'Winter Scene' by J. de Momper and J. Brueghel, shown on the front cover of *The Connoisseur,* Dec. 1972) and was not a Roman type.

32. *Newstead,* 337, pl. 69, 2 for a one-piece felloe, also from Bar Hill *PSASc* XL, 497, fig. 34; jointed felloe, *ib.* 492, fig. 33, 4. Prices: S. Lauffer, *Diokletians Preisedikt* XV, 31 ff.(*vitutis rotis*—one piece; *arcuatis*—jointed).

33. *Esp.* 4155 shows a linch-pin. Small, with slot at lower end, *102,* 50, fig. 7, 7—8 for normal type: stepped, *57,* 247, fig. 4; cf. W. Manning, *Verulamium Excav.* I, 174, fig. 64, 76; an example from Cambodunum, *CK,* Abb. 50, 2, combines step and slotted end in a rather delicately made specimen.

CHAPTER 12 *(The Amphitheatre)*

1. *Stukeley,* 170; J. Ward, *Phil. Trans.* XLV, 603.

2. Hearne's reaction to Stukeley's discovery is worth quoting (*Hearne,* VIII, 265): 'This Dr Stukeley is a very conceited man, and 'tis observ'd by all that I have talked with, that what he does hath no manner of likeness to the Originals . . . . he pretended to have discover'd a Roman amphitheatre at Silchester. . . . This is . . . fancy. I have been at Silchester [1714]. There is nothing like it. . . .'

3. *46, 346.* I have seen one large coping-stone at this spot, with mouldings quite different from the coping of the wall, but could not find it again in 1970.

4. *AJ* XVI, 156; XLIV, 17, pl. 20, XLVII, 185, 188, fig. 2.

5. *Isca* (1972), 89–101.

6. *B* II, 243, fig. 2.

7. At Chester there was a *Nemeseum* in a similar position, *JRS* LVII, 203, 5, cf. pls. 13, 3 and 17, 1. Shrines of this goddess were frequently to be found in amphitheatres or near by.

8. RCHM *Dorset* II.3, 590–1.

9. *JRS* LXI, 116.

10. The late Mr Billy Smart told me that the diameter of his ring was 12.8 m.

11. A good general account of the games: J. P. V. D. Balsdon, *Life and Leisure in Ancient Rome,* ch. 8; see also M. Grant, *Gladiators.*

12. *Isca* (1972), 101.

13. *Camden,* 127, on Claudian, *De consulatu Stilichonis* III, 301.

14. K. Painter, *BMQ* XXXIII, 121 ff. for general survey. Aldborough (Isurium Brigantum) should be added to the list of amphitheatres, and a Caerleon carved stone, *Isca* (1972), fig. 65, to the other evidence cited.

15. Balsdon, *o.c.,* 298.

16. Boon, *AJ* XXXVIII, 327, pl. 25, with refs. to continental finds notably at Aquincum; M. R. Hull, *Roman Potters' Kilns* 90, fig. 49, shows a fragment of mould, of Bacchic type.

17. Of Severus Alexander and Julia Mamaea his mother, A.D. 228; it has a brass rim shrunk on to a bronze centre. Villainously cleaned prior to 1950, it is as Gnecchi, *I medaglioni romani* III, 84, no. 2, but smaller (36 mm., 32.85 g.).

18. In general, see J. M. Pullan, *Hist. of the Abacus,* and Kretzschmer, *TZ* XX, 96 ff.

19. Numbers are scratched on the edge or the face, sometimes both and different; cf. *Chichester Excav.* I. fig. 5, 15; and *B* 111, 358, fig. 21.

20. *JRS* XLIX, 132, and G. Meates, *Lullingstone Roman Villa* (Official Guide), 24. Cf. from Welwyn a handsome glass set, Belgic, four groups of six, I. Stead, *101*, 14, pl. 1.

21. Wrongly described in *RS* as a whipping-top: it will not work as such. Daremberg and Saglio, *Dict. des antiquités grecques et romaines* III.2, 994 show an analogous gaming-piece from Halicarnassus.

22. *57*, pl. 27; *58*, 31 fig. 4. In general see Balsdon *o.c.*, 154 ff; R. C. Bell, *Board Games*, 91 ff.; and for a parallel to the large tile, *RA* 1966–i, fig. 55, Vienne.

23. The remarkable primitive dolls in the Lovett Coll. (National Museum of Wales, now on loan to the Museum of Childhood, Edinburgh) include some made from pieces of wood or bone or even of stones, with a few spots of ink to indicate features and a few rags for clothing. Such were the dolls of the poorest children until very recent times, and such, no doubt, were those of the Callevan children also.

CHAPTER 13 *(Temples and Pagan Religion)*

1. *61*, 479, pl. 83.

2. Cf. *Lydney*, 41; *Ross*, 176.

3. S. Loeschcke, *Tempelbezirk im Altbachthal* I, 12; II, 24: Ritona temple and no. 41.

4. *61*, 206, 474, pl. 23. *Lewis* errs in adding a large base on L. of the entrance, which he saw with the model at Calleva Museum: in reality this is loose, and represents the altar-base found E. of the temple, the case being too small to place it in proper relationship. An altar-base in much the same position as at Silchester, at Harlow: *CA* I, 289, fig., R. Palisade or hedge, as suggested at the end of this paragraph: cf. *ib.*, fig. L., and Varro, *De re rustica* I, 14.

5. P. Lambrechts, *Contrib. à l'ét. des divin. celt.*, 146; cf. e.g. *RIB*, 131; *Ross,* pl. 59B.

6. *61*, 209, fig. 5; *May,* pl. 87A (lost).

7. *52*, 744, pl. 30; *58*, 414, pl. 28.

8. *62*, pl. 1.

9. For similar close settings, cf. *Lewis, passim.*

10. *52*, 749; cf. *HG* VIII, 314; H. Koethe, *Ber. RGK* XXIII, Abb. 8, 32, and various others.

11. *Lewis*, 20; but his suggestion of a timber superstructure is improbable.

12. *ArJ* XI, 57.
13. W. Frend, *JBAA* ser. 3 XVIII, 1 ff.
14. *58*, 418, pl. 32.
15. D. Smith, *AA* ser. 4 XL, 66.
16. *58*, 423.
17. L. de Vesly, *Les fana de la région normande*, fig. 23.
18. *ArJ* XI, 57; *58*, 422. Seven in the Stair Coll., seen 1821; four at Reading; one at Stratfield Saye; one is pierced for suspension. The spear mentioned below was earlier thought to be a surgical instrument, indentified in *RS*. In general, see J. R. Kirk, *Oxon* XV, 32.
19. *58*, 423; cf. de Vesly, *o.c.*, 85, pl. 16; and one in a fourth-century grave at Lavoye, G. Chenet, *La céramique d'Argonne du 4e siècle*, pl. 1; cf. *Ross*, 49, n. 1.
20. *RIB* 126, cf. 309 (Caerwent).
21. *50*, 267; *54*, 20, 206, 222, pl. 16; *Journal* 10 and 13 Sept., 11 and 25 Oct., 11 Nov. 1872.
22. Koethe, *l.c.*, no. 27A.
23. 'Alabaster', cf. R. Schindler, *Landesmuseum Trier: Führer durch die vorgeschl. und römische Abteilung* (1970), Abb. 243; graffito, *54*, 238.
24. *57*, 95, pl. 8.
25. *Lewis*, figs. 76, 78.
26. RCHM *Eburacum*, no. 32; complete plan unknown.
27. W. Kleiss, *Die öffentlichen Bauten von Cambodunum*, Beilage 4; *CK*, Abb. 17.
28. *54*, 201, pl. 16.
29. *56*, 237, pl. 11; *Lewis*, 106, fig. 105.
30. *Mithraea* in Britain, Boon, *AC* CIX, 165, fig. 11. Mithraism, introduction: M. J. Vermaseren, *Mithras: the Secret God*.
31. *56*, 236.
32. *46*, 346.
33. *Lewis*, figs. 93, 74; *ARB*, fig. 50.
34. *57*, 234, fig. 2, pls. 29–30.
35. *53*, 279, pl. 23; cf. pl. 24 for column found in it, and for similar base (?) of shrine (?) at Caerwent, Ho. 8N, *62*, 409, fig. 3, pl. 57. XXVIII.1 and XXXIV.1, *58*, 421, pl. 28; *60*, 439, pl. 40.
36. *57*, pl. 32; *56* pl. 11.
37. *58*, 32, pl. 1.
38. *54*, pl. 18; *58*, pl. 2; *60*, pl. 40; *57*, pl. 8, for mosaic, *40*, pl. 23. It may be pointed out that Pompeian *lararia* are often in niches in the thick-

ness of the walls well above the floor and no such evidence could survive at Silchester.

39. *55*, 237, pl. 15.
40. Pompeian *lararia*, G. K. Boyce, *MAAR*, XIV.
41. *Genius*, not in *46*, cf. *Journal* 30 April 1869; at Stratfield Saye. *Lar, PSAL* XVI, 74, fig.; *55*, 239, fig. 4; lost in fire at Wasing House during the war, information from Sir William Mount. *Lares*, cf. E. B. Thomas, *Folia Archaeologica* XV, 21 ff.
42. Devizes, W. Musgrave, *Belgium Britannicum* (1719), 123, pls. Others mentioned, Felmingham (British Museum); Lamyatt (Bristol City Museum). In general see my article in *JRGZ* forthcoming.
43. *58*, 148, figs. 6–7, pl. 8.
44. P. Lambrechts, *L'exaltation de la tête dans la pensée et dans l'art des Celtes*, esp. 67–9.
45. Wheeler, *Y Cymmrodor* XXXIII, fig. 33. Cohors I Sunicorum, *RIB* 430. A rude stone Mercury, Wheeler *l.c.* fig. 50, left, re-used as a door-sill in an adjacent building, may have stood on this base.
46. J. J. Deiss, *Herculaneum*, 67.
47. *55*, 224, 238, pl. 11.
48. *58*, 19, pl. 2.
49. F. Oelmann, *Festschrift-Oxé*, 183. The Titelbierg *aedicula*, *Esp.* 4193 is often taken to represent a Romano-Celtic temple. It has a disproportionately large doorway where a small figurine was probably placed. There is a great variety of *aediculae* in the same region.
50. RCHM *Dorset* II.3, 556, pl. 220.
51. *54*, 458 (Pit 'B' by error); *102*, 31.
52. Cf. E. Wightman, *BJ* CLXX, 220.
53. *58*, 32 (nine vessels); *57*, 96 (four jugs below a gravel layer); cf. A. Ross in *Stud. Ancient Europe*, 258, 264; *PF, passim*.
54. E.g. *57*, 246, pits in Insula XXIII yielding thirteen and seven whole vessels.
55. 1890: *52*, 742, cf. *53*, pl. 21; *54*, 39 ff.; vessels, grey jug, *May* pl. 56 104, other omitted; cist, cf. Ross, *l.c.* n. 53, fig. 64 (Jordon's Hill), and *PF passim*. 1900: *57*, 246, pl. 30; was wrapped in cloth sack? (photographic evidence): vessels, *May* pl. 56, 100, other again omitted.
56. J. Leach, *AA* ser. 4 XL, 33 ff.; *Ross*, 379; and on ironwork 'hoards', W. Manning, *B* III, 224 ff.
57. Carrawburgh, *AA* ser. 4 XXIX, 6, 18, 86; *Verulamium*, 118. The Carrawburgh cones were said to have been roasted, i.e. carbonised, for fuel. The Silchester ones display the same phenomena (gentle charring,

smoke, pine odour) but I think the effect is more probably natural. Cultivation in Britain, J. Loudon, *Arboretum et Fruticetum Britannicum* IV (1838), 2230.

58. *JRS* XLVI, 141; in a ritual pit at Trier, see next note; cf. *PF,* 243 and *passim.*

59. Cf. D. Wortmann, *BJ* CLXX, 252 ff., with list, not all sepulchral instances.

60. Cf. n. 57; but the price of 3 *denarii* apiece was cheap, not dear, in the late third century.

61. *58,* 426. Box sprays in a leaden sarcophagus at Roden Downs (Berks.), *Trans. Newbury District Field Club* IX, 47. Pliny, *Epistulae* II, 17.

62. *PW* 2.II, 1083, etc.

63. *57,* 110, figs. 8–9; Boon, *B* IV, 107–14, for much of what follows.

64. Cf. H. Idris Bell, *Cults & Creeds of Graeco-Roman Egypt,* 20.

65. BMC *Coins of Alexandria,* pl. 12, no. 1298, reproduced by Boon, *l.c.* n. 63.

66. Cited, *ib.* Cf. also a Nîmes head, *Esp.* 2671.

67. It is suggested in *RA* 1966–i, 182, that the Insula XXXV temple could have been an *Iseum* and that the statue of Sarapis, or bust, could have belonged there. *Peregrini* using this temple may have worshipped Isis, and Silchester is not impossibly far from London where the worship of Isis was early established (*LRT,* pl. 5). But there is no reason not to believe this to be an ordinary Romano-Celtic *fanum.* Cf. Trier Altbachthal no. 50 (*Lewis,* fig. 110) for such a one with open-air offering-altar and plinth in *cella.*

68. *60,* 163, a small marble arm and a pedestal with the outline of a foot, hard chalk (Fox Coll. IV, 57); note a lost 'alabaster' head in Stair's collection, seen by Gough in 1768: Gough's *Camden* (1806) I, 205, 7.6 cm. high (rough drawing in Bodl., Gough Maps (Hampshire).

69. *57,* 250; *Journal,* 6 July 1874; *53,* 561; *PSAL* XVI, 74—no reason to doubt it. A seated Victory in brass, *53,* 562, is modern and was probably introduced by one of the workman: from a clock or the like.

70. *57,* 250, fig. 8.

71. *53,* 269; *46,* 354 (cock and 'bear'); compositions, e.g. Babelon-Blanchet, *Bronzes antiques de la Bib. Nat.,* 355. A spread eagle found by Joyce is exactly like several others in Britain and is also probably modern; his 'toy gridiron' is a book-clasp of perhaps the seventeenth century.

72. *Journal,* 17 Oct. 1870; *46,* 354.

73. *RIB,* 276, pl. 6: note (cf. our p. 111) the metal is priced in *denarii,* the work in *sestertii.*

74. *53*, 284; *55*, 239; *58*, 423; *60*, 163; *92*, pl. 30D. These figurines have been studied for Britain by F. Jenkins, *ACt* LXXI-LXXII.
75. *57*, 81.
76. Cf. J.–J. Hatt, 'Les croyances funéraires des gallo-romains' *RAE* XXI, 48 ff.
77. *60*, 163.
78. *Ross*, pls. 50a, 49a. This writer often identifies protuberances on the heads of crude carvings as horns, when it is clear, in some cases, that figures of Mercury are in question, e.g. pl. 51a from London (with 'catapult'!).
79. *63*, 561 fig. 3; *56*, 120; *92*, 127 pl. 36c, *102*, 52; and other fragments; from all of which a grey plaster restoration at Reading was made, sometimes mistaken for an original. Dorchester, *JRS* XLVI, 143, pl. 16, 2. Caerleon, *Isca* (1972), fig. 14c. Cf. also *Esp.* 5568 (Brumath), 'horned'.
80. *Ib.* fig. 14A, E, F and perhaps D.
81. E.g. *May*, pls. 47, 52–4; *58*, 4; *50*, 75. The votive character of these is not certain. On the last cf. *CIL* XIII, 10018.3. Lamps, pl. 46A, 8, and our p. 224.
82. *Ib.* pl. 71, 165; *Verulamium*, 118; *AC* LXXXVII, 319, fig. 61, etc.
83. *Journal*, 27 Oct. 1870. A lion-mask on one shows that the point was uppermost.
84. *RIB* 82; but too little remains for sense to be made of it; cf. 217.
85. *102*, 45 no. 16, fig. 5.
86. *56*, 241; cf. Schindler, *o.c.* Abb. 241, centre left.
87. *HG* V, 64, paraphrasing Petronius, *Saturae*, 17.
88. *61*, 241, probably a harness-ornament. Such objects usually have holes for attachment by laces.
89. *55*, 429; cf. Babelon-Blanchet, *o.c.*, 1175 (three phalli).
90. Cf. *Folklore* LXXVIII, 147, for mention of modern Italian mascots in red plastic with a phallic significance.
91. *56*, 241; *54*, 492; *ArJ* VIII, 245, illus.; cf. my note *AC* CIX, 163 (Segontium Mithraeum; there is also a bell, unpublished, from Carrawburgh Mithraeum).
92. *B* I, pl. 27c.
93. *57*, 111. Cf. Campbell Bonner, *Stud. in Magical Amulets*, 123, 325. Iaō from the Aramaic *Ya'u*, and this from the Hebrew *YHWH* familiar to us as Jehovah or Yahweh: see Bell, *o.c.* 29, 73. Gnosticism in brief, *ib.*, 91. The only other gem with a cock-headed anguipede

recorded from Britain, so far as I know, is in a ring of the *'Aesica'* find, *55*, 180, fig. 3; it is unknown whether the reverse is inscribed.

94. *RIB* 436.

95. Gough's *Camden* (1789) I, 142. See Preisendanz in Roscher's *Ausfürliches Lexicon der grch. und römischen Mythologie, s.v.,* for a very rare magical word or name written ZAC, ZACAP, (*Zas, Zasar*). But to find it, rather than some commoner and more powerful word, on a gem would be unlikely, Dr A. A. Barb pointed out to me: he suggests either an acrostic or an acclamation as the correct interpretation (*in litt.,* 28 April 1970).

CHAPTER 14 *(The Church)*

1. *The Times,* 10 June 1892; *53,* 563 ff., fig. 4, pls. 40–41; *JRS* LII, 185: the official report by S. S. Frere is forthcoming in *AJ.*

2. See p. 72 and p. 311, n. 24.

3. In *CB;* H. Kähler, *Die frühe Kirche.*

4. J. M. C. Toynbee, *JBAA* ser. 3 XVI, 7, figs. 3–4. The character of the P. Maggiore building has been questioned by P. Mingazzini, *Festschrift-Mercklin,* 90, Gortyna, *Monumenti Antichi* I, 8ff.

5. F. Fremersdorf in *Neue Ausgrabungen,* 329; Toynbee, *l.c.,* 6, figs., pl. Others, P.D.C. Brown, *B* II, 227, fig. 1.

6. G. Leroux, *Les origines de l'édifice hypostyle,* 311. A. Grabar, *Martyrium* 303–4, n. 1, fig. 98, adduces from Montano (Soria, *Scielta di varii tempietti antichi,* 1624) an apparently transeptal building; but Montfaucon (*L'Antiquité expliquée* II.1, 1719) had already characterised it as being 'd'une disposition assez bizarre' as indeed are many plans in the *Scielta.* Caerleon, *AC* CXIX, 15, fig. 12.

7. E.g. S. Gsell, *Les monuments antiques de l'Algérie* II, fig. 123, Guesséria. The side-chambers are at a lower level than the apse.

8. In 1892 it was not thoroughly cleared, and its true character was exposed by Richmond.

9. *Cabrol-Leclercq* IV.1, 733 n. 4; XII.2, 1950–1. Radford, *MA* XV, 4.

10. *Cabrol-Leclercq* I.2, 3159, fig. 1123, showing a simple table as altar. The Silchester mosaic is roughly matched by one of *c.* 300 in *Verulamium,* pl. 48B, but the design is far too simple to be used as an index of date, and is known to appear much earlier, e.g. *Fishbourne* I, pl. 73C, etc. The excavators compared a presumably late pavement in a corridor at Wroxeter forum, *JBAA* XVII, facing 100, fig. D.

11. Radford, *l.c.* 25, plan, 26; Kähler *o.c.* Abb. 9, 11–13. Trier, T. Kempf in *Neue Ausgrabungen* 368, Abb. 3, or *Grenier* III, fig. 187.

12. Kähler, *o.c.,* Abb. 13; Radford, plan, 26.

13. *Cabrol-Leclercq* VIII.2, 1551–2; Krautheimer-Corbett, *Ant* XXXIV, 201, fig. 2; G. Bovini, *Edifici cristiani di culto d'età costantiniana a Roma,* 60, figs. 6–7; Kähler, *o.c.* Abb. 17–18.

14. *Cabrol-Leclercq* XV.2, 3328, n. 3; Toynbee, *JRS* XLIII,7; Bovini, *o.c.* 373, fig. 46. Plans based on Alfarano's are found in many books, e.g. Banister Fletcher.

15. *Cabrol-Leclercq* XIV.2, 2918, fig. 10646; II.1, 571, fig. 1435.

16. G. Soteriou, *Archaiologike Ephemeris* 1927–8, 200, fig. 32 (transept not projecting); Daphnousi, *ib.* fig. 38.

17. E.g. a late fifth-century church at Como, A. Clapham, *Eng. Romanesque Archit.,* fig. 5; *Cabrol-Leclercq* XV.1, fig. 10865, Carolingian church at Seligenstadt.

18. *Cabrol-Leclercq* II.1, 553, fig. 1418.

19. Cf. Grabar, *Martyrium,* 303; P. Lemerle, *Philippes et la Macédonie . . . ,* 375; J. G. Davies, *Origin and Development of Early Christian Archit.,* 39.

20. I.e. towards the choir, the men participants being in the south aisle on his right, and women in the north aisle on his left: *Cabrol-Leclercq* XII.2, 2666.

21. It is impossible to match the situation of this panel in a pagan temple. At Springhead, Kent, there is a panel 1.5 m. in front of a hollow-fronted platform for cult-objects, but a *lateral* significance is lacking: *JRS* XLIX, 134, fig. 27, R.

22. The pit is behind the base when viewed from the east, and Richmond pointed out that a pagan blood-trench would have been in front. Radford (*MA* XV, 3) prefers Hope's explanation; but in the absence of the official report of the 1961 work was unaware of the evidence relating to the pitching around the base.

23. *Cabrol-Leclercq* II.1, *s.v.* 'baptême' and esp. 259, 261, 298, 301, and 392 for heating in baptisteries. The candidates were naked for the ceremony and stood facing east. In our case we imagine that the bishop was already in position at the east end of the baptistery.

24. *Ib.,* 395 shows two neophytes standing in a font on a pedestal. Cf. also the Aquileia gravestone, fifth century, *ib.* I.2, fig. 871.

25. Brown, *l.c.*

26. Toynbee, *l.c.,* 15 or *Art in Roman Britain,* 182, on the Walesby tank with part of a baptismal scene upon it. The Pulborough (Sussex)

tank has a very large Chi-Rho, *AJ* XXIII, pl. 28. The tanks range from 67 to 99 cm. diam. and 31 to 48 cm. deep, and their capacity is from about 72.5 to 290 l. (*ib.*, table, 156).

27. *Cabrol-Leclercq* II.1, 455, fig. 1371.

28. Two small silver ring-settings, one certainly late Roman, have intaglio heads and inscriptions IVL BELLATOR VIVAS and VIVAS. Some supposed Christening-spoons from the Mildenhall treasure and elsewhere bear personal names and VIVAS and may be associated with other spoons bearing the Christian monogram; but *Vivas* is too commonplace a salutation for us not to miss the diagnostic . . . *in Deo:* see K. Painter, *JBAA* ser. 3 XXVIII, 10. *Potens vivas* on a Paris spoon also bearing fishes is certainly Christian because of the symbolism of the latter, see Toynbee, *Festschrift-Gerke*, 47.

29. *46, 363; Journal* 9 June 1869, from the *'tabularium'* (which thus got its name), i.e. the central room of the three south of the *aedes*.

30. *BMGRB*, fig. 23.

31. Fr. de Ficoroni, *I piombi antichi*, pl. 9, 5.

32. Lamp, see p. 313, n. 31; glass, *58*, 32, fig. 5. In Britain, see D. Charlesworth, *AA* ser. 4 XXXVII, 46, and another at Caerleon, 1970, dating *c.* 200, with M, palm and fish. Continental, see F. Fremersdorf, *Denkmäler des römischen Köln* VIII, 142, Taf. 308; N. Walke, *Das römische Donau-Kastell Straubing-Sorviodurum*, 144, Taf. 75.

33. Discoveries made since the date of Professor Toynbee's 1953 article, *JBAA* ser. 3 XVI, have not significantly altered the general picture. Christianity is attested in at least one other *civitas*-capital, Caerwent (Boon, *BBCS* XIX, 338–44) where a building had already (improbably, in my opinion) been claimed as a church, see *80, 235*, pl. 78, 3. There is a good summary of evidence for churches in Radford's article in *MA* XV, cited above; on Lullingstone see also K. Painter, *BMQ* XXXIII, 131 ff., and in general his paper in *Studi di antichità cristiana, Actas del VIII congresso intern. di arqueologia cristiana*, 149–66. Bede refers (*Hist. ecclesiastica gentis Anglorum* I, 26) to churches in the vicinity of Canterbury, notably that 'close to the city itself on the east side, erected in ancient times, while the Romans still dwelt in Britain, in honour of S. Martin' where Ethelbert's Frankish queen worshipped and which became the headquarters of the mission of Augustine in 597 (for its remains, cf. H. M. and J. Taylor, *Anglo-Saxon Archit.* I, 143, fig. 63), presumably a *martyrium* in a cemetery-area as at St. Albans (Bede I, 29) or Caerleon (Gildas, *De excidio*, 10), and perhaps as at Stone near Faversham in Kent (*AJ* XLIX, 273 ff.). Indeed

Christian places of worship cannot have been as rare as they would seem to be in the extreme rarity of their known remains, even if in more than one town the 'house-church' type, so difficult to identify today without the clinching evidence which so seldom is available (Caerwent, Ho. VII N. with the sealed ritual deposit?), remained very probably in use. We may therefore hope that, either in Britain or in western Europe, a close parallel for the Silchester basilica will one day appear.

CHAPTER 15 *(Cemeteries)*

1. Pre-Roman cremation, *102*, 34. Burial described by Karslake, *62*, 330. The best general book on funerary matters is J. M. C. Toynbee, *Death and Burial in the Roman World*.
2. *62*, 327.
3. No proper record exists; cf. *53*, pl. 25 for site and stone base.
4. Cf. Boon, *Isca* (1972), 110, fig. 77 for a glass sprinkler-bottle from a Caerleon interment: both this and the pottery bottle were presumably used to scatter perfume over the corpse.
5. *JBAA* XVI, 92. For the photographs I am indebted to Mr John Hampton (p. 49). It is difficult to say whether there would have been rich burials, and on the whole the parallels are against it, cf. e.g. A. Down and M. Rule, *Chichester Excav.* I, 67, where a large number of simple 'inurnments' were found, with or without ancillary vessels, and on the whole few offerings of consequence. Most of the Caerleon burials were poor. Rich burials have of course occurred at York and Colchester and various other places.
6. *RIB* 87, now in the Museum of Archaeology and Ethnology, Cambridge.
7. *60*, 163, figs. 2–3; cf. my note *BBCS* XXV, 356.

CHAPTER 16 *(Houses: Plan and Structure)*

1. *54*, 448, pl. 45.
2. Cf. XVII.5, *56*, pl. 5.
3. T. Kléberg, *Hôtels restaurants et cabarets dans l'antiquité romaine*, *passim*.
4. *AA* ser. 4 X, pl. 28, some with furnaces or hearths, as at Silchester. Genre scenes, cf. those cited in connexion with the forum, our p. 322, nn. 15, 18; and e.g. R. Calza and E. Nash, *Ostia* figs. 102 (butcher), 103 (eggs and chickens), 104 (greengrocer), 106 (cobbler); R. Meiggs, *Ostia*, pl. 27A (cutler), 27B (butcher).

5. *58*, 420, pl. 28 (Insula wrongly numbered XXVII in text; and in *61*, pl. 22, the numbers of the houses are transposed).
6. *53*, 280, cf. pl. 23. Underlying remains: aerial photograph.
7. *59*, 338, pl. 73.
8. *JRS* XLI, 25 (but XXXIIIA.3 is not an early single-corridor, nor are VI.1 and XXXIIA.1 early double-corridor, houses).
9. *Camulodunum*, 89, fig. 19 (our interpretation differs).
10. *57*, pl. 32; *54*, pl. 45; *53*, pl. 22; *60*, pl. 21.
11. *62*, pl. 57; *Verulamium*, pl. 20; cf. Ditchley, *ARB* fig. 46, or Mansfield Woodhouse, *ib.*, or Hambleden, *71*, pl. 13.
12. *57*, pl. 30.
13. *TSAS* LVII, 124, fig. 30; *ACt* XXII, 49, plan.
14. *56*, pl. 7; *57*, pl. 32.
15. *60*, pl. 21; *58*, pl. 28.
16. *57*, pl. 30; *58*, pl. 2; *54*, pls. 17–18; *57*, pl. 30; *55*, pl. 23; *57*, pl. 8.
17. *55*, pls. 10–11.
18. *53*, pl. 21; *60*, pl. 21; *56*, pl. 1; Chedworth, *ARB* fig. 50.
19. *54*, pl. 17–18; *56*, pl. 11; *60*, pl. 40.
20. *57*, pl. 30; J. Ward, *Romano-British Buildings and Earthworks*, fig. 42.
21. *55*, pls. 10, 15.
22. *40*, 405, pl. 23.
23. *53*, pl. 23, Room 13, north-west corner; *60*, pl. 21, Room 4; *54*, pl. 17, Room 11.
24. *54*, 153, fig. 21; A. Maiuri, *Pompeii* (1960), fig. 76 for raised hearth with grid, etc.
25. Brickwork, e.g. on *Esp.* 5268; Holt, W. F. Grimes, *Y Cymmrodor* XLI, fig. 60, 9.
26. *56*, 104, pl. 5, Room 3; *ib.*, 106, Room 11: neither very likely. In XIV.2 there were large rough supports for a slab-table, *55*, 245, pl. 15, Room 6; cf. at Spoonley Wood villa, *52*, 654, pl. 17, Room 14.
27. *55*, 416; *53*, 560; cf. *AJ* XXXIX, pl. 5B, Verulamium.
28. *58*, 19, pl. 2 (the 'chases' in the walls would be for the flues of a superseded hypocaust, not for timbers: photographs show them to have been larger than he implies). XXXIIA.1, *58*, 417.
29. *53*, 285: votive offering?
30. Cf. instances collected by *Callender*, 32–4: pierced or upside-down for drainage.
31. *56*, 111; *May*, pl. 69B. Fractional sign, R. Cagnat, *Cours d'épigraphie* (1914), 33.
32. *56*, pl. 11, Rooms 24–25, with furnace, 26.

33. *40, 411*, pl. 34: another at Frocester Court villa, Glos., H. Gracie, *TBGAS* LXXXIX, 23, pl. 1c. Similar in numerous auxiliary forts, beneath floor of *aedes*.

34. *60, 439*, figs., pl. 40, Room 27. Sill, Fox Coll. V, 29. Monolithic sills are only common where stone is abundant and near, e.g. at Kingsweston villa, Glos., *TBGAS* LXIX, 27, plan facing 48.

35. *Fishbourne* I, 120, fig. 38 (but the 'bedding-trenches' may be root-pruning trenches, see J. Wacher in a review, *ArJ* CXXVIII, 276). Frocester, plan, *CA* II, 285, fig. It is difficult to believe that the summer glory of the Silchester hedges, honeysuckle *(Lonicera periclymenum,* well-attested for the Roman period) was not grown.

36. Edging, Pliny, *Epistulae* II, 17; topiary-work, *Pliny* XVI, 16, cf. XII, 2 *nemora tonsilia;* also Martial, *Epigrammata* III, 58.

37. *57, 255; 59, 367; 60, 449; 57, 427.* Portugal laurel is marked as doubtful in *57, 255* and may have given rise to hesitation in *Godwin,* 109: but certain, *59, 368.* The rose is disappointing, in view of its known popularity and numerous varieties, *Pliny* XXI, 4. Of course the botanical record is not complete.

38. *60, 436*, fig. 2, pl. 40. D. Neal records similar traces at Boxmoor villa, *B* II, 176. Some think a rough graffito on plaster from Hucclecote villa, *JRS* XXIV, 221, fig. 8, represents part of the elevation of a half-timbered building.

39. *58, 417*, pl. 30, foreground, left. Note also 57, pl. 31 for a basal tile-bedding of partition-walls in XXIV.2, for sole-beams.

40. *Vitruvius* VI, 5.

41. *58, 23.* Good parallels at *Verulamium,* 140, pl. 100; *AJ* XXXVIII, pl. 2 shows a sheet of fallen plaster with the imprint of the pattern on the underside. Actual wattling at Ribchester, *B* I, pl. 32A. External colour-washing, e.g. *54, 221.*

42. Arch, *58, 28*; piles at baths, *59, 362* n. *a.* our pl. 16, alder (cf. *Pliny* XVI, 40 on this); raft, *60, 439, Journal* June 1875.

43. *58*, pl. 30.

44. Half-column, *53*, pl. 24, fig. 5; porches, *54*, pl. 18, *57*, pl. 30, etc.

45. Seeds, *57, 253.* Thatching-implement, *102*, 51, fig. 7A: common, esp. on Iron Age sites. When the tips are polished by use, as here, another explanation is difficult to find.

46. *58, 32.*

47. *55, 237*; negative 1182. Arrangement of tiles, Ward, *o.c.*, fig. 76.

48. *Journal,* 1866, end of vol. I.

49. Ridge-block, Fox Coll. IV, 68; finials, *ib.* 63, 68; *53,* pl. 24, fig. 8, *58,* 29. Arrangement of slabs, Ward, *o.c.,* fig. 78; cf. Fox, 52, pl. 18 (Spoonley Wood villa).

50. *54,* 217; Verulamium, *AJ* XXXIX, pl. 1 (Brit. Mus.); N. Davey, *B* III, 264, figs. 11–12, esp. 12 with painted guilloche panelling like that of floors; Smith, lecture, 1972.

51. Stone sills, *56,* 231, *55,* 412; impression of wooden, *58,* 25. Doors, e.g. *Richter,* figs. 660–1, 663; W. Altmann, *Die römischen Grabaltäre der Kaiserzeit, passim.* Actual, *PF,* 150, figs. (fragment 70 cm. wide, over 135 cm. long, five half-lap jointed 3 cm. boards with moulded battens over junction; circular iron lock-plate with L-shaped hole; shown upside-down; wood not stated).

52. Odyssey XXI, 47, ἄντα τιτυσκόμενη 'aiming straight'.

53. *Primitive Locks and Keys,* 24.

54. The wooden statuette of a Celtic goddess found near a temple at Winchester holds just such a key (?to the doors of the after-life), *B* III, pl. 24B.

55. *AJ* XLVII, 280, refs.

56. Cupboards, e.g. *Richter, figs.* 583, 586.

57. The type is well-described by W. Manning, *BBCS* XXII, 410 (a Caerleon example).

58. *57,* 247, fig. 5; another in a similar late 'hoard' from Gt. Chesterford, Essex.

59. *56,* 241, fig. 2.

60. *RCHM Dorset* II.3, 555–6, fig., pl. 220; in general, D. B. Harden, *Stud. Building History,* 49.

61. P. 324, n. 8.

62. Cast panes, Boon, *JGS* VIII, 41 (figs. 3, 5, 6, 8 from Silchester). Analyses, H. Cole, *ib.* 46 (but I now believe the 'decoloration' was accidental and due to the inclusion of colourless or possibly manganese-pink scrap: see p. 365, n. 41). Largest pane, Red House baths, Corbridge, D. Charlesworth, *AA* ser. 4 XXXVII, 166; others, A. Kisa, *Das Glas im Altertume,* 382.

63. Boon, *l.c.,* 42, fig. 1; cf. M. Green, *Arch. News-Letter* VII, 227 on the process, but he errs in thinking that all Roman window-glass was thus made.

64. Glazing-bar, Saalburg-Museum. Red cement on a Gravesend fragment, *B* III, 147, cf. J. Miln, *Fouilles faites à Carnac* (1877), 116, 120, pl. 2. Tile, Boon *l.c.* 44, n. 9; cf. Harden in *Shakenoak* I, 81, and *SHA Firmus etc.,* 3 (fixed with pitch).

65. Cf. K. Painter, *BMQ* XXXI, 122, with list.

66. *55*, 240. Such finds are not uncommon, and little attention could have been paid to wet or dry rot ensuing.

67. *60*, 161.

68. *57*, 230, pl. 27 (cf. also *40*, 409, pl. 25); *57*, 238. The third example is laid as the floor of a summerhouse at Wasing House, and is the 'mosaic' mentioned by S. Chandler, *History of Silchester* (1837), 33. The late Mr Francis Needham kindly measured it in 1961: it consists of hexagonal tiles 16 cm. across the flats. Possibly it came from the south-east corner of Insula I where *54*, 268 mentions the finding of a hexagonal tile. Such tiles do not seem to have been used in hypocausts, though octagonal tiles are sometimes in evidence in *pilae*, e.g. *58*, pl. 31.

69. Caersws, *AC* ser. 3 III, 160. Danube: personal inspection; also in Italy, *Mem. Amer. Acad. Rome* VIII, 147, pl. 43; cf. *Vitruvius* VII, 1.7. *Opus sectile* in Britain, e.g. *Fishbourne* II, 33.

70. E.g. *Verulamium*, 100, pl. 103A; Wiggonholt baths, *JRS* XXVIII, pl. 28, top.

71. *55*, 215 for these and others; also e.g. *52*, 736.

72. I.1 (*46*, pl. 11); XIV.2 (*55*, 240, pl. 15, our pl. 32); XVI.1 (*55*, 416, pl. 23); XVII.1 (*56*, 104, pl. 5, also freestanding hearth in N. hall); XXVII.1 (*58*, 21, pl. 2); XXVII.2 (*58*, 26, pl. 2); XXXIIA.1 (*58*, 417, pl. 32); XXXIIB.3 (*55*, 429, fig. 4); XXXIIIA.B2 (*59*, 335, pl. 72, with long hearth and round furnace adjacent); XXXV.1 (*61*, 203, pl. 32).

73. Newport, *JBAA* ser. 2 XXXVI, 81, figs., over tessellation; Star, *PSAS* CVIII, 58, fig. 5, pl. 6B, neatly made of re-used roofing-slabs.

74. Coal, p. 324 n. 10.

75. *55*, 226, pl. 13.

76. Julian, *Misopogon* 341D. '. . . I would not allow the servants to heat the room in which I slept, though the cold increased more and more daily, in case it should draw out the damp from the walls [*i.e. he had forbidden the hypocaust to be lit*]. I merely ordered some lighted brands and a few live coals to be brought in. These drew out so much vapour [ἀτμούς] from the walls that my head felt heavy and I fell asleep, and narrowly escaped suffocation. I was carried into the fresh air, however, and upon disgorging the food I had recently swallowed, by my doctor's advice—though I did not bring up very much—I was immediately relieved, passed a comfortable night and was ready for business.' The young emperor Jovian (A.D. 363–4) was rumoured to have died in similar circumstances, cf. Ammianus Marcellinus XXV, 10, 13.

CHAPTER 17 *(Houses: Interior Decoration)*

1. *Vitruvius* VII, 3, 7.

2. *56,* 241, analysed with other British finds by Jope and Huse, *Nature* CXLVI, no. 3688, 26—copper, calcium, silica, and a little sodium; mode of manufacture, *ib.* On colours in general, see S. Augusti, *I colori pompeiani;* analyses of British pigments closely coincide; cf. J. Plesters on those from Downton villa paintings, *WAM* LVIII, 237. Medium, *Vitruvius* VII, 10 etc. and Plesters, *l.c.*

3. *62,* 326, poorly described. Not a plasterer's float, for which see W. Manning, *Verulamium Excav.* I, 168, fig. 62, 8, with reference to the Sens relief *(Esp.* 2767); see also a Pompeian painting, H. Lamer, *Römische Kultur im Bilde,* Abb. 122, for a clearer illustration.

4. For a wide, flat brush of strikingly modern appearance, see *Esp.* 5226.

5. *52,* 756.

6. In general see J. M. C. Toynbee, *Art in R.B.* figs. 195–205; J. Liversidge, *Britain in the Rom. Emp.,* 84; N. Davey, *B* III, 251–68 for many valuable drawings of schemes, including ceiling plaster.

7. E.g. A. Maiuri, *Roman Painting* (Skira, 1953).

8. Cf. *55,* 249.

9. *58,* pl. 12, 2; *60,* pl. 19. There is much greater depth at Caerwent and much more plaster, mostly unpublished, was recovered, including some fine figured work shown *Art in Wales* (Welsh Arts Council 1964), figs. 57a–b.

10. *56,* 233.

11. *57,* 241.

12. *58,* 19. It is hard to believe that these gay draperies did not correspond to reality, and a relief still retaining traces of its original red and yellow garment-colouring is mentioned by *Esp.,* 5154.

13. *58,* 22; floor, pl. 3.

14. *55,* 249, fig. 5; floor, pl. 12. Corncockle was Fox's identification, but but there is a petal too few.

15. *60,* 154: pieces survive at Reading.

16. *55,* 249.

17. Porphyry, *60,* 155: the exact find-spot of a piece from Insula XXXV, now at Calleva Museum, is unknown. Similar pieces and various marbles at Canterbury, *JRS* XLVI, 144. Part of a small moulded porphyry base from XXXIIB.3 (*55,* 249) probably came from the pedestal of a bust or statuette, perhaps belonging to the temples nearby.

18. *53,* pl. 23, 3.

19. See n. 9.

20. It is presumed that the mouldings noted from one of the Insula XXX temples (52, 747) were of this type.

21. Floor-cloth, Dr Woolaston, *Thermae Romano-Britannicae* (1864), 25; cart, T. Morgan, *Romano-British Mosaic Pavements* (1886), 94–5.

22. The gazetteer of Mrs A. Rainey's *Mosaics in Roman Britain*, 136–40, describes all recorded Silchester floors worth mention.

23. K. Painter, *BMQ* XXXII, 22–3; cf. also D. Smith, in *RVB*, 110–11.

24. Materials, 52, 737; 60, 158 (soft chalk, samian ware) and *passim*. My statement in *RS* that glass cubes do not occur is quite wrong. They occur in I.1 across the centre of the *cantharus* now at Stratfield Saye, where it can be seen that they are of blue-green glass, translucent. Glass cubes also occurred in XIV.2, where two shades of blue and mentioned by Fox (55, 242). One is royal blue, the commonest colour for glass tesserae in Britain: the other, however, must really be jade-green, for no other glass cubes are in the Silchester collection.

25. E.g. 53, 266. Cf. evidence of tessera-knapping at Kingsweston villa, Glos., *TBGAS* LXIX, 11, and see further Smith, *RVB*, 107–8, n. 1.

26. E.g. 53, 738; 54, 214. Remains of scrubbing-brushes of very modern appearance can be seen in the Vindonissa-Museum, Brugg (*Vindonissa Illustrata*, 41, bottom right).

27. In I.2 there was a fragment of rainbow outer bordering, consisting of graduated colours laid lozengewise (Fox Coll. V, 13); this is exceedingly rare; the few other instances are of the third or fourth century, e.g. at Colliton Park, Dorchester (*RCHM Dorset* II.3, pl. 218), after 341. Probably unique as an *outer* border.

28. The *cantharus* (cf. 57, pl. 28, in XXIII.2) is therefore a very suitable motif for a dining-room. Gadrooned examples often appear on funerary reliefs, e.g. *Esp.* 1225–6, 1298, 1300, sometimes with guardian animals, dolphins, or issuant scrolls. The funerary symbolism, at once simple and complex, has regard to the after-life, and it may not be bizarre to suppose that a similar connotation attached to floors. There appear to be no actual examples of gadrooned *canthari* preserved. For a bronze *cantharus* with dolphin-handles (cf. the example in XIV.1, 55, pl. 14) see e.g. the Xanten and Cambodunum pieces, *BJ* CLXIX, 406, Abb. 14a, *CK* Abb. 41, 4.

29. First-century at Eccles villa, Kent, *ACt* LXXX, frontispiece, restored; *Fishbourne*, pls., 'second period'.

30. I have been much indebted to Dr David Smith over the years for help and guidance in the matter of the Silchester mosaics, though I must assume responsibility for what is said about them here.

31. Second-century schools, see David Smith in the forthcoming publication of papers delivered to the Second International Colloquium on Ancient Mosaics (Vienne, 1971). Fourth-century schools, Smith in *MGR*, 95 ff., and *RVB*, 95 ff., also *AJ* XLIX, 235 ff. See also D. Johnstone on *canthari* of the 'Corinium' school, *TBGAS* LXXXVI, 102 ff., and distribution-map of fourth-century schools' work, *CA* III, 160.

32. *55*, pl. 13.

33. Pompeii, M. Brion, *Pompeii & Herculaneum*, fig. 39; Fishbourne, e.g. *Fishbourne* pl. 75.

34. *55*, pls. 12, 14.

35. XXI.4, cf. *57*, 94: Fox. Coll. V, 18; I.2, *46*, pl. 13: glass cubes, see n. 24.

36. *Verulamium*, pl. 40.

37. *AJ* XL, pl. 1; *Ar J* CXXIII, pl. 7.

38. E.g. *Verulamium*, pl. 45A; Colchester, *l.c.* n. 37; Chichester, A. Down and M. Rule, *Chichester Excav* I, pl. 13. Smith thinks the Silchester floor is so carefully done that it is probably the earliest.

39. *57*, pl. 28.

40. *58*, pl. 3.

41. Fox. Coll. V, 1.

42. *AJ* XL, pl. 1 and *Fishbourne* pl. 47 are mid-second century examples; Dyer-st., Cirencester, Buckman and Newmarch, *Remains of Roman Art* (1850), facing 36 is probably third-century (Smith). Rudstone, Yorks. and Hinton St. Mary, Dorset, are fourth-century and clearly later stylistically than the others: *RVB* pls. 3.20, 29.

43. *Surrey Arch. Colls.* LX, 26, pl. 7.

44. *60*, pl. 41 (good drawing, poor colouring). The small panel drawn *ib.* does not belong to it, but to a fragmentary panel from I.1 lifted by Joyce and reset in Stratfield Saye House; cf. *46*, 337 and pl. 11, east end of south wing.

45. *AJ* XLIX, pl. 41. Cf. also others including the Constantinian Whittington Ct., Glos. instance, *TBGAS* LXXI, pl. 2.

46. *58*, 21; not in Fox Coll., drawn from a tracing made by myself. The shading is reminiscent of 'Corinium' work; cf. Buckman-Newmarch, *o.c.*, pl. 5.

47. Shown small on the plan, *55*, pl. 15; Fox Coll. V, 7.

48. Too little survives for certainty, but perhaps cf. Itchen Abbas, Hants., *JBAA* XXXIV, facing 504. Baskets of flowers: the extant jade-green glass cubes (see n. 24) presumably appeared in the foliage hanging

from the basket preserved. Basket of fruits, Chedworth, cf. J. M. C. Toynbee, *Art in R.B.,* figs. 214–15; Woodchester, S. Lysons, *Woodchester* (1797), pl. 19, *RVB* pl. 3.14. For an actual basket of this type, 26 cm. high, 'honeysuckle', see *PF,* 79, fig. 2.

49. *57,* 232, Fox. Coll. V, 19. There are many instances of similar work elsewhere, e.g. at Castor, E. T. Artis, *Durobrivae* (1828), pl. 19— squares.

50. *53,* pl. 23. In II.1 were two very coarse panels, presumably late, containing a rosette and a bud: *53,* 272–3; Fox. Coll. V, 14–15.

51. *55,* pl. 15, In XXIII.2, Room 15 had a coarse red and buff striped floor, *57,* 232.

52. *52,* pl. 28, for example, shows a panel of fine fretwork in the corridor.

53. *Ib.* and pl 29.

54. *JRS* LVII, pl. 15, 2.

55. *56,* 245 ff., pl. 14; cf. pl. 11.

56. Note esp. the Verulamium mosaic, *AJ* XXXIX, pl. 4A, destroyed in late second cent.; otherwise cf. *Verulamium* pl. 44B and at Colchester *ArJ* CXXIII, pls. 7–8, all three however with the great underlying circle not present at Silchester; and the contents of the panels are very different. In general, fourth-century floors exhibit the designers' *horror vacui,* but Low Ham, *RVB* pl. 3.5, is an exception.

57. *RVB,* pl. 3, 27.

58. Cf. *MGR passim.*

59. Smilax, *Pliny* XVI, 35; XXI, 9. Caerleon, my *Isca* (1972), fig. 42, Severan(?); Lyon, *MGR,* 235, fig. 1 bottom L., topmost of three, of which the lowest was covered with ashes thought to be from the 197 destruction of Lyons. Cf. a floor at Italica, Garcia y Bellido, *Italica,* pl. 16.

60. *Ib.* pl. 15.

61. *Verulamium,* pl. 42, right; Chedworth, Woodchester, Bignor, conveniently set out by Fox, *56,* pl. 15.

62. *Ib.* pl. 16. Straying tendrils, perhaps cf. *ArJ* CXXIII, pl. 16, an early-looking Colchester floor. Painted scroll, e.g. at Verulamium, *AJ* XXXVII, pl. 4a; *B* III, 256, fig. 4.

63. *RVB,* pl. 3.5.

64. A close study of photographs, all rather oblique, hints at this.

65. Profile busts on mosaic are so rare that the following may be cited: Claudian, G. Becatti, *Scavi di Ostia* IV, *I Mosaici,* pls. 122–3; second-third century at Alba-Iulia (Apulum), I. Berciu, *Studii şi Comunicări* Acta Musei Regionalis Apulensis, IV), pls. 11-12, coloured: winds, not

winged, named ZEPHE (Zephyrus) and IIVR (Eurus). Winds, not profile, on British mosaics, Brading, *RVB*, pl. 3.8; Frampton, *ib*. pl. 3.28.

66. *VCH Som.* I, figs. 71–2, and the Littlecote Park mosaic, Wilts., *RVB* pl. 3.16, and in colour I. A. Richmond, *Roman Britain* (1947), facing 33.

CHAPTER 18 *(Houses: Furniture and Equipment)*

1. General works: *Liversidge, Richter*. Note esp. *Richter*, 97: 'there was... a uniform style throughout the Roman domains, bearing out the closely-knit character of the Empire'.

2. 55, 430 ('turned out of some kind of hard wood'), identified by myself in 1952; *Liversidge*, fig. 35. *Richter*, fig. 514, shows a turned wooden leg from Egypt.

3. Stools, *ib.* figs. 515–18; couches, figs. 530–2—dining; reliefs, British, *Liversidge, passim*.

4. Cf. the couch inlaid with bone and glass, *Richter*, fig. 531. There is some bone inlay in the collection; porphyry, p. 213. Cf. 102, fig. 8a for fragment of Alexandrian glass inlay; there are also pieces of millefiori and turquoise-colour; cf. *G* XI, fig. facing 16, from Xanten.

5. *Liversidge*, 9–10; *Richter* overstates the case against it, I think: the armchair, *Esp.* 5155 is stuffed. Gilt upholstery leather from London, *Liversidge*, fig. 22.

6. Petronius, *Saturae*, 97–8. Actual remains, Colchester, *B* IV, 302.

7. Simpelveld, *Esp.* 7795; *Richter,* fig. 584 for an excellent photograph. Caşei, S. Ferri, *Arte romana sul Danubio*, fig. 412 (*Römer in Rumänien,* Taf. 90). The edge of the coverlet seems to show that a fleece is not in question, but a textile *(tapete:* the British was the best, cf. *JRS* XLV, 114).

8. Cf. n. 3. Dining customs, J. Carcopino, *Daily Life in Ancient Rome* (1956), 262 ff.

9. *Esp.* 4062, 4097, 5155, 6489 etc., for seated diners; 5839, two reclining and one seated man. Women in Gaul are usually shown seated in basket chairs, and the metropolitan fashion of reclining seems not to have been adopted by them.

10. Dr Liversidge's original identification of the legs as those of tables, *Ant* XXIV, 25 ff. Examples in reliefs, *id., o.c.* for Britain; *Richter*, figs. 567 ff.

11. *Esp.* 5155, 5839, 7806 etc.

12. *Liversidge*, fig. 54. Dorchester, *ib.* figs. 44–5. Classical, see n. 10.

13. *Liversidge,* fig. 61; cf. A. Lawson, *Archaeologia* forthc. on all Silchester shale and jet. Several other tops are known, e.g. *B* I, pl. 35c, very like the larger Silchester piece.

14. *60, 163:* perhaps part of a service of dishes, if found together, as the reference may imply; cf. Lawson, *l.c.*

15. Reliefs, *Esp.* 5155, etc.; feet, Liversidge, *RVB,* pl. 4.23.

16. *50,* pl. 16, bottom right.

17. *HG* V, 236: *solennel,* because deities were shown seated in such chairs (our pl. 34a).

18. R. Goodburn in *Verulamium Excav.* I, 149, cf. pl. 49. The earliest identification of these objects was at Pompeii, when the hollow left by a chest in the ashes was cast in plaster: *Revue des Deux Mondes,* 1 July 1870, cited *PF,* 333–4.

19. *BMGGRL,* 166.

20. *Richter,* 119; cf. *Esp.* 5268, etc., for curtains on rings.

21.. *53, 574; May,* pl. 46A; S. Loeschcke, *Lampen aus Vindonissa,* Taf. 6, 65.

22. J. Holwerda and W. C. Braat, *Oudheidkundige Mededeelingen* n.s. XXVI, Supplement, 38, nos. 10–11, pl. 21, 3a–b, 5a–b. A very uncommon type probably with a metal original e.g. *BMC Lamps* pl. 5, 37.

23. J. M. C. Toynbee, *AJ XXXVIII,* 90, pl. 15. After Joyce's death it became customary for the Silchester labourers to bring their finds to Stratfield Saye from time to time, and the piece may have been lost on such an occasion.

24. *54,* 153, fig. 20.

25. *May,* pl. 46B.

26. *57, 250.* Several other examples of this type are published.

27. R. J. Forbes, *Stud. Ancient Technology* VI, 126, observes that in recent times at least a thin strip of stem was left to support the pith wick of rush-lights, and had the property of drawing the burnt portion to one side, in the same way as the strained thread in modern candle-wicks, introduced in 1825.

28. *Esp.* 4097, 5155 etc. where the heavy, fringed table-cloth may also be noted, cf. 5839.

29. M. Biddle, *AJ* XLVII, 230 ff.; cf. *Esp.* 7806 for tray on table.

30. Biddle *l.c.* has a list of examples, including the Silchester pieces, *58,* 422.

31. Hare-and-hound knives, cf. a complete one, *CA* III, 275, fig.; Primania's spoon, *EE* IX, 1311a.

32. The *patera* was a handleless vessel, as used in sacrifices.

33. The ivory is *BMC Early Christian Antiqs.*, pl. 6A. For the remaining matter see H. U. Nuber, 'Kanne und Griffschale', *Ber. RGK* LIII, 1–232, many figs.

34. *55*, 418, perhaps Campanian, but the mask is not very good, so probably Gaulish. Cf. M. H. P. den Boesterd, *Descr. Colls. Rijksmuseum Kam at Nijmegen, the Bronze Vessels*, 72, pls. 11, 16, no. 260B. Manufacture, cf. A. Mutz, *Die Kunst des Metalldrehens bei den Römern*.

35. *55*, 429. One with identical fretting is in Bangor Museum from the Abergele hoard; cf. Ellis Davies, *Preh. & Roman Remains of Denbs.*, fig. 9; Campanian.

36. *58*, 32, as in the Appleshaw hoard, *56*, 11, fig. 8, as noted by the excavators; cf. the Caerwent bowl with Christian monogram, *BBCS* XIX, 339, fig. 1. Inscription, *JRS* XLVII, 107, no. 25.

37. *55*, 231, from a pit below a wall of the west range of XIV.1. For Roman glass in general see D. B. Harden, 'Ancient Glass II: Roman', *ArJ* CXXVI, 44–77, illus., refs. There are numerous other catalogues, well-illustrated; but for its illustration of similar forms in other materials cf. especially P. la Baume, *Römisches Kunstgewerbe*.

38. *55*, 430. Cf. Corning Museum of Glass, *Glass from the Ancient World*, 138, for 'lug'. In colourless glass, a very few are known, see my note in *Monmouth Antiq.* III.2 forthcoming.

39. Boon, *Ann. du 4e Congrès des Journées internat. du Verre*, 93.

40. The mould-blown prototype, e.g. *Glass from the Ancient World*, 72, or BM. *Masterpieces of Glass*, 62. In the Guildhall Museum, London, is a nearly complete tall colourless beaker with relief-cut round or pear-shaped motifs.

41. *RS* called this piece 'Alexandrian', wrongly, comparing it with a London vessel (Harden, *l.c.*, pl. 10B). On these cups cf. D. Charlesworth, *JGS* XIII, 34.

42. E.g. *Glass from the Ancient World*, 90–1.

43. Pottery copy of a ribbed bowl, e.g. *AC* CXV, 56, fig. 2, 4 (Caerleon).

44. Flanged bowl copying samian Form 38, cf. O. Doppelfeld, *Römisches und frankisches Glas in Köln*, Taf. 85: jar, e.g. *Verulamium Excav.* I, fig. 76, 25–6; beaker, e.g. M. Vanderhoeven, *Verres romains tardifs et mérovingiens du Musée Curtius, Liège*, pl. 18, 62.

45. E.g *Verulamium Excav.* I, fig. 78, 48–50, a common type, very widespread; cf. N. Sorokina, *Ann. du 4e Congrès, etc.*, 76, Abb. 5, 12—common at Tanaïs etc.

46. Cf. F. Fremersdorf, *Denkmäler des römischen Köln* V, Taff. 30 ff. The Silchester piece was illustrated by W. A. Thorpe, *English Glass*, fig. 2K.

47. See D. B. Harden, *97*, 203 ff., 207, pl. 69H, cf. pl. 67F–G; other British example, from Gt. Staughton, Hunts., *ib.* 212. To the list of cage-cups or *'diatreta'* add O. Doppelfeld, *G* XXXVIII, 403 ff.

48. Lawson *l.c.,* n. 13.

49. On samian-ware see, in brief, B. R. Hartley in *ARB,* ch. 13 (available as separate); C. M. Johns, *Arretine & Samian Pottery* (B.M.), where, pl. ii, a marbled vessel is shown (colouring too 'hot').

50. Not in *May:* G. Simpson, *JRS* XLII, 69, fig. 5, 3: the 'Aldgate' potter. The two masks in black gloss, *May* pl. 35, with two of Pan in lower relief; better, G. Simpson, *AJ* XXXVII, pl. 14, in a useful article on this type of samian, to which now add *AJ* LIII, 42 ff.

51. Boon, *RAC* VII, 321, figs. 1–2, form wrongly suggested.

52. *55*, 253, fig. 6; *May,* 100–1, pl. 40A; on it, K. Greene, *Guide to Pre-Flavian Fine Wares* (privately printed, Cardiff 1972), 12, 38, fig. 12, 8.

53. Most but not all the samian is in *May,* e.g. marbled, pl. 39A, 1–4, 7–8; barbotine, pls. 33, 36, 41, all except 3 (black); cut-glass, pl. 37; rouletted, pl. 29, lower, and cf. 38, Argonne; applied moulded (black), see n. 50. Other plates are given to plain wares, the text still fairly good but out-of-date in some points of ascription and chronology.

54. *May,* pls. 40C, 42A, bronzed, 48. The distinction between Rhenish and Lezoux black-gloss wares is well brought out by N. Brewster, *AA* ser. 4 L, 205–16.

55. These vessels were a puzzle for many years. A list was drawn up by G. Behrens, *G* XXX, 110–11, illus.; examples from Colchester and Caerleon (two, one inscribed but illegibly) may be added, and another from Heddernheim, H. U. Nuber, *Rei Cretariae Romanae Fautorum Acta* XI/XII, 70–5, with an inscription which settled the matter. The central orifice was plugged when the wine, etc. was poured in and the bowl was then inverted so that the contents would be strained through the perforations.

56. *May,* pls. 44–5. In general see B. R. Hartley, *Notes on the Roman Pottery Industry in the Nene Valley* (Peterborough Mus. Pbln. II). Continental finds, e.g. S. de Loë, *Belgique ancienne* III, figs. 66–7; H. Brunsting, *400 Jaar romeinse Bezetting van Nijmegen* (1969), fig. 20.

57. On Oxfordshire and New Forest pottery see progress-reports by Chr. Young and Mrs V. Swan respectively, *Current Research in Romano-British Coarse Pottery* (Council for British Archaeology, Res. Rept. 10), 105 ff., 117 ff.

58. *May*, pls. 52, 85, 87, 89; 54–6 *passim;* rosette-stamped, pl. 57; painted, 55, cf. 65, no. 140.

59. *Ib.* pls. 58–9, maroon-glazed. Much of the red colour-coated ware once thought to be New Forest is now known to be Oxfordshire.

60. *Ib.* pl. 50, 73; sometimes found in glass, and it is to glass that the diagnostic reference from Soranus, cited by W. Hilgers, *Lateinische Gefässnamen,* 80, refers.

61. *54,* 153, fig. 21; other British examples have since come to light; cf. p. 340, n. 24.

62. Incomplete; cf. e.g. *Bull. Inst. of Arch.* I, 68, fig. 11a, Brading villa.

63. E.g. *May,* pl. 49, 68, first-second century.

64. *57,* 249.

65. *57,* 248; D. H. Kennett, *JRGZ* XVI, 145, with a note on the type, in an article on late Roman bronze vessel 'hoards' in Britain.

66. *56,* 241, fig. 3 (XIX.1); cf. *Esp.* 7762. Chains, *57,* 247, 1900 'hoard': Dr Manning tells me that there are parts of one simple 'Stanfordbury' type (i.e. with figure-of-eight links) and two of 'Chesterford' type (with loop-in-loop chains and decorative cage-top).

67. *61,* 485, fig. 4; cf. Liversidge in B. Flower and E. Rosenbaum, *The Roman Cookery Book,* 30, pl. 2, 2.

68. The best general surveys in a subject in which there is much current research are *Gillam* and *ARB,* ch. 14.

69. On mortaria, see Hilgers *o.c.,* 68. The account by Mrs K. Hartley in *Richborough* V, 172 ff. is particularly valuable; but she now informs me that the potter *Verecundus,* there suggested as having worked near Silchester, is known to be continental. There are no stamps of his at Silchester, cf. *May,* pl. 83A.

70. *53,* 285; not illustrated by May. The material requires re-examination, being described prior to the researches of Lyell and Reid.

71. F. Oswald, *AJ* XXIV, 45. But there can be no doubt that mortaria were used to mix food, not indeed by *pounding,* but by *rubbing,* and many are found worn or worn through by this means. Some may have been used for souring milk, see next note.

72. *55,* 245, cf. pl. 15 for location. Parts of two other vessels are in the collection and there is another from Silchester in Brighton Museum (inf. Mrs Hartley).

73. General account, *56,* 117 ff. For those made of lava, cf. *Ant* XXIX, 68 ff.

74. *56,* 240, fig. 1.

75. *54,* 452, pl. 46 marked G.

76. *61*, 478. The staves mentioned must belong to a bucket.
77. *61*, 477, fig. 1, perhaps from the bottom of a bottle-case (our p. 361, n. 171). The most handsome basketry to survive from Roman times, said to be of honeysuckle and found containing resin, are three vase-shaped handled baskets about 25 cm. high; one is illustrated by F. Baudry and L. Ballereau, *PF*, 129.
78. *May*, pl. 85, 26; *VCH Hants.* I, 284.

CHAPTER 19 *(Agriculture and Food)*

1. In general, see *Applebaum*, and K. D. White, *Roman Farming*.
2. *PHFC* XV, 159.
3. At about SU 644608. I am indebted to Mr J. Hampton for drawing my attention to this discovery.
4. *Applebaum*, 13–14, pl. 1. For a more highly Romanised example at Cromwell villa (Northants.), *JRS* LI, pl. 11, 3.
5. Applebaum, *PHFC* XVIII, 136.
6. Kennet valley, H. Peake, *Archaeol. of Berks.*, gazetteer; *JRS* XLV, 142, LIII, 149. A. L. F. Rivet, *Town and Country in R.B.* (1964) but see below, p. 266.
7. *102*, 20: the line of the track eastwards to a junction with the main road near the reduced outer earthwork appears on some photographs, e.g. our pl. 9.
8. *102*, 21, and aerial photographs.
9. *Ib.*, 19.
10. As perhaps at Ditchley, *Oxon* I, 52.
11. Kromayer-Veith, *Heerwesen und Kriegführung der Griechen und Römer*, 280, 425 (850 g. per day). Military diet, R. Davies, *B* II, 122 ff. The modern intake (1938) is given as 4.5 bushels per head annually, i.e. 163.65 litres (imperial standard bushel = 36.3677 l., information kindly supplied by the Weights and Measures Dept. of Cardiff Corporation; we take it henceforward as 36 l., in view of the very approximate nature of our calculations).
12. Cited by J. Percival, *Wheat in Gt. Britain* (1934), 51.
13. This phrase is from his article, *Agricultural Hist. Rev.* VI, 85: but we do not know how, or how high, grain was stacked in granaries.
14. *PPS* XX, 112.
15. G. Duby, *L'économie rurale et la vie des campagnes dans l'occident médiéval* I, 184 ff., esp. 187.

16. *Columella* III, 3.4; Varro, *De Re Rustica* I, 44 mentions much higher returns, exceptional—or legendary.

17. Weedy crops, *Applebaum*, 113. Possibly the presence of leguminous seeds in grain e.g. at Downton villa (Wilts.), *WAM* LVIII, 328, is attributable to the germination of plants ploughed in as green manure, *Columella* II, 14 etc. See also n. 22.

18. Taking the figure of G. Simpson, *Britons and the Roman Army*, 119 and adding 15,500 for the three legions. C. F. C. Hawkes, *ArJ* CIV, 79, suggests on the basis of grain-pits that three-fifths of the harvest at the Cranborne Chase villages may have been taken for the *annona*. But these villages are believed to be part of an imperial domain. The remainder of his calculations are unfortunately upset by a false metric equation of the bushel (see n. 11).

19. Rotations, White *o.c.*, 118 ff., and cf. P. Brunt, *JRS* LXII, 156, in a review.

20. That is, allowing a third extra to local needs.

21. *57*, 256; *58*, 35 (*Triticum sativum:* but there is doubt as to how correct such old identifications may have been; cf. H. Helbaek, *PPS* XVIII, 201. On the other hand it would be difficult to confuse *T. sativum = vulgare* with e.g. the longer kernals of T. *spelta*).

22. *Godwin*, 342, makes the point about the association of *Agrostemma githago=Lychnis githago* with rye; but see *Newstead*, 359 for numerous seeds associated with wheat chaff.

23. *61*, 210.

24. E.g. at Downton, n. 17 and Verulamium, *PPS* XVIII, 213.

25. *60*, 449; *57*, 254.

26. Cabbage seeds were found at Gt. Casterton, P. Corder, *First Interim Rept.*, 19.

27. Carrot, *58*, 246; radish, *59*, 367; parsnip, *57*, 255 cf. *59*, 368. Another brassica 'not *B. alba*', *58*, 35, appears to have been identified later as ?turnip, which is known at Pevensey, *Sussex Arch. Colls.* LII, 94.

28. *57*, 255, etc.

29. Though poorly represented: *57*, 254; *58*, 35; also at Pevensey, n. 27; cf. *PPS* XVIII, 212.

30. *61*, 210, 212, fig. 8; *57*, 255; *60*, 164.

31. *59*, 367 etc.; cf. *Pliny* XIX, 8, in egg-glaze.

32. *57*, 256 (*Lycopus europaeus;* cf. F. H. Knapp, *Botanical Chart of Br. Flowering Plants* (1846), 274); *58*, 426 (*Galium verum* and *Serratula tinctoria, ib.*, 193, 408: of the first he says 'the roots are used by the Highlanders for dyeing red; they boil them with the yarn,

adding alum to fix the colour. Curtis says these roots yield a better red dye than madder. . . .'). Neither madder nor woad is at present known from the Romano-British period.

33. *57*, 255 etc.
34. *Ib.;* Apicius, *De Re Coquinaria,* 128: a kind of fruity foo-yung (see B. Flower and E. Rosenbaum: *The Roman Cookery Book).*
35. *Palladius* III, 25.19; cf. XI, 16; *Pliny* XIV, 16.
36. *Pliny* XXIV, 8.
37. *57*, 252, cf. *Pliny* XV, 25: glimpsed, cf. our p. 237.
38. *57*, 255 etc.
39. *59*, 368.
40. *Ib.*
41. *57*, 255; *Pliny* XV, 13.
42. *59*, 367: possibly the Gallic medlar of *Pliny* XV, 20.
43. *60*, 449, cf. our p. 198.
44. *57*, 253, *58*, 427 etc.; cf *Applebaum,* 117; *SHA Probus* 18, 8.
45. Pips and skins from wine-making, *TBGAS* LV, 74. The typical fortunes of a modern British vineyard are described by A. Pettigrew, *Trans. Cardiff Nats. Soc.* XVI, 6 ff. See also Ed. Hyams in *The Times,* Supplement, 20 Nov. 1963, p. iii. Pepys drank 'very good red wine of my Lady's own making [at Walthamstow] in England', *Diary* (ed. Latham and Matthews) I, 317 (1660).
46. *57*, 256; *58*, 427 etc. Julian, *Misopogon* 341A, 'himatia'.
47. Distribution of the fertilised fig, Hegi, *Illustrierte Flora von Mittel-Europa* (1957) III.1, 279 Abb. 126. Dried figs, e.g. *Columella* XII, 15; in amphorae, *Callender,* ch. 4.
48. *Ib.;* stones at Neuss, hospital, K–H. Knörzer, *Novaesium* IV, 98. Almond, Wiggonholt bath-house (Sussex), Winbolt, *SAC* LXXXI, 65 (but ?identification).
49. Hazel-nut, *57*, 256 etc. Walnut, *Godwin,* 290; sweet chestnut, *SAC* LII, 94; see Applebaum, 119.
50. Quoted from Lynn S. White, *Medieval Technology and Social Change,* 73.
51. *Pliny* XI, 41: '*butyrum* is the scum of milk'. Its use was mainly as an ointment in classical lands.
52. *53*, 285 ff; *53*, 572 states that the average measurements of metacarpals and metatarsals of ox found in 1892 were 192 and 210 mm., thus indicating animals a trifle larger than those studied by Pitt Rivers *ECC* I, table, 187; II, table, 224.

53. *58*, 423 ff. Cf. J. C. Ewart in *Newstead*, 374 ff.: Ewart tried to reconstruct the Romano-British type by breeding, cf. *ib.* pl. 97, 4, and has some interesting speculations on the colour of the coat, brown or black.

54. *54*, 238: not *Bos longifrons* as suggested by the excavators.

55. *ECC* II, 218 ff., fig. p. 222.

56. E.g. *JRS* LIV, 56, fig. 4b; White, *Agricultural Implements of the R. World*, pl. 11B.

57. *ECC* II, 221 ff., fig. p. 222; Ewart, *l.c.* 573, pl. 97, 3. The Woodcuts and Rotherley sheep seem also to have been smaller than the Silchester sheep: *53*, 572 gives metacarpal and metatarsal measurements of 124 and 128 mm.

58. Birds, *53*, 288; pheasant, *58*, 20, *59*, 369, *60*, 167. Cf. P. Lowe, *Ibis* ser. 3 III, 334 ('domestic fowl'); but the most recent comment is that of Dr. M. I. Platt of the Roy. Scottish Museum (*in litt.*, Reading Museum, 27 Feb. 1951): '. . . I have looked carefully at the . . . avian relics and find I have no occasion to doubt the original identification—they compare very favourably with the pheasant skeletons we have.'

59. Painting, Verulamium, *AJ* XXXVII, pl. 5 in colour; pavement, Caerleon 1692, Boon, *Isca* (1972), 133, n. 267, fig. 40—brown long-tailed birds.

60. S. Lauffer, *Diokletians Preisedikt*, 4.17–20. Luxuries earlier, cf. *SHA Elagabalus*, 31; *Pertinax*, 12; *Severus Alexander*, 37; *Tacitus*, 12. Pets at first? cf. Martial, *Epigrammata* III, 58, 16.

61. *Palladius*, I, 29.

62. *53*, 288 etc.

63. *53*, 287; *57*, 111; *60*, 165.

64. This expression used of the Maiden Castle dog, *Maiden Castle*, 371 f. A dog from Blewburton is more carefully described by J. E. King, *BAJ* LIII, 60, tables 3–4.

65. *53*, 288; *58*, 424; *ECC* I, 172 ff., pl. 69.

66. F. Zeuner, *Hist. of Domesticated Animals*, 393.

67. *60*, 449.

68. Ff. G. Payne, *ArJ* CIV, 89, 110 f., fig. 1. More recently, Manning has suggested that these may have been the cutting-edges of peat-spades, in A. Gailey and A. Fenton, *The Spade in Northern and Atlantic Europe*, 26. There is peat in the Kennet valley and the suggestion is certainly one to be borne in mind.

69. *JRS* LIV, 60: two coulters and two bars in 1890 'hoard', cf. *54,* 144, 141; four and four in the 1900 'hoard', *57,* 247 (but here only three coulters are mentioned). Coulters, Payne *ArJ* CIV, pl. 35B; bar, Manning *JRS* fig. 5A, pl. 8, 2–3. The Gt. Chesterford and Dorchester (Oxon.) 'hoards' furnished like numbers of coulters and bars.

70. Ploughs and ploughing: in addition to Payne's basic study in *ArJ* CIV, see Manning, *l.c.* n. 69, and *Applebaum,* ch. 6.

71. Withy rope, Cf. G. Payne, *Yr Aradr Cymreig,* 150 and n.; instanced at Glastonbury, A. Bulleid and H. St. G. Gray, *The Glastonbury Lake-Village* I, 341. The last plough-team of oxen, Lord Bathurst's at Cirencester Park, has now been discontinued; see a photograph in *The Field,* 14 May 1959, 914.

72. P. V. Glob, *Acta Archaeologica* (Copenhagen), XVI, 109–10.

73. E.g. White, *Agricultural Implements of the R. World* pls. 11A, 10B.

74. So Payne, *ArJ* CIV, 92.

75. *Pliny,* XVIII, 20. Two asymmetrical winged shares from Britain 'confirm in the most satisfactory way the evidence deducible from some of the coulters [i.e. that they have been 'set' to cut preferentially one way] that the fixed mould-board had arrived in the Romano-British period'—Payne, *Agricultural Hist. Rev.* V, 78. Moveable coulter, A. Aberg, *Gwerin* I, 181, fig. 8 (La Tène or Roman, Austria).

76. *Pliny,* XVIII, 18.

77. Clear diagrams appear in H. C. Bowen, *Ancient Fields.*

78. Manning in *The Spade,* 21, fig. 2D, with marks where the iron was attached.

79. *Ib.,* 21–4; Silchester examples, figs. 3A, H, round and square-ended.

80. *Ib.,* 19, 20, 26.

81. Cf. *Applebaum,* 79, citing *Newstead,* pl. 61, 17.

82. Forks, *57,* 247; *bidens,* White, *o.c.* pl. 26; cf. Manning, *The Spade,* 20–1, fig. 2.

83. *Applebaum,* 80, mentions a wooden hay-fork from Chew Park villa (Som.), but the fork in question seems far too small. I have seen and used a wooden hay-fork on a small farm in the Forest of Dean before the war.

84. Scythes, *Applebaum,* 76. Mower's anvils, *54,* 143, fig. 5; *57,* 247.

85. E. J. T. Collins, *Sickle to Combine* (Mus. of English Rural Life, Reading, 1969), 9, gives figures showing that a man using a scythe can cut three times as much corn in a day as a man reaping high with a sickle, and more than twice as much as a man reaping low, though not much more than a man using a bagging-hook.

86. *57*, 256.
87. *57*, 254.
88. *57*, pl. 30.
89. *55*, pl. 10.
90. *56*, pl. 5.
91. *56*, pl. 11.
92. *57*, pl. 30.
93. *JRS* LVII, 187, fig. 9; *Applebaum*, 183, fig. 39; *JRS* XLV, 131, fig. 32; Roach Smith, *Collectanea Antiqua* II, 9, fig.
94. *Applebaum*, 123 ff. Shackles were found at Park Street villa (H. O'Neil, *ArJ* CII, 33, 66, fig. 9), Belgic or Roman; a better parallel for ours, *Roman Colchester* 111, pl. 21A, for what must almost surely have been an underground slave-barrack *(ergastulum)*. In general see also White, *op. cit., passim.*
95. *57*, pl. 32.
96. *53*, pl. 21.
97. *61*, pl. 23 ('east court').
98. *JRS* LVII, 192, fig. 15; LX, 232, fig. 31; and see n. 93.
99. *56*, 230, pl. 11, 242.
100. *55*, pl. 10.
101. P. Corder and J. L. Kirk, *A Roman Villa at Langton*, fig. 38.
102. *54*, pl. 46.
103. *ArJ* CIV, 48; *Applebaum*, 175, fig. 36.
104. *57*, pl. 30; see p. 160 above.
105. *56*, pl. 5.
106. *61*, pl. 83.
107. *53*, pl. 21.
108. The type of granary with cross-walls supporting an elevated floor does not apparently occur at Calleva: I.2, south end of east wing, might be considered an example but the work of two or three periods is clearly involved and it is not possible to say what the final arrangement was. The cross-wall granary is rare in villas, occurring at Ditchley, *Oxon* I, 48, fig. 8; *Shakenoak* I, 18, fig. 4; and very large (in excess of 30 by 18 m.) at Horton Kirby (Kent), *Kent Arch. Rev.* 1972–3, 304, fig. p. 302.
109. *57*, 242, pl. 32.
110. *Oxon* I, 45, fig. 8; *Langton*, 40, fig. 47; *ArJ* LXVI, pl. 1, not a shrine, surely?
111. Flail, Lynn S. White *o.c.*, 152 ff.
112. *Applebaum*, 5.

113. Helbaek, *PPS* XVIII, 232–3, n. 1; cf. *Pliny* XVIII, 10 on treatment of *far* (emmer).
114. E.g. at Downton, see n. 17.
115. *59*, 335, fig. 1, pl. 73; Atworth, R. G. Goodchild, *AJ* XXIII, 148 ff., fig. 1, pl. 27A. A West Blatchington example appears to be of second to third century date, *Sussex Arch. Colls.* LXXXIX, 27 ff., fig. 7, 8A.
116. *60*, pl. 17.
117. *Ant* XXV, 197, fig. 1.
118. *71*, pl. 13, 151 ff.
119. *57*, pl. 32; *56*, pl. 11; *57*, pl. 30.
120. *56*, pl. 11 ('tank'); *58*, pls. 28–9 (misunderstood).
121. H. O'Neil, *ArJ* CII, 110, pl. 6A; P. Corder, *Second Interim Report* 19 ff., 23, fig. 9; grain, 22; Old Sleaford (Lincs.), *JRS* LI, 170, fig. 19.
122. *54*, pl. 47, 1.
123. *JRS* XLVII, 221, fig. 28.
124. *Ant* XXV, 199, fig. 2.
125. *53*, pls. 21, 28.
126. *Duplicia bubilia: Columella* 1, 6. 4, width 10 or 9 *pedes* (3 or 2.7 m.); also *ibid.* I, 6.6.
127. *57*, 98, pl. 9: very solid flint-packed post-holes curiously described as 'drains'.
128. *58*, pl. 32.
129. *58*, pl. 2.
130. *57*, pl. 8.
131. *Applebaum*, 175, fig. 36, follows A. Moray-Williams, *ArJ* LXVI, 49, in suggesting that piers at 2.4 m. intervals at Stroud villa designated ox-stalls.
132. *55*, pl. 23: probably a reception-room in an early house nearly obliterated.
133. *55*, pl. 23.
134. *58*, pl. 2.
135. *53*, pl. 22.
136. *JRS* XLIX, 135, fig. 26, right: *Applebaum*, 180, fig. 38 (byre on the other side).
137. *60*, pl. 40: other traces of buildings hereabouts. The long building might be compared with the supposed sties at Pitney, n. 136.
138. *57*, pl. 30.
139. *61*, 483, pl. 83. Hen Waliau: V. E. Nash-Williams, *The R. Frontier in Wales* (1969), 63.

140. *53*, pl. 21.
141. *55*, pl. 10.
142. *55*, pl. 10.
143. *56*, pl. 5.
144. *56*, pl. 11.
145. *56*, pl. 11.
146. *57*, pl. 30.
147. *57*, pl. 30.
148. *57*, pls. 30, 32.
149. *57*, pl. 32.
150. *58*, pl. 2.
151. *60*, pl. 40.
152. *53*, 286, 572; *58*, 424; *59*, 369; *60*, 167, including sea-fish and molluscs.
153. Salted, e.g. *Columella* VIII, 17. Ham was smoked, Horace *Sat.* II, 2, 117, thus probably fish also.
154. Mr H. Carter, of Reading Museum, kindly checked the molluscs for me. He reports the presence of the common and edible snail, *Helix aspersa,* but not the escargot, *H. Pomatia,* which occurred, however, at Shakenoak *(Shakenoak* III, 162), and may have been reared there; cf. *Pliny* IX, 56 on rearing four sorts of snails commercially.
155. *Rutupino edita fundo Ostrea, Sat.* IV, 141.
156. *57*, 252.
157. Sussex and Hants., cf. R. Bradley, *Sussex Notes and Queries* XVII, 23–4, a reference owed to Miss Jane Evans. In general see J. Nenquin, *Salt* (Dissert. Arch. Gandenses VI) with gazetteer of British and other salt-making sites.
158. On *defrutum,* etc., see B. Flower and E. Rosenbaum, *The Roman Cookery Book,* 23 ff.
159. *Columella* V, 8; *Palladius* IX, 9. With the exception of Cato, the ancient writers on agriculture give considerable space to apiculture, including Pliny and Virgil, thus attesting the importance of honey in the diet.
160. *WAM* LVII, 240; A. T. Morley-Hewitt, *Roman Villa* . . . (1963), 33, fig.
161. *May,* pl. 64, 120; 148, ref. to inscriptions on similar vessels.
162. *Callender,* ch. 4.
163. *Ib.,* 45; resin or pitch applied, *Pliny* XIV, 20; resinated wine, *ib.,* and e.g. *Columella* XII, 21, 23. Cf. R. Dion, *Hist. de la vigne et du vin en France des origines au XIXe siècle,* 118 ff., esp. 120.

164. M. B. Lloris, *Las anforas romanas en España*, 485 ff. (Form V= *Callender*, Form 11).

165. *May*, 278 ff., pl. 83B; a south Spanish stamp L C ANT (cf. *Callender*, no. 820) is a recent stray find. G. Antonius Quietus distribution, *Callender*, fig. 25.

166. Cork, *Pliny* XVI, 8, cf. Horace, *Carm.* III, 8, 10; *Callender*, 43, Lloris, *o.c.*, 70 ff. 'Pine' bungs, *Newstead*, 317. The wood of the Silchester bung was kindly identified afresh by Mr J. Davies of the Botany Dept., National Museum of Wales.

167. Route, Lloris, *o.c.*, fig. 44. Cases, *Callender*, pl. 5; long-bodied, *Esp.* 6699.

168. At entry to amphora-cellar, R. Laur-Belart, *Führer durch Augusta Raurica*, 133, Abb. 101; also in *Callender*.

169. Cylindrical bottles, Boon, *Annales du 4e congrès des Journées internationales du verre*, 95; square, D. Charlesworth, *JGS* VIII, 26 ff. (but with error in the computation of Roman measure, not affecting conclusions). There are two from the same mould of the smaller base figured, with a tree-motif, damaged by pontil-scar; and an imperfect base reading S[I]L retrograde, of which several examples are elsewhere known, one at the Trentholme Drive cemetery, York. The small hexagonal perfume-bottle is matched by e.g. M. Vanderhoeven, *Verres romains (Ier-IIIe siècles) des Musées Curtius et du Verre* (Liège), no. 125.

170. Frontinian stamp, cf. A. Kisa, *Das Glas im Altertume*, 944, no. 45. Frontinian bottles in general, C. Isings, *Roman Glass from Dated Finds*, form 89.

171. Wicker cases, *Esp.* 5154, also *ib.* without cases; Boon, *Annales*, on this point.

172. *56*, 121 ff., pl. 8, including Haverfield's note on the inscriptions then seen.

173. *Bayerische Vorgeschichtsblätter* XXIV, 6 ff., Abb. 9 for distribution-map.

174. W. H. Manning and R. P. Wright, *AJ* XLI, 238, pl. 46 for additional inscriptions found in 1960 when the barrel was dismantled. London: *JRS* LI, 195, 24.

175. Cf. n. 172; for *-os* and *-us* see respectively the mid first-century and second-century potters' accounts on shards, from La Graufesenque: F. Hermet, *La Grauf.*, pt. ii, pls.; A. Albenque, *RA* ser. 6 XXXVII, 184–6, fig.

176. Cf. n. 172.

177. 55, 414.

178. *Pliny* XIV, 7 mentions a variety of Chian wine, *Arvisium,* and the letters AR on an amphora at Rome have been held to refer to this (*CIL* XV, 4537). It is hardly a possibility here. The Côte d'Or *Pagus Arebrignus* was noted in the late empire for its wines, cf. Dion, *o.c.* 139: probably too late. If GI were really GE or (the same) GII it might stand for *Gemellum,* a variety of Italian Aminean wine, *Pliny* XIV, 2, cf. *CIL* XV, 4572 etc.: but the suggestion is very unlikely.

179. M. Hopf, *JRGZ* XIV, 215. Harelbeke, J. Viérin, Ch. Léva, M. Renard and Ed. Frison, *Collection Latomus* XX, 759 ff., = *Archaeologia Belgica* LIX, a most important group of studies. *Picatum,* cf. n. 163. It has recently been pointed out, however, that a resinous lining was not confined, in the case of amphorae, to those meant for wine: one vessel is labelled 'fish-sauce' (A. J. Parker in D. J. Blackman (ed.), *Marine Archaeology,* 371.

180. 57, 253, 256: *Abies pectinata* = *A. alba.*

181. Viérin *et al., l.c.,* pl. 40 for distributions; cf. also *Flora Europaea* I, 30, 32. Determination of the Harelbeke and Aardenburg staves, Frison, *l.c.,* 800, 803.

182. *Pliny,* XIV, 21; cf. XVI, 10 *ad fin.*

183. Finds of barrels: Ulbert, map *l.c.;* epigraphical, cited by Renard, *l.c.,* 793 and n.3; axe-hammers, *ib.* 799, cf. pl. 43; Epfach, H. Dannheimer, *Bayerische Vorgeschichtsblätter* XXXVI, 322-4, inscribed DONAT(i).

184. Tablets, *LRT,* 56; *AJ* XXXIII, 207, 'fir'; Silchester, *Abies alba* (identified by Mr R. Perry of the Dept. of Botany, National Museum of Wales, from a splinter); Chew Park villa, Som., larch, *JRS* XLVI, 115; 'pine', *Newstead,* 308, probably silver fir?. Abroad, *Abies alba* at Vindonissa, dendrochronologically dated *c.* A.D. 55, *Gesellschaft Pro Vindonissa* 1971, 87; ditto at Valkenburg, W. Glasbergen, *De romeinse Castellum te Valkenburg Z.H., Opgravingen 1962* (1972), 67; Tolsum, Friesland, W. van Es, *De Romeinen in Nederland,* fig. 149. Small stave-built buckets were also of fir *in genere,* cf. p. 316, n. 7.

185. 60, 101.

186. *Esp.* 3232, 5193, etc.; F. B. Florescu, *Die Trajanssäule,* Taff. 3, 45–6, 107. There is no certain representation of an amphora on the Column, a point of some importance.

187. A small second-century? pot was dredged from the Loddon at Stanford End, on the north side of Stratfield Saye Park, some years ago and is

kept at Stratfield Saye. The find-spot would be close to the line of the Roman road.

188. J. Déchelette, *Les vases céramiques ornés de la Gaule romaine* I, 120, n. 2.

189. The clearest instance, at Caerleon: H. Helbaek, *The New Phytologist* LXIII, 158 ff. Remains of 'caramelised barley-malt' and 'fermented material' in a re-used amphora at Alzey, W. Unversagt, *Schumacher-Festschrift*, 314–15, are actually of honey, M. Hopf, *JRGZ* X, 68.

CHAPTER 20 (*Industry, Crafts and Trade*)

1. General: R. F. Tylecote, *Metallurgy in Archaeology.*

2. *102*, 6; bloom, H. Cleere and N. Bridgewater, *BHMG* I. 7, 30 ff.

3. H. H. Coghlan, *Notes on prehistoric and early Iron in the Old World,* 148.

4. To be published in my report on the Fortress Baths in *AC.*

5. Cf. the deposit mentioned p. 272, which is of a very common type.

6. *52, 742, 54,* 139ff, *57,* 246ff. (where the '1890' total is given as 66, probably a misprint for 60).

7. Manning, *B* III, 239, n. 98.

8. The beaked type is uncommon: cf. Lindenschmit, *Altertümer unserer heidnischen Vorzeit* V, Taf. 46, 747. The usual type is cubical or slightly pyramidal; cf. *Esp.* 8442.

9. The white-hot blanks were inserted into the tapering holes at either end of these implements and bushed over to form the heads.

10. 1908; Gowland, *PSAL* XXII, 532: 'one insignificant piece of slag was sufficient evidence of copper-refining . . . a new industry for Silchester . . . purifying the crude copper obtained by smelting ore. . . .'

11. *102*, 51, fig. 7c; a 'tray' where filings, etc. were collected was recognised in 1961 by Miss M. Wilson (north edge of Insula VII opposite the forum); cf. *Verulamium Exc.* I, 18.

12. Boon and P. A. Rahtz, *ArJ* CXXII, 41–3. There are a partly-melted coin of Valentinian II, one of Carausius and one of Diocletian in the collection, probably connected with counterfeiting. Cf. Boon, in G. Wainwright, *Coygan Camp* (Cambrian Arch. Assn., 1967), 124, pl. 10, 17.

13. *O.c.,* 136.

14. Cf. Cleere, *B* II, 208.

15. A few lumps of raw and partly smelted galena occur, e.g. *102,* 52: the latter points to cupellation, but on a small scale.

16. *57, 417*, Pb 62% Sn%. Solder also mentioned *58, 412* (no analysis). *Pliny,* XXXIV, 18 mentions *tertiarium*—two-thirds lead, one-third tin, to which no Silchester solder corresponds; but a multiplicity of types exists for specific purposes.

17. *50, 278; 57, 415*, fig. 15B.

18. *PSAL* XXII, 58, wrongly given as Insula VIII. In general see W. Wedlake, *Camerton,* 82 ff.; P. D. C. Brown, *Cornish Arch.* IX, 107 ff.; I. Goodall, *Yorks. Arch. Journ.* XLIV, 34–6. with ref. to base-ring inner mould on Fox's Silchester drawing and an outer mould from Wiltshire.

19. *BMGRB,* 32. The southern group of Wedlake's map, *o.c.* pl. 19, could well arise from a Silchester industry. Dishes, cf. C. A. Peal, *PCAS* LX, 19 ff.

20. *58, 422.* A similar torque in gold, *Gesellschaft Pro Vindonissa,* 1971, 88, Abb. 1.

21. *54, 221.* The most recent account of the industry is unfortunately confused, *CC,* 80.

22. See n. 15.

23. *54, 455,* pls. 45–6; *57,* 113 ff.; Gowland, 1905, *PSAL* XX, 214. The lead phosphate on coins from hollows in the church (p. 312, n. 24) may be connected with this last find.

24. See Boon, *Apulum* IX, 465 ff. on all this matter.

25. Cf. L. Cope and H. Billingham, *BHMG* I. 9, 1 ff., II. 1, 51 ff.

26. In *Hengistbury,* 72 ff. Though generally supposed to be of the Iron Age, one site at least produced Roman coins and pottery. Cupellation at Wroxeter (*Apulum* IX, 473) may have depended on argentiferous copper from Llanymynech (Mont.) not far away. Slight confirmation of connections between Silchester and Cornwall is supplied by a cuprite bugle, or long bead, in the collection.

27. *ArJ* CXXII, 45–6. See n. 23.

28. *61, 485.* Replacement capital, see p. 107 and *53,* pl. 37, 1.

29. *AJ* VI, 75–6. Prof. C. F. C. Hawkes recalled (*in litt.* 2 Aug. 1968) Karslake's 'belief in' and 'pride in having published' the stamp, but on various visits in the early and mid 1930's does not recall having been shown it or other material.

30. *PHFC* XVI, 59.

31. Accession-no. 1957: 16, gift of V. Burton Esq., Ordnance Survey.

32. A. W. G. Lowther, *Stud. of Patterns on Roman Flue-Tiles and their Distribution* (Surrey Arch. Soc. Occas. Paper I, 1948).

33. E. M. Clifford, *JRS* XLV, 68 ff. An LHS tile of Gloucester type in the collection is probably not truly provenanced; this might apply also to

the 'Virgilian' tile from the same source; cf. Haverfield, *VCH Hants.* I, 282.

34. W. F. Grimes, *Y Cymmrodor* XLI. Civil, e.g. at Cranleigh, Surrey, *AJ* XVI, 463. Clamps, Grimes *l.c.*, 60, schedule nos. 18, 81.

35. *52, 757.*

36. *May,* pl. 86, 8 gives an incorrect outline of the tile; *ib.* 9, was probably a (delighted) *Sa*[*tis*].

37. *RLÖ* XIII, 106 ff. for some comparative material. Latest tile, information from Prof. J. E. Bogaers, cf. *SJ* XXV, 102, including V KAL OCTO (Sept. 27), from Siscia.

38. *62, 327* ff., cf. 326 for supports from ditch; *May,* 192. Cf. *ArJ* CXIV, pl. 6A for details of base of dome, lined with pot-lids (wasters).

39. See in general P. Corder, *ArJ* CXIV, 10 ff. Nearly all Romano-British pottery-kilns are of this 'up-draught' type. Several examples of pairs of kilns, as here, are given.

40. I hope to publish Mr Cole's report *in extenso* in *JGS.*

41. These decolorants do not normally appear together and here strongly indicate the use of scrap of diverse origin. Analysis (wt. %) of glass on crucible: SiO_2 70.1—CaO 5.2—MgO 0.6—Fe_2O_3 0.5—Al_2O_3 3.3—Na_2O 18.2—K_2O 0.6—Sb_2O_3 0.1—Mn_3O_4 0.2—SO_3 1.0.

42. 'On heating a piece of clay-refractory material, the usual expansion first occurs. . . . At a certain temperature, however, major crystalline changes take place, and with further increase in temperature the test specimen shows very marked contraction. At higher temperatures still, normal relatively low linear expansion takes place. On cooling, the specimen contracts linearly so that at room-temperature it is smaller than originally. A second heating over the same temperature-range shows only normal expansion, and, on cooling, normal contraction. . . . Thus, if a specimen, on heating, exhibits the contraction-phenomenon, it means that in its previous thermal history it had never been at temperatures above its maturing temperature (i.e. at which marked contraction occurs). . . . It is obvious that . . . the crucible had never been above 1000° . . . approximately' (Mr H. Cole).

43. Tooling and grain, Boon, *JGS* VIII, 43, figs. 6–8, 9–11. Glass-making sites, C. Isings, *Roman Glass from Dated Finds,* 4 ff.; O. Doppelfeld, *Römische und frankische Gläser,* introd. In Britain, notably at Caistor St. Edmund, *CC* 78, fig. 14. Glass was probably made in the Silchester manner at many sites, but it is important to remark that evidence of crucibles and siege is required to attest them, not merely 'glass wasters' which could arise from accidental burning of fragments.

44. But the wood-screw was not in use, and the specimen recorded from a pit in Insula IV (*53*, 561) was a workman's practical contribution to the collection and not a Roman screw. This battered coach-bolt with machine-cut thread was made on a lathe of a type quite unknown to the Romans, and could not have been produced before 1849 at the earliest. See an article by H. W. Dickinson, *Trans. Newcomen Society* XXII, 79 ff. Roman threads, A. Mutz, *Wire* July/Aug. 1973, 183.

45. Frame-saw blades 70–80 cm. long are to be seen in the Luxembourg museum; they have very coarse, irregular-set teeth. Setting, *Pliny* XVI, 43. W. L. Goodman, *Hist. of Woodworking Tools*, 115 ff. for a good account of sawing. *60*, 154 refers to a 'saw-pit', but Goodman points out that saw-pits were an English phenomenon, no earlier than the eighteenth century. Sawing on trestle, Goodman *o.c.* and e.g. *Esp.* 4702. Sir J. Evans miscalled the saw-files with notches 'paring knives'.

46. E.g. *60*, 446.

47. *54*, 151, fig. 18.

48. Goodman's section, *o.c.* 43 ff. is excellent. The angle of the blade of the Silchester specimen could not have been less than 49°; 45° is the optimum.

49. Bobbins, *Newstead*, 311, fig. 45; *PSASc.* XL, 502, pl. 24, 6 (Bar Hill), wider shank, with thread attached.

50. *54*, 149.

51. A. Lawson, *l.c.* p. 349, n. 13. For armlet-industry, see J. B. Calkin, *PDAS* LXXV, 45 ff.

52. Occurrence of manufacturing débris: Iron Age, A. Bulleid and H. St. G. Gray, *Glastonbury Lake-Village* I, 261, fig. 54, κ4; Post-Roman, L. Alcock, *Dinas Powys*, 176, fig. 39 (probably introduced as curiosities). Evidence from West Park villa, Fordingbridge, Hants., A. T. Morley-Hewitt, *Roman Villa* . . . (1969), 21. The two 'unfinished dishes' mentioned *RS* are *well*-finished pedestals for figurines, probably.

53. E.g. box-fittings from Caerleon, *Isca* (1972), 72; fan from York, Richmond, *ArJ* XCIII, 79, figs. 12, 14.

54. *55*, 421.

55. *102*, 51, III.2.

56. Bulleid and Gray, *o.c.* II, 568 ff. Saxon, *Shakenoak* III, 48 and fig. 21.

57. *Wild*, 136, lists only four occurrences besides Silchester. He suggests that weights could have been of unbaked clay, but since earlier and later weights are baked, this is improbable. The two-beam vertical loom, *ib.* 69 ff. There are good accounts of textile processes in this book, and clear diagrams.

58. See Frere, *AJ* XXXVII, 219, pl. 26A for fourth-century specimens from a pot found at Charlton, Hants., and cf. *AJ* XXXVIII, 244. The teeth are not very different, though sharper, than e.g. *Wild* fig. 16B: perhaps the plates were set, like those of bone combs, in a frame.

59. Cf. *Wild,* 73–4, table 140–1, including Silchester.

60. *Wild,* 60 mentions two knitting-needles in a wooden case from an unpublished Dutch grave. Otherwise he has little to say about knitting, which must have been a commonplace activity, cf. a review of his book by W. Endrei, *Textile History* III, 125–7. Dura knitting ('crossed eastern stitch'), R. Pfister and L. Bellinger, *Excav. at Dura-Europos, Final Rept.* IV. ii, 4, 54–6, 26. D. Burnham, *Textile History* III, 116–24, suggests that these were made by a one-needle technique. The use of double needles is attested by the Dutch find and e.g. by Coptic knitted socks, *Textile History* I, 193, pl. 1. Some of the large Roman needles from Silchester and elsewhere, with splayed heads, may have been intended for single-needle work.

61. *54,* 459 ff.

62. *54,* 461, figs. 3–4.

63. There are about twenty-five such furnaces, disposed as follows (though the listing is incomplete, being confined to *Archaeologia* references): Insulae IV, V, VI, XII, XIV, XV, XVII, XX, XXII, XXVIII (one); XXXIII (two); XI, XIII (three); XXIII (four) X (seven). In other insulae, none seems to have been noted, though long hearths may occur.

64. The number is said to have been the same as in Insula II, *53,* 284.

65. *CC,* 81. The fire-flues show that they cannot have been bake-ovens.

66. *Shakenoak* I, 18, fig. 10, 1 for furnace containing over 9 kg. of melted lead; plan, fig. 4, second-third century. Contrast the plan of the furnace with e.g. the bake-oven in the West Park villa, Morley-Hewitt *o.c.,* 9 and plan. I am indebted to Mr Morley-Hewitt for full information regarding this and other installations in the kitchen of the villa.

67. *56,* 112 ff., pl. 7. A fragment of one quern was found. One wonders to what extent the 'roughly defined circular blocks' were cleaned up, and how the wall-bottoms related to their level. The flint-packed post-holes ('drains') in XXIIA.1 (p. 259) were 1.2 m. across, with holes for posts 60 cm. wide and 76 cm. deep, *57,* 98. Other large post-holes occurred at Stroud villa (Hants.), 1.2 m. across and 60 cm. deep, see A. Moray-Williams, *ArJ* LXVI, 39, pls. 2–3.

68. One in London and another at Corfe Castle, Dorset, both Mayen lava: *LRT,* 109, fig. 43; *RCHM Dorset* II.3, 601, fig.

69. *56*, 114. The sarcophagus with reliefs cited by Fox in support of his suggestion regarding the bases is more likely to illustrate dough-mixing equipment; cf. L. Moritz, *Grain Mills and Flour in Classical Antiquity*, 82.

70. Manning, *AJ* XLIV, 38 ff.

71. *Vitruvius* X, 5; cf. Moritz, *o.c.*, 122 ff.

72. *Esp.* 3685.

73. *60*, 156, 165–7.

74. *61*, 480.

75. *53*, 572.

76. *60*, 448.

77. *53*, 562, 573 and n. The measurement stated to be 'thickness' is clearly 'depth from surface', as a photograph shows.

78. R. J. Forbes, *Stud. Ancient Technology* V, 1 ff., for tanning; cf. also J. G. Jenkins, *Country Life*, 15 June 1961, 1414, traditional methods at Rhayader.

79. Caerwent, *61*, 579. Clermont, *HG* V, 197, nn. Little is in reality known of this deposit and in a letter of 28 December 1968 M. Pierre Fournier urges extreme caution.

80. *60*, 446 ff., fig. 8. The connection of this tank with the curious system of timber conduits leading under part of this house from another tank in the south part of VI.1 (cf. *60*, 158, 445, pls. 21, 40), and with a square wood-lined pit and trough in the west court of XXXIV.1 is difficult to make out, but suggests that both houses had come into the same ownership and were being used in late times for industrial purposes, probably tanning.

81. On the question of the Roman pound, see P. Grierson, presidential address, *NC* 1964, xi–xiv; he concludes that 'starting from scratch', 325 g. might be best. On Celtic weights, see Th. Schwarz, *Schweizerische Münzblätter* XIII/XIV, 150–7 (rather ambitious): besides the 309 g. weight actually attested, he deduces a heavy Celtic pound of 640 g.

82. For other examples cf. *CIL* V, 8119.4; *CIL* XIII, 10030.13; *RA* 1966–i, 132, fig. 26; Schwarz, *loc.cit.*, 154–5, Abb. 4. Sets from Aquileia and Brimeux near Boulogne are inscribed as having been 'tested to the standard of the Temple of Castor' (for Brimeux, see Cagnat-Chapot, *Manuel d'archéologie romaine*, I, 496, fig.) and of these the Aquileia set is very good. The whole matter of the weights found requires proper examination, and the actual figures checked.

83. Apollo, at Stratfield Saye, *JBAA* I, 147, fig. 1=XV, 94, fig. 3.

84. See p. 318 n. 17 for Silchester and Caerleon; others, *LRT,* 83–4, fig. 21; *BMGGRL,* 184, fig. 203.

85. The Silchester coins at Reading were summarised by J. W. E. Pearce, *NC* 1929, 328 ff., but those at Stratfield Saye were not included; they have now been deposited at Reading and only choice specimens, mounted in glazed frames by Joyce, remain there. Counterfeits: see my brief essay in *PUBSS* XIII.1, 75–9, with refs., and my forthcoming article in the proceedings of the 1973 Institute of Archaeology, London, seminar. The best published collection is still in C. H. V. Sutherland's *Coinage and Currency in Roman Britain* (1937), but the interpretation is now in some respects out of date: in particular, it is now established that counterfeits were current in the period of currency of the prototypes and not later, as used to be thought in the case of late, very small varieties: cf. Boon, *NC* 1961, 191 ff., refs. Lightweights, Boon, *NC* 1965, 164–5, 173, in a general study of these; including two *subferrati.* Value of counterfeit radiates, *PUBSS* XIII.1, 78. No general account of the Silchester radiate or fourth-century copies has yet appeared; 'Carausius II', Boon, *NC* 1955, 235, but for the latest see J. P. C. Kent, *NC* 1971, 210. Silchester hoards, Boon, *NC* 1960, 243 ff., but add those mentioned here pp. 311–12, nn. 21, 27. General on the Roman coinage, H. Mattingly, *Roman Coins* (1960); R. Reece, *Roman Coins.*

86. Arm-purse, *58,* 469. Cf. Eric Birley, *AA* ser. 4 XLI, 5–17.

Index

The contents are limited to persons and matters related directly to Silchester, and are divided into three parts: (1), Persons; (2), Buildings; and (3), Subjects. *Italic* figures refer to pages on which illustrations appear.

PART 2: BUILDINGS

PART 3: SUBJECTS